Variants in Economic Theory

ECONOMISTS OF THE TWENTIETH CENTURY

General Editors: David Colander, *Christian A. Johnson Distinguished Professor of Economics, Middlebury College, Vermont, USA* and Mark Blaug, *Professor Emeritus, University of London, UK, Professor Emeritus, University of Buckingham, UK and Visiting Professor, University of Amsterdam, The Netherlands*

This innovative series comprises specially invited collections of articles and papers by economists whose work has made an important contribution to economics in the late twentieth century.

The proliferation of new journals and the ever-increasing number of new articles make it difficult for even the most assiduous economist to keep track of all the important recent advances. By focusing on those economists whose work is generally recognized to be at the forefront of the discipline, the series will be an essential reference point for the different specialisms included.

A list of published and future titles in this series is printed at the end of this volume.

Variants in Economic Theory

Selected Works of Hal R. Varian

Hal R. Varian

Dean, School of Information Management and Systems,
Professor, Haas School of Business,
Professor, Department of Economics,
Class of 1944 Professor,
University of California at Berkeley, USA

Economists of the Twentieth Century

Edward Elgar

Cheltenham, UK • Northampton, MA, USA

Published by
Edward Elgar Publishing Limited
Glensanda House
Montpellier Parade
Cheltenham
Glos GL50 1UA
UK

Edward Elgar Publishing, Inc.
136 West Street
Suite 202
Northampton
Massachusetts 01060
USA

A catalogue record for this book
is available from the British Library

Library of Congress Cataloguing in Publication Data
Varian, Hal R.
  Variants in economic theory : selected works of Hal R. Varian.
  (Economists of the twentieth century)
  A collection of 21 articles and book chapters, with some corrections, previously published between 1967-1995, plus a "biographical reflections" chapter written by Varian.
  Includes bibliographical references.
  1. Varian, Hal R. 2. Economists—United States.
3. Microeconomics. 4. Econometrics. 5. Finance. I. Title.
II. Series.
HB119.V37A25 1999
330'.092—dc21   99-12891
                                                    CIP

ISBN 1 85898 326 6

Printed and bound in Great Britain by Bookcraft (Bath) Ltd.

CONTENTS

vi

Acknowledgements

The publishers wish to thank the following who have kindly given their permission for the use of copyright material.

Academic Press for article: "Equity, Envy, and Efficiency," in *Journal of Economic Theory*, **9**, pp. 63–91, September 1974.

American Economic Association for articles: "A Model of Sales" in *American Economic Review*, **70**, pp. 651–659, September 1980; "Price Discrimination and Social Welfare," *American Economic Review*, **75**, pp. 870–875; "A Solution to the Problem of Externalities when Agents are Well-Informed," *American Economic Review*, pp. 1278–1293, December 1994.

Blackwell Publishers for article: "Divergence of Opinion in Complete Markets," *Journal of Finance*, **40**, pp. 309–317, 1985.

The Econometric Society for articles: "Non Walrasian Equilibria" in *Econometrica*, **45**, pp. 573–590, April 1977; "The Nonparametric Approach to Demand Analysis," *Econometrica*, **50**, pp. 945–972, July 1982; "The Nonparametric Approach to Production Analysis," *Econometrica*, **52**, pp. 540–597, May 1984; "Estimating Risk Aversion from Arrow-Debreu Portfolio Choice," *Econometrica*, **56**, pp. 973–980, July 1988.

Elsevier Science for articles: "Two Problems in the Theory of Fairness," *Journal of Public Economics*, **5**, pp. 249-260, 1976; "A Remark on Boundary Restrictions in the Global Newton Method," *Journal of Mathematical Economics*, **4**, pp. 127–130, 1977. "Nonparametric Analysis of Optimizing Behavior with Measurement Error," *Journal of Econometrics*, **30**, pp. 445–458; "Goodness of Fit in Optimizing Models," *Journal of Econometrics*, **46**, pp. 125-140; "Sequential Provision of Public Goods," *Journal of Public Economics*, **53**, pp. 165–186, 1994.

IEEE for article "Pricing Congestible Network Resources" (with Jeff MacKie-Mason), *IEEE Journal on Selected Areas in Communications*, **13**, September 1995.

Kluwer Academic Publishers for article "Economic Incentives in Software Design," *Computational Economics*, **6**, pp. 201–217; and "Differences of Opinion and the Volume of Trade," in C. C. Stone (ed.), *Financial Risk: Theory, Evidence, and Implications*, 1988; "A Bayesian Approach to Real Estate Assessment," *Bayesian Econometrics and Statistics*, S. Fienberg and A. Zellner (ed.), pp. 195–208, 1974.

Texas A&M University for article "Catastrophe Theory and the Business Cycle," in *Economic Inquiry*, **17**, January 1979, pp. 14-28.

University of Michigan Press for "How to Build an Economic Model in Your Spare Time," in Szenverg (ed.) *Passion and Craft, How Economists Work,* 1995.

To my teachers

Chapter 1

BIOGRAPHICAL REFLECTIONS

I was born in Wooster, Ohio, a small Midwestern town about 50 miles south of Cleveland. My brother and I grew up on an apple orchard owned by my father and grandfather. In many respects I had an idyllic childhood—I remember long summer days of playing among the apple trees and lying on the hillside watching the shapes form in the clouds. However, despite the appeals of this pastoral life, I always felt trapped on the orchard. There was a whole wide world out there beyond Wooster, Ohio that I was missing out on.

I was an avid reader, especially of science and science fiction, and spent virtually every Saturday morning at the library picking out the next week's set of books. When I was about 12 I joined some mail order bookclubs. One of the initial three offerings was Isaac Asimov's *Foundation Trilogy*, which was a series of novels revolving around the predictions of a "psychohistorian" who created an elaborate mathematical model of the Galactic Empire. The idea that one could construct mathematical models of human behavior made a big impression on me; perhaps this is why I eventually became an economist.

My mother has always professed surprise at my career choice. She says that she was sure I would become a scientist. I keep explaining that economics *is* a science, but I don't think I have yet convinced her.

In 1958 the Russians shot Sputnik into orbit, an event that was to have a great impact on my life. The perceived lag in US education prompted the National Defense Education Act, which provide scholarship and loans without which I would have probably been unable to pay for college.

I did very well in grade school and high school. In the summer of 1964, I was chosen to attend a National Science Foundation Summer Science camp at Ohio University. I spent about six weeks there, previewing college life. Among other things I learned to program in Fortran II on an IBM 1620. We had to feed an entire box of punched cards into the computer just to load the compiler, with my own puny little 80-card program stuck at the end.

My science project was to estimate the angular distribution of cosmic rays, and by the end of the summer, I actually succeeded in writing the curve-fitting program and analyzing the data. The fall of my senior year I applied to MIT, since I was convinced that it was the best place for science. I had never visited the campus—indeed, I had barely been out of Wooster—yet I was supremely confident that this was the right choice.

1.1 MIT

I entered MIT in the Fall of 1965, very much the typical smug freshman who had always been at the top of his class. At one orientation meeting, the leader asked how many of us had at least one perfect score on our college entrance exams. I proudly raised my hand ... and then noticed that virtually the entire room also had their hands up. The lesson was clear—I wasn't in Wooster any more!

I had a great time in college. I took my classes, and did reasonably well, maintaining a B average, and making dean's list for a few semesters. But I also went through the standard experience of a small-town boy discovering life in the big city. I suppose I could have studied more, and done better, but I would have missed a lot of other experiences.

During the summer of 1966, I got a programming job writing assembly language code for a Univac 1108. This was incredibly tedious—if I was lucky I was able to run two jobs a day. At the end of the summer both my boss and I were leaving the company. He called me aside and told me to take all the comment cards out of my deck. "But then," I said, "no one will be able to figure out what we did." "Exactly," he replied, "if they want to make any changes they'll have to hire us back as consultants!" Since then I have always insisted that my own programmers write liberal comments in their code.

While at MIT I was still inspired by the vision of mathematical modeling of human behavior, but I wasn't sure what subject dealt with that: I looked into psychology, operations research, and, finally, economics. In my sophomore year I took intermediate microeconomics from Joe Stiglitz and decided that this was the subject for me.

MIT is known as a technical university, but it has a remarkably good set of courses in the arts and humanities. I took music, art, philosophy, and several other such courses, all of which I enjoyed very much. One semester I was president of the MIT Student Art Association.

During my senior year, I took the first-year graduate course in micro theory, taught by Bob Bishop. I didn't do all that well, mostly because I was distracted by extra-curricular activities, but this didn't discourage me. My senior thesis advisor was Duncan Foley, who apparently saw hope in me and encouraged me to go to Berkeley. I dutifully followed his advice.

1.2 Berkeley

I was admitted to Berkeley, and vividly remember sending in my letter of acceptance one day in the spring 1969. After dropping my letter in the mailbox, I picked up the student newspaper, only to see that the top news story of the day involved helicopters gassing students in Sproul Plaza! I contemplated retrieving my admissions letter, but figured that the tear gas should dissipate by the time I arrived.

I got a summer job at Berkeley doing computer programming for the Center for Real Estate and Urban Economics, and drove West with some friends in June of 1969.

Berkeley in the early seventies was a remarkable place. Something new was happening every day. I look back now and ask how we all could have been so silly, but at the time, it was an exciting experience. Despite the temptation to describe the entire range of what was *really* going on, I will devote my attention solely to my academic development during this period.

When the term started, I was encouraged to take an advanced placement exam for the graduate micro sequence. Having taken the equivalent course at MIT, I easily passed placement exam, and so created a hole in my schedule. The graduate advisor, George Akerloff, encouraged me to take an advanced micro course from Dan McFadden, and also suggested I go "take something" in the mathematics department.

Somehow I discovered that John Kelley was teaching a 3-quarter course in general topology, function spaces and measure theory. I had no idea what these topics were, but I had heard that Kelley was an excellent teacher, so I signed up for the courses. This turned out to one of the great intellectual experiences of my life. This is ironic, since if I had understood clearly what I was getting into, I would have realized the subjects were much too advanced for me!

Berkeley had the best mathematics department in the world, and all of the other students had been top math undergraduates. I, on the other hand, had only taken the three required math courses at MIT and never had taken a "real" math course involving proofs. Nevertheless, I persevered, and by the end of the term I was doing as well as the best students in the class. It was only much later that I learned that topology was a generalization of real analysis, which one is supposed to study first!

I went on to take several other math courses at Berkeley and eventually accumulated enough credits for a masters degree. Despite this accomplishment, I have never considered myself a very good mathematician. My main shortcoming is that I am too sloppy and not careful enough in my proofs. Luckily, peer review has caught most of my really egregious errors! (One nice benefit of compiling this volume of selected works is that I have been able to fix some of the small bugs in my papers—perhaps it should be called "corrected works.")

McFadden's course in micro theory was also a very nice course, but I have to say, I didn't really appreciate its importance at the time. During this year I also took a course from a philosopher, Hubert Dreyfus, on existential philosophy, which had a big influence on me. During subsequent terms I took several philosophy courses on Heidegger, Kierkegaard, Wittgenstein, and various analytic philosophers.

This period in my life was intensely exciting—I was taking courses in economics, mathematics, statistics, and philosophy, as well as enjoying the pleasures of the Bay Area. Looking back, I wonder how I had the energy for it all!

Tom Rothenberg encouraged me to apply for an NSF Fellowship, which I received, thereby relieving me from financial worries for the next three years. I had a stipend of $10,000 a year, paid a rent of $50 per month, a good dinner cost $3, and I could take any course I wanted at one of the best universities in the world. What a life!

At the beginning of my fourth year, I attended a seminar by Menachem Yaari, who talked about a theory of "fairness". Interestingly enough, the particular formalization of fairness that he described was first proposed by my former undergraduate advisor, Duncan Foley. I found the concept intriguing, and ended up writing my thesis on it. The thesis was published in the *Journal of Economic Theory*, and is reprinted as Chapter 2 in this collection.

1.3 Back to MIT

I went on the job market in the spring of 1973 and was invited to speak at a number of schools, including Minnesota, Michigan, Harvard, Penn, and MIT. I received an offer at MIT, which was then the best economics department in the country. Clearly, that was the job to take.

I was asked to teach one of the four core micro courses. Bob Bishop taught the first course, on Marshallian economics. Marty Weitzman taught the second on activity analysis. I taught the third on duality, and Paul Samuelson taught the fourth. The students referred to these courses as "curves, vectors, sets, and jokes."

My course, sets, was supposed to be "Berkeley economics," which meant duality, general equilibrium, and other topics that had been developed in the 1970s by Dan McFadden, Gerard Debreu, Erwin Diewert and other Berkeley researchers. The trouble was that there was no textbook to teach from. There were a few advanced journal articles, but these were inaccessible to beginning students. Bob Hall gave me 20 pages of lecture notes he had written, and I also had the 50 or so pages of notes written by Dan McFadden and Sid Winter for the course I had taken at Berkeley.

I wrote up some more notes myself, trying to make this material more accessible to the students. This had the side effect of making it more accessible to myself. As is commonly observed, teaching is the best method for learning.

MIT had just purchased one of the first wordprocessors, an IBM desk-sized computer that stored each page on a magnetic card. I had the operator enter my notes on that machine because I realized that they were going to be revised frequently. One defect of this system was that it didn't handle Greek characters, which is why the first edition of *Microeconomic Analysis* had no Greek.

Each time I taught the course, the notes got bigger. One day Don Lamm, an acquisitions editor from W. W. Norton, was visiting my office. He asked the obligatory question: "Are you working on any books?" "Of course not," I replied, "that would be a foolish way to spend time as an assistant professor." "What's that pile of paper over there?" Don asked. "Oh," I said, "that's just class notes." "Well," said Lamm, "that's close enough for me." He left the office with the notes and sent me a book contract a month later.

I continued to do some work in economic theories of equity, and a little bit of mathematical economics, but in the early 70s, the most exciting intellectual work at MIT was in macroeconomics, and I found myself gravitating to that area. I was particularly interested in "disequilibrium theory," a way of approaching macro that has since fallen into disrepute. (Unjustly so, in my opinion.) My work in this area is represented by the chapters on non-Walrasian equilibrium and catastrophe theory.

During this time I taught undergraduate courses in statistics, mathematical economics, and macroeconomics. These were great teaching assignments, because they compelled me to actually learn this material. I had some tremendous students while at MIT. Paul Krugman, Olivier Blanchard, and Jeff Frankel were among the graduate students I taught there. I also taught mathematical economics to Carl Shapiro and Larry Summers, as well as supervising their senior theses.

In the spring of 1975 I got calls from both Berkeley and Stanford asking me if I would like to come visit for a year. It was, and is, a common recruiting tactic for schools like this to invite young assistant professors to visit. They were comparatively cheap, and it gave the schools a chance to look you over to see if they wanted to make you a pre-emptive offer when tenure time came.

I also got a call from the University of Michigan in the fall of 1996 inviting me out for a "job talk." I enjoyed the visit to Ann Arbor, but didn't take the "job" part all that seriously.

I spent the winter of 1977 at Stanford and the spring at Berkeley. During this time I worked on the manuscript for *Microeconomic Analysis.* Carl Shapiro was also at Berkeley, as a first-year student in mathematics and I hired him as an RA for the book. I like to think that this experience had something to do with his deciding to pursue economics as a profession.

1.4 Michigan

During the spring of 1977 I received an offer from Michigan as a full professor, with a salary double what I was making at MIT. It also meant that I would move directly from assistant to full professor, while less than four years out of grad school. This opportunity was too attractive to turn down, so I moved to Ann Arbor that summer.

At Michigan I became interested in industrial organization and public finance and wrote my papers on "A Model of Sales" and "Redistributive Taxation" I formed a long and fruitful collaboration and friendship with Ted Bergstrom, from whom I have learned many things over the years.

In the early 1979, I was chosen as a Guggenheim Fellow, and decided to spend the year at Oxford, at the invitation of Jim Mirlees, whom I had met at MIT. This was a wonderful year. I spent about six weeks in the summer with a Eurail pass exploring the capitals of Europe, also finding time to teach courses in Stockholm and Helsinki.

I lived "in college" at Nuffield, which meant I didn't have to worry about mundane details of life and spent nearly all my time on research. This is where I wrote most of my papers on "nonparametric methods," which, being rather mathematical, required more sustained concentration than most work. I couldn't have done nearly as much in this area in a less sequestered environment.

I returned to Michigan in the summer of 1980. At this time Michigan was a pretty backwards place, compared with the east and west coast schools, and we struggled to convince the administration to modernize the department.

In mid-80s I was able to attract Roger Gordon and Michelle White, who made a huge difference in the intellectual life of the department. In the late 80s I helped bring Ken Binmore to Ann Arbor, who added a much-needed capability in game theory.

Around 1986 I decided to write a textbook in intermediate microeconomics. I had several motivations. By this time my graduate text had become the standard, and people kept asking me what their students should read to prepare them for the graduate book. I was also quite unhappy with the existing books, which were becoming more and more dumbed down. I vividly remember the event that got me to actually start writing: I had to prepare a midterm exam for my course and, looking through the textbook I had used, I found it hard to think of anything substantive that the students had learned!

It was something of a painful experience writing the book, since the students were quite critical of the slightest error or ambiguity, but their criticisms ultimately produced a better book. My colleague Ted Bergstrom collaborated with me on the workbook, which turned out to be a great success. I can say that in all due modesty since most of the best material in the workbook came from Ted.

This book has gone on to be translated into 10 languages and is used around the world. I just finished the fifth edition a few months ago, and it seems to be going strong, despite the very competitive market in this area.

1.5 Computers

During the eighties I also spent a lot of time with microcomputers. I had bought an IBM PC back in 1981, shortly after it first came out, and continued to upgrade to each new model. I helped to organize a users' group in Ann Arbor, and spent a lot of time hacking. There was a serious side to all this—I was using computation much more in my research—but, I have to say, that was more of an excuse than a motivation.

In the early 90s, one of my colleagues asked me a difficult question: "Who pays for my email? You're an economist and a computer geek, so you should know." I had to admit there was some logic in his view, so I set out to find the answer.

At that time the main US Internet backbone, the NSFNET, was managed in Ann Arbor, so the resources were close by. I teamed up with my colleague Jeff MacKie-Mason and a few months later we wrote our paper on "The Economics of the Internet."

This paper was the first that married my interest in computers with my interest in economics. As I learned more and more about digital technology, I saw that there were a huge number of fascinating economic questions waiting to be answered, and I spent more and more time thinking about pricing information, intellectual property, and other similar topics.

1.6 Back to Berkeley

In 1993 the President of University of Michigan did a very strange thing: he appointed Dan Atkins, the Associate Dean of Engineering, to be the new Dean of the Library School. This seemingly inexplicable appointment was prescient: within the year it had become clear that management of digital information was going to require a whole new profession which combined traditional library skills with skills in information technology.

Dan wanted to create a new interdisciplinary degree program within the library school to deal with information management, he asked me to serve on the committee organizing this new school. Sometime during this period I received a letter from Berkeley inviting me to apply to be dean of a similar school that was being established there. I tossed the letter in the wastebasket, as I had done with previous offers to be dean here and there, but then thought that I should take a look at what Berkeley was doing. I read the proposal for the new school at Berkeley and was very impressed—this was just what we were trying to do at Michigan, only their thinking was much further along. One thing led to another, and before I knew it, I was dean of the new school at Berkeley.

My administrative duties have cut into my research productivity, but not my enthusiasm about economics. I am more convinced than ever of the value of economic modeling in helping us to understand the economics of digital goods. However, this experience has also convinced me that we economists should spend more time and effort into trying to explain what we do to non-economists. *We* know our work is valuable. With a little more effort on our parts, everyone else will know it, too.

My latest effort, a book titled *Information Rules: A Strategic Guide to the Network Economy*, is an attempt to do just that. Co-authored with my former student, Carl Shapiro, the book describes the economics of networks and information technology in a way that we hope is both accurate and enlightening. It has also been quite successful, being Editor's Choice for "business books of the year" at Amazon.com, and receiving very favorable reviews in the *New York Times* and *The Economist*.

***

When Edward Elgar asked to publish my collected works, my first reaction was: "But they aren't done yet!" I still think this is true (despite having been a dean for 5 years) but I finally agreed that this is a good time to collect together the first 20 years of my research efforts.

This volume contains some selections from those two decades of research. As the reader has seen from my remarks earlier in this essay, I have worked in many different areas of economics. My criterion in selecting papers for this volume was to select works that were of high quality and were also representative of this breadth of interests. I hope that you enjoy reading them as much as I have enjoyed writing them.

Chapter 2

EQUITY, ENVY, AND EFFICIENCY

I consider the problem of dividing a bundle of goods among several agents so that the allocation is Pareto efficient and so that no agent prefers any other agent's bundle of goods to his own. I establish conditions under which these allocations exist, examine the extension of the concept to production economies, and various generalizations concerning coalitions.

Consider the problem of dividing a fixed amount of goods among a fixed number of agents. If, in a given allocation, agent i prefers the bundle of agent j to his own, we will say i *envies* j. If there are no envious agents at allocation x, we will say x is equitable. If x is both Pareto efficient and equitable, we will say x is fair.

Section 1 motivates and examines these definitions, and compares this approach to some other theories of normative economics. Section 2 examines the relationship between envy and efficiency and establishes some quite general results concerning the existence of fair allocations.

Section 3 considers the problem of fair allocation of goods and leisure when production is possible. It is found that fair allocations will not in general exist in this case, even under very regular conditions. Accordingly, the concept is generalized in two ways which will exist under weak conditions, and these new concepts are characterized in terms of income and wealth distribution.

Finally, Section 4 considers an extension of the concept of equity where we allow comparisons to be made between coalitions of agents. In this case it is shown that the *only* allocations that are coalition-fair in a large economy are competitive equilibria with equal incomes.

2.1 The concept of fairness

What is a fair way to divide society's product? The importance of this question can hardly be denied, but the amount of economic analysis relevant to it is rather small. In this paper I attempt to apply some of the

I wish to thank Daniel McFadden, David Gale, Gerard Debreu, and Carl Futia for helpful suggestions and comments. Of course, I am solely responsible for any remaining errors. I wish also to thank the National Science Foundation for fellowship support during the writing of this paper.

standard tools of theoretical economics to the analysis of certain formal definitions of fairness.

I begin by considering the case of pure fair division: There is some fixed amount of resources to be divided among n agents. I will define an allocation as *equitable* if no agent prefers some other agent's bundle to his own.[1] If an allocation is both equitable and Pareto efficient, I will say it is *fair*.[2] Finally, if some agent does prefer another agent's bundle to his own at a given allocation, I will say that the first agent envies the second.

These definitions formalize a recurrent theme in ethical thought· namely, considerations of *symmetry* in distributive justice. The equity comparison allows each agent to put himself in the place of each other agent and then forces him to evaluate the other agent's position on the same terms that he judges his own. Thus it allows an interpersonal comparison of a sort, but it restricts the way in which this comparison can be made; in particular, there can be no "double standard" for evaluating others' positions as compared to one's own position.

Of course this definition can only be a minimal requirement for fairness; after all, the only facts taken into account are the preferences of the agents and the physical amount of goods to be divided. In many cases other facts may be relevant to the fair division problem; examples of such other considerations might be the strengths of the agents' preferences, the moral worth of the agents, or the history of how each of the agents contributed to the formation of the original bundle.

But the simplicity and minimal informational requirements of this definition should count as a strength of this approach rather than a weakness. As I expand the problem of fair allocations to include the possibility of production, coalition formation, and so on, the criteria for what should count as a "fair" allocation may certainly change. But we must walk before we can run, and it will pay us to examine the implications of this simple definition in some detail.

Before I proceed to that task, I want to spend a small amount of time comparing this approach to the "standard" approach of specifying a social welfare function of the form $W(u_i(x))$ and choosing a division that maximizes it. The "fairness" of the allocation resulting from this approach depends critically on the particular welfare function used. Furthermore, it is well known that finding a "reasonable" social welfare function may be a very difficult problem; I am referring, of course, to the various impossibility results of social decision theory. (For a good survey of these results see Sen (1970).)

Social decision theory views the specification of the social welfare func-

---

[1] The definition of equity is due to Foley (1967).

[2] The definition of fairness is due to Schmeidler and Yaari (1972). Schmeidler and Vind have also considered the related notion of "fair net trades." (1972).

tion as a problem in aggregating individual preferences. Its chief results are of the form "There are no reasonable ways to aggregate individual preferences."

Why do we get such a pessimistic conclusion from this approach? It seems to me that there are two problems:

(i) Social decision theory asks for too much out of the aggregating process.

(ii) Social decision theory does not put enough into the aggregating process.

Social decision theory asks for too much out of the process in that it asks for an entire *ordering* of the various social states (allocations in this case). The original question asked only for a "good" allocation; there was no requirement to rank all allocations. The fairness criterion in fact limits itself to answering the original question. It is limited in that it gives no indication of the merits of two nonfair allocations, but by restricting itself in this way it allows for a reasonable solution to the original problem.

Social decision theory puts too little into the social decision problem in that we generally allow individual preferences to be defined over the entire set of social states. In the particular problem of distributive justice, this means that individual preferences are defined over entire allocations. I think that this degree of generality contains too little structure to produce any satisfactory *positive* results. The fairness approach, on the other hand, restricts preferences to be defined only on individual bundles and thus allows for a symmetric comparison of the agents' relative positions.

Besides the generally negative results concerning the specifications of such functions, the specific welfare functions that have actually been used are all of the Bergsonian variety; that is where the utility functions were defined only on the individual bundles: $W(u_i(x_i))$. The allocations that maximize such functions have the desirable property of being Pareto efficient; however, the restriction to the Bergsonian form eliminates the information available for the "envy" comparison. Welfare functions consistent with the idea of fairness would have a form where utility evaluations of other agents bundles were allowed; that is, the welfare function would have the form of $W(u_i(x_j))$. A specific example would be: $W(x) = \alpha \sum u_i(x_i) - \beta \sum (u_i(x_j) - u_i(x_i))\delta_{ij}$, where δ_{ij} is unity if the "envy" term is positive and zero otherwise. The parameters α and β can be interpreted as weighing the relative importance of the "efficiency" and the "equity" considerations.

Comparison to Rawls

John Rawls has considered in some detail the meaning of the concept of justice. Since many economists are familiar with his work, it may be useful to compare the fairness idea to Rawls' approach.

Rawls argues that the principles of justice in a society should be principles that would be agreed upon by free and rational persons in an "original position" of "ignorance" as to their actual positions in the society in question. The original position is to be regarded only as a hypothetical state. Formally it adds nothing to an analysis of what a just state is; it only gives us a restriction on what type of *reasons* can be given for choosing one particular principle of justice over another. The restriction is of course that the only reasons allowed are reasons that could be appealed to in the original position. Thus Rawls spends considerable effort in delineating exactly what information is available to the agents in the original position.

This, it seems to me, is a well-directed inquiry. For what should count as reasons in a moral discussion is an important and interesting question; although the idea of the original position simply leaves us with the same problem, its particular picturesque description allows for a certain insight. By appealing to the initial anonymity of the agents, Rawls appeals to the same symmetry instinct to which fairness appeals.

When Rawls eventually tries to answer the question of what principles would be chosen in the original position, he arrives at two principles, which I abbreviate as the "equal liberties principle" and the "difference principle." Much of the book is spent in clarifying these principles and analyzing their consequences. To justify the choice of these particular principles of justice, Rawls states that "it is useful as a heuristic device to think of the two principles as the maximin solution to the problem of social justice." [Rawls (1971), p. 152.]

Many economists have jumped on this statement as implying that Rawls favors a maximin social welfare function. The arguments against such a maximin welfare function are rather strong, primarily resting on the fact that people are usually not all that pessimistic in their choice behavior (Arrow (1973).) But note that Rawls appeals to the maximin argument only as a *heuristic* principle. His fundamental assertion is that the two principles of justice mentioned before would be chosen; the maximum behavior is only an attempted explanation of why they would be chosen.

The question that concerns me here is not how the theory of fairness compares to a maximin social welfare function, but rather whether the theory of fairness could be the outcome of the original position as described by Rawls. It seems to me that it could, and in fact I believe Rawls himself argues to this effect.

Rawls discusses the concept of "envy" in Sections 80 and 81. It is important to take note of his terminology; Rawls thinks of envy as "the propensity to view with hostility the greater good of others even though their being more fortunate than we are does not detract from our advantages" [Rawls (1971), p. 532]. In the particular case of distributive justice I am considering, this definition seems to describe a case where preferences are defined over entire allocations, and increasing the bundle of one agent results in decreasing the utility of the other agents. Hence it is clear that the theory of fairness rules out what Rawls calls envious behavior since preferences are required to be defined on individual bundles.

On the other hand, Rawls does allow that resentment is a legitimate moral category. For Rawls claims.

"If we resent our having less than others, it must be because we think that their being better off is the result of unjust institutions. Those who express resentment must be prepared to show why certain institutions are unjust..." [Rawls (1971), p. 533].

I believe that envy, as I have defined it, is very similar to Rawls' concept of resentment, for the existence of envy is clear-cut evidence that agents are being treated asymmetrically. In the above quotes, Rawls implies that a just society would be free from resentment.

Hence it would seem that a just allocation of goods in Rawls' sense must satisfy the criterion of fairness as I have defined it.

2.2 Fair division

In this section I will present some theorems concerning the problem of fair division previously introduced and discuss some of the relationships between the concepts of equity, envy, and efficiency. We will first restate the previous definitions in somewhat more formal terms.

An allocation x is *weakly efficient* (x *is in* PW) iff there is no feasible allocation y such that $y_i \succ_i x_i$ for all agents i. An allocation x is *strongly efficient* (x *is in* PS) iff there is no feasible allocation y such that $y_i \succeq_i x_i$ for all agents i and there is some agent j such that $y_j \succ_j x_j$. An allocation x is equitable iff $x_i \succeq_i x_j$ for all agents i and j. If $x_i \preceq_i x_j$, we will say that i *envies* j at the allocation x. If an allocation x is both equitable and strongly efficient, we will say x is fair. If the allocation x is equitable but only weakly efficient, we will say x is weakly fair.

A fundamental relationship between envy and efficiency is given in the following theorem.

THEOREM 2.1.   *If x is a strongly efficient allocation, then there is some agent that envies no one and there is some agent that no one envies.*

Thus there is a "top" and a "bottom" to the set of agents in a strongly efficient allocation. It is possible to extend this partial order to the whole set of agents by disregarding the nonenvious agents and their bundles and considering the resulting allocation; this allocation is still strongly efficient, and thus there are nonenvious agents. (These are the agents who envied only the original nonenvious agents.) We can consider these agents to be the "second best off," and then continue to extend the ordering. Unfortunately, simple examples show that the ordering which comes from disregarding the unenvied agents, those at the bottom of the pile, will not in general be consistent with the ordering just described. Nevertheless, it is of some interest to note that we can get a natural measure of how well off each agent is in any strongly efficient allocation.

Moving on to the concept of equity, we recall that a classical notion of equity in the context of a market economy is that of an equal-income competitive equilibrium, which is also, of course, an efficient allocation. It is therefore reassuring to notice that equal-income competitive allocations are indeed fair by our definition.

THEOREM 2.2.   *Suppose that preferences are monotonic. Then if* (x, p) *is a competitive equilibrium with* $p \cdot x_i = p \cdot x_j$ *for all i and j, then x is fair.*[3]

Interestingly enough, a competitive equilibrium from an equitable allocation is not necessarily fair, and not all fair allocations have equal incomes. Furthermore, there will in general be points in the equal division core which are not fair.

A primary concern about the usefulness of the concept of fair allocations is the question of whether they exist in general circumstances. The above theorem gives us an immediate result on this existence question.

THEOREM 2.3.   *If preferences are convex and monotonic, then fair allocations exist.*[4]

The primary restriction of the above theorem is that of convexity of preferences. As fair allocations can easily exist in the absence of this condition, the above result is somewhat unsatisfactory.

It turns out that a more general condition for the existence of fair allocations is that the topological structure of the set of efficient allocations be especially simple; that is, that it consist of one piece with no "holes" in it. The next theorem investigates conditions under which this is the case; here

$$PW_+ = \{x \text{ in } PW: x_i \neq 0 \text{ for any } i\},$$
$$u(PW_+) = \{(u_1(x_1), \ldots, u_n(x_n)): (x_1, \ldots, x_n) \text{ is in } PW_+\}.$$

THEOREM 2.4.   *Suppose that every agent prefers any nonzero bundle to the zero bundle; then* $u(PW_+)$ *is homeomorphic to the interior of*

---

[3] The first part of Theorem 2.2 is of course Koopmans' first optimality theorem. Since the definitions are slightly different, I have repeated the proof, inserting the necessary changes. The assumptions can be relaxed somewhat.

[4] The idea of Theorem 2.3 is due to Schmeidler and Yaari (1972).

*an $(n-1)$-dimensional simplex. Furthermore, if there are no two alloca-
tions in PW_+ which all agents regard as indifferent, then PW_+ is itself
homeomorphic to the interior of an $(n-1)$-dimensional simplex.*[5]

COROLLARY. *If preferences are monotonic and strictly convex, then
$\mathrm{PW} = \mathrm{PS}$ and both are homeomorphic to an $(n-1)$-dimensional simplex.*[6]

The assumptions that underly the above theorem, when coupled with the
results of Theorem 2.1, are enough to give the existence of fair allocations.

THEOREM 2.5. *If preferences are monotonic and there are no two
allocations in* PW *which all agents regard as indifferent, then fair allocations
exist.*[7]

The restrictive assumption in the above theorem is clearly the assumption about the two "Pareto indifferent" efficient allocations. This is, of
course, precluded by strict convexity of preferences, but as Example 2.1
(see the appendix to section 2) shows, this condition cannot be dispensed
with if we want the efficient set to be homeomorphic to a simplex and if we
want the existence of fair allocations. However, we can weaken the notion
of fairness somewhat and find a more general concept (though ethically less
satisfactory) that will exist without the above condition.

Consider the fair division problem as a bargaining process. Given a
strongly efficient allocation x, we will say that agent i *objects* to agent j
if (i) i envies j and (ii) i can propose a new allocation y that all agents
regard as indifferent to x where no one envies j. An objection to this new
allocation y by any other agent can be called a *counterobjection*. Then we
can define the *fair set of allocations, F,* as being the set of strongly efficient
allocations where every objection has a counterobjection. Thus in the fair
set there are either no envies, or the envies tend to "cancel out." We can
show that

THEOREM 2.6. *If preferences are monotonic, then fair sets exist.*

A fundamental fact of our ethical notions is that "equals should be
treated equally." In the context of the fair division problem, we can interpret "equals" as agents who have exactly the same preferences. Then it

---

[5] The first part of Theorem 2.4 is a generalization of a lemma due to Arrow and Hahn
(1971), p. 111, which had required the use of convexity.

[6] The corollary to Theorem 2.4 is not new, although I have been unable to discover the
exact reference.

[7] The idea of using the Knaster-Kuratowski-Mazurkiewicz Lemma here is due to Schmeidler and Yaari (1972). The hypothesis of monotonicity can be replaced by the hypotheses that PS = PW and any nonzero bundle is preferred to the zero bundle.

is obvious from the definition of fairness that at a fair allocation "equals are treated equally" in the sense that they are indifferent to each other's bundles. Further results in this direction follow.

THEOREM 2.7.   *Suppose the preferences of agent i are identical with those of j and both are strictly convex; then, if x is a fair allocation, $x_i = x_j$.*

In particular, if all agents have identical strictly convex preferences, then equal division is the unique fair allocation. However, we can relax this condition of strict convexity to get a rather general result on existence in the special case of equal tastes.

THEOREM 2.8.   *If any bundle is preferred to the 0 bundle and all agents have identical preferences, then weakly fair allocations exist.*

The theorem is not true if we replace "weakly fair" by "fair"; a counter-example can be constructed by using two agents with identical utility functions $u = \min(x_1, x_2)$ and an initial bundle to be divided of $(2, 1)$.

2.3 Fairness and production

In Section 2 an important characteristic of the problem of fair division was that the bundle of goods to be divided was fixed; that is, there were no possibilities for production. Since the social resources were regarded as fixed, it is not surprising that we were able to discover an appealing definition of fairness and a relatively general theorem of existence. When the resources are fixed and no information but preferences is available, it is only natural to assume that everyone has an equal prior claim to the social resources. Thus any perceived asymmetry by the agents, such as envy, cannot be tolerated. The situation is radically different when production is possible. For in this case the agents may contribute differently to the social product, and thus there is an inherent asymmetry to the problem. Indeed, the deepest problems of distributive justice are concerned precisely with this question: How do we divide the social product when agents can contribute differently to the formation of that product? We will try to investigate this question by extending the approach of fair division discussed in the last section.

We will assume that there is a fixed initial bundle of consumption goods w in R_+^k; furthermore, each agent can hold up to one unit of his own leisure. Thus the final bundles held by the ith agent are of the form $(x_i, 1 - q_i)$, where x_i is the ith agent's bundle of commodities, q_i is his amount of labor time, and thus $1 - q_i$ is his amount of leisure time. We will incorporate the technological production possibilities into the analysis by considering

the set of all feasible allocations X, a subset of $R^{n(1+k)}$. The definition
of strongly efficient allocations is similar to the previous definition; an
allocation is equitable iff $(x_i, 1 - q_i) \succ_i (x_j, 1 - q_j)$ for all agents i and
j, and an allocation is fair iff it is both equitable and strongly efficient.
Thus, if we have an efficient allocation where each agent (weakly) prefers
his consumption-leisure bundle to any other agent's, that allocation is fair.

The problem with this approach is simply this: Fair allocations, as defined above, will not in general exist even in very regular cases. The problem becomes apparent when we examine the proof of Theorem 2.6; for this
theorem we need the results of both Theorem 2.4 (that the efficient set is
homeomorphic to a simplex) and Theorem 2.1 (that at an efficient allocation there is some agent that no one envies.) There is no problem with
Theorem 2.6; the efficient set will still be homeomorphic to a simplex if
we assume that (i) zero consumption and zero leisure is the worst possible
bundle, and (ii) the set of feasible allocations is *regular*—i.e., it is compact
and convex, and if $(x, 1 - q)$ is in X, every allocation that is smaller than
$(x, 1 - q)$ is in X.

The problem comes in Theorem 2.1. Surprising as it may seem, it is
possible to have strongly efficient allocations where two agents each envy
the other. Consider the following two-person two-good example:

$$u_1(x_1, q_1) = \log x_1 + \log(35 - q_1),$$
$$u_2(x_2, q_2) = \log x_2 + \log(25 - q_2),$$
$$x_1 + x_2 = (1/5)q_1 + q_2.$$

Consider the allocation $((6, 5), (10,15))$. It is easy to check that the marginal rates of substitution equal the marginal rates of transformation so
that this allocation is efficient. However,

$$u_1(x_1, q_1) = 6 \times 30 = 180,$$
$$u_1(x_2, q_2) = 10 \times 20 = 200,$$
$$u_2(x_2, q_2) = 10 \times 10 = 100,$$
$$u_2(x_1, ql) = 6 \times 20 = 120,$$

so that each agent envies the other. Since the crucial relationship between
envy and efficiency does not go through to the production case, the proof
of Theorem 2.6 does not work. In fact the following economy[8] has no fair
allocations at all, even though it exhibits constant returns to scale and
homogeneous utility functions:

$$u_1(x_1, q_1) = (11/10)x_1 + (1 - q_1),$$
$$u_2(x_2, q_2) = 2x_2 + (1 - q_2),$$
$$x_1 + x_2 = (1/10)q_2 + q_1,$$
$$0 \leq q_1 \leq 1, \qquad 0 \leq q_2 \leq 1.$$

---

[8] This example is due to Pazner and Schmeidler (1972a).

The intuitive reason for this is clear: Efficiency will always require that agent 1 do all the work and agent 2 compensates him for it by allowing him larger consumption. But in such a situation agent 2 will envy agent 1 because he consumes more of the goods and agent 1 will envy agent 2 because he consumes more leisure.

The fundamental problem here is that agent 2 really "envies" the ability of agent 1 as revealed in any efficient allocation. Since this ability cannot be traded, we cannot hope to get a fair allocation. Similarly, one person might envy another person's talent or good looks. However, there is an important difference between talent and productive ability; I may not be able to produce as fine a painting as Picasso could, but I could produce as many if I just worked more (and lived long enough). In economic activities with a well-defined product an agent with less ability may be able to produce as much as an agent with more ability simply by working longer and harder. It is this type of substitution that will allow us to define another notion of "fairness" in the productive case.

It is also important to notice that this nonexistence is not due solely to the fact that there are different types of labor or different abilities. The effect of different tastes is crucial, for one can show that Theorem 2.8 goes through unchanged so that, if all agents have the same preferences, a fair allocation exists even though agents' abilities may differ.

Apparently, to get a satisfactory notion of fairness in the production context, we will have to change our definition of "equity." We will consider two possible generalizations of the notion of fair allocations, each concentrating on different aspects of the concept of equity.

We will consider production technologies where it makes sense to associate with each agent the amount of goods that agent produces at a given allocation. Thus we can consider bundles of the form $(x_i, 1 - q_i, z_i)$, where x and q are as before and z_i is the amount of all commodities produced by the ith agent, so that z_i is an element of R^k. In what follows we will make the Independence Assumption: that z_i is independent of permutations of the other z_j's. Thus the production of the ith agent may depend on what others produce, but not on who produces it.

Under this assumption, it makes sense to ask how much j would have to work to produce what i produces at some particular allocation $(x, 1 - q, z)$; this will just be the amount of j's labor necessary to produce the output z_i assuming $z - z_i$ is held constant, and we will denote this amount of labor by $Q_j(z_i)$.

We shall now define an allocation as equitable* iff $(x_i, 1 - q_i, \succeq_i (x_j, 1 - Q_i(z_j))$ for all agents i and j. Of course, if it is impossible for agent i to produce what j produces, $Q_i(z_j)$ will be undefined, and we will regard the equity* condition as being vacuously satisfied for these two agents.

Admittedly this definition is not entirely ethically satisfactory. Perverse cases arise when one agent is the sole producer of some good, since in that case no complaint against him could be justified. It is especially bad if this agent is the sole producer of some good that gives utility only to him! However, in cases where there is a reasonable amount of substitution possibilities between agents' labor, the definition has a certain appeal. It only allows you to complain about another agent's consumption if you are willing to match his contribution to the social product. Otherwise your complaint cannot be considered legitimate. Thus I may "envy" a doctor who only works one day a week doing brain surgery and yet has substantial consumption; but unless I am willing to put in enough labor time to match his production of services—for example, 6 years of medical school required—my complaint against him cannot count as legitimate in the sense of equity*.

This definition does happily provide us with an existence theorem for fair* allocations; for the analog of Theorem 2.1 goes through.

THEOREM 3.1.   *If the Independence Assumption is satisfied, and if $(x, 1 - q)$ is a strongly efficient allocation, then there is some agent that envies* no one and some agent that no one envies*.*

And so the existence theorem works.

THEOREM 3.2.   *Let X be regular, let preferences be monotonic, and suppose that there are no two allocations in PW, which all agents regard as indifferent. Then fair* allocations exist.*

(Of course the analog of Theorem 2.6 concerning the existence of fair sets goes through also.)

Recall that in the case of fair division, a competitive equilibrium from an equal division was fair. An analogous result holds for fair* allocations. Suppose that we have a particularly simple kind of technology where there we can associate with each agent an "ability," a_i, so that if the ith agent works for q_i hours he contributes $a_i q_i$ "labor power." Production then depends only on the amount of "labor power," not on the amount of time worked by agents. In this special case, an allocation is equitable* iff $(x_i, 1 - q_i) \succ_i (x_j, 1 - (a_j/a_i)q_j)$ for all i and j. Then we have the following theorem.

THEOREM 3.3.   *Suppose that preferences are convex and monotonic; then if we choose an initial endowment where each agent gets w/n of the consumption goods and one unit of his own leisure, the resulting competitive equilibrium is fair*.*

So the "natural" equilibrium, with equal division and no compensation for abilities, has the property of equity*; if any agent preferred some other agent's bundle to his own, he would not be willing to produce what that other agent produces.

The intuition here is clear: If two agents produce the same output, efficiency requires that they be paid the same total amount, even though their wages may differ. Hence, if I prefer to produce what another agent produces and our initial endowments of goods are the same, I should be able to also afford his consumption bundle. This argument also shows how we could extend the theorem to more complex technologies; we only need require that agents evaluate consumption-output bundles rather than consumption-leisure bundles. Then the result should go through for any technology where an individual's output is defined.

We will now discuss the second concept of "fair allocations" that I mentioned earlier. If we have the classical conditions of convexity, monotonicity, and so on, every efficient allocation is a competitive equilibrium for some initial endowment. Thus with each efficient allocation $(x, 1 - q)$ we can associate a competitive price vector (p, r), where p is the price vector of the consumption goods and r is the vector of wage rates for the various kinds of labor. We can then associate with each agent an implicit income $y_i = (p, r) \cdot (x_i, 1 - q_i)$, where each agent's leisure is evaluated at his particular wage rate. We will then say that an allocation is income-fair iff $y_i = y_j$ for all agents i and j.

It is easy to prove that income-fair allocations will always exist; we simply divide the total consumption-leisure bundle up evenly by giving each agent an equal share of all consumption goods and an equal share of each other agent's leisure time and then trade to a competitive equilibrium. Since a given agent presumably only cares about his own leisure, Pareto efficiency implies that no agent will hold any other agent's leisure time at the competitive equilibrium. Stated formally:

THEOREM 3.4. *Suppose that preferences are convex and monotonic; then if we choose an initial endowment where each agent gets w/n of the consumption goods and l/n of each agent's leisure, the resulting competitive equilibrium is income fair.*[9]

Theorems 3.3 and 3.4 demonstrate the fundamental ambiguity of equity in the production case: Should we view labor time on an *individual* basis and give each agent the same amount of his individual leisure, or should we view labor time on a *social* basis and give each agent the same amount of "labor power"? In the first case we have equal wealth but no correction for ability, and in the second case we have equal incomes and total correction for ability.

2.4 Coalition fairness

The concept of equity allows comparisons between agents to be made only on an individualistic basis; each agent compares his own bundle to the

---

[9] Pazner and Schmeidler (1972b) prove a similar result.

bundle of each of the other agents. A stronger notion of equity might be one in which comparisons were allowed between *groups* of agents. For example, each group of agents could compare its aggregate bundle to the aggregate bundle of any other group of the same size. A concept of this type will be called *coalition fairness,* or, more briefly, c-fairness. Before we can state the formal definitions, we will need to set up some machinery.

We consider a collection of agents, C, which may be finite or infinite, and the set of coalitions of agents in C, $\mathcal{C}$, which we will assume to be a sigma-algebra of C. We have a measure on $\mathcal{C}$, $\lambda : \mathcal{C} \to R_+$, which measures the size of a coalition. If C is finite, λ will just be the normalized counting measure, while if C is a continuum we will assume that λ is an atomless measure, normalized so that $\lambda(C) = 1$.

Suppose that we have some fixed bundle of goods, w in R_+^k, to be divided among the agents of C. An allocation α will be a measure, $\alpha : C \to R_+^k, \alpha(C) = w$ that assigns to each coalition its aggregate bundle. [In the finite case it is sometimes convenient to use the standard definition of allocation as an nk vector $x = (x_1, \ldots, x_n)$.] Coalitions are assumed to have a preference ordering over possible allocations; we write "coalition A prefers α to β" as "$\alpha \succ\succ_A \beta$." Preferences are interpreted as "$\alpha \succ\succ_A \beta$" means "(almost) all agents in A prefer α to β" (see Debreu (1967)).

Finally, we denote by $R_e(\alpha)$ the e range of $\alpha : R_e(\alpha) = \{\alpha(A) : \lambda(A) = e\}$, and by $P_e(\alpha)$ the e-preferred bundles, $P_e(\alpha) = \{\beta(A) : \beta \succ\succ_A \alpha$ and $\lambda(A) = e\}$. $R_e(\alpha)$ consists of all aggregate bundles held by coalitions of size e in the allocation , and $P_e(\alpha)$ consists of all aggregate bundles that can be distributed among the agents of a coalition of size e to form a preferred (partial) allocation.

We can now succinctly state the definition of c-fairness.

DEFINITION.   *An allocation is c-fair iff* $P_e(\alpha) \cap R_d(\alpha) = \emptyset$ *for* $0 \leq d \leq 1, 0 < e \leq 1, d \leq e$.

In other words, an allocation α is c-fair iff no coalition of size e prefers any aggregate bundle of any coalition of the same size or smaller.[10]

Notice that this definition requires that a c-fair allocation be (weakly) Pareto efficient, since for $e = \lambda(C) = 1$ we require that $P_1(\alpha) \cap R(\alpha) = \emptyset$, so that there is no way to rearrange the allocation to make every agent better off.

The first question is, of course, when do c-fair allocations exist? Since the concept of c-fairness includes the concept of fairness, every c-fair allocation must certainly be fair but not vice verse. However, we do have the following.

---

[10] The definition of c-fairness is due to Vind (1971).

THEOREM 4.1. *If α is a competitive equilibrium with initial endowment $i(A) = \lambda(A)w$ for all A in $\mathcal{C}$, then α is c-fair.*[11]

In other words, equal-income competitive equilibria are c-fair.

Are there any other c-fair allocations? In general, the answer is "yes"; it is easy to construct examples in the two-person two-good Edgeworth box case. However, in an important sense, equal-income competitive equilibria are the only c-fair allocations for a fair division problem with many agents.

There are two approaches to formalizing and demonstrating this proposition: one is by considering a replicated economy in the manner of Debreu and Scarf (1963); the other is by considering an economy with an atomless continuum of agents in the manner of Vind (1964, 1971). We begin with the replicated economy.

Suppose that we have only a finite number of types of agents $i = 1, \ldots, m$. Here, by saying that two agents are of the same type, I only mean that they have the same preferences. We will assume that these preferences are strongly convex, continuous, and insatiable, as do Debreu and Scarf (1963). Under these assumptions, it is clear that c-fair allocations must have the equal-treatment property; that is, if α is c-fair, then agents of the same type must get the same bundle. (This is proved formally in Lemma 4 in the appendix to section 4).

Now consider a given allocation $x = (x_1, \ldots, x_n)$ which is c-fair, and let the economy replicate; that is, consider an economy with r agents of each type and r times the original bundle w to be divided among them. (Admittedly this is not quite the fair division problem, since the bundle to be divided keeps increasing as the economy replicates; however, since the number of agents keeps growing also, the problem is essentially the same from the viewpoint of an individual agent.)

Since c-fair allocations have the equal treatment property, we only need to consider their projection into the m-type space, so clearly we will get no more of them in the replicated economy; the question is, will we get fewer? The answer is "yes"; in fact, we have the following theorem.

THEOREM 4.2. *If $(x_1, \ldots, x_m)$ is c-fair for all replications r, then it is a competitive equilibrium with equal incomes—that is, with initial endowment $\omega_i = w/m$ for $i = 1, \ldots, m$.*

In the two-person two-good Edgeworth box case there is a simple diagrammatic argument which is presented as Example 4.1 (see the appendix to Section 4).

---

[11] Theorem 4.1 was stated and proved by Vind in (1971). A quite general theorem on the existence of a competitive equilibrium with a continuum of agents may be found in Auman (1966).

If c-fair allocations are equal-income competitive allocations in the limit, we would expect that to be the case when we start out with a continuum of agents. As usual, we can also dispense with the assumption of convexity of preferences in the continuum case.

First we note the following.

THEOREM 4.3.   *If $(C, \mathcal{C}, \lambda)$ is an atomless economy and α is a c-fair allocation, then α is atomless.*[12]

Thus we only need to consider atomless allocations as candidates for c-fair allocations. We now have the following theorem.

THEOREM 4.4.   *If $(C, \mathcal{C}, \lambda)$ is an atomless economy, then α is c-fair implies that α is a competitive equilibrium with $i(A) = \lambda(A)w$ for all A in $\mathcal{C}$.*[13]

The implication of Theorems 4.2 and 4.4 seems to be that, if we wish to divide things fairly among a large number of agents so that the allocation is stable with respect to envy among coalitions, then our only choice is an allocation that is a competitive equilibrium with equal incomes.

It has been suggested to me that a more general and more symmetric definition of coalition fairness might be one where each coalition compares its "average" bundle to the "average" bundle of each other coalition.[14] In this way, each coalition can consider the aggregate bundles of all other coalitions, not just coalitions of the same size or smaller. We can formalize this notion in the following definition:

DEFINITION.   *An allocation α is c'-fair iff $P_e(\alpha) \cup (e/d)R_d(\alpha) = \emptyset$ for all $0 < d \le 1$ and $0 < e \le 1$.*

Thus each coalition examines the aggregate bundle of each other coalition, weighting the aggregate bundle by their relative sizes; if any such weighted bundle is preferred by the examining coalition, the allocation cannot be c'-fair.

It is clear that the notion of c'-fairness implies the notion of c-fairness, and one would suspect that it is a strictly stronger notion; that is, that there are c-fair allocations that are not c'-fair. However, that is not the case.

---

[12] Theorem 4.3 was stated by Vind (1971).

[13] Theorem 4.4 is a generalization of a theorem by Vind (1971), which had required the additional hypothesis that the dimension of $\cup R_e(\alpha)$ be k. Since this hypothesis is economically meaningless, the present version is a substantial improvement.

[14] Andreu Mas-Collel and Michael Scriven made this suggestion.

THEOREM 4.5.   *Let (C, C, λ) be an atomless economy; then an allocation α is c'-fair if and only if it is c-fair.*

2.5 Appendix to section 2

The set of feasible allocations will be denoted by

$$X - \{x \text{ in } R_+^{nk} : \sum x_i \leq w\}.$$

We assume $w \gg 0$. We will assume that each agent i has preferences $\succeq_i$ defined on the commodity space R_+^k and that these preferences are complete, transitive, and closed. Thus these preferences can be represented by continuous utility functions $u_i \colon R_+^k \to R$.

Preferences are said to be convex iff for $x' \neq x$, $x' \succ_i x$ implies

$$ax + (1 - a)x' \succeq_i x \quad \text{for } 0 \leq a \leq 1.$$

Preferences are strictly convex iff, in the above case, $ax + (1 - a)x' \succ_i x$ for $0 < a < 1$. Preferences are monotonic iff $x \leq x'$ and $x \neq x'$ implies $x \prec_i x'$.

An allocation x is a competitive equilibrium with prices p and initial endowment ω iff $x' \succ_i x_i$ implies that $p \cdot x' > p \cdot x$, and $p \cdot x_i \leq p \cdot \omega_i$ for $i = 1, \ldots, n$.

$$S^{n-1} = \{x \text{ in } R_+^n : \sum x_i = \text{ the unit simplex }\}.$$
$$\text{int } S^{n-1} = \{x \text{ in } S^{n-1} : \sum x_i > 0 \text{ for all } i = 1, \ldots, n\}.$$
$$S_j^{n-1} = \{x \text{ in } S^{n-1} : x_j = 0\} = \text{ the } j\text{th side of } S^{n-1}.$$

THEOREM 2.1.   *If x is a strongly efficient allocation, then there is some agent that envies no one and there is some agent that no one envies.*

Proof. Suppose to the contrary that each agent envies some other agent. Then, since there are only a finite number of agents, there is some cycle $(i_1, \ldots, i_m)$ such that i_1 envies i_2 envies $\cdots$ envies i_m envies i_1. Then the allocation x' where each agent in the cycle receives the bundle of the agent he envies and agents outside the cycle remain the same is feasible and dominates the original allocation x. This contradicts the fact that x is strongly efficient.

The proof of the second assertion is similar. ∎

THEOREM 2.2.   *Suppose that preferences are monotonic. Then if (x, p) is a competitive equilibrium with $p \cdot x_i = p \cdot x_j$ for all i and j, x is fair.*

Proof. Proof. First we will show that x is strongly efficient. Assume not; then there is some allocation y such that $y_i \succeq_i x_i$ for $i = 1, \ldots, n$ and, for some j, $y_j \succ_j x_j$. We can choose y so that it itself is strongly efficient.

For each j that strictly prefers y_j to x we have $p \cdot y_j > p \cdot x_j$. Consider some agent i that is indifferent between x_i and y_i, if any such agents exist. If $p \cdot y_i < p \cdot x_i$, the agent could afford to buy a slightly more expensive bundle, and by monotonicity he could find a bundle strictly better than x_i, contradicting the fact that x_i is a competitive equilibrium. Thus

$$p \cdot y_i \geq p \cdot x_i$$

so that

$$\sum p \cdot y_i > \sum p \cdot x_i.$$

Since preferences are monotonic,

$$\sum y_i = \sum x_i = \sum \omega_i,$$

but this gives us

$$p \cdot \sum \omega_i > p \cdot \sum \omega_i.$$

This is a contradiction, so it must be that x is strongly efficient.

To show that x is also equitable, we suppose that agent i envies agent j: $x_i \prec_i x_j$. Then by definition of competitive equilibrium, $p \cdot x_i < p \cdot x_j = p \cdot x_i$, which is a contradiction. ∎

THEOREM 2.3. *If preferences are convex and monotonic, then fair allocations exist.*

Proof. Let the initial allocation ω be defined by $\omega_i = w/n$. Under the assumptions of the theorem, standard existence proofs show that a competitive equilibrium (x, p) will exist, be in PS, and $p \cdot x_i = p \cdot x_j = p \cdot (w/n)$. By Theorem 2.2 this will be fair. ∎

THEOREM 2.4. *Suppose that every agent prefers any nonzero bundle to the zero bundle; then $u(\mathrm{PW}_+)$ is homeomorphic to the interior of an $(n-1)$-dimensional simplex. Furthermore, if there are no two allocations in PW_+ that all agents regard as indifferent, then PW_+ is itself homeomorphic to the interior of an $(n-1)$-dimensional simplex.*

Proof. We will, without loss of generality, normalize the utility functions so that $u_i(0) = 0$ and $u_i(w/n) = 1$. The proof proceeds in a number of steps.

STEP 1. If x is feasible, $x_i \neq 0$ for any i, and x is not in PW, then there exists a feasible allocation z and a real number $t > 1$ such that $u_i(z_i) = t u_i(x_i)$ for all $i = 1, \ldots, n$.

Proof. If x is not in PW, then there exists some feasible y such that $u_i(y_i)/u_i(x_i) > 1$ for $i = 1,\ldots,n$. Let $t = \min_i u_i(y_i)/u_i(x_i)$. The functions $f_i\colon [0,1] \to R$ defined by $f(e) = u_i(ey)/u_i(x)$ are continuous, $f_i(1) \geq t$, $f_i(0) = 0 < t$. Therefore, by the intermediate value theorem, there is a set of e_i' such that $f_i(e_i') = t$; the allocation defined by $z_i = e_i'y_i$ is feasible and satisfies the above requirements.

STEP 2. Let $p\colon u(\mathrm{PW}_+) \to \operatorname{int} S^{n-1}$ be defined by $p(u) = u/\sum u_i$. The function p is certainly continuous on $u(\mathrm{PW}_+)$, since the denominator can not vanish. Furthermore, I claim it is one to one on $u(\mathrm{PW}_+)$.

Proof. Assume not; then there exists u, v in $u(\mathrm{PW}_+)$ such that

$$u\Big/\sum u_i = v\Big/\sum v_i = z \text{ in int} S^{n-1}.$$

Therefore the u and v are scalar multiples of each other with no zero coordinates, so that one is strictly greater than the other, which contradicts the fact that both are in $u(\mathrm{PW}_+)$.

STEP 3. The set $T(y) = \{t \text{ in } R\colon ty \text{ is in } u(X)\}$ contains a nonzero element for each y in S^{n-1}.

Proof. The set of functions $g_i\colon [0,1] \to R$ defined by

$$g_i(e_i) = u_i(e_i(w/n))$$

are continuous, $g_i(1) = 1$, $g_i(0) = 0$. Applying the intermediate value theorem again, we find that for y in S^{n-1} there exists e_i' in $[0,1]$ such that $u_i(e_i'(w/n)) = y_i$ and the allocation $e_i'(w/n)$ for $i = 1,\ldots,n$ is certainly feasible. Therefore 1 is in $T(y)$.

STEP 4. The function $p\colon u(\mathrm{PW}_+) \to \operatorname{int} S^{n-1}$ is onto.

Proof. Given y in int S^{n-1}, the set $T(y)$ defined above is compact and nonempty. Then there exists $0 \neq t' = $ the maximum t such that t is in $T(y)$. Suppose that $t'y$ is not in $u(\mathrm{PW}_+)$; then by Step 1 there is some t'' such that $t''t'y$ is in $u(X)$. But then $t''t' > t'$, which contradicts the maximality of t'.

STEP 5. p^{-1} is continuous on int S^{n-1}.

Proof. Let K be an arbitrary closed set in $u(\mathrm{PW}_+)$. Then K is compact since it is a subset of a compact set, namely, $u(\mathrm{PW})$. For p^{-1} to be continuous, we need $(p^{-1})^{-1}(K)$ to be closed. Since p is one to one and onto, this set is just $p(K)$, which is closed by compactness of K.

STEP 6. p is a homeomorphism between $u(\mathrm{PW}_+)$ and int S^{n-1}.

Proof. It is one to one, continuous, and onto. Furthermore, if there are no two allocations x and y in PW_+ such that $u_i(x_i) = u_i(y_i)$ for $i = 1, \ldots, n$ the map u restricted to PW_+ will be one to one. It is clearly continuous and onto, so composing it with p will give us a homeomorphism between PW_+ and int S^{n-1} ∎

COROLLARY. *If preferences are strongly monotonic and strictly convex, then* $\text{PS} = \text{PW}$ *and both are homeomorphic to an* $(n-1)$*-dimensional simplex.*

Proof. That PW contains PS is obvious. We will show that PS contains PW. Suppose the allocation x is not in PS; then there is some allocation y such that $u_i(y_i) \geq u_i(x_i)$ for all i, and $u_j(y_j) > u_j(x_j)$ for some j. By continuity we can remove a positive fraction $1 - \theta$ of all commodities from y_j and still have $u_j(\theta y_j) > u_j(x_j)$. Then define an allocation z by $z_j = \theta y_j$, $z_i = y_i + (1 - \theta)y_j/(n-1)$ for $i = 1, \ldots, n$, $i \neq j$. The allocation z has the property that $u_i(z_i) > u_i(x_i)$ for all $i = 1, \ldots, n$, so that x is not in PW.

We now need to show that there are no two allocations in PW which all agents regard as indifferent. Suppose that x and y are two such allocations; then $\frac{1}{2}x + \frac{1}{2}Y$ is feasible, at least as good for all agents, and strictly preferred to both x and y by agents for whom $x_i \neq y_i$, which contradicts the efficiency of x and y.

The fact that the homeomorphism p is one to one and onto on the boundary of PW can be verified from the fact that $\text{PS} = \text{PW}$ and the steps of the theorem. ∎

THEOREM 2.5. *If preferences are monotonic and there are no two allocations in* PW *which all agents regard as indifferent, then fair allocations exist.*

Proof. By the remarks in Step 6 of Theorem 2.4, we see that u is a homeomorphism between PW_+ and $u(\text{PW}_+)$. In Theorem 2.6 we see that the intersection of the $u(M_j)$'s is nonempty, and thus the intersection of the M_j's is nonempty. Any allocation in this intersection is fair. ∎

LEMMA (*Knaster, Kuratowski, and Mazurkiewicz*). *Let* $M_1, \ldots, M_n$ *be a family of closed subsets of* S^{n-1} *with the property that the* j*th face of* S^{n-1} *is contained in* M_j*, and that* S^{n-1} *is contained in the union of the* M_j*. Then the intersection of the* M_j *is nonempty.*

Proof. See Scarf (1973), p. 68. ∎

THEOREM 2.6. *If preferences are monotonic, then fair sets exist.*

Proof. Define the set of allocations where no agent envies agent j: $M_j = \{x \text{ in PS} : u_i(x_i) \geq u_i(x_j) \text{ for all } i = 1, \ldots, n\}$. Then the union of these sets for $j = 1, \ldots, n$ covers PS by Theorem 2.1, and by the Corollary to Theorem 2.4 PW = PS. Since the functions u_i are continuous, M_j is closed, and, since any bundle is preferred to the zero bundle, M_j contains all allocations in PS where $x_j = 0$.

Now take the image of these sets M, under the map pu: PS $\to S^{n-1}$ defined by

$$\mathrm{pu}(x) = (u_1(x_1) \cdots u_n(x_n)) \Big/ \sum u_i(x_i) \,.$$

The sets $\mathrm{pu}(M_j)$, $j = 1, \ldots, n$, satisfy the hypotheses of the lemma of Knaster, Kuratowski, and Mazurkiewicz, so that their intersection is not empty.

Let z be in this intersection; then $z \gg 0$ since, if $z_i = 0$ for some i, there would be some j such that $Z_j > 0$ and therefore $p^{-1}(z)$ would not be in $u(M_j)$. Since the points where $z \gg 0$ form the interior of S^{n-1}, p is a homeomorphism on such points, so that the intersection of the $u(M_j)$ is nonempty for $j = 1, \ldots, n$. Let v be in this intersection and consider the set $u^{-1}(v)$, which I claim is a fair set, F.

This is true because

(i) $u_i(x_i) = u_i(y_i)$ for all x, y in F, $i = 1, \ldots, n$.

(ii) Suppose that $u_i(x_j) > u_i(x_i)$, so that x is not in M_j for some x in $F = u^{-1}(v)$. But v is in $u(M_j)$, so there must be some other allocation y in $u^{-1}(v)$ that is in M_j, which means $u_i(y_i)u_i(y_j)$ for $i = 1, \ldots, n$ and $u_i(y_i) = u_i(x_i)$ for $i = 1, \ldots, n$. ∎

THEOREM 2.7.   *If the preferences of agent i are identical with those of j and both are strictly convex, then, if x is a fair allocation, $x_i = x_j$.*

Proof.   Assume that $x_i \neq x_j$, and consider the allocation $z = (1/2)x_i + (1/2)x_j$. Since x is fair and i and j have the same preferences, $x_i \sim_i x_j$ and $x_j \sim_j x_i$, so that $z \succ_i x_j$ and $z \succ_j x_j$. Since giving z to both i and j is feasible, this contradicts strong efficiency. ∎

THEOREM 2.8.   *If any bundle is preferred to the zero bundle and all agents have identical preferences, then weakly fair allocations exist.*

Proof.   If an allocation is to be fair in these circumstances, it must give equal utility to each agent and also be weakly efficient. Let pu be the map defined in Theorem 2.4, Step 2; then $(\mathrm{pu})^{-1} (1/n, \ldots, 1/n)$ is a set of weakly efficient allocations with equal utilities. ∎

EXAMPLE 2.1. Monotonicity does not imply the existence of fair allocations. (However, the allocations x and y form a fair set.)

To see that there are no fair allocations in Fig. 1, imagine a point such as x_0 or y_0 that moves along one of the components of PS. As x_0 moves along the left component, its swap x_0 always lies on a higher indifference curve than does x_0, showing that x_0 cannot be fair. The point y_0 behaves similarly.

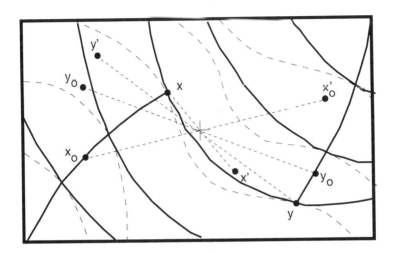

Figure 1. Nonexistence of fair allocations.

2.6 Appendix to section 3

THEOREM 3.1.   *If the Independence Assumption is satisfied and y $(x, 1 - q)$ is a strongly efficient allocation, then there is some agent that envies* no one, and some agent that no one envies*.*

Proof. The proof is similar to the proof of Theorem 2.1. Suppose that each agent envies* some other agent. Since there are only a finite number of agents, there must be some cycle. Performing the "swap" among the agents in the cycle is feasible because of the definition of envy* and the Independence Assumption; the resulting allocation dominates the original one, contradicting efficiency. ∎

THEOREM 3.2.   *Let X be regular, let preferences be monotonic, and suppose that there are no two allocations in PW which all agents regard as indifferent. Then fair* allocations exist.*

Proof. The proof is similar to those of Theorems 2.5 and 2.6. The first hypotheses allow the proof of Theorem 2.4 to work in this case, which makes the efficient set homeomorphic to a simplex. Since Theorem 4.1 provides the analog to Theorem 2.1, the application of the Knaster-Kuratowski-Mazurkiewicz Lemma can proceed as before. ∎

THEOREM 3.3. *Suppose that preferences are convex and monotonic; then, if we choose an initial endowment where each agent gets w/n of the consumption goods and one unit of his own leisure, the resulting competitive equilibrium is fair*.*

Proof. The assumptions imply the existence of a competitive equilibrium with prices p and wages r. We can normalize the wage of labor with ability of unity to have $r_i = 1$; since in the competitive equilibrium all wages will be proportional to ability in this case, the normalization will make $r_i = a_i$ for $i = 1, \ldots, n$. By the definition of competitive equilibrium, we have

$$(p, ai) \cdot (xq_i) = p \cdot w/n + a_i,$$

or, by rewriting,

$$p \cdot x_i - a_i q_i = p \cdot w/n \quad \text{for } i = 1, \ldots, n.$$

It is clear that $(x, 1-q)$ is efficient; assume then that some agent i envies* some agent j. Then

$$(x_i, 1 - q_i) \prec_i (x_j, 1 - (a_j/a_i)q_j),$$

which implies

$$(p, a_i) \cdot (x_i, q_i) < (p, a_i) \cdot (x_j, (a_j/a_i)q_j).$$

Expanding and substituting, we get

$$p \cdot w/n = p \cdot x_i - a_i q_i < p \cdot x_j - a_j q_j = pw/n$$

which gives us the contradiction. ∎

EXAMPLE 3.1. The following economy has no fair allocations:

$$u_1(x_1, q_1) = (11/10)x_1 + (1 - q_1),$$
$$u_2(x_2, q_2) = 2x_2 + (1 - q_2),$$
$$x_1 + x_2 = q_1 + (1/10)q_2 \quad \text{for } 0 \le q_1 \le 1, 0 \le q_2 \le 1$$

Proof.
   (a) In any efficient allocation we must have
   (i) $q_1 = 1$, since if q_1 were strictly less than 1 we would have $u_1(x_1+(1-q_1), 0)$ strictly greater than $u_1(x_1, q_1)$, and that bundle would be feasible for agent 1;

(ii) $q_2 = 0$, since if q_2 were strictly greater than 0 we would have $u_2(x_2 - e/10, q_2 - e)$ strictly greater than $u_2(x_2, q_2)$, and that bundle would be feasible for agent 2, for small enough e.

(b) If $x_2 = 0$ we would have

$$u_2(x_1, q_1) = 2 > 1 = u_2(x_2, q_2),$$

which is certainly not fair.

(c) We are left which the case where the allocation is of the form $(x(x_2, 0))$ with $x_1 + x_2 = 1$. For an allocation of this form to be fair, we must have

$$u_1(x_1, q_1) \geq u_1(x_2, q_2),$$
$$(11/10)x_1 \geq (11/10)x_2 + 1,$$

and

$$u_2(x_2, q_2) \geq u_2(x_1, q_1),$$
$$2x_2 + 1 \geq 2x_1$$

But these two inequalities, along with the equality $x_1 + x_2 = 1$, imply that $3/4 \geq x_1 \geq 21/22$, which is a contradiction. ∎

2.7 Appendix to section 4

Definitions

An allocation α is in the (equal division) core iff there is no allocation and coalition B such that $\beta \succ\succ_B \alpha$ and $\beta(B) = \lambda(B)w$ for $\lambda(B) > 0$.

An allocation α is a competitive equilibrium from $i(A) = \lambda(A)w$ iff there exists a price vector p in R^k such that $p \cdot \alpha(A) = p \cdot i(A)$ for all A in $\mathcal{C}$ and $p \cdot x > p \cdot i(A)$ for all x in $P_e(\alpha)$, A in $\mathcal{C}$ such that $\lambda A(A) = e > 0$.

A coalition A is an atom for a measure μ iff, $\mu(A) > 0$ and $B \subset A$ implies that $\mu(B) = \mu(A)$ or $\mu(B) = 0$.

Assumptions on Preferences

(a) In the replication case we make the assumptions of Debreu and Scarf (1963): namely,

(i) *Insatiability.* Given a commodity bundle x, we assume there is a commodity bundle x' such that $x' \succ_i x$.

(ii) *Strong convexity.* Let x' and x be arbitrary commodity bundles, $x' \neq x$, $x' \succ_i x$, and let $0 < a < 1$. We assume that

$$ax + (1-a)x' \succ_i x.$$

(iii) *Continuity.* We assume that $\{x : x \succeq_i x'\}$ and $\{x : x' \succeq_i x\}$ are closed.

(b) In the continuum case we make the assumptions of Vind (1964): namely,

(1) *Independence.* The preferences of a coalition A are independent of the values of the allocation outside of A.

(ii) *Monotonicity.* If an allocation α gives at least the same amount as β to all subcoalitions of A and more of at least one commodity to all subcoalitions of A with $\beta(B) \neq 0$, then A prefers α to β and to any allocation worse than β.

(iii) *Continuity.* If β is preferred to α by A, then any commodity bundle in a neighborhood of $\beta(A)$ can be allocated to A in such a way that the new allocation is still preferred to α by A.

Facts

THEOREM (*Debreu and Scarf*).   *If the assumptions of (a) above are met and if $(x_1, \ldots, x_m)$ is in the (equal division) core for all replications r, then it is a competitive equilibrium with equal incomes.*

THEOREM (*Vind*).   *If the assumptions of (b) above are met, then for $(C, \mathcal{C}, \lambda)$ an atomless economy, the (equal division) core exactly coincides with the set of allocations that are competitive equilibria from $i(A) = \lambda(A)w$ for A in $\mathcal{C}$.*

THEOREM (*Lyaponov*).   *The range of a vector-valued measure is closed and convex.*

LEMMA 4.0.   *If preferences are strongly convex, then c-fair allocations have the equal treatment property; that is, if x is a c-fair allocation and the preferences of agent i are exactly the same as the preferences of agent j, then $x_i = x_j$.*

Proof. Suppose that the total number of agents is n, and let $e = 2/n$. Setting $z = x_i + x_j$, we have that z is in $R_e(\alpha)$, for α the measure corresponding to the allocation x.

Since x is c-fair, $x_i \sim_i x_j$ and $x_j \sim_j x_i$. Assuming that $x_i \neq x_j$, we have that $y = (1/2)x_i + (1/2)x_j$ is preferred by both i and j to their present bundles by strong convexity, and thus the aggregate bundle $2y = z$ is in

$P_e(\alpha)$ Since $P_e(\alpha)$ and $R_e(\alpha)$ are thus not disjoint, the allocation x cannot be c-fair. This is a contradiction. ∎

THEOREM 4.1.   *If α is a competitive equilibrium with initial endowment $i(A) - \lambda(A)w$ for all A in C, then α is c-fair.*

Proof. Assume not; then there is some coalition A that prefers to have the bundle of some coalition B with $\lambda(B) \leq \lambda(A)$. Thus, $p \cdot \alpha(B) > p \cdot \alpha(A)$. But $i(A) = \lambda(A)w \geq \lambda(B)w = i(B)$, so that $p \cdot i(B) \leq p \cdot i(A)$, which contradicts the definition of a competitive equilibrium. ∎

THEOREM 4.2.   *If $(x_1, \ldots, x_m)$ is c-fair for all replications r, then it is a competitive equilibrium with equal incomes; that is, with initial endowment $\omega_i = w/m$ for $i = 1, \ldots, m$.*

Proof. Suppose that $x = (x_1, \ldots, x_m)$ is c-fair but is not in the (equal division) r-core for some replication r. Then we wish to show that eventually x cannot be c-fair.

If x is not in the r-core, then it is blocked by some coalition S that has s members, $N_i(S)$ members of each type, $i = 1, \ldots, m$. Let z be the (partial) allocation that is preferred by S that is feasible for it; we have

$$\sum_{i=1}^{m} \sum_{q=1}^{r} z_{iq} = \frac{sw}{m}.$$

(Here z_{iq} refers to the bundle of an agent of type i in replication q, for agent iq in S.)

Let MS be the coalition consisting of $mN_i(S)$ agents of type $i = 1, \ldots, m$. This is just an m-times replication of S and thus has ms members. Furthermore, it blocks $(x_1, \ldots, x_m)$ via the (partial) allocation z', where z' is just the m-times replication of z, and thus

$$\sum_{i=1}^{m} \sum_{q=1}^{rm} z'_{iq} = \frac{smw}{m} = sw.$$

Consider now the coalition SM consisting of s copies of each of the original m types of agents. SM is the same size as MS; furthermore, at the original allocation x, SM holds $s \sum_{i=1}^{m} x_i = sw$, so that the (partial) allocation z' is feasible for it and the allocation z' is preferred by MS to its allocation, which shows that x is not c-fair.

Therefore, if x is c-fair for every replication r, it must eventually be in every r-core, and thus it must be a competitive equilibrium with equal incomes, by the Theorem of Debreu and Scarf. ∎

THEOREM 4.3.   *If $(C, \mathcal{C}, \lambda)$ is an atomless economy and α is a c-fair allocation, then α is atomless.*

Proof. Assume not and let A be an atom for α; by definition of atom, $\alpha(A) > 0$. There are two cases:

(a) $\lambda(A) = 0$. Since there can be at most only a countable number of atoms of α, we can find a nonatomic coalition B with $\lambda(B) > \lambda(A)$ and $\alpha(B) < \alpha(A)$. This contradicts the assumption that α is c-fair.

(b) $0 < \lambda(A) \leq 1$. Let $A = B \cup D$ with $\lambda(B) = \lambda(D) = (1/2)\lambda(A)$. Then $\alpha(B) + \alpha(D) = \alpha(A)$, and yet either

(i) $\alpha(B) = 0$ and $\alpha(D) = \alpha(A)$, or

(ii) $(D) = 0$ and $\alpha(B) = \alpha(A)$.

In either case, α is not c-fair. ∎

THEOREM 4.4.   *If $(C, \mathcal{C}, \lambda)$ is an atomless economy, then α is c-fair implies that α is a competitive equilibrium with $i(A) = \lambda(A)w$ for all A in $\mathcal{C}$.*

Proof. Assume that α is not a competitive equilibrium with $i(A) = \lambda(A)w$ for all A in $\mathcal{C}$. Then α is not in the (equal division) core. Thus there are (β, B) such that $\beta \succ\succ_B \alpha$ and $\beta(B) = i(B) = \lambda(B)w$, so $\lambda(B)w$ is in $P_e(\alpha)$ for $e = \lambda(B)$.

Consider now the range of the vector valued measure (α, λ). Certainly $(\alpha(C), 1)$ is in it and certainly $(0, 0)$ is in it; by convexity $(\lambda(B)\alpha(C), \lambda(B))$ is in it. Since $\alpha(C) = w$, this implies that $\lambda(B)w$ is in $R_e(\alpha)$ for $e = \lambda(B)$, which contradicts the fact that α is c-fair. ∎

THEOREM 4.5.   *Let $(C, \mathcal{C}, \lambda)$ be an atomless economy; then an allocation α is c'-fair iff it is c-fair.*

Proof. Proof.

(i) *Sufficiency.* This is equivalent to "α is not c-fair" implies that "α is not c'-fair." If α is not c-fair, then for some d less than or equal to some e, $P_e(\alpha) \cup R_d(\alpha) \neq \emptyset$, so that there is some bundle x in the intersection. Then $(e/d)x \geq x$ so that $(e/d)x$ is in $P_e(\alpha)$ by monotonicity, which implies that α is not c'-fair.

(ii) *Necessity.* If α is c-fair, it is a competitive equilibrium with prices p such that $p \cdot \alpha(A) = p \cdot \lambda(A)w$ for all A in $\mathcal{C}$, by Theorem 4.4. Suppose that α is not c'-fair; then $(e/d)\alpha(B)$ is in $P_e(\alpha)$ for some B with $\lambda(B) = d$. By definition of competitive equilibrium, we have

$$p \cdot (e/d)\alpha(B) > p \cdot we.$$

But $p \cdot \alpha(B) = p \cdot \lambda(B)w$, so that $p \cdot \lambda(B)w(e/d) > p \cdot we$, which implies that $p\dot{w}e > p \cdot we$, since $\lambda(B) = d$. This is a contradiction. ∎

EXAMPLE 4.1. Consider the example depicted in Fig. 2, where x is c-fair, since it is preferred by both agents to its swap x', but x is not a competitive equilibrium with equal incomes or even in the (equal division) 1-core.

Let the economy replicate once so that we have two agents of each type, and consider the coalition AA consisting of two agents of type A and the coalition AB consisting of one agent of type A and one agent of type B.

Since x is outside of the core, both agents of type A prefer the allocation $w/2$ to what they hold at x. But the allocation $w/2$ is feasible for the coalition AB, and thus AA prefers the aggregate bundle of AB, so x is not c-fair.

A similar argument can be made for any allocation that is outside of the r-core for any replication r. Since the core shrinks down to the competitive equilibrium, this is the only allocation that can be c-fair for all r.

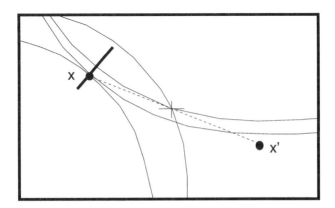

Figure 2. Coalition-fair allocations and replication.

References

K. Arrow (1973) "Some Ordinalist-Utilitarian Notes on Rawls' Theory of Justice," *Journal of Philosophy*, **70**, 245-263.

K. J. Arrow and F. J. Hahn (1971) *General Competitive Analysis*. San Francisco, CA: Holden-Day.

R. Auman (1966) "Existence of Competitive Equilibria in Markets with a Continuum of Traders," *Econometrica*, **34**, 1-17.

G. Debreu (1967) "Preference Functions on Measure Spaces of Economic Agents," *Econometrica*, **35**, 111-122.

G. Debreu and H. Scarf (1963) "A Limit Theorem on the Core of an Economy," *International Economic Review*, **4**, 235-246.

D. Foley (1967) "Resource Allocation and the Public Sector," *Yale Economic Essays*, **7**.

E. Pazner and D. Schmeidler (1972a) "A Difficulty in the Concept of Equity," Tel-Aviv University, Technical Report.

E. Pazner and D. Schmeidler (1972b) "Decentralization, Income Distribution, and the Role of Money in Socialist Economies," Technical Report No. 8, The Foerder Institute for Economic Research, Tel-Aviv University.

J. Rawls (1971) *A Theory of Justice*. Cambridge, MA: Harvard University Press.

A. Sen (1970) *Collective Choice and Social Welfare*. San Francisco, CA: Holden-Day.

H. Scarf (1973) *The Computation of Economic Equilibria*. New Haven, CT: Yale University Press.

D. Schmeidler and M. Yaari (1972) "Fair allocations," unpublished.

D. Schmeidler and K. Vind (1972) "Fair Net Trades," *Econometrica*, **40**, 637-642.

K. Vind (1964) "Edgeworth Allocations in an Exchange Economy with Many Traders," *International Economic Review*, **5**, 165-177.

K. Vind (1971) "Lecture Notes for Economics 288," Stanford University.

Chapter 3

TWO PROBLEMS IN THE THEORY OF FAIRNESS

An allocation is called fair iff it is Pareto efficient and no agent prefers the bundle of any other agent to his own. This paper briefly discusses the conceptual foundations of this definition and then considers two problems in the theory of fairness. The first involves clarifying the sense in which equal income competitive equilibria are "especially fair", and the second involves a suggestion for using the fairness idea for "second best" comparisons of arbitrary allocations.

An allocation x is called *equitable* iff no agent prefers another agent's bundle to his own. If at a given allocation some agent does prefer another agent's bundle to his own, we will say that the first agent *envies* the second. An allocation x is called *fair* iff it is both equitable and Pareto efficient. These and related definitions have been analyzed by several authors, among them Feldman and Kirman (1974), Foley (1967), Kolm (1972), Schmeidler and Vind (1972), Pazner and Schmeidler (1974), and Varian (1974, 1975). There are many interesting relationships between these ideas and the classical concepts of general equilibrium analysis. In this paper, we will consider briefly the conceptual foundation of the notion of equity and then discuss two problems in the theory of fairness. The entire discussion will be limited to the case of a pure exchange economy.

3.1 The concept of equity

How does the formal definition of equity relate to our intuitive notions of distributive justice? I believe that the fundamental feature of the definition of equity is its emphasis on *symmetry*: we require each agent to find his own position at least as good as that of any other agent. The nice thing about this particular kind of symmetry is that it is an *internal* measure, depending specifically on the individual tastes of the agents involved. Thus the theory of fairness, based on symmetry, emphasizes yet another aspect of the concept of justice and can fruitfully be compared with, and contrasted

I wish to thank Martin Weitzman and Kenneth Arrow for several helpful suggestions on these issues. Work supported in part by the Urban Institute grant, "Efficiency in Decision Making".

to, the basically utilitarian theory of welfare economics, the contractual theory of Rawls (1971), and the procedural theory of Nozick (1973).

I have discussed the relationship of fairness to Nozick's theories in Varian (1975), and will consider some relationships to welfare economics in the last section of this paper. Here I want to describe an interesting viewpoint on Rawls' theory that stems from the idea of equity.

Rawls has provided us with a rich theory of justice which involves many concepts. A particular concept that has attracted much attention among economists is the maximin criterion [see Rawls (1971, 1974), Arrow (1973), and Alexander (1974)]. Rawls suggests that a just allocation is one that maximizes the utility of the worst-off individual. This rule has been criticized by several authors, but this is not our purpose here. I am not so concerned with Rawls' justification for the maximin rule, but rather with its operational meaning. How are we to determine who is the worst-off individual in some given circumstances? Any such determination would, it seems, require some "external" comparison of utilities, a task which is often quite difficult. It would be nice if we had a version of the maximin rule which involved only an "internal" interpersonal comparison in the way that the equity comparison is internal.

I suggest the following definitions: at any allocation we will define the *worst-off* person as being one whom no one envies; similarly, the *best-off* person will be one that envies no one. It can be shown that at any Pareto efficient allocation there is someone that no one envies, and someone that envies no one; thus, the best-off and the worst-off person are well defined, at least if we limit ourselves to Pareto efficient allocations. [See Varian (1974, theorem 1.1).]

The nice property of these definitions is that they are internal: interpersonal comparisons are being made, but they are being made by the agents involved, and are not being imposed by any external observer. One can now interpret the maximin rule as suggesting that a just allocation is a Pareto efficient allocation where the worst-off agent—the one that no one envies—is made best off—that is, envies no one. In other words, a just allocation would be one where all agents were unenvious, that is, a fair allocation. In this sense, fair allocations and "maximin" allocations are compatible notions of distributive justice.[1]

3.2 Fairness and equal incomes

It is clear that an equal income competitive equilibrium is a fair allocation. However, the converse is not true; in general there will be many other fair

---

[1] Pazner and Schmeidler (1973) suggest another way in which fairness and the maximin rule are compatible.

allocations that do not have equal incomes. Nevertheless, it seems some-how that the equal income fair allocation is, in several senses, "especially fair". One sense of this has already been examined in a previous paper: if we require not only that no individual envies another, but also that no group of agents envies the average bundle of any other group, the only fair allocations in large economies are the equal income competitive equilibria [Varian (1974)].

However, the "coalition-envy" concept is by no means as compelling as the original envy concept. Are there other senses in which equal income allocations are privileged ?

Opportunity fairness

Let us refer to Fig. 1, where we have an example of a fair allocation with unequal incomes. Since the allocation is efficient we know that it can be supported by prices p; since neither bundle lies in the preferred set of the other agent the allocation is fair.

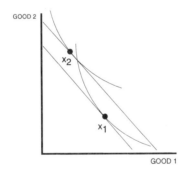

Figure 1. A fair allocation with unequal incomes.

If we imagine now that there is a market so that agents can trade their bundles at competitive prices, this allocation loses some of its normative significance. For, even though agent 2 doesn't envy agent 1 *directly*, he does envy agent 1's *possibilities*: there are points in agent 1's budget set that agent 2 prefers to his own bundle x_2.

It is clear that we can define a concept of "opportunity-fairness" which re-quires that each agent prefers his bundle to any bundle in any other agent's budget set. A moment's reflection will convince us that under an assump-tion of local nonsatiation of preferences, an allocation is opportunity-fair if and only if it is a competitive equilibrium with equal incomes.

The original notion of fairness still makes sense here: if all we know about the problem are the agents preferences and what the feasible bundles are, all fair allocations seem equally reasonable. If we know more about the problem—for example, what agents' possibilities are under some particular institutional setup—we may well want to restrict the set of fair allocations further.

Robustness of fair allocations

Let us refer again to the example in Fig. 1. It is well known that if all agents have identical, strictly convex preferences, the unique fair allocation is equal division. Thus, in a sense, it is the differences in tastes that allow for the existence of these nonequal income fair allocations.

But are these nonequal income allocations really robust against a variety of tastes? Imagine agents being continually born and being assigned randomly to one of the two income classes. Imagine further that the agents have considerable variation in preferences in the following sense: at given prices and income, there is some probability that any point on the budget hyperplane will be demanded by some agent.

Then eventually some agent will be assigned to the higher income level and demand a point lying in the preferred set of one of the lower income agents. If, on the other hand, an equal income fair allocation were specified, the fairness of the allocation would be robust against adding new agents.

In this sense the equal income allocation is especially fair in that it works no matter what the agents distribution of tastes is, or how that distribution changes. It therefore places many fewer informational demands on the allocative mechanism.

Equal incomes and a continuum of tastes

Some further consideration of Fig. 1 offers this analysis: the problem is that there are gaps in the taste patterns of the agents. For it is clear that if an agent has tastes very similar to mine and a higher income, then I will envy his chosen consumption bundle. Now if there were a continuum of agents, each similar to his neighbors, then certainly each agent could have no larger income than his neighbors—or else envy would result.

The natural model for this situation is that of a continuum of economic agents. There is an extensive literature on such economies which involves considerable use of measure theory [see for example Aumann (1966) and Hildenbrand (1969)]; here I will concentrate on a simpler model emphasizing the topological properties of the continuum. The set of agents is regarded as the open unit interval I. Agent t in I will be endowed with a continuously differentiable strictly concave utility function u_t. We want nearby agents to have similar tastes; I therefore make the following assumption.

ASSUMPTION 1. $u : I \times R_+^k \to R$ defined by $u(t, x) = u_t(x)$ is a continuous function.

Let $P = \{x$ in $R_+^k : w^i > x^i > 0$ for $i = 1, \dots, k\}$ be the possible consumption set of the agents; here w is the original bundle to be divided.

Definition 1. A fair allocation is a function $x : I \to P$ such that (1) x is Pareto efficient, and (2) $u_t(x(t)) \geqq u_t(x(s))$ for all s, t in I.

For the purposes of this paper, I will define Pareto efficiency in the following way.

Definition 2. An allocation x is Pareto efficient iff it is feasible and there is no set of agents A and no feasible allocation y such that $u_t(y(t)) > u_t(x(t))$ for all t in A, and $\sum_{t \text{ in } A} y(t) = \sum_{t \text{ in } A} x(t)$ (or $\int_A y(t) = \int_A x(t)$, whichever is appropriate to the cardinality of A).

That is, an allocation is Pareto efficient iff there is no set of agents, of any size, that can benefit from trade.

It is intuitively clear that under appropriate assumptions this will require that all marginal rates of substitution between each pair of goods be equal to a common value which we can take to be the competitive price ratio between the two goods. Rather than spell out these conditions precisely, I will simply make the following assumption.

ASSUMPTION 2. x is a competitive equilibrium for some price vector p and some income distribution $y : I \to R$. That is, for each t, $x(t)$ maximizes u_t on agent t's budget set, $B_t = \{z$ in $P : p \cdot z = y(t) = p \cdot x(t)\}$.

A natural requirement of an equity concept is that equals be treated equally, or, even more, that nearly equals be treated nearly equally. That is, if x is a fair allocation and agent s is similar to agent t, then $x(s)$ should be close to $x(t)$. It is reassuring to discover that fair allocations have this property.

LEMMA 1.   Let $x : I \to P$ be a fair allocation; then x is a continuous function.[2]

Unfortunately, continuous functions can still exhibit quite perverse behavior. To get the next result, we need to specialize a bit more.

---

[2] For a proof see the appendix.

THEOREM 1.   *Let $x : I \to P$ be a fair allocation which is differentiable; then $y(t) = p \cdot x(t)$ is a constant function.*[3]

In other words, a differentiable fair allocation must award equal incomes to all agents. the differentiability of preferences is an important hypothesis of the above proposition, as it is easy to construct counter-examples if indifference curves have kinks. I do not know if the differentiability of the allocation is equally important.

There is an easy geometrical argument for this proposition. Under the assumptions of the theorem, the fair allocation will be some curve in the commodity space P. Consider some point on this curve, say $x(t)$, and consider agent t's indifference curve through this point. This indifference curve cannot cross the allocation curve or else envy would result; hence it is tangent to the allocation curve, which is the envelope of all the agents' indifference curves.

But remember that the fair allocation is Pareto efficient, and therefore each agent's indifference curve is tangent to his budget line. This implies that the allocation line itself is tangent to each agent's budget line; which in turn implies that all agents have equal incomes.

In summary, we have found three reasons why equal income allocations are especially fair: they provide equal opportunities for all agents, they are robust against changes in tastes or adding agents with new tastes, and they are the only kind of fair allocation when tastes vary continuously across many agents.

3.3 Second-best fairness

The fairness approach to normative economies specifies a globally "best" allocation by appealing to the agents' preferences and to considerations of symmetry. The more classical approach of welfare economics specifies a "best" allocation by maximizing an a priori given welfare function over the set of feasible allocations.

Both of these approaches have their advantages and disadvantages: fairness gives an explicit solution to the problem, while the welfare function approach simply pushes the problem back one stage to the specification of the welfare function; on the other hand, the fairness criterion is of no use in comparing the social value of two *arbitrary* allocations, while the welfare function handles this problem easily. When we use the welfare function approach we have the problem of *specifying* the form of the function; while in the fairness approach we have the problem of *extending* the fairness criterion to order all alternatives.

---

[3] For a proof see the appendix.

Perhaps by combining these two approaches we can achieve a reasonable solution to both problems.[4] Suppose that we limit our choice of welfare functions to those of the linear-in-utility form:

$$W(x) = \sum_{i=1}^{n} a_i u_i(x_i).$$

This form is especially simple, and can in fact be axiomatically characterized [see Fishburn (1973), Fleming (1952), Harsanyi (1969) and Vickrey (1969)].

Vickrey's characterization is especially interesting for our purposes. Imagine an economic agent in a Rawlsian 'original position' of ignorance as to his role in society and even as to his own particular utility function. When faced with this situation an agent might well attempt to choose that distribution of goods that maximizes his "expected utility"—the expectation being taken over the possible cardinal utilities involved in the various outcomes. This formulation of the problem has the advantage of introducing the particular von Neumann-Morgenstern cardinalization of the utility functions at the outset, as well as leading to a welfare function that is a weighted sum of utilities.

This form does have certain other advantages which make it quite useful; namely, that under certain assumptions:

(1) every maximum of such a function is Pareto efficient, and

(2) every Pareto efficient allocation is a maximum of such a function for some choice of the weights, $a_1, \ldots, a_n$.

The first proposition is trivial; the second rests on the fact that under concavity assumptions a necessary and sufficient condition for x to maximize $W(x)$ on the set of feasible allocations is that there exist a price vector $\hat{p}$ such that $a_i Du_i(\hat{x}) - \hat{p} = 0$. But since x is Pareto efficient, each agent is maximized on his budget set so $Du_i(\hat{x}) = \lambda_i \hat{p}$. Choosing $a_i = 1/\lambda_i$ then shows $\hat{x}$ maximizes $W(x)$. [For a more detailed proof, the reader should consult Negishi (1960)].

We still have the problem of how to choose the weights. If we adopt the view of fairness, a fair allocation is the "best of all possible allocations". Hence we would want to require that $W(x)$ reach a global maximum at a fair allocation. We have already seen that an equal income competitive allocation is necessarily fair, and, furthermore, this type of allocation is especially fair in several important senses.

Since an equal income competitive allocation is efficient, it maximizes $W(x) = \sum_{i=1}^{n} a_i u_i(x_i)$ for some set of a_i. We therefore normalize our

---

[4] Feldman and Kirman (1974) have used the fairness idea to make second-best comparisons in a quite different way.

welfare function by choosing that set of a_i as weights. The resulting welfare function can be used to make comparisons among arbitrary allocations.

What is the economic interpretation of these weights? The above argument tells us that these weights are the inverses of the marginal utilities of income evaluated at the equilibrium values. Thus

$$a_i = \frac{1}{D_y u_i(x_i(p^*, y^*))} = \frac{1}{\lambda_i^*},$$

where x_i — ith agent's demand function, p^* = equilibrium vector of prices, and y^* = equilibrium income, equal for all agents.

Notice that the natural units of a_i are in dollars/util. The welfare evaluation of an arbitrary allocation is then measured in dollars: our criterion leads us to evaluate *utilities* at any allocation in terms of dollar evaluations that are appropriate at a "utopian" position; in this sense, it is a kind of "consumer surplus" measure.

This welfare function has a property which is very convenient for evaluating small changes around the fair allocation: suppose we are currently at the fair allocation (x, p) and we are considering undertaking a new small project which will result in a new allocation, z. Then this project increases social welfare if and only if $\sum_{i=1}^{n} p \cdot x_i < \sum_{i=1}^{n} p \cdot z_i$; i.e., if and only if national income is greater when evaluated at the current prices.

We can verify this proposition by expanding the welfare function in a Taylor series around the original allocation x:

$$\sum_{i=1}^{n} \frac{u_i(z_i)}{\lambda_i} = \sum_{i=1}^{n} \frac{u_i(x_i)}{\lambda_i} + \sum_{i=1}^{n} \frac{D u_i(x_i)}{\lambda_i} \cdot (z_i - x_i) + o(z - x).$$

But since the original allocation is an equal income competitive equilibrium, each agent is maximized on his budget set and therefore $D u_i(x_i) = \lambda_i p$. Inserting this into the above equation we get

$$W(z) - W(x) = \sum_{i=1}^{n} \frac{u_i(z_i)}{\lambda_i} - \sum_{i=1}^{n} \frac{u_i(x_i)}{\lambda_i}$$

$$= \sum_{i=1}^{n} p \cdot (z_i - x_i) + o(z - x),$$

which says that for small changes aggregate welfare is greater if and only if national income is greater.

Of course this property follows from the assumption of efficiency, not the assumption of equity. At any efficient allocation, the economy can be viewed as implicitly maximizing a weighted sum of utilities, with poorer agents, those with higher marginal utilities of income, receiving less weight. Any small project that increases national income increases this implicit welfare function.

But at an arbitrary nonfair allocation the implicit welfare function may not be the *right* welfare function. An allocation that increases national income may well decrease a welfare function normalized on a fair allocation. If the utopian goal of society is equal incomes, then cost-benefit studies must be done with care—the appropriate criterion is not whether benefits exceed costs but whether *weighted* benefits exceed *weighted* costs.

What are the defects of this approach? It certainly has an appeal when x is close to x^*; however, when x is far from x^*, the weights chosen may appear to be somewhat arbitrary. Secondly, if the endowment of the economy changes, the welfare function may change. Of course if preferences are homothetic and the endowment changes in a balanced way, the welfare function will remain constant. Thirdly, although the welfare function reaches a maximum at fair allocations, it may also reach a maximum at very unfair allocations.

For example, suppose that utility functions are concave, homogeneous of degree one, and identical. In a pure exchange economy, the unique fair allocation will then be equal division; that is, $x_i^* = w/n$ for $i = 1, \ldots, n$. In this case we can normalize all the λ_i's to be equal to 1. For $n = 2$, and for arbitrary $1 > t > 0$, we have

$$u_1(x_1^*) + u_2(x_2^*) = tu_1(x_1^*) + (1 - t)u_2(x_2^*)$$
$$= u_1(tx_1^*) + u_2((1 - t)x_2^*).$$

Thus there are very many nonegalitarian distributions which also achieve maximum welfare; the linear in utility welfare function ignores the *distribution* of utility. One way to remedy this situation is to consider a social welfare function of the following form:

$$V(x) = \sum_{i=1}^{n} a_i u_i(x_i) - b \sum_{i=1}^{n} \sum_{j=1}^{n} a_i(u_i(x_j) - u_i(x_i))\delta_{ij},$$

where (a_i) and b are parameters and δ_{ij} is one when the preceding term is positive and zero otherwise.

This welfare function is actually much more in the spirit of fairness than the preceding one. The first term can be seen as expressing a measure of efficiency, while the second expression measures the total "envy" in the distribution. This method of introducing distributional characteristics into the welfare function is more appealing than measures of variance of income, etc., since it measures the distribution in *utility* terms.

Let x^* be the equal income fair allocation. Then a natural choice for a_i is again, $1/\lambda_i^*$. This also ensures that V reaches its global maximum at such a point. For let y be any other feasible distribution; then

$$\sum_{i=1}^{n} \frac{1}{\lambda_i^*} u_i(x_i^*) \overset{\geq}{=} \sum_{i=1}^{n} \frac{1}{\lambda_i^*} u_i(y_i^*),$$

since $W(x)$ is maximized at x^*, and

$$b\sum_{i=1}^{n}\sum_{j=1}^{n}\frac{1}{\lambda_i^*}(u_i(x_j^*) - u_i(x_i^*))\delta_{ij} \leq b\sum_{i=1}^{n}\sum_{j=1}^{n}\frac{1}{\lambda_i^*}(u_i(y_j^*) - u_i(y_i^*))\delta_{ij},$$

since the envy term is 0 at the fair allocation and nonnegative elsewhere. In particular, welfare will be strictly lower than $V(x^*)$ at any nonequitable allocation.

The welfare function $V(x)$ is a function of a non-Bergsonian variety; that is, $V(x)$ is of the form $F(u_i(x_j))$ rather than $F(u_i(x_i))$. The welfare of a nonefficient allocation may well be higher than that of Pareto dominating allocations; this type of function thus reveals the often mentioned but seldom analyzed "equity-efficiency tradeoff".

3.4 Appendix: equal incomes and a continuum of tastes

LEMMA 1.   *Let $f : X \to Y$ be a function from a metric space to a compact metric space. Let (x_i) be a sequence in X converging to x_0, and let $(f(x_i))$ be the corresponding sequence in Y. If every convergent subsequence of $(f(x_i))$ converges to $f(x_0)$, then the function f is continuous at x_0.*

Proof.   This proposition is well known, but it is easier to prove it than to find a suitable reference. Suppose that f is not continuous at x_0. Then there is some neighborhood of $f(x_0)$, N, such that the sequence $(f(x_i))$ does not remain in N as i goes to infinity. It is therefore possible to choose a subsequence of $(f(x_i))$ that converges to some point y which is not equal to $f(x_0)$.

LEMMA 2.   *Let $x : I \to P$ be a fair allocation; then x is a continuous function.*

Proof.   Let (t_i) be a sequence in I converging to t_0 and let $(x(t_i))$ be the corresponding sequence in P. We will show that every convergent subsequence of $(x(t_i))$ converges to $x(t_0)$.

We first note that by compactness $(x(t_i))$ has a convergent subsequence that converges to some point x^* in the closure of P. Suppose that $u_{t_0}(x^*) > u_{t_0}(x(t_0))$. Then for $x(t_i)$ close to x^*, $u_{t_0}(x(t_i)) > u_{t_0}(x(t_0))$, contradicting equity. Similarly, suppose that $u_{t_0}(x^*) < u_{t_0}(x(t_0))$. Then for t_i close to t_0 and $x(t_i)$ close to x^*, we have $u_{t_i}(x(t_i)) < u_{t_i}(x(t_0))$, which again contradicts equity. Therefore $u_{t_0}(x^*) = u_{t_0}(x(t_0))$.

Now if x^* is not equal to $x(t_0)$, strict concavity of utility implies that $u_{t_0}(\frac{1}{2}x^* + \frac{1}{2}x(t_0)) > u_{t_0}(x^*) = u_{t_0}(x(t_0))$. Therefore for t_i close to t_0 and for $x(t_i)$ close to x^*,

$$u_{t_0}\left(\frac{1}{2}x(t_i) + \frac{1}{2}x(t_0)\right) > u_{t_0}(x(t_0)).$$

Since u is continuous in t, we also have

$$u_{t_i}(\frac{1}{2}x(t_i) + \frac{1}{2}x(t_0)) > u_{t_i}(x(t_0)).$$

But these two inequalities contradict the hypothesis of Pareto efficiency. Therefore $x^* = x(t_0)$ and x is a continuous function. ∎

THEOREM 1. *Let $x : I \to P$ be a fair allocation which is differentiable; then $y(t) = p\ x(t)$ is a constant function.*

Proof. Choose an agent t_0 and define a differentiable function $v : I \to R$ by $v(t) = u_{t_0}(x(t))$. Since x is a fair allocation, $v(t)$ reaches a maximum at t_0 and therefore its derivative must vanish. This implies that

$$Dv(t_0) = D_t u_{t_0}(x(t_0)) = D_x u_{t_0}(x(t_0)) \cdot D_t x(t_=) = 0. \qquad \text{(A.1)}$$

But x is a competitive equilibrium, so agent t_0 is maximized on his budget set, which means

$$D_x u_{t_0}(x(t_0)) = \lambda_{t_0} p. \qquad \text{(A.2)}$$

Putting expressions (A.1) and (A.2) together we get

$$p \cdot D_t x(t_0) = 0. \qquad \text{(A.3)}$$

Consider the income function y defined above, and use (A.3) to calculate its derivative:

$$D_t y(t - 0) = D_t[p \cdot x(t_0)] = p \cdot D_t x(t_0) = 0$$

The choice of t_0 was arbitrary, which implies y is a differentiable function with everywhere a zero derivative. It must therefore be a constant function. ∎

References

Alexander, S. (1974) "Social evaluation through national choice," *Quarterly Journal of Economics*, **88**, 597–624.

Arrow, K. (1973) "Some ordinalist utilitarian notes on Rawls's theory of Justice," *Journal of Philosophy*, **70**, 245–263.

Aumann, R. (1966) "Existence of a competitive equilibrium in markets with a continuum of traders," *Econometrica*, **34**, 1–17.

Feldman, A. and A. Kirman (1974) "Fairness and envy," *American Economic Review*, **64**, 995–1005.

Fishburn, P. (1973) "Summation social choice functions," *Econometrica*, **41**, 1183–1196.

Fleming, J. (1952) "A cardinal concept of welfare," *Quarterly Journal of Economics*, **66**, 366–384.

Foley, D. (1967) "Resource allocation and the public sector," Yale Economic Essays 7

Harsanyi, J. (1969) "Cardinal welfare, individualistic ethics, and interpersonal comparisons of utility," in *Readings in welfare economics*, ed. K. Arrow, and T. Scitovsky. Homewood, IL: Irwin.

Hildenbrand, W. (1969) "Pareto optimality for a measure space of economic agents," *International Economic Review*, **10**, 363–372.

Kolm, S.C. (1972) *Justice and Equite*. Paris: Editions du Centre National de la Recherche Scientifique.

Negishi, T. (1960) "Welfare economics and the existence of an equilibrium for a competitive economy," *Metroeconomica*, **12**, 92–97.

Nozick, R. (1973) "Distributive justice," *Journal of Philosophy and Public Affairs*, **3**, 45–126.

Pazner, E. and D. Schmeidler (1973) "Social contract theory and ordinal distributive equity," *Journal of Public Economics*, **5**, 3/4, 261–268.

Pazner, E. and D. Schmeidler (1974) "A difficulty in the concept of fairness," *Review of Economic Studies*, **41**, 441–443.

Rawls, J. (1971) *A theory of justice*. Cambridge: Harvard University Press.

Rawls J. (1974) "Some reasons for the maximin criterion," *American Economic Review*, **64**, 141–145.

Schmeidler, D. and K. Vind (1972) "Fair net trades," *Econometrica*, **40**, 637–642.

Varian, H. (1974) "Equity, envy, and efficiency," *Journal of Economic Theory*, **9**, 63–91.

Varian, H. (1975) "Distributive justice, welfare economics, and the theory of fairness," *Journal of Philosophy and Public Affairs*, **4**, 223–247.

Vickrey, W. (1969) *Readings in welfare economics*. Homewood, IL: Irwin.

Chapter 4

CATASTROPHE THEORY AND THE BUSINESS CYCLE

We use the approach of R. Thom's "Catastrophe Theory" to construct a generalization of Kaldor 's 1940 trade cycle. The model allows for cyclic behavior which exhibits either rapid recoveries (recessions) or slow recoveries (depressions).

In this paper we examine a variation on Kaldor's (1940) model of the business cycle using some of the methods of catastrophe theory. (Thom (1975), Zeeman (1977)). The development proceeds in several stages. Section I provides a brief outline of catastrophe theory, while Section II applies some of these techniques to a simple macroeconomic model. This model yields, as a special case, Kaldor's business cycles. In an appendix to this paper, we provide a more rigorous treatment of the cyclic behavior of the model following the work of Chang and Smyth (1971).

In Section III, we describe a generalization of Kaldor's model that allows not only for cyclical recessions, but also allows for long term depressions. Section IV presents a brief review and summary.

This paper is frankly speculative. It presents, in my opinion, some interesting models concerning important macroeconomic phenomena. However, the hypotheses of the models are neither derived from microeconomic models of maximizing behavior, nor are they subjected to serious empirical testing. The hypotheses are not without economic plausibility, but they are far from being established truths. Hence, this paper can only be said to present some interesting stories of macroeconomic instability. Whether these stories have any empirical basis is an important, and much more difficult, question.

4.1 Catastrophe theory

Catastrophe theory is a branch of applied mathematics that was originated by Rene Thom in order to describe certain kinds of biological processes.

University of Michigan. I wish to thank Winston Chang, Paul Evans, Richard Schmalensee, Robert Solow, and Ramu Ramanathan for some helpful comments on an earlier version of this paper. This work was supported in part by a grant from the National Science Foundation.

(Thom (1975)). It has subsequently been applied to a wide range of biological, physical and social phenomena, most notably by Christopher Zeeman. (A complete collection of Zeeman's work is available in Zeeman (1977). One of the nicest applications is Zeeman's study of the heartbeat (Zeeman (1972)) which is a good starting point for any systematic study of catastrophe theory.)

Applied catastrophe theory is not without its detractors (Sussman and Zahler (1978)). Some of the applied work in catastrophe theory has been criticized for being ad hoc, unscientific, and oversimplified. As with any new approach to established subjects, catastrophe theory has been to some extent oversold. In some cases, applications of the techniques may have been overly hasty. Nevertheless, the basic approach of the subject seems, to this author at least, potentially fruitful. Catastrophe theory may provide some descriptive models and some hypotheses which, when coupled with serious empirical work, may help to explain real phenomena.

Catastrophe theoretic models generally start with a parameterized dynamical system, described explicitly or implicitly by a system of differential equations:

$$\dot{x} = f(x, a).$$

Here x is an n-vector of state variables, $\dot{x}$ is the n-vector of their time derivatives, and a is a k-vector of parameters. These parameters may also change over time, but at a much slower rate than the state variables change. Thus, it makes sense to model the system as if the state variables adjust immediately to some "short run" equilibrium, and then the parameters adjust in some "long run" manner. In the parlance of catastrophe theory, the state variables are referred to as "fast" variables, and the "parameters" are referred to as "slow" variables. This distinction is, of course, common in economic modeling. For example, when we model short run macroeconomic processes we take certain variables, such as the capital stock, as fixed at some predetermined level. Then when we wish to examine long run macroeconomic growth processes, we imagine that economy instantaneously adjusts to a short run equilibrium, and focus exclusively on the long run adjustment process.

Catastrophe theory is concerned with the interactions between the short run equilibria and the long term dynamic process. To be more explicit, catastrophe theory studies the movements of short run equilibria as the long run variables evolve.

A particularly interesting kind of movement is when a short run equilibrium jumps from one region of the state space to another. Such jumps are known as catastrophes. Under certain assumptions catastrophes can be classified into a small number of distinct qualitative types. An example of the simplest type of catastrophe, the fold catastrophe, is given in Figure 1.

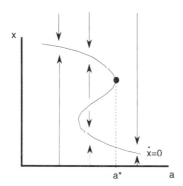

Figure 1. The fold catastrophe.

Here we have depicted a system with one fast variable, x, and one slow variable a. For any fixed value of a, the fast variable adjusts to a locally stable equilibrium, This means that the system moves rapidly to either the upper or the lower leaf of the $\dot{x} = 0$ locus, depending on initial conditions. For definiteness, we imagine that initially a is rather small, so that x adjusts to a short run equilibrium position on the upper leaf of the $\dot{x} = 0$ locus.

We now suppose that a slowly increases. Then the short run equilibrium will move continuously to the right along the $x = 0$ locus, until it reaches the fold point a^*. Any further increase in a necessitates a jump from the upper leaf to the lower leaf of the $\dot{x} = 0$ locus. This movement is an example of the fold catastrophe. Note that any sort of return to the upper leaf of the $\dot{x} = 0$ would involve a similar jump when a declined past the other fold point.

It can be shown that in a system with one state variable and one parameter, this is essentially the only kind of catastrophe that can occur—any sudden jumps in such two-dimensional systems are generally locally topologically equivalent to Figure 1.[1]

In higher dimensions things get a bit more complicated. Suppose we have a three dimensional system with one fast variable, x, and two slow variables, a and b:

$$\dot{x} = f(x, a, b).$$

Then the $\dot{x} = 0$ locus will generally be some two dimensional surface in R^3. This surface locally sits over the plane R^2 in one of three possible ways, which are depicted in Figure 2.

---

[1] More precisely, one should qualify this statement by requiring that the catastrophe be "stable" in the sense that its geometry is qualitatively unaffected by any small perturbations. The word "generally" really should be "generically."

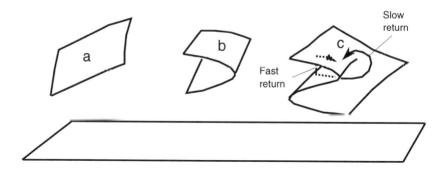

Figure 2. Classification of two-dimensional singularities.

Figure 2a is of course the no catastrophe case: any small movements of the slow variables a and b result in a continuous adjustment of the short run equilibrium. Figure 2b depicts the two-dimensional analog of the fold catastrophe: it is essentially equivalent to the one dimensional case described earlier. Figure 2c presents the only new and interesting case, namely, the cusp catastrophe.

The cusp catastrophe is essentially a fold that disappears at some point (the cusp point). This feature allows for a new kind of movement. Let us imagine that we have established a short run equilibrium on the upper leaf of the cusp. Now we let a and b vary so that we fall over the fold, down to the lower leaf of the $\dot{x} = 0$ locus. Let us consider how the system might return to the upper leaf.

It is apparent that there are two possible paths, both illustrated in Figure 2c. One path is to move back under the fold and then have a jump return to the top leaf. The other route to the top would be to move around the cusp, and eventually return to the original starting point. The first type of return would generally be much faster than the second since the second return relies exclusively on the movements of the slow variables. Which type of return occurs depends of course on the nature of the slow dynamics, the extent of the perturbations and so on. We will return to this point later in the context of a specific example. For now, we simply note that any system that allows for both fast and slow returns of the sort described above must be locally equivalent to the cusp catastrophe.[2] (Of course, globally the shape of the $\dot{x} = 0$ locus may be very complex, and the resulting dynamics may be quite complicated.)

In higher dimensions things get even more complex. In order to establish a reasonable classification system it is necessary to limit oneself to gradient

---

[2] Again, a rigorous statement of this result would involve the qualification in footnote 1.

dynamical systems. In this case Thom has shown that when $k \leq 4$, there are generically only 7 kinds of local catastrophes. For a development of some of the mathematical ideas involved in this classification theorem the reader should consult Golubitsky (1978), Wasserman (1974), Lu (1976), Thom (1975), or Zeeman (1977).

In the economic model that follows we will only utilize the two simplest catastrophes, the fold and the cusp. In these low dimensional cases, there are no restrictions on the nature of dynamical systems involved. In some ways, the material that follows is more closely related to the mathematical theory of the singularities of maps, rather than catastrophe theory per se. (For an elementary survey of singularity theory see Callahan (1974); for a more advanced exposition see Golubitsky and Guillemin (1973)).

4.2 A model of recessions

Let us begin with a simple dynamic model of national income adjustment.

$$\dot{y}/s = C(y) + I(y, k) - y$$
$$\dot{k} = I(y, k) - I_0.$$

Here y is (gross) national income, k is the capital stock, $C(y)$ is the consumption function, $I(y, k)$ is the gross investment function and $I(y, k) - I_0$ is the net investment function. The autonomous component of the investment function, I_0, represents investment for the purpose of replacing depreciated equipment.[3] The parameter s represents the speed of adjustment of the first process, which we generally believe is quite rapid at least when compared to movements of the capital stock.

The dynamic relations postulated are, I believe, relatively standard. However, they are not without problems. First, note that the specification of the k equation implies that any long run equilibrium must involve zero net investment, and any cyclical behavior by the model must involve a declining capital stock over part of the cycle. Since such declines are rarely observed, this feature has cast doubt on the relevance of nonlinear models of the business cycle such as espoused here (c.f. Rose (1967), p. 153). However, this point is easily dealt with. The k variable is presumably measured relative to trend; thus the capital stock may well continually increase—but sometimes it may grow at a more rapid pace than at other times. The cyclic aspect of the model would then be concerned with these fluctuations about the trend level of growth.

---

[3] Some sort of distinction between gross and net investment is necessary if we wish savings to be positive even when investment is negative The usual formulation is to make replacement investment proportional to k. But this tends to obscure some of the calculations in the appendix. The autonomous investment formulation is a compromise for the purposes of exposition.

Secondly, there is a problem with the $\dot{k}$ equation when the y equation is out of equilibrium; namely, that when desired savings is less than desired investment, actual investment—and thus actual capital accumulation—will presumably be constrained. One might argue that this disequilibrium constraint shows up as an involuntary accumulation or decumulation of inventories, but this raises even more vexing problems. (See Blinder (1977)). Another way to deal with this problem would be to specify an adjustment equation of the form $\dot{k} = \min[I(y,k), S(y)]$. However, the nondifferentiability in this formulation raises technical difficulties.

Instead, we will take a less satisfying, but perhaps more expeditious approach, and simply ignore this problem. Since we will be postulating that the y equation adjusts exceedingly fast, I cannot believe that this approximation will cause any serious difficulties.

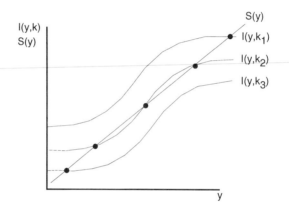

Figure 3. Savings and investment behavior which generate the fold catastrophe.

We will now proceed to characterize the dynamic behavior of the system by describing qualitative features of the functional forms. First, we will suppose that the consumption function is linear so that $C(y) = cy + D$. This seems uncontroversial.

For the investment function we will postulate a somewhat more unusual shape, namely, the sigmoid shape shown in Figure 3. Kaldor (1940) has argued for this shape as follows:

(The marginal propensity to invest) ... "will be small for low levels of activity because when there is a great deal of surplus capacity, an increase in activity will not induce entrepreneurs to undertake additional construction: the rise in profits will not stimulate investment. (At the same time the level of investment will not be zero, for there is always some investment undertaken for long-period development purposes which is independent of current activity.) But it will also be

small for unusually high levels of activity because rising costs of construction, increasing costs and increasing difficulty of borrowing will
dissuade entrepreneurs from expanding still faster—at a time when
they already have large commitments." Kaldor (1940), p. 81.

We can express this a bit more systematically as follows. Let us suppose
that prices and wages are fixed, or at least sticky. Then an increase in
national income should initially stimulate investment through the usual
sort of expectations effect. However, an increase in national income will
also push up interest rates through the liquidity balance effect, and this
increase in interest rates might well choke off ensuing investment. The net
results of such interactions could easily be the shape depicted in Figure 3.

Of course, investment also depends on the level of the capital stock. We
will make the natural assumption here: as k increases, other things being
equal, the investment function will shift down. Again, this hardly seems a
controversial assumption.

Now let us describe the shape of the $\dot{y} = 0$ locus. This is the set of all
y and k such that the demand for output equals the supply of output or,
equivalently where investment equals savings. In Figure 3 we have super-
imposed the linear savings function and the sigmoid investment function,
for three different values of k. When k is very low, we will have a high level
of investment and thus a high short run equilibrium level of income. As
k increases, we get three possible equilibrium values for y, two stable and
one unstable. Finally when k is rather large (relative to trend), investment
will be small, and thus equilibrium income will be small. These simple
observations allow to depict the $\dot{y} = 0$ locus in Figure 4. Note that it has
the shape of the fold catastrophe.

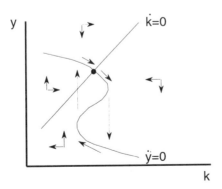

Figure 4. The (y, k) phase space.

We now proceed to the $\dot{k} = 0$ locus. It is clear that this must be an
upward sloping line in the (y, k) phase space. It turns out that as long

as the marginal propensity to consume is less than one, the $\dot{k} = 0$ locus intersects the $\dot{y} = 0$ locus in exactly one point. This fact is proved in the appendix.

There are thus three possibilities: we could have a long run equilibrium on the upper, middle, or lower leaf of the $\dot{y} = 0$ locus. The upper and lower cases are symmetric, so we will omit a discussion of the lower intersection. The middle intersection is the case considered by Kaldor (1940) and, more rigorously, by Chang and Smyth (1972). It has been shown by Chang and Smyth that when the speed of adjustment parameter is large enough, and certain technical conditions are met, there must exist a limit cycle in the phase space. In the appendix I prove a slightly simplified and modified version of this result.

This "business cycle" proposition is clearly the result intuited by Kaldor thirty years ago. However, the existence of a regular, periodic business cycle causes certain theoretical and empirical difficulties. Recent theoretical work involving rational expectations (Lucas (1975)) and empirical work on business cycles (McCullough (1975), (1977), Savin (1977)) have argued that (1) regular cycles seem to be incompatible with rational economic behavior, and (2) there is little statistically significant evidence for a business cycle anyway.

However, there does seem to be some evidence for a kind of "cyclic behavior" in the economy. It is commonplace to hear descriptions of how exogenous shocks may send the economy spiraling into a recession, from which it sooner or later recovers. Leijonhufvud (1973) has suggested that economies operate as if there is a kind of "corridor of stability": that is, there is a local stability of equilibrium, but a global instability. Small shocks are dampened out, but large shocks may be amplified.

The catastrophe model just described offers a way of rationalizing these features. Let us suppose that the long run equilibrium (or the long run equilibrium growth path) occurs on the upper leaf of the $\dot{y} = 0$ locus, as is shown in Figure 4. Then the resulting equilibrium is easily seen to be locally stable. However, it is globally unstable.

The nature of this instability is rather interesting. Suppose for some reason firms acquire too much capital, perhaps by overinvesting in inventories. Then the investment function might shift down so far that the only short run equilibrium level of income would be very low. As inventories are gradually decumulated, k falls and investment begins to recover. At a critical value of k, income jumps rapidly back to the upper leaf and k eventually returns to its long run equilibrium level. Such a movement is depicted in Figure 4.

Such a story seems to me to be a reasonable description of the functioning of the commonly described "inventory recession." It may also describe other longer term fluctuations in the pattern of capital accumulation. In either case the cyclic behavior of the model rests on the assumed sigmoid nonlinearity in the investment functions. Although the postulated nonlinearity has some inherent plausibility, there is no explicit evidence that in reality investment does behave as suggested.

However, let us, for the sake of argument, accept such a story as providing a possible explanation of the "cyclic" behavior of an economy. Then there is yet another puzzle. Each recession in this model will behave rather similarly: first some kind of shock, then a rapid fall, followed by a slow change in some stock variables with, eventually, a rapid recovery. Although this story seems to be descriptive of some recessions, it does not describe all types of fluctuations of income. Sometimes the economy experiences *depressions*. That is, sometimes the return from a crash is very gradual and drawn out.

Now the fold catastrophe could be shaped so as to exhibit a long drawn out recovery—simply bend the lower leaf up towards the upper leaf so that the slow capital adjustment is a bigger fraction of the total movement. However, the fold catastrophe does not allow for both kinds of movement: the rapid recovery characterizing a recession and the slow recovery characterizing a depression. To get such behavior we will have to utilize the cusp catastrophe.

4.3 A model of depressions

In order to describe a model with both fast and slow recoveries, we need to utilize the cusp catastrophe. The cusp catastrophe requires two slow variables. One of these must be the capital stock, but what will the other be? It seems natural to choose the other stock variable of short run macro-economic theory, namely private wealth. By wealth here, I mean wealth very broadly construed—including human capital, expectations of future employment, all types of assets, and in fact any type of stock variable that affects consumption decisions up to, and including, "consumer sentiment."

Well, how should changes in wealth affect consumption decisions? It is generally agreed that an increase in wealth will, other things being equal, increase consumption. Conversely, a decrease in wealth results in a decrease in consumption, presumably because consumers wish to save more in order to rebuild their stocks of wealth.

We are going to assume such a positive relationship between consumption and wealth and a bit more; namely that there is a positive relationship between wealth and the marginal propensity to consume. That is, not only does an increase in wealth increase the level of the consumption function, it also increases the slope of the consumption function.

In the linear consumption function case that we have been using, this assumption means that we can write $C(y,w) = c(w)y + D(w)$ with $c'(w) > 0$ and $D'(w) > 0$. Again this assumption seems quite plausible, but I know of no theoretical or empirical evidence to support it.

Nevertheless, this simple assumption about wealth effects is sufficient to generate the cusp catastrophe. The argument is illustrated in Figure 5. For "intermediate" values of k and w we have the same story as with the fold catastrophe: shifts in k generate the fold part of the cusp catastrophe, with the characteristic three sheets of short run equilibria, two stable sheets and one unstable. If, on the other hand wealth becomes very small, the savings function shifts upward *and* becomes more steep. If the savings function becomes steep enough, then no amount of shifting k will result in multiple equilibria: that is, if the marginal propensity to save exceeds the marginal propensity to invest for all levels of income, then there can be only one intersection of the savings and investment functions.

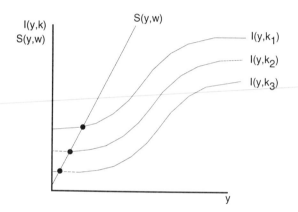

Figure 5. Savings and investment behavior which generate the cusp catastrophe.

Putting these facts together, we see that the $\dot{y} = 0$ locus will be three sheeted for some values of k and w, but will be one sheeted for sufficiently low values of w. This characterizes the geometry of the cusp catastrophe.[4]

It remains to describe the movements of the slow variables k and w. We will suppose that there is some long run equilibrium $(y^*.k^*, w^*)$ located on the top sheet of the $\dot{y} = 0$ surface. We will also suppose that this equilibrium is locally stable: when k is greater than k^*, k is negative; when w is less than w^*, w is positive and so on. An interesting configuration consistent with these assumptions is illustrated in Figure 6. In this figure the flow lines illustrating the $\dot{y}$ movement and the flow lines hidden beneath the fold have been omitted for clarity.

---

[4] Zeeman has referred to the a and b parameters as representing "normal" and "splitting" factors involved in some underlying dynamical system. The method of generating the cusp catastrophe described in the text seems perfectly general and suggests that a more descriptive terminology for a and b would be to call them the the "shift" and the "tilt" factors.

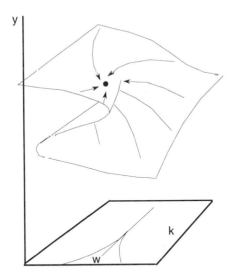

Figure 6. Depressions and recessions with the cusp catastrophe.

Here is the interesting feature of the model. Suppose as before, that there is some kind of perturbation in one of the stock variables. For definiteness let us suppose that some kind of shock (a stock market crash?) affects w. If the shock is relatively small, we have much the same story as with the inventory recession: a gradual decline in k, then a jump return to the upper sheet, and an eventual return to the long run equilibrium. If on the other hand the shock is relatively large, wealth may decrease so much as to significantly affect the propensity to save. In this case, when k declines, national income will remain at a relatively low level rather than experience a jump return. Eventually the gradual increase in wealth due to the increased savings will move the system slowly back towards the long run equilibrium. (See Figure 6.)

According to this story the major difference between a recession and a depression is in the effect on consumption. If a shock affects wealth so much as to change savings propensities, recovery may take a very long time, and differ quite substantially from the recovery pattern of a recession. This explanation does not seem to be in contradiction with observed behavior, but as I have mentioned earlier, it rests on unproven (but not implausible) assumptions about savings and investment behavior.

4.4 Review and summary

We have shown how nonlinearities in investment behavior can give rise to cyclic or cycle like behavior in a simple dynamic macroeconomic model.

This behavior shares some features with empirically observed behavior. If savings behavior also exhibits nonlinearities of a plausible sort, the model can allow for both rapid recoveries which characterize recessions, as well as extended recoveries typical of a depression.

4.5 Appendix: the existence of business cycle

In this appendix we examine the behaviur uf the following dynamical system:

$$\dot{y} = s[C(y) + I(y, k) - y]$$
$$\dot{k} = I(y, k) - I_0.$$

We shall make the following maintained assumptions:

ASSUMPTION. *The consumption and investment functions are continuously differentiable functions of y and k. Furthermore, the domain of the dynamical system can be chosen to be some compact region S of R_+^2, diffeomorphic to a disk, and $(\dot{y}, \dot{k})$ points inward on the boundary of S.*

The last part of this assumption simply states that the system is eventually self-correcting: for large enough k, $\dot{k}$ is negative, for large y, $\dot{y}$ is negative and so on,

We will use two results from the mathematical theory of dynamical systems, (For a survey of dynamical systems which describes these and other useful theorems, see Varian (1978)).

The first theorem gives a criterion for the existence and uniqueness of equilibria.

THEOREM (Poincare-Hopf). *Let $\dot{x} = f(x)$ be a dynamical system on the k-disk that points inward on the boundary of the disk. Furthermore, suppose that all equilibria x_i^* are regular in the sense that each Jacobian matrix $Df(x_i^*)$ is nonsingular. Then one can define the index of each equilibrium x_i^*, $i = 1, \ldots, n$ by*

$$\text{index}(x_i^*) = \begin{cases} +1 & \text{if } \det(-Df(x_i^*)) > 0 \\ -1 & \text{if } \det(-Df(x_i^*)) < 0 \end{cases}$$

and these indices have the property that

$$\sum_{i=1}^{n} \text{index}(x_i^*) = +1.$$

Proof. Proof: See Milnor (1965) or Guillemin and Pollack (1974). ∎

We can apply this theorem directly to the problem at hand. The Jacobian matrix referred to in the Poincare-Hopf theorem takes the form:

$$-Df(x) = \begin{bmatrix} s\left[1 - \frac{\partial C(y)}{\partial y} - \frac{\partial I(y,k)}{\partial y}\right] & -s\frac{\partial I(y,k)}{\partial k} \\ -\frac{\partial I(y,k)}{\partial y} & -\frac{\partial I(y,k)}{\partial k} \end{bmatrix}$$

The determinant of this matrix is easily seen to be

$$\det(-Df(x)) = -s\left(1 - \frac{\partial C(y)}{\partial y}\right)\frac{\partial I(y,k)}{\partial k}.$$

Thus as long as the marginal propensity to consume is less than one, all equilibria must have index +1. The Poincare-Hopf theorem then implies that there is exactly one equilibrium.

The second mathematical result used requires a bit of notation. Again we let $\dot{x} = f(x)$ be a dynamical system on the k-disk and we let $\phi_t(z)$ be the state of the system at time t, if the system was in state x at time zero. The function $\phi_t(x)$ is called the flow of the dynamical system. A point x is a limit point of $\hat{x}$ if there is some sequence $t_n \to \infty$ such that $\lim_{n\to\infty} \phi_{t_n}(x) = \hat{x}$. The set of all limit points of x is called the limit set of x. For a description of the properties of limit sets as well as some other aspects of the qualitative theory of differential equations, see Hirsch and Smale (1974).

Intuitively speaking, the limit sets of a system are where the flow ends up as time goes to infinity. One example of a limit set is an equilibrium such as x^*. If we start at x^*, then we stay there forever more so it is certainly a limit set. Another example of a limit set is a closed orbit. If we start at any point on a closed orbit, we can find a sequence (t_n) such that the flow converges to any other point. The Poincare-Bendixson theorem shows that these are about the only examples of limit sets for dynamical systems in the plane.

THEOREM (Poincare-Bendixson). *A nonempty compact limit set of a continuously differentiable dynamical system in the plane, which contains no equilibrium point, is a closed orbit.*

Proof. See Hirsch and Smale (1974), Chapter 11. ∎

Let $\dot{x} = f(x)$ be a dynamical system with equilibrium x^*. We will say that x^* is totally unstable if x^* is an asymptotically stable equilibrium of the system $\dot{x} = -f(x)$. The following lemma is an immediate consequence of the Poincare-Bendixson theorem:

LEMMA. *Let (y^*, k^*) be the unique equilibrium of the macrodynamic system (1). Suppose that (y^*, k^*) is totally unstable. Then if $(y, k) \neq (y^*, k^*)$ is any other point of S, the limit set of (y, k) is a closed orbit.*

Proof. Proof: Let $(y, k) \neq (y^*, k^*)$ be a point of S. The limit set of (y, k) is compact and nonempty since S is compact. It cannot contain (y^*, k^*) since (y^*, k^*) is totally unstable, and it cannot contain any other equilibrium point since (y^*, k^*) is the unique equilibrium. By the Poincare-Bendixson theorem, the limit set of (y, k) must be a closed orbit. ∎

We now apply this lemma to the macrodynamic system (1). We already know that (y^*, k^*) is the unique equilibrium of the system; hence we only need consider configurations where (y^*, k^*) is totally unstable. We reexamine the Jacobian matrix of the system as given in expression (2). Since the determinant of this matrix is positive, both eigenvalues have the same sign. The trace of the Jacobian matrix is:

$$\mathrm{Tr}(Df(x^*)) = s\left[\frac{\partial C(y^*)}{\partial y} + \frac{\partial I(y^*, k^*)}{\partial y} - 1\right] + \frac{\partial I(y^*, k^*)}{\partial k}.$$

(Remember that (2) is the *negative* of the Jacobian matrix.)

The second term of this expression is negative by assumption—an increase in the capital stock will tend to decrease investment. If the long run equilibrium is located on the upper leaf of the $\dot{y} = 0$ locus, then the first expression will also be negative and the long run equilibrium will be locally stable.

If, however, the long run equilibrium is located on the middle leaf of the $\dot{y} = 0$ locus, the first term will be positive. If the speed of adjustment parameter s is large enough this term will dominate, and the trace will be positive. This, along with the positive determinant, implies that both eigenvalues of the Jacobian matrix have positive real part, and hence (y^*, k^*) will be totally unstable. Applying the earlier lemma completes the argument.

4.6 Relationship to previous work

The applicability of the Poincare-Bendixson Theorem to the Kaldor model was first noticed by Chang and Smyth (1971). Their proof utilized a different version of the theorem and differs in some details, but is essentially similar to that given above. Rose (1967) has applied Poincare-Bendixson to a rather different sort of business cycle model, while Ichimura (1954) has examined a parameterized version of the model and has shown it to give rise to a form of Lienard's equation.

References

Blinder, A. (1977) "A Difficulty with Keynesian Models of Aggregate Demand," in *Natural Resource Uncertainty, and General Equilibrium Systems*, ed. A. Blinder and P. Friedman. New York: Academic Press.

Callahan, J. (1974) "Singularities and Plane Mapsm," *American Mathematical Monthly*, March 1974.

Chang, W. and Smyth D. (1971) "The Existence and Persistence of Cycles in a Nonlinear Model: Kaldor's 1940 Model Reexamined," *Review of Economic Studies*, **38**, 37–44.

Golubitsky, M. (1978) "An Introduction to Catastrophe Theory and its Applications," *SIAM Review*, **20**, 352–387.

Golubitsky, M. and Guillemin, V. (1974) *Stable Mappings and Their Singularities*. New York: Springer-Verlag.

Guillemin, V. and Pollack, A. (1974) *Differential Topology*. Englewood Cliffs, New Jersey: Prentice Hall.

Hirsch, M. and Smale, S. (1974) *Differential Equations, Dynamical Systems, and Linear Algebra*. New York: Academic Press.

Ichimura, S. (1954) "Towards a General Nonlinear Macrodynamic Theory," in *Post Keynesian Economics*, ed. K. Kurihara. New Brunswick, New Jersey: Rutgers University Press.

Kaldor, N. (1940) "A model of the Trade Cycle," *Economic Journal*, March 1940.

Kaldor, N. (1971) "A Comment," *Review of Economic Studies*, **38**, 45–46.

Leijonhufvud, A. (1973) "Effective Demand Failures," *Swedish Journal of Economics*, , 27–48.

Lu, Y. (1976) *Singularity Theory and an Introduction to Catastrophe Theory*. New York: Springer-Verlag.

Lucas, R. (1975) "An Equilibrium Model of the Business Cycle," *Journal of Political Economy*, **83**, 1113–1144.

McCullough, J. (1975) "The Monte Carlo Cycle in Business Activity," *Economic Inquiry*, **13**, 303-321.

McCullough, J. (1977) "The Monte Carlo Hypothesis: Reply," *Economic Inquiry*, **15**, 618.

Milnor, J. (1965) *Topology from the Differentiable Viewpoint*. Charlottesville: University of Virginia Press.

Rose, H. (1967) "On the Nonlinear Theory of the Employment Cycle," *Review of Economic Studies*, **34**, 153–173.

Savin, N. (1977) "A Test of the Monte Carlo Hypothesis: Comment," *Economic Inquiry*, **15**, 613–617.

Sussman, H. and Zahler, R. (1978) "Catastrophe Theory as Applied to the Social and Biological Sciences: A Critique," *Synthese*, **37**, 1–216.

Thom, R. (1975) *Structural Stability and Morphogenesis.* New York· Benjamin.

Varian, H. (1978) "Dynamical Systems with Applications to Economics," in *Handbook of Mathematical Economics*, ed. K. Arrow and M. Intriligator. Amsterdam: North-Holland Press.

Wasserman, C. (1974) *Stability of Unfoldings.* New York: Springer-Verlag.

Zeeman, C. (1972) "Differential Equations for the Heartbeat and Nerve Impulses" in *Towards a Theoretical Biology 4: Essays*, ed. Waddington, Edinburgh University Press.

Zeeman, C. (1977) *Catastrophe Theory.* New York: Addison-Wesley.

Chapter 5

NON-WALRASIAN EQUILIBRIA

This paper presents a general equilibrium model which exhibits non-Walrasian equilibria. In Walrasian models economic agents act only on the basis of relative prices. In this model agents take quantity signals into account as well: firms maximize profits subject to a constraint on expected sales, and consumers maximize utility subject to a constraint on realized income. With such a specification it is shown that a non-Walrasian equilibrium will generally exist. Furthermore, the non-Walrasian equilibrium will be a stable equilibrium of an appropriate dynamical system while the Walrasian equilibrium will be unstable.

There has recently been a resurgence of interest in specifying more completely the relationship between Walrasian microeconomic models of economic behavior and Keynesian macroeconomic models. On the face of it, these two approaches to economic reality seem very different. The Walrasian model assumes agents engage in maximizing behavior taking as given a common perception of relative prices. Their relative prices then adjust to equilibrate the system. The Keynesian model specifies that agents' behavior obeys certain rules relating quantity variables of the system. These quantities then adjust to equilibrate the system.

Keynesian analysis is often thought to concern itself primarily with a case where price signals are fixed or adjust very slowly; Walrasian analysis examines cases where realized and expected quantity signals do not affect agents' behavior. Microeconomics concerns itself with long run equilibrium phenomena, while macroeconomics concerns itself with short run equilibria and dynamic phenomena.

In simple dynamic Walrasian models where the rate of change of prices depends on excess demands, the only equilibria of the system are those where excess demand is zero; i.e., the Walrasian equilibria. A fundamental feature of such equilibria is the fact that the assumption of maximizing behavior implies that they must be Pareto efficient.

Many of my colleagues have contributed valuable suggestions on an earlier draft of this paper. In particular, Robert Solow, James Mirrlees, Martin Weitzman, Axel Leijonhufvud, Lars Svensson, and Vincent Crawford provided very helpful remarks. I especially wish to thank Carl Futia for several readings of earlier rough drafts and his valuable comments on them. Of course, I am solely responsible for any remaining errors.

On the other hand, macroeconomic models often allow for extended periods of underemployment of resources. The question of whether such non-Walrasian equilibria can persist in models with flexible prices is very important. In this paper I present some simple dynamic models with flexible prices that exhibit non-Walrasian equilibria. A fundamental feature of these models is that the economic agents do not behave in the standard Walrasian manner. Walrasian firms maximize potential profits calculated only on the basis of observed prices; here we require firms to maximize profits given a constraint on expected sales. Walrasian consumers maximize utility on a potential budget set; here we require consumers to maximize utility on their actual budget set, as constrained by realized sales. Thus the economic agents' behavior depends on quantity signals as well as on price signals. It is this dependence that allows for the existence of the non-Walrasian equilibria.

Similar concepts of non-Walrasian behavior have been discussed by Leijonhufvud (1968, 1973), Benassy (1973), Barro and Grossman (1971), Futia (1975), Patinkin (1965, Chapter 13), Solow and Stiglitz (1968), and Varian (1976). The most direct antecedent of the equilibrium concept presented here is Benassy's concept of the "monopoly line" (1973, p.49).

Money plays two very important roles in these models: (i) it allows the markets for goods and for labor to be separated; and (ii) it allows for a gap between savings and investment. Despite these important roles, money is not directly referred to in the formal structure of the models. To incorporate money into such a formal structure, one would need to specify a more complete theory of why economic agents hold money; such a theory must invoke many considerations which are not directly relevant to the main points of this paper. Hence, I have tried to avoid an explicit discussion of monetary phenomena.

5.1 A graphic example

We will consider first a very simple example which displays in a concrete way the phenomena I wish to discuss. We imagine a flow economy with two goods: a perishable consumption good (c) and labor (q). Associated with each good is its price; the price of the consumption good will be denoted by p, the nominal wage rate will be denoted by v, and the real wage rate will be denoted by $w = v/p$. There are two types of agents in the economy, producers and consumers.

We imagine that the technology available to producers can be described by a production function, $f(q)$, which we will assume to exhibit decreasing returns to scale. Given a real wage, a classical Walrasian profit maximizing firm would choose an amount of labor that maximizes profits; such behavior gives rise to the *Walrasian demand for labor* function, which we will denote by $Q_d(w)$.

This behavioral hypothesis is very restrictive. It requires firms to base their behavior only on relative prices and to ignore any signals they receive concerning other economic conditions such as the effective demand for their product, the probability of actually completing desired transactions, and so on. If we allow firms to take account of such other signals, their "optimal" behavior may be quite different from the above.

Let us imagine that firms have some point expectations about the demand for their product. At any point in time, this *expected demand* will be denoted by y. On the basis of this expected demand, firms choose a production plan that maximizes profits given the constraint that output be less than or equal to y. In the case of the production function defined above, such behavior will give rise to a *constrained demand for labor,* which we denote by $Q_d(w, y)$. It is clear that $Q_d(w, y) = f^{-1}(y)$ when w is less than the marginal product of labor at output y and $Q_d(w, y)$ will equal the unconstrained profit maximizing level of demand otherwise. We will primarily be interested in the case where expectations actually constrain the demand for labor.

We turn now to the behavior of consumers. Faced with a real wage rate w, consumers determine a utility maximizing supply of labor and planned demand for consumption. We will assume for now that consumers attempt to spend all of their labor income, and at least part of their profit income, on consumption. The consumption function of profit income will be given by $P(w, y)$. We will later be interested in three specifications for this function: (i) $P(w, y)$ as real realized profits; (ii) $P(w, y) = P^*$, the Walrasian level of profits; and (iii) $P(w, y)$, as an arbitrary function of w and y. In the first case consumers spend all of their profit income, in the second case expenditure from profit income is constant, and in the third case we have an arbitrary profit consumption function.[2]

The supply function of labor will be denoted by $q_s(w)$ so that the Walrasian demand for consumption is simply $wq_s(w) + P(w, y)$. If consumers cannot sell all of the labor they wish to—that is, if $Q_d(w, y) < q_s(w)$—their Walrasian demand for consumption will be constrained. This constrained demand for consumption—which we call *effective demand*—will be the demand that is actually presented to the market. Let $Q(w, y) = \min(q_s(w), Q_d(w, y))$ be the actual amount of labor sold; the effective demand for consumption will then be $Y(w, y) = wQ(w, y) + P(w, y)$.

We now turn to a specification of the dynamics of the economy just described.

If the firm's desired demand for labor is not equal to the supply of labor, the nominal wage rate will adjust. I assume this can be described by the

---

[2] Other interpretations of $P(w, y)$ are possible. For example, one could say that consumers base their demand for output on *expected* profit payments; or, one could say that firms pay out profits according to some payment function.

following differential equation:

(1) $\dot{v} = Q_d(w, y) - q_s(w)$ (wages).

Similarly, if the expected demand for output is not equal to the actual effective demand for output, firms adjust their expectations; I assume this process can be described by the following differential equation:

(2) $\dot{y} = Y(w, y) - y$ (expectations).

Thus, if actual demand is greater than expected demand, firms raise their expectations; if actual demand is less than expected demand, firms lower their expectations.

If actual demand is less than effective supply of output, prices will also change. I assume that this adjustment can be described by an equation of the form:

(3) $\dot{p} = Y(w, y) - f(Q(w, y))$ (prices).

The complete dynamical system is now described by the three equations (1), (2), and (3). We are interested in the equilibria of this system; these are pairs of (y, w) such that (i) the expected demand equals actual demand so expectations are unchanging, (ii) actual demand for consumption equals the actual supply of consumption so the price level is unchanging, and (iii) the actual supply of labor equals the conditional demand for labor so that the wage rate is unchanging.[3]

In Figure 1 I have drawn the production possibilities set as a function of leisure (i.e., $1 - Q$), and the indifference curves of the consumers between consumption and leisure.[4] at the Walras equilibrium (w^*, y^*) we have the familiar tangency condition that the marginal rate of transformation equals the marginal rate of substitution, so the economy is Pareto efficient.

---

[3] It is clear from inspecting the prices equation (3) that if $\dot{p} = 0$, then $P(w, y)$ must equal real realized profits; that is, there can be no savings or dissavings in any equilibrium of this model. To see this, simply notice that $\dot{p} = 0 = wQ(w, y) + P(w, y) - f(Q(w, y))$ implies $P(w, y) = f(Q(w, y)) - wQ(w, y)$.

[4] Carl Futia suggested part of the diagrammatic exposition that follows.

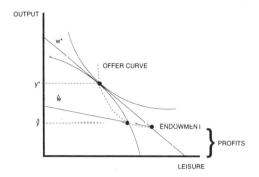

Figure 1. The non-Walrasian and the Walrasian equilibria.

Let us assume that the profit consumption function is given by $P(w,y) = P^*$ so that the equilibrium of the above system is compatible with the Walrasian equilibrium. Let us now imagine the following experiment: vary the real wage while keeping "exogenous" demand for output fixed at P^*. This variation of the real wage will sweep out the offer curve of the consumer, which is depicted in Figure 1. At $w = w^*$, the offer curve passed through the Walras equilibrium point; at $w = 0$, the consumer remains at his endowment point. The offer curve intersects the production frontier in two points; one is the Walrasian equilibrium, (w^*, y^*), the other is a non-Walrasian equilibrium, here denoted by $(\hat{w}, \hat{Y})$. At $(\hat{w}, \hat{Y})$ the *effective* demand for labor equals the supply of labor, the demand for consumption equals the effective supply of consumption, expectations are being satisfied, and actual profits are equal to P^*. This is an equilibrium of the effective demand system.

What is happening at this non-Walrasian equilibrium? Firms have pessimistic expectations for the demand for their product; thus they demand little labor. The low real wage induces consumers to supply little labor. Hence, demand equals supply and the system is in equilibrium. *There are no signals to tell any agent to change his behavior.*

If all profits are spent, there are many non-Walrasian equilibria of the above system. Figure 2 shows how to construct such equilibria. Pick any point on the production frontier to the right of the Walrasian equilibrium. Draw the tangent line to the indifference curve at this point; find the level of profits $\hat{P}$ that makes this the budget line of the consumer. If $P(w,y) = \hat{P}$, the entire system will be in equilibrium at the expected level of output. This is easy to see algebraically. Real realized profits will be given by $R(w,y) = f(Q(w,y)) - wQ(w,y)$. If consumers spend all profits so that

$P(w,y) = R(w,y)$, we have:

$$\dot{y} = wQ(w,y) + f(Q(w,y)) - wQ(w,y) - y$$
$$= f(Q(w,y)) - y.$$

Under conventional assumptions $f(Q(w,y))$ will equal y when $w \leq w^*$ and $y \leq y^*$ so that in this region $\dot{y}$ is identically zero. Hence, the system will be in equilibrium when $Q_d(w,y) - q_s(w) = 0$. Since we have only one equation in two unknowns, it is clear that wo will, in general, have a one-dimensional set of equilibria. (This set of equilibria is what Benassy calls the monopoly line.)

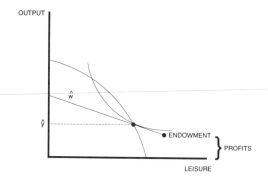

Figure 2. Construction of a non-Walrasian equilibrium.

A natural question to ask about such equilibria is the question of stability. If all profits are spent the stability issue is rather simple. As we have seen, in this case the consumption market is automatically in equilibrium, so that we only have to worry about equilibrium in the labor market. If expectations are perturbed downward, the demand for labor goes down, and the real wage falls to equate demand with supply at the lower level of output.

A more interesting case arises when we have a more interesting profit consumption function. For example, if $P(w,y) = P^*$ we have the following surprising feature: the Walrasian equilibrium will be an unstable equilibrium and the non-Walrasian equilibrium will be stable. This can be seen by considering the following experiment.

We start at the the Walrasian equilibrium $(w,^*, y^*)$ and consider a perturbation to a $y < y^*$. If expectations are perturbed downwards, firms will lower both their demand for labor and their supply of output. Since price $= p =$ marginal cost $= v(dq/dy)$ at the Walrasian equilibrium we have (heuristically) that $p\, dy = v\, dq$ so that the decrease in labor's income is exactly equal to the decrease in value of output. Thus the nominal price level remains unchanged. But there is now excess supply in the labor market, so the nominal wage rate falls, implying the real wage falls. This contributes a term of the form $dv\,q$. The total effect is that aggregate income falls further than the value of aggregate supply. Thus, effective demand will be less than expected demand and firms will adjust their expectations downward even further.

Consider the situation at the non-Walrasian equilibrium, $(\hat{w}, \hat{Y})$. Suppose we perturb expectations upward to a $y > \hat{y}$. At $(\hat{w}, \hat{Y})$ price is greater than marginal cost; therefore, $p\,dy > v\,dq$ so that the incremental value of consumption supply is greater than the increment to income. Thus, the gap between actual demand and expected demand is negative, which implies that firms revise their expectations downward, returning to $(\hat{w}, \hat{Y})$.

The above arguments show that the non-Walrasian equilibrium is stable with respect to small changes in expectations. It will be shown later that the non-Walrasian equilibrium is also stable with respect to perturbations of the real wage. This has some very interesting consequences.

Since price is greater than marginal cost at the non-Walrasian equilibrium, there is an incentive for firms to cut their prices that is not captured in the behavioral equation (3). Let us therefore consider an adjustment process of the following sort: in the short run firms adjust their prices according to the supply and demand conditions, but in the long run they may attempt to increase sales by lowering prices when price is greater than marginal cost. We will imagine that the economy is at the non-Walrasian equilibrium and ask what happens when some firm lowers its price.

Presumably this firm will get more customers, which in turn implies other firms will lose customers. Since the demand facing the other firms falls, they will also cut their prices, which implies the total price level of the economy falls. The real wage therefore rises. Consumers will then wish to increase their supply of labor. Labor supply is now greater than labor demand and, therefore, the money wage falls. The process continues until equilibrium is re-established at the old real wage—but now with lower nominal wages and prices.[5]

Since firms can only control their nominal prices, and the non-Walrasian equilibrium is stable with respect to perturbations of the real wage, the money wage will always adjust to re-establish equilibrium. Firms cannot succeed in selling more goods by lowering their nominal prices.

In a world where demand responds slowly to price cuts, a decision to cut prices trading off the immediate loss in profits with an eventual increase in profits. If firms know from past experience that there will not be an eventual increase in sales, they may choose not to cut prices. In such

---

[5] Here one really needs to explicitly introduce monetary phenomena. I am assuming an accommodating money supply. If the money supply were fixed at some constant value, the equilibrium would be established at the old real wage with the same nominal prices and wages.

a case, the economy will remain at the non-Walrasian equilibrium with stable nominal prices and wages.

If we allow variable consumption as a function of profits, the above heuristic analysis still applies, with the proviso that $D_w P(w, y)$ is small and that $D_y P(w, y)$ is positive; that is, the slope of the profit consumption function is positive. These assumptions do not seem unrealistic.

The effective demand system described above has been shown (nonrigorously) to have some extremely unpleasant properties. Not only does there exist a non-Walrasian equilibrium, but it is a stable equilibrium of the system while the Walrasian equilibrium is unstable. In this effective demand model, this type of inefficient "self-fulfilling expectations" is the rule, not the exception. The Walrasian equilibrium is *always* unstable, and there will always exist non-Walrasian equilibria, at least under some quite plausible economic assumptions. The precise statement of the general model and a demonstration of this assertion are the content of the next section.

5.2 A model with one factor of production

In this section I examine a more general and abstract model which includes the example discussed in the previous section. We now allow for different speeds of adjustments of expectations, prices, and wages. The dynamical system is therefore represented by:

(4) $\qquad \dot{y} = G_0(Y(w, y) - y) \qquad$ (expectations),

(5) $\qquad \dot{p} = G_1(Y(w, y) - f(Q(w, y))) \qquad$ (prices),

(6) $\qquad \dot{v} = G_2(Q_d(w, y) - q_s(w)) \qquad$ (wages).

The functions G_i, $i = 0, 1, 2$, are assumed to be smooth sign-preserving functions of their arguments.

There are three main points that need to be discussed: (i) the dynamics of the real wage as opposed to the nominal wage; (ii) the description of the state space and global dynamics of the system; and (iii) the profit consumption function.

The first point is the most straightforward. By the quotient rule for derivatives,

$$\dot{w} = \frac{p\dot{v} - v\dot{p}}{p^2}$$

(7) $\qquad \dot{w} = \dfrac{G_2(Q_d(w, y) - q_s(w))}{p} - \dfrac{wG_1(Y(w, y) - f(Q(w, y)))}{p}$

(realwage)

To save on notation we will subsume the $(1/p)$ factor into G_1 and G_2. The system described by (4) and (7) now gives us a complete description of the dynamics of the economy in terms of the state variables y and w. This dynamical system will be referred to as the "real system" (RS). It is given by:

(8) $\dot{y} = G_0(Y(w,y) - y)$ (expectations);

(9) $\dot{w} = G_2(Q_d(w,y) - q_s(w)) - wG_1(Y(w,y) - f(Q(w,y)))$
         (real wage.)

We now turn to the specification of the state space of the economy. The natural structure for this state space is that of a rectangle in R_+^2, $YW = \{(y,w) \text{ in } R_+^2 : \underline{y} \le y \le \overline{y} \text{ and } \underline{w} \le w \le \overline{w}\}$. The parameters $\underline{y}$ and $\underline{w}$ are lower bounds on expectations and wages—these are presumably small positive numbers—while $\hat{y}$ and $\hat{w}$ are upper bounds on the same variables. These bounds will be given explicitly below. For reasons that will become apparent, we will actually want to think of the state space as being a smooth manifold-with-boundary; to ensure this, we need to round off the corners of the above rectangle. This smoothed rectangle will be denoted by M.

We now turn to the problem of analyzing the existence and stability of the Walrasian and non-Walrasian equilibria. The problem is complicated by the fact that the dynamical system under consideration is nondifferentiable. To get around this, we resort to a kind of n-dimensional "one-sided" derivative. Our strategy will be as follows: we will define a new, "virtual" dynamical system on M which coincides with the "real" dynamical system at all relevant equilibria. If we can show that the virtual dynamical system has non-Walrasian equilibria, then we will have shown that the real dynamical system has non-Walrasian equilibria. If we can show the Walrasian equilibrium is *unstable* for the virtual dynamical system, then it will in general be unstable for the real dynamical system.

We will assume that there exists an interior Walrasian equilibrium to the real dynamical system which we will denote by (w^*, y^*). The assumptions required to establish this existence are well known by now; they primarily involve the continuity of the Walrasian excess demands, and some desirability assumptions. In general we must allow for the possibility of nonzero profits at (w^*, y^*). We will denote this level of real profits by P^*.

Let $e(w,y) = wq_d(w,y)$ denote the conditional cost function of the firm; by this I mean the costs incurred by a firm required to produce an output equal to y. The conditional cost function satisfies two familiar derivative properties; namely, that price equals marginal cost at an (unconstrained) maximum profit point and that the derivative of $e(w,y)$ with respect to w gives the conditional demand for labor, $q_d(w,y)$. I will assume without further comment that $q_d(w,y)$ and $q_s(w)$ are smooth functions on the domain M.

Under an assumption of diminishing returns to scale the marginal cost curves of the firms are monotonically declining to the left of the Walras equilibrium level of output, so that cost minimization will be equivalent to constrained profit maximization for y less than y^*. For no constrained profit maximizer would operate at a point where price was less than marginal cost since he could make a higher profit by cutting output. Likewise, if price is greater than marginal cost, a constrained maximizer will produce the maximum amount he thinks he can sell, namely, y.

Consider the following dynamical system on M, which we will call the *virtual system* (VS):

(8) $y = G_0(e(w, y) + P^* - y)$ (virtual expectations);

(9) $\dot{w} = G_2(q_d(w, y) - q_s(w))$ (virtual real wage.)

This virtual system differs from the real system in three ways: (i) it assumes realized labor income is $e(w, y) = wq_d(w, y)$ rather than $wQ(w, y)$; (ii) it assumes the level of real profits distributed is always P^*; (iii) it ignores the effect of the consumption market on the real wage.

For now we will simply fix profit payments to be P^*; the subsequent analysis applies equally well for variable profit behavior, as long as $D_y P(w, y)$ is positive and $D_w P(w, y)$ is small, and certain boundary conditions are met. Formally, this behavior can be subsumed in the more general case of a consumption function which will be discussed in more detail below.

Given such profit behavior, the virtual system is a well-defined dynamical system on the state space M. We know that it has at least one zero, the Walras equilibrium (w^*, y^*); we want to know if it has any other equilibria. Suppose that we can find one of these other equilibria $(\hat{w}, \hat{Y})$ where price is greater than marginal cost. Then this must be an equilibrium of the real system. For, if price is greater than marginal cost, we have already argued that cost minimizing behavior is equivalent to constrained profit maximizing behavior so that $e(w, y)$ represents actual factor payments and $q_d(w, y)$ is the same as $Q_d(w, y)$. Furthermore, since $q_d(w, y) = q_s(w)$, we have $y = f(q_s(w))$ so that the desired amount of output is actually produced and thus the consumption market clears. Hence, $(\hat{w}, \hat{Y})$ is also an equilibrium of the real system.

We have now reduced the problem of the existence of a non-Walrasian equilibrium of the real dynamical system to the study of the existence of a non-Walrasian equilibrium of the virtual dynamical system. In order to ensure the existence of such an equilibrium, we need to restrict the behavior of VS near the boundary of M.

We now introduce a concept from differential topology. Consider an arbitrary smooth dynamical system on M defined by $\dot{x} = f(x)$. The *Gauss map on the boundary* M is defined by $g(x) = f(x)/\|f(x)\|$ where x is restricted to lie on the boundary of M and $\| \ \|$ is the ordinary Euclidean norm. Thus the Gauss map is a smooth map from the boundary of M to the unit sphere. If this map is *not* onto the unit sphere, we will say the Gauss map is *nullhomotopic*. The Gauss map will be nullhomotopic if there is some direction such that $\dot{x}$ never points in that direction along the boundary of M.

Consider the following economic assumptions; for sake of generality they are stated for n factors of production:

Assumption B1: $P^* > 0$; Walrasian profits are positive.

Assumption B2: There is a maximum level of output; i.e., there is at least one indispensable factor of production in limited supply. Choose $\bar{y}$ to be greater than this maximum level of output.

Assumption B3: There are some constants $k_i > 0$ such that $f(q_1, \ldots, q_n) > 0$ iff $q_i > k_i$ for $i = 1, \ldots, n$. That is, all factors are indispensable. Choose $\hat{w}_i$ such that $\overline{w}_i k_i - \bar{y} + P^* > 0$.

Assumption B4: For any w, $e(w, y) = 0$. For any w such that $w_i = 0$, $q_s^i(w) = 0$.

It is shown in the appendix that these natural boundary assumptions imply that the Gauss map of VS is nullhomotopic on the boundary of M. This fact allows us to invoke the following elementary consequence of the Poincaré-Hopf theorem:

Theorem: *Let $v: M \to TM$ be a smooth vector field on the disk with the Gauss map nullhomotopic to the boundary of M and that has a finite number of isolated zeroes $p_1 \ldots p_n$ with $\det(Dv(p_i)) \neq 0$ for $P-i = 1, \ldots, n$. Then one can define the index of each zero as being:*

$$index(p_i) = \begin{cases} +1 & \text{if } \det(-Dv(p_i)) > 0 \\ -1 & \text{if } \det(-Dv(p_i)) < 0, \\ & \text{an integer depending on topological considerations if} \\ & \det(-Dv(p_i)) = 0, \end{cases}$$

and furthermore,

$$\sum_{i=1}^{n} index(p_i) = 0.$$

The proof of this theorem is an easy modification of the Hopf lemma on page 36 of Milnor (1972). (See also the excellent discussion in Guillemin and Pollack (1974).) It is clear from this theorem that if we can show that the Walrasian equilibria must all have index -1, then we can conclude that there must exist other equilibria to the virtual system.

We consider the negative of the system VS and compute it's Jacobian at a Walrasian equilibrium (w^*, y^*). This will be:

$$\det V = \det \begin{bmatrix} -D_y\dot{y}(w^*, y^*) & -D_w\dot{y}(w^*, y^*) \\ -D_y\dot{w}(w^*, y^*) & -D_w\dot{w}(w^*, y^*) \end{bmatrix},$$

where

$$-D_y\dot{y}(w^*, y^*) = -DG_0(0)[D_ye(w^*, y^*) - 1],$$
$$-D_y\dot{w}(w^*, y^*) = -DG_2(0)[D_yq_d(w^*, y^*)],$$
$$-D_w\dot{y}(w^*, y^*) = -DG_0(0)[q_d(w^*, y^*)],$$
$$-D_w\dot{w}(w^*, y^*) = -DG_2(0)[D_wz(w^*, y^*)].$$

Here I have denoted $q_d(w, y) - q_s(w)$ by $z(w, y)$ and made repeated use of the fact that the derivative of the conditional cost function is the conditional factor demand, $q_d(w, y)$.

Let us check the signs of each of these terms. We first recall that since (w^*, y^*) is a Walras equilibrium, firms are maximizing profits, and therefore price equals marginal cost. This implies that real marginal cost, $D_ye(w^*, y^*)$, must be equal to 1. Thus, $-D_y\dot{y}(w^*, y^*) = 0$. Since the derivative of the conditional demand for labor with respect to output is presumably positive, $-D_y\dot{w}(w^*, y^*) = 0$ must be negative.

The conditional demand for labor is certainly positive so $-D_w\dot{y}(w^*, y^*)$ must be negative. Finally we assume that the excess demand for labor is globally downward sloping which implies that $-D_w\dot{w}(w^*, y^*)$ is positive. Putting this all together, we find that the Jacobian matrix V has sign pattern

$$\operatorname{sign} V \begin{bmatrix} 0 & - \\ - & + \end{bmatrix}$$

This clearly has a negative determinant and, therefore, every Walrasian equilibrium must have index -1. By the theorem, there must therefore exist other, non-Walrasian, equilibria with positive index. The only sign that can change in the above Jacobian is the sign of $-D_y\dot{y}$. In order for the determinant of V to be nonnegative, we need to have $-D_y\dot{y}$ positive, which means that price must be greater than marginal cost. Hence, this virtual equilibrium is also a real equilibrium and the proof is done.

There is one further remark concerning this method of proof. We have assumed that the speed of adjustment function, the $G_I(\cdot)$ functions, are globally sign-preserving. We could just as well have assumed some more interesting behavior; for example, that at large unemployment levels real wage adjustment becomes sticky and the real wage refuses to fall. With such an adjustment process it is very possible to get true "unemployment equilibria". The techniques presented in this section can easily be modified to demonstrate the existence of such equilibria.

We turn now to the question of the stability of the equilibria. Let $U = \{(w, y) \text{ in } M : q_d(w, y) \le q_s(w) \text{ and } 1 \le D_ye(w, y)\}$. This is the set of states of the economy where labor demand is no greater than labor supply and price is no greater than marginal cost. Consider the following virtual dynamical system (VS') on M:

$$\dot{y} = G_0(e(w,y) + P^* - y) \qquad \text{and}$$

VS':

$$\dot{w} = G_2(q_d(w,y) - q_s(w)) - wG_1(e(w,y) + P^* - y).$$

According to the previous discussion, VS' coincides with RS on the subspace U. We will discuss the stability of VS' at (w^*, y^*) and $(\hat{w}, \hat{Y})$, which will give us information about the "one-sided stability" of the real system at the two equilibria. It is easy to check that the additional term involving the consumption market does not affect the sign pattern of the matrix V. Since the matrix $-V$ has a negative determinant, we can conclude that the virtual system must be unstable at (w^*, y^*).

What about the behavior of the real dynamical system? We know that it coincides with the virtual system on the subspace U, and that (w^*, y^*) is in U. As long as U contains points other than points along the one stable ray, there will be points near (w^*, y^*) that have no tendency to return to (w^*, y^*) under the influence of the real dynamical system. Hence, we can conclude that even the real dynamical system is unstable at any Walrasian equilibrium. Qualitative features of the real and virtual systems are depicted in Figures 3 and 4.

What about the stability of the non-Walrasian equilibrium? Here the situation is a bit more complicated; to show the Walrasian equilibrium is unstable, we only needed to show it was unstable on one side. To show the non-Walrasian equilibrium is stable we have to show it is stable on both sides.

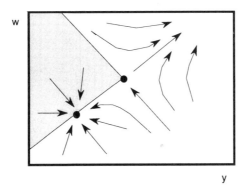

Figure 3. The virtual system (the set U is shaded.)

We already know that at least some of the non-Walrasian equilibria have index $+1$, and that the sign pattern of the Jacobian matrix at $(\hat{w}, \hat{Y})$ must be of the form:

$$\text{sign}(-V) = \begin{bmatrix} - & + \\ + & - \end{bmatrix}.$$

This matrix has negative trace and a positive determinant (since the index is $+1$) so the virtual system is stable at the non-Walrasian equilibrium.

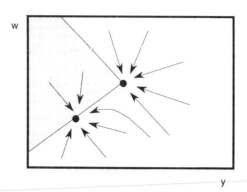

Figure 4. The real system (the set U is shaded.)

To analyze perturbation on the other side, we must consider the following system (VS″, which coincides with the real system on $M \setminus U$:

VS″:
$$\dot{y} = G_0(w q_s(w) - y) \qquad \text{and}$$

$$\dot{w} = G_2(q_d(w, y) - q_s(w)) - w G_1(w q_s(w) - f(q_s(w))).$$

The conditions for stability are not especially informative, and are rather messy so I will not examine them here. However, it is perfectly reasonable to assume they are met at both equilibria. Hence, we now have a clear picture of the dynamics around both equilibria: one-sided instability at the Walras equilibrium, and stability at the non-Walrasian equilibrium.

5.3 An n-factor model

It is possible to extend the above model to a case with more than one factor of production. The restriction that there be only one kind of output is more fundamental. Of course, if all output behaves similarly with respect to factor price movements, the previous analysis is still possible. This is really the case where the Hicksian aggregation conditions are satisfied so that output can be treated as a composite good with respect to factors. These conditions are restrictive but not unreasonably so.

The virtual dynamical system (VS) in the n-factor case will be the natural generalization of the one-factor system:

$$\dot{y} = G_0(Y(w,y) - y),$$

VS·

$$\dot{w}_1 = G_1(q_d^1(w,y) - q_s^1(w)),$$

$$\vdots$$

$$\dot{w}_1 = G_n(q_d^n(w,y) - q_s^n(w)).$$

Now realized income is just the constrained cost function $c(w,y)$ plus some given level of profits P^*. As before, $-D_y \dot{y}(w^*, y^*) = 0$, $-D_{w_i} \dot{y}(w^*, y^*)$ is negative, $-D_y \dot{w}_i(w^*, y^*)$ is negative, and if all excess demand curves are downward-sloping, $-D_{w_i} \dot{w}_i(w^*, y^*)$ will be positive. We will also assume that cross price effects are small; that is, that $-D_{w_j}(w^*, y^*) \approx 0$. This is a strong assumption, but is not unreasonable in the present context. It simply assumes that there is little short run substitution possibility between factors. Thus when expectations decline and relative prices shift, *all* factor payments will decline, so the economic analysis can proceed as before. (Futia (1975)] has shown that the cross price effects can be large as long as the $D_w \dot{w}$ matrix satisfies the Gale-Nikaido conditions.)

In order for the formal analysis to proceed, we need to ensure that the Jacobian of the negative of the virtual dynamical system just described has index -1. By the above assumptions on signs of the individual terms, this matrix will have sign pattern:

$$\text{sign } V = \begin{bmatrix} 0 & - & - & \cdots & - \\ - & + & & & \\ - & & + & & \\ \vdots & & & \ddots & \\ - & & & & + \end{bmatrix}.$$

The omitted off-diagonal terms are all zeroes. Such a matrix must alway have a negative determinant. My original proof of this was by induction and involved an expansion by cofactors on the last column. Subsequently Robert Solow discovered the following simple proof: notice that we can multiply each row of the matrix by a positive constant and add it to the first row in a way that cancels out each of the negative elements to the right of the left-hand corner element. The resulting matrix has sign pattern:

$$\text{sign } V_2 = \begin{bmatrix} 0 & - & 0 & \cdots & 0 \\ - & + & & & \\ - & & + & & \\ \vdots & & & \ddots & \\ - & & & & + \end{bmatrix},$$

which obviously has a negative determinant. This argument allows one to see clearly the geometrical structure of the dynamical system around (w^*, y^*): all of the eigenvectors point inward except for one which points outward. The Walrasian equilibrium is a saddle point of the system, with index $(w^*, y^*) = -1$. As before, if we assume the boundary behavior of B1– B4, we can apply the Poincaré-Hopf theorem and argue for the existence of a non-Walrasian equilibrium.

5.4 A model with savings and investment

Consider a macroeconomic model where all labor income is spent and all profit income is saved. There is an exogenous demand for investment which is equal to the level of profits at the Walrasian equilibrium, so that $I = P^*$.[6] The demand for output is now given by: $e(w, y) + I$, and the condition for equilibrium in the output market is that this demand for output is equal to the supply of output: $e(w, y) + I = y$. This condition can be written as: $y - e(w, y) = I$ which is just the condition that savings equals investment.

The dynamical system for this model is given by:

$$\dot{y} = G_0(e(w, y) + I - y) \qquad \text{and}$$
$$\dot{w} = G_1(q_d(w, y) - q_s(w)).$$

This system is exactly the same as that analyzed earlier. We have seen that it has two equilibria: one unstable and efficient, the other stable and inefficient. As in simple macroeconomic models, the equilibria must be compatible with the level of exogenous expenditure. But there is more than one level of output associated with a given level of investment.

At the equilibrium with a lower level of output we have a small demand for output for consumption and a fixed investment demand. The usual case is thought to be that, at low levels of expectations, investment demand would be low. We clearly need to analyze the case where investment depends on expectations.

Let us therefore postulate an investment function, $I(w, y)$ which represents the real demand for output for investment when firms face a real wage w and expect the demand for their product to be y. As before, we will do a "one-sided" analysis and consider only the case where firms can realize their desires, where they can hire enough labor to satisfy the demand for current output and for investment purposes. In such circumstances, labor's realized income will be $Y = e(w, y) + P(w, y)$, composed, respectively, of income from the production of output and profits. Since profits are by definition equal to $y - e(w, y)$, the above equation reduces to $Y = y$.

---

[6] If we chose some $I \neq P^*$, the "Walrasian" equilibrium would not be efficient. However, there would still, in general, be multiple equilibria.

We now postulate a consumption function $C(Y) = C(y)$. At a demand limited state of the economy, the following seems to be an appropriate expectations adjustment equation:

$$\dot{y} = G_0(Cy) + I(w, y) - y.$$

Exactly as before, firms revise their expectations about the demand for consumption upwards when demand exceeds their expectations, and revise their expectations downwards when the reverse is the case. The adjustment equation for wages is the same as the previous virtual adjustment equation:

$$\dot{w} = G_2(q_d(w, y) - q_s(w)).$$

Suppose that (w^*, y^*) is an equilibrium of the above system; then realized income $Y^* = y^* = C(Y^*) + I(w^*, y^*)$. Hence, savings must equal investment, which is a familiar macroeconomic equilibrium condition.

Let us suppose that (w^*, y^*) is an efficient equilibrium in some appropriate sense, and ask ourselves what factors influence its index. Evaluating the various derivatives we find:

$$-D_y\dot{y} = -g_0(D_Y C(Y^*) + D_y I(w^*, y^*) - 1),$$
$$-D_w\dot{y} = -g_0 D_Y C(Y^*) D_w I(w^*, y^*),$$
$$-D_y\dot{w} = -g_0 D_y q_d(w^*, y^*),$$
$$-D_w\dot{w} = -g_2 D_w z(w^*, y^*).$$

Here $g_i = DG_i(0)$ for $i = 0, 2$ and $z(w, y) = q_d(w, y) - q_s(w, y)$.

It is not obvious what sign to attach to $D_w I(w^*, y^*)$; it seems reasonable to assume it is positive since an increase in the real wage should stimulate investment in an attempt to substitute capital for labor. If this is the case, all the signs of the Jacobian matrix will be the same as before with the exception of the term in the upper left-hand corner. This term will be negative when the marginal propensity to consume plus the marginal propensity to invest is greater than one. This is exactly the macroeconomic condition for instability. Thus macroeconomic instability is a sufficient, but not necessary, condition for (w^*, y^*) to have index -1. A necessary condition can be found by tracing through the elementary row operations used earlier; it is the following:

$$[D_Y C(Y^*) + D_y I(w^*, y^*) - 1] - \frac{D_y q_d(w^*, y^*) D_w I(w^*, y^*)}{D_w z(w^*, y^*)} > 0.$$

Even when the economy is macroeconomically stable, the positive effect of the last term may be sufficient to allow unstable behavior to reveal itself through the income feedback loop. In this case we can put together a stable Keynesian system with a stable Walrasian system and get an unstable system! (This possibility has been noticed by Leijonhufvud (1973).)

If the efficient equilibrium (w^*, y^*) does have index -1 and the appropriate boundary conditions are met, we know that there must be another virtual equilibrium of the system with index $+1$. Such an equilibrium must be macroeconomically stable. However, it is difficult to assert with certainty that this virtual equilibrium must be a real equilibrium. For a proof of existence, it seems that one must analyze the real dynamical system in a more explicit manner. This analysis should be possible through use of some new techniques developed by Carl Futia (1975).

5.5 Summary

We have shown that when one introduces a new state variable into the Walrasian system one allows for the existence of non-Walrasian equilibria. Stated this way, the result should not be too surprising. After all, the Walrasian model is a complete equilibrium model. If one adds more state variables we will have more unknowns than equations; the implicit function theorem then implies that we will have a continuum of equilibria. This is precisely the idea behind Benassy's "monopoly line". If we then add a new relationship—such as a consumption function—only certain points of this set of equilibria will be equilibria of the complete system. This is the content of the main theorem of this paper.

If one specifies a stable dynamics for the Walrasian system, the stability of the non-Walrasian system will depend on the specification of the consumption function. In the case described in Section 1 of this paper the marginal propensity to consume was one, which is the borderline case for macroeconomic instability. The income feedback through the factor market was enough to push the system into unstable behavior. Here the important point is that the stability of the Walrasian equilibrium and the existence of non-Walrasian equilibrium are intimately related.

The techniques used in this paper should be of use in describing other non-Walrasian systems. In Walrasian economics, where one is interested in existence of a Walrasian equilibrium, fixed-point theorems provide an appropriate tool. In models where one is interested in existence of equilibria *other* than Walrasian equilibria, the implicit function theorem and the Poincaré-Hopf theorem should be useful.

5.6 Appendix

Proposition: *Under assumptions B1 through B4, the Gauss map is null-homotopic on the boundary of M.*

Proof. We will show the degree of the Gauss map is zero on the boundary of YW; a simple continuity argument gives the desired result. To show that the degree of the Gauss map is zero, it suffices to show that there is some vector in the unit ball that is *not* in the image of the Gauss map. We will show that there is no point (w, y) on boundary YW where $\dot{y} < 0$ and $\dot{w} < 0$, $i = 1, \ldots, n$, which will establish the proposition.

Consider the possible cases: (i) Can $w_i = 0$ for any i? No, for by Assumption B4 we would have demand no smaller than supply in some market. (ii) can $y = 0$? No, for Assumptions B1 and B4 imply $\dot{y}$ would then be positive. (iii) Can $y = \overline{y}$? No, for Assumption B2 implies there would be excess demand for some factor. (iv) Can $w_i = \overline{w}_i$? No, for Assumption B3 implies that $\sum_j \overline{w}_i q_d^j(\overline{w}, y) + P^* \geq \overline{w}_i k_i + P^* - \overline{y} > 0.$ ∎

References

Barro, R., and H. Grossman (1971) "A General Disequilibrium Model of Income and Employment," *American Economic Review*, **61**, 82–93.

Benassy, J-P. (1973) "Disequilibrium Theory," Ph.D. Dissertation, University of California at Berkeley, June.

Futia, C. (1975) "The Existence of Non-Walrasian Equilibria," Bell Laboratories Working Paper, Murray Hill, New Jersey.

Guillemin, V., and A. Pollack (1974) *Differential Topology*. Englewood Cliffs, NJ: Prentice-Hall.

Hirsch, M. and S. Smale (1974) *Differential Equations, Dynamical Systems, and Linear Algebra*. New York: Academic Press.

Leijonhufvud, A. (1968) *On Keynesian Economics*. Oxford: Oxford University Press.

Leijonhufvud, A. (1973) "Effective Demand Failures," *Swedish Journal of Economics*, **75**, 27–48.

Milnor, J. (1972) *Topology from the Differentiable Viewpoint*. Charlottesville: University Press of Virginia.

Patinkin, D. (1965) *Money, Interest, and Prices*. New York: Harper and Row.

Solow, R. and J. Stiglitz (1968) "Output, Employment, and Wages in the Short Run," *Quarterly Journal of Economics*, **82**, 537–560.

Varian, H. (1975) "A Third Remark on the Number of Equilibria of an Economy," *Econometrica*, **43**, 985–986.

Varian, H. (1976) "On Persistent Disequilibrium," *Journal of Economic Theory*, **10**, 218–227.

Chapter 6

A REMARK ON BOUNDARY RESTRICTIONS IN THE GLOBAL NEWTON METHOD

This remark shows how Smale's method of computing fixed points can be extended to problems involving very general boundary behavior.

6.1 Introduction

Consider a smooth vector field on the unit disk defined by $\dot{x} = f(x)$, $f : D^n \to R^n$. If this vector field "points inward" on the boundary of the disk, then it is well known that there exists an equilibrium x^* where $f(x^*) = 0$.

Recently, Smale (1976) and Kellog, Li, and Yorke (1976) have suggested algorithms to compute such an equilibrium. In particular, Smale has shown that if the vector field satisfies some rather strong boundary conditions, there is a differential equation whose solution tends to some equilibrium x^* when one starts at almost any point on the boundary of D^n. The differential equation is given implicitly by

$$Df(x)\frac{\mathrm{d}x}{\mathrm{d}t} = -\lambda(x),$$

where λ is a scalar function of x such that sign λ = sign det $Df(x)$.

Smale's boundary conditions are rather complicated to state and in any practical problem they may be difficult to verify. The purpose of this note is to show how these boundary conditions can be significantly relaxed. In particular, I show that under the condition that $f(x)$ points inward on the boundary of D^n one can find an equilibrium by following the above differential equation through the use of an appropriate trick.

This research was funded in part by National Science Foundation grant number SOC76-09414. I wish to thank Steve Smale for some helpful conversations.

6.2 The method

Let us suppose initially that the vector field meets the very strong condition that it points *radially* inward on the boundary of D^n, that is, $f(x) = -x$ on the boundary of D^n. First, I will outline a description of Smale's method in this simple case, and then show how the general case may be modified so as to fit into this framework.

Define M to be the unit disk excluding the set of equilibria. Then the "Gauss map" $g : M \to S^{n-1}$ given by $g(x) = f(x)/\|f(x)\|$ is well defined. Sard's theorem shows that for almost all e in $S^n - 1$, $g^{-1}(e)$ is a one-dimensional manifold; that is, a finite union of circles and line segments with the boundaries of the segments coinciding with the boundary of M.

Now, since $f(x) = -x$ on the boundary of D^n, there is one *and only one* point x_e on this boundary in $g^{-1}(e)$. But the other end of the line segment starting at x_e must lead to a point on the boundary of M. Therefore it must lead to an equilibrium.

Let us parameterize this path by $x(t)$; by the definition of g, $x(t)$ must satisfy the identity

$$f(x(t)) \equiv e\|f(x(t))\|$$

Differentiating this with respect to t gives

$$Df(x(t))\frac{\mathrm{d}x}{\mathrm{d}t} = ea(t) = \frac{f(x(t))a(t)}{\|F(x(t))\|} = f(x(t))\lambda(t),$$

where $a(t)$ and $\lambda(t)$ are some scalar constants; since they only indicate the speed at which we move along the path, their magnitude is unimportant. However, the *sign* of $\lambda(t)$ is important. An orientation argument shows that the appropriate sign is that of $\det -Df(x)$. Thus if we start at almost any point on the boundary of D^n and follow the differential equation given above, we will be led to an equilibrium.

The derivation is exactly the derivation used by Smale applied in the special case where $f(x) = -x$ on the boundary of D^n. Smale's boundary assumption was actually somewhat weaker than this; it essentially implied that the Gauss map defined above is one-to-one on the boundary of the disk. This means that there are no two points x and y on the boundary of the disk where $f(x)$ and $f(y)$ point in the same direction. When stated in this way Smale's boundary assumption seems very restrictive.

It turns out that this boundary assumption can be relaxed significantly. In fact, one only needs to assume that the vector field defined by $f(x)$ never points radially outwards on the boundary of the disk:

Boundary Condition.   *At all x on the boundary of D^n, there is no positive scalar r such that $f(x) = rx$.*

It is clear that this condition is compatible with the requirement that $f(x)$ points inward on the boundary of D^n. We now reduce this general boundary condition to the previous case.

Let D_2^n be a disk in R^n of radius 2. Let $s = \|x\| - 1$ and define the following vector field on D_2^n:

$$h(x) = -\frac{sx}{\|x\|} + (1-s)f\left(\frac{x}{\|x\|}\right), \qquad 1 < \|x\| \leq 2,$$
$$\quad - f(x), \qquad\qquad\qquad 0 \leq \|x\| \leq 1.$$

This field coincides with the original field on the unit disk and is a continuous extension on $D_2^n \setminus D^n$. In fact, a vector in this portion of D_2^n is simply a linear combination of the vector $x/\|x\|$ and $f(x/\|x\|)$ with the weights being given by the radial distance. The important thing to note is that this extension introduces no new equilibria. For suppose x^* in $D_2^n \setminus D^n$ were such that $h(x^*) = 0$; then

$$\frac{-sx^2}{\|x\|} + (1-s)f\left(\frac{x^*}{\|x\|}\right) = 0, \qquad 0 < s < 1,$$

$$f\left(\frac{x^*}{\|x\|}\right) = \frac{s}{(1-s)}\frac{x^*}{\|x^*\|},$$

but this contradicts the assumption that no vector on the boundary of D^n points radially outward. It is therefore clear that Smale's method can be applied directly to the above system.

6.3 Some remarks on the method

(1) There is a slight problem which was pointed out to me by James Mirlees. The extension defined above is not differentiable in a radial direction at the boundary of D^n. However, Smale's proof can easily be modified to take account of such a well behaved non-differentiability. The essential step is to choose e to be a regular value of g restricted to D^n, g restricted to $D_2^n \setminus D^n$, and g restricted to the boundary of D^n. This ensures that $g^{-1}(e)$ will intersect the boundary of D^n transversely and will therefore be a 1-manifold with a finite number of kinks. Hence Smale's differential equation will still be well defined as long as one chooses the correct Jacobian matrix when crossing the boundary of D^n.

(2) The boundary condition described above is very natural from an economic point of view. Nishimura (1981) has shown that if one has the condition of free disposal and the assumption of no boundary equilibria, it follows that the vector of excess demand can never point radially outward on the boundary of the price simplex.

(3) Some geometrical insight into the method can be gained by examining fig. 1. By construction, the vector $f(x)$ points in the direction e at each x along the path $g^{-1}(e)$. If there are two points on the boundary of D^n where $f(x)$ points in the direction e they may be connected by a component of $g^{-1}(e)$. However, degree considerations show that there must be *some* component of $g^{-1}(e)$ that starts at the boundary of D^n and leads to an equilibrium. The extension suggested here gives a way of finding such a path.

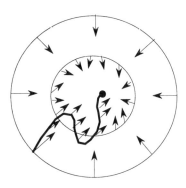

Figure 1. The vectors along the path $g^{-1}(e)$ are all parallel to each other.

References

Smale, S. (1976) "Convergent processes of price adjustment and Global Newton methods," *Journal of Mathematical Economics*, **3**, 107–120.

Kellog, B., T.Y. Li and J. Yorke (1976) "A method of continuation for calculating a Brouwer fixed point," S. Karamdiar, ed., in *Computing fixed points with applications*, Academic Press, New York, **3**, 107–120.

Nishimura, K. (1981) "The exclusion of boundary equilibria," *International Economic Review*, **22**, 475.

Chapter 7

THE NONPARAMETRIC APPROACH
TO DEMAND ANALYSIS

This paper shows how to test data for consistency with utility max-imization, recover the underlying preferences, and forecast demand behavior without making any assumptions concerning the parametric form of the underlying utility or demand functions.

The economic theory of consumer demand is extremely simple. The ba-sic behavioral hypothesis is that the consumer chooses a bundle of goods that is preferred to all other bundles that he can afford. Applied demand analysis typically addresses three sorts of issues concerning this behavioral hypothesis.

(i) Consistency. When is observed behavior consistent with the prefer-ence maximization model?

(ii) Recoverability. How can we recover preferences given observations on consumer behavior?

(iii) Extrapolation. Given consumer behavior for some price configura-tions how can we forecast behavior for other price configurations?

The standard approach to these questions proceeds by postulating para-metric forms for the demand functions and fitting them to observed data. The estimated demand functions can then be tested for consistency with the maximization hypothesis, used to make welfare judgments, or used to

This work was financed by grants from the National Science Foundation and the Guggenheim Memorial Foundation. I wish to thank Erwin Diewert, Avinash Dixit, Joseph Farrell, Angus Deaton, and Sydney Afriat for comments on an earlier draft.

forecast demand for other price configurations. This procedure will be satisfactory only when the postulated parametric forms are good approximations to the "true" demand functions. Since this hypothesis is not directly testable, it must be taken on faith.

In this paper I describe an alternative approach to the above problems in consumer demand analysis. The proposed approach is *nonparametric* in that it requires no ad hoc specifications of functional forms for demand equations. Rather, the nonparametric approach deals with the raw demand data itself using techniques of finite mathematics. In particular I will show how one can directly and simply test a finite body of data for consistency with preference maximization, recover the underlying preferences in a variety of formats, and use them to extrapolate demand behavior to new price configurations. Thus each of the issues of concern to demand analysis mentioned above is amenable to the nonparametric approach.[1]

7.1 Testing for consistency with the maximization hypothesis

Let $p^i = (p_1^i, \ldots, p_k^i)$ denote the ith observation of the prices of some k goods and let $x^i = (x_1^i, \ldots, x_k^i)$ be the associated quantities. Suppose that we have n observations on these prices and quantities, $(p^i, x^i), i = 1, \ldots, n$. How can we tell if these observations could have been generated by a neoclassical, utility maximizing consumer?

DEFINITION: A utility function $u(x)$ *rationalizes* a set of observations $(p^i, x^i), i = 1, \ldots, n$, if $u(x^i) \geq u(x)$ for all x such that $p^i x^i \geq p^i x$.

At the most general level there is a very simple answer to the above question: any finite number of observations can be rationalized by the trivial constant utility function $u(x) = 1$ for all x. The real question is when can the observations be rationalized by a sufficiently well behaved nondegenerate utility function? The best results in this direction are due to Sydney Afriat (1967, 1972, 1973, 1976, 1977).

AFRIAT'S THEOREM. *The following conditions are equivalent:*

(1) There exists a nonsatiated utility function that rationalizes the data.
(2) The data satisfies "cyclical consistency"; that is,

$$p^r x^r \geq p^r x^s, \qquad p^s x^s \geq p^s x^t, \qquad \ldots, \qquad p^q x^q \geq p^q x^r$$

---

[1] Another concern of applied demand analysis is the issue of testing for restrictions on the form of the utility function or budget constraint such as homotheticity, separability. etc. I address these questions in Varian (1980, 1981).

implies

$$p^r x^r = p^r x^s, \qquad p^s x^s = p^s x^t, \qquad \ldots, \qquad p^q x^q = p^q x^r.$$

(3) There exist numbers $U^i, \lambda^i > 0, i = 1, \ldots, n$, such that

$$U^i \leqq U^j + \lambda^j p^j (x^i - x^j) \qquad for \;\; i, j = 1, 1, \ldots, n.$$

(4) There exists a nonsatiated, continuous, concave, monotonic utility function that rationalizes the data.

Proof. See Appendix 1.

There are several remarkable features of Afriat's Theorem. First, the equivalence of (1) and (4) shows that if some data can be rationalized by any nontrivial utility function at all it can in fact be rationalized by a very nice utility function. Or put another way, violations of continuity, concavity, or monotonicity cannot be detected with only a finite number of demand observations. Secondly, the numbers U^i and λ^i referred to in part (3) of Afriat's theorem can be used to actually construct a utility function that rationalizes the data. The numbers U^i and λ^i can be interpreted as measures of the utility level and marginal utility of income at the observed demands. This is described in more detail in Appendix 1.

Thirdly, parts (2) and (3) of Afriat's theorem give directly testable conditions that the data must satisfy if it is to be consistent with the maximization model. Condition (3) for example simply asks whether there exists a nonnegative solution to a set of linear inequalities. The existence of such a solution can be checked by solving a linear program with $2n$ variables and n^2 constraints. Diewert and Parkan (1978) describe some of their computational experience with this technique using actual demand data. Unfortunately the fact that the number of constraints rises as the square of the number of observations makes this condition difficult to verify in practice for computational reasons.[2]

Condition (2) seems rather more promising from the computational perspective. As it turns out, there is an equivalent formulation of condition (2) which is quite easy to test. In addition this equivalent formulation is much more closely related to the traditional literature on the revealed preference approach to demand theory of Samuelson (1948), Houthakker (1950), Richter (1966), and others. In order to describe this formulation we must first consider the following definitions:

DEFINITIONS. Given an observation x^i and a bundle x:

---

[2] One can always use the duality theorem of linear programming to construct an equivalent problem with n^2 variables and $2n$ constraints, but this problem may also be computationally difficult.

(1) x^i is *directly revealed preferred* to x, written $x^i R^0 x$, if $p^i x^i \geqq p^i x$.

(2) x^i is *strictly directly revealed preferred* to x, written $x^i P^0 x$, if $p^i x^i > p^i x$.

(3) x^i is *revealed preferred* to x, written $x^i R x$, if $p^i x^i \geqq p^i x^j, p^j x^j \geqq p^j x^l$, $\ldots, p^m x^m \geqq p^m x$ for some sequence of observations $(x^i, x^j, \ldots, x^m)$. In this case we say that the relation R is the *transitive closure* of the relation R^0.

(4) x^i is *strictly revealed preferred* to x, written $x^i P x$, if there exist observations x^j and x^l such that $x^i R x^j$, $x^j P^0 x^l$, $x^l R x$.

Note that in the above definitions we do not require x^i, x^j, x^l, etc. to be distinct observations. We also adopt the convention that $x R x$ for all bundles x.

DEFINITIONS. A set of data satisfies the:

(1) *Strong Axiom of Revealed Preference, version 1* (SARP 1) if $x^i R x^j$ and $x^j R x^i$ implies $x^i = x^j$;

(2) *Strong Axiom of Revealed Preference, version 2* (SARP 2) if $x^i R x^j$ and $x^i \neq x^j$ implies not $x^i R x^j$;

(3) *Strong Axiom of Revealed Preference, version 3* (SARP 3) if $x^i R x^j$ and $x^i \neq x^j$ implies not $x^i R^0 x^j$;

(4) *Generalized Axiom of Revealed Preference* (GARP) if $x^i R x^j$ implies not $x^j P^0 x^j$.

The most common statement of the Strong Axiom is probably SARP 2.[3] It is clear that SARP 1 is equivalent to SARP 2. It is not quite so clear that SARP 3 is equivalent to SARP 2, but nevertheless they are equivalent. One can easily show that SARP 1, SARP 2, and SARP 3 imply GARP, but not vice versa. Basically SARP (in any of its formulations) requires single valued demand functions while GARP is compatible with multivalued demand functions. For example, the data in Figure 1 violate SARP but are quite compatible with GARP.

This is why we refer to GARP as the Generalized Axiom of Revealed Preference. It turns out to be a necessary and sufficient condition for data to be consistent with utility maximization, and is in fact equivalent to Afriat's cyclical consistency condition.

FACT 1. *A set of data satisfies cyclical consistency if and only if it satisfies GARP.*

Proof. Suppose that we have some data containing a violation of cyclical consistency so that $p^r x^r \geqq p^r x^s, \ldots, p^j x^j > p^j x^i, \ldots, p^q x^q \geqq p^q x^r$. Then

---

[3] See Richter (1979) for several variations on revealed preference axioms. Note that Richter considers a framework where the entire demand correspondence is given, rather than only a finite number of observations. This leads to a number of differences in the analysis.

$x^i R x^j$ by going around the cycle, and $x^j P^0 x^i$ directly. Hence we have a violation of GARP.

On the other hand, suppose we have some data that has a violation of GARP. Then writing out the violation in the above form shows we have a violation of cyclical consistency also. ∎

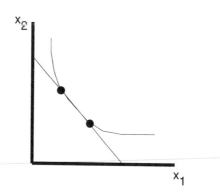

Figure 1. The data violation SARP, but are consistent with GARP.

The equivalence of GARP and cyclical consistency is trivial from the mathematical point of view, but is quite important from the computational point of view, since GARP is quite simple to check in practice, as we discuss below.

First, let us note that GARP can be restated as: if $x^i R x^j$ then $p^j x^j R p^i x^i$ for $i, j = 1, \ldots, n$. Hence verifying that some data satisfies GARP is trivial once we know the relation R – the transitive closure of the direct revealed preference relation R^0.

It is clear that the computation of the transitive closure of a finite relation is a finite problem. The only issue is how one might compute it efficiently. This question has been addressed in the economics literature by Koo (1963, 1965, 1971), Dobell (1965), and Uebe (1972), and in the computer science literature by Warshall (1962) and Munroe (1971), among others.

Most of the algorithms in the economics literature compute the transitive closure of a relation in time proportional to n^4. The computer scientists, utilizing the law of comparative advantage, do a bit better. Warshall's algorithm computes the transitive closure in n^3 steps, and Munroe describes a process that does it in time proportional to $n^{2.74}$. Warshall's algorithm is especially easy to implement and quite ingenious. It seems fast enough for the problems encountered in economics, as well. We therefore describe Warshall's algorithm in Appendix 2.

At this point it might be worthwhile to be rather explicit about how one represents the relations R^0 and R in a form suitable for computation and how one actually verifies GARP in a systematic way.

Let us construct an n by n matrix M whose $i - j$ entry is given by:

$$m_{ij} = \begin{cases} 1 & \text{if } p^i x^i \geq p^i x^j, \text{ that is, } x^i R^0 x^j; \\ 0 & \text{otherwise.} \end{cases}$$

M is constructed directly from the data; it summarizes the relation R^0. Warshall's algorithm, described in Appendix 2, operates on M to create a matrix MT where

$$mt_{ij} = \begin{cases} 1 & \text{if } x^i R x^j, \\ 0 & \text{otherwise.} \end{cases}$$

MT can be used to check GARP in the following way.

ALGORITHM 1.   *Checking data for consistency with GARP.*

Inputs: $(p^i, x^i), i = 1, \ldots, n$, and the matrix MT representing the relation R.

Outputs: whether the data satisfies GARP or not.

1. Is $mt_{ij} = 1$ and $p^j x^j > p^j x^i$ for some i and j? If so, we have a violation of GARP.

Algorithm 1 is easily implemented on a computer. According to Afriat's theorem and Fact 1 we can use Algorithm 1 to simply and directly test a finite amount of data with the utility maximization model. If some data satisfies GARP then there is a nice utility function that will rationalize the observed behavior. If the data contains a violation of GARP then there does not exist a nonsatiated utility function that will rationalize the data. Hence we have a straightforward and efficient way to check a finite amount of data for consistency with the neoclassical model of consumer behavior.

7.2 Recoverability: ordinal comparisons of consumption bundles

Let us turn now to a somewhat different issue, namely the recoverability question described in the introduction. The revealed preference relation R which we discussed in the previous section summarizes all of the preference information contained in the demand observations. Any complete preference ordering that rationalizes the data must contain R, and every completion of R that rationalizes the data is a possible preference ordering that generated the data.

However, economists typically assume certain regularity conditions on the allowable preference orderings. For example we might restrict ourselves to preference orderings representable by utility functions that are nonsatiated, monotonic, and concave. Afriat's theorem implies that we can always impose such restrictions with no loss of generality; and conversely, that it is impossible to detect violations of these restrictions with a finite amount of demand data.

Suppose then that we are given two new consumption bundles x^0 and x' that have not been previously observed. Suppose that every continuous, nonsatiated, concave, monotonic utility function $u(x)$ that was consistent with $(p^i, x^i), i = 1, \ldots, n$, implied that $u(x^0) > u(x')$. Then we might well be justified in concluding that x^0 was in fact preferred to x'.

Alternatively we could adopt the following viewpoint. Suppose that *every* price vector p^0 at which x^0 could be demanded – and that was consistent with the data $(p^i, x^i), i = 1, \ldots, n$, – also implied that x^0 was revealed preferred to x'. Then certainly we could conclude x^0 would be preferred to x' by any consistent consumer. Let us consider this approach in a bit more detail.

First it is clear that if x^0 has already been observed – so we know the price at which x^0 is demanded – there is no problem in verifying whether $x^0 R x'$. Hence we concentrate on the case where x^0 has not previously been observed. In this case we do not know what price to associate with x^0 for purposes of the revealed preference comparison. However, we do know what the set of *possible* prices could be:

DEFINITION: Given any bundle x^0 not previously observed we define the set of prices that *support* x^0 by:

$$S(x^0) = \left\{ p^0 : (p^i, x^i), i = 0, \ldots, n, \text{satisfies GARP and } p^0 x^0 = 1 \right\}.$$

This is simply the set of prices at which x^0 could be demanded and still be consistent with the previously observed behavior. (The requirement that $p^0 x^0 = 1$ is a convenient normalization.) We note that Afriat's theorem implies $S(x^0)$ is nonempty for all x^0 – just let p^0 be the supporting price at x^0 of any concave utility function that rationalizes the data.

We can use the definition of GARP to provide a convenient description of $S(x^0)$:

FACT 2.   *A price vector p^0 is in $S(x^0)$ if and only if it satisfies the following system of linear inequalities:*

$$p^0 x^0 = 1, \tag{1}$$

$$\begin{aligned} p^0 x^0 &\leq p^0 x^i & for\ all\ x^i\ such\ that\ x^i R x^0, \\ p^0 x^0 &< p^0 x^i & for\ all\ x^i\ such\ that\ x^i P x^0. \end{aligned} \tag{2}$$

Proof. Follows immediately from the definition of GARP. ∎

According to Fact 2, $S(x^0)$ is simply the solution set to a certain system of linear inequalities constructed from the data $(p^i, x^i), i = 1, \ldots, n$, and the relations R and P.

We can use $S(x)$ to describe the set of observations "revealed worse" than x^0 and "revealed preferred" to x' in the following way.

$$RW(x^0) = \{x : \text{for all } p^0 \text{ in } S(x^0),$$
$$p^0 x^0 \overset{\geq}{=} p^0 x^i \text{ for some } x^i P x \text{ or}$$
$$p^0 x^0 > p^0 x^i \text{ for some } x^i R x, \}$$

$$RP(x') = \{x : \text{for all } p \text{ in } S(x),$$
$$px \overset{\geq}{=} px^i \text{ for some } x^i P x' \text{ or}$$
$$px > px^i \text{ for some } x^i R x'\}.$$

More succinctly, and with only a slight abuse of our earlier definitions, we might write:

$$RW(x^0) = \{x : \text{ for all } p^0 \in S(x^0), x^0 P x\},$$

$$RP(x') = \{x : \text{ for all } p \in S(x), x P x'\}.$$

These definitions formalize the idea described earlier: if x' is in $RW(x^0)$, then whatever the price at which x^0 is demanded – as long as it is consistent with the previous data – that price will necessarily make x^0 revealed preferred to x'. Thus *every* concave monotonic utility function that rationalizes the data must rank x^0 ahead of x'. Of course $RP(x')$ has a similar interpretation. In fact it is clear from the definitions that x^0 is "revealed preferred" to x' if and only if x' is "revealed worse" than x^0. We record this fact for future reference.

FACT 3. x^0 *is in* $RP(x')$ *if and only if* x' *is in* $RW(x^0)$.

$RP(x^0)$ and $RW(x^0)$ are extremely important to the rest of our discussion so it is worthwhile presenting a few two-dimensional examples. The simplest case – with one data point – is presented in Figure 2. Let us verify that Figure 2 is correct.

First, we consider $RP(x^0)$. In this simple case, $RP(x^0)$ is simply the convex monotonic hull of all points revealed preferred to x^0: namely x^1 and x^0 itself. To verify this, let x be any point in $RP(x^0)$, and let p be any (nonnegative) price vector at which x could be demanded. It is geometrically clear that, whatever budget line is chosen, x will be revealed preferred to x^0 – either directly, or indirectly through the observation x^1. (The reader might check his understanding of this point by indicating the region where x will be *directly* revealed preferred to x^0 by all supporting prices, and the region where x will only be *indirectly* revealed preferred to x^0 for some supporting prices.) So much for $RP(x^0)$.

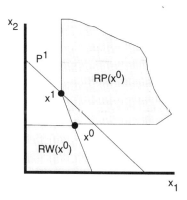

Figure 2. Determining the sets RP and RW; simple case.

In order to verify the construction of $RW(x^0)$, we have to consider all of the prices at which x^0 could be demanded and still be consistent with the previous data point (p^1, x^1). In this case GARP imposes an important restriction on p^0: the budget line through x^0 can be no steeper than the indicated angle θ. If it were steeper we would create a violation of GARP: we would have $x^1 R x^0$, and $x^0 P^0 x^1$. $RW(x^0)$ is the set of points that lie below all budget lines consistent with GARP – exactly as illustrated in Figure 2.

Figure 3 presents a more complex example. As before $RP(x^0)$ turns out to be the convex monotonic hull of all the points revealed preferred to x^0. $RW(x^0)$ is a bit more interesting. For all budgets that support x^0 and satisfy GARP, x^0 is revealed preferred to x^1, and *a fortiori* to all the points beneath x^1's budget set ... including x^2, x^3 and so on.

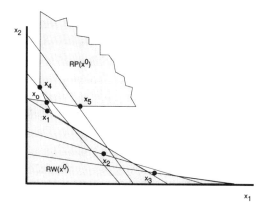

Figure 3. Determining RP and RW; more complex case.

Now Figure 3 presents us with quite a bit of information about the indifference curve passing through x^0: it cannot intersect $RP(x^0)$ or $RW(x^0)$ so it must lie in between the two. Put another way, *the set of bundles preferred to x^0* (using the true utility function) *must always contain $RP(x^0)$, and must be contained in the complement of $RW(x^0)$.* This last set, the complement of $RW(x^0)$, will be useful later on; we will call it $NRW(x^0)$ for "not revealed worse" than x^0.

It is clear from Figure 3 that $RP(x^0)$ and $NRW(x^0)$ are not only "inner" and "outer" estimates of the set of bundles preferred to x^0, they are also the tightest inner and outer estimates. If a point x' is not contained in either of these sets then there is a nice utility function that rationalizes the data for which $u(x^0) \gtreqless u(x')$ ... and there is a nice utility function that rationalizes the data for which $u(x') \gtreqless u(x^0)$.

These statements are obvious for the two dimensional example given in Figure 3, but in fact they are true in general. In order to establish this we need the following criterion for membership in $RW(x^0)$.

FACT 4. *A bundle x' is in $RW(x^0)$ if and only if there does not exist a $p^0 \gneqq 0$ that satisfies the following system of linear inequalities:*

$$p^0 x^0 = 1, \tag{1}$$

$$p^0 x^0 \leqq p^0 x^i \quad \text{for all } x^i \text{ such that } x^i R x^0, \tag{2}$$

$$p^0 x^0 < p^0 x^i \quad \text{for all } x^i \text{ such that } x^i P x^0,$$

$$p^0 x^0 \leqq p^0 x^j \quad \text{for all } x^j \text{ such that } x^j R x', \tag{3}$$

$$p^0 x^0 < p^0 x^j \quad \text{for all } x^j \text{ such that } x^j P x'.$$

Proof. Suppose x' is in $RW(x^0)$. Then any p^0 that satisfies the first set of inequalities is a supporting price for x^0 by Fact 2. By the definition of $RW(x^0)$ it must therefore violate one of the inequalities in the second set.

Conversely suppose x' is not in $RW(x^0)$. Then there is some supporting price p^0 at which x^0 is not revealed preferred to x' by any chain. That is, p^0 satisfies (2) and (3). ∎

Fact 4 gives us an explicit way to check whether x' is revealed worse than x^0. And by Fact 3 we can see whether x' is revealed preferred to x^0 just by checking whether x^0 is revealed worse than x'. Hence we can recover all of the ordinal information in the data by checking whether there exists a solution to a simple set of linear inequalities. This is easily accomplished by solving a simple linear program. Note that the number of constraints in this program will at most be $2n + 1$ – and generally be considerably smaller than $2n + 1$.

We can now verify the intuitively plausible statements made earlier concerning the relationship between $RP(x^0)$, $RW(x^0)$, $P(x^0) = \{x : u(x) > u(x^0)\}$, and $W(x^0) = \{x : u(x^0) > u(x)\}$.

FACT 5. *Let $u(x)$ be any utility function that rationalizes the data. Then for all x^0, $RP(x^0) \subset P(x^0) \subset NRW(x^0)$.*

Proof. Obvious from the fact that $x^0 P x'$ implies $u(x^0) > u(x')$ for any utility function that rationalizes the data. ∎

FACT 6. *Suppose that x' is not in $RW(x^0)$; then there exists a nonsatiated, continuous, concave monotonic utility function that rationalizes the data for which $u(x^0) \geqq u(x')$. An analogous statement holds if x' is not in $RP(x^0)$.*

Proof. Suppose x' is not in $RW(x^0)$. Then by Fact 4 there exists a p^0 supporting x^0 such that not $x^0 P x'$. Hence by using Fact 16 in Appendix 1, there is a utility function with the stated properties. ∎

FACT 7. *Let $x^0 R x'$. Then $RP(x^0) \subset RP(x')$. Assume further that x' is observed as a chosen bundle at some price p'. Then $RW(x^0) \supset RW(x')$ and $NRW(x^0) \subset NRW(x')$.*

Proof. Let $\hat{x}$ be in $RP(x')$. Then for all $\hat{p}$ that support $\hat{x}$ we have xRx^0. Since by hypothesis $x^0 R x'$, transitivity implies $\hat{x} R x'$. Hence $\hat{x}$ is in $RP(x')$.

Let $\hat{x}$ be in $RW(x')$. Since x' is actually chosen at price p' this implies $x' R \hat{x}$. Since by hypothesis $x^0 R x'$, transitivity implies $x^0 R \hat{x}$. Hence $\hat{x}$ is in $RW(x^0)$. ∎

7.3 Recoverability: ordinal comparisons of budgets

In many applications of demand analysis the natural objects of interest are not bundles of goods but are budgets – i.e. prices and expenditures. For example. if one wants to compare proposed changes in the tax structure, it is natural to compare alternative price configurations: given two proposed lists of prices and expenditures (p^0, y^0) and (p', y') we want to know which one is preferred by some individual consumer.

If we had a measure of the consumer's indirect utility function $v(p, y)$ we could simply compute $v(p^0, y^0)$ and $v(p', y')$ and compare the two numbers. If we have only a finite number of observations on a consumer's behavior

(p^i, x^i), $i = 1, \ldots, n$, we could postulate a specification of an indirect utility function, derive the associated demand functions, and estimate the parameters of the resulting demand system. These estimated parameters of the demand system translate directly back to parameters of the indirect utility function which can then be used to make the welfare comparison between the two budgets.

However, the parametric specification necessarily involves an unwarranted maintained hypothesis of functional form. How can we proceed to make a nonparametric comparison of (p^0, y^0) versus (p', y')?

Let us recall the notion of *indirect revealed preference* of Sakai (1978), Little (1979), and Richter (1979).

DEFINITION: Given an observed budget (p^i, y^i) and a budget (p, y), we say:

(1) (p, y) is *directly revealed preferred* to (p^i, y^i), written $(p, y)R^0(p^i, y^i)$, if $px^i \leqq y$.

(2) (p, y) is *strictly directly revealed* preferred to (p^i, y^i), written $(p, y)P^0$ (p^i, y^i), if $px^i < y$.

(3) (p, y) is *revealed preferred* to (p^i, y^i), written $(p, y)R(p^i, y^i)$, if R is the transitive closure of R^0.

(4) (p, y) is *strictly revealed preferred* to (p^i, y^i), written $(p, y)P(p^i, y^i)$ if there exist observed budgets (p^j, y^j) and (p^l, y^l) such that $(p, y)R(p^j, y^j)$, $(p^j, y^j)P(p^l, y^l)$, $(p^l, y^l)R(p, y)$.

Note that the indirect revealed preference relation works exactly opposite to the way the revealed preference relation works. To tell whether x^0 is revealed preferred to something we need to know the price p^0 at which x^0 is demanded – and then x^0 is revealed preferred to the infinite number of bundles beneath its budget line. To tell whether (p^0, y^0) is revealed worse than some budget we need to know the bundle x^0 that is demanded at (p^0, y^0) – and then (p^0, y^0) is revealed worse than the infinite number of budgets (p, y) for which $px^0 \leqq y$.

Nevertheless we can apply the same approach to ordinal comparisons to construct dual versions of the results in Section 3. This duality is most clearly exhibited if we normalize prices by dividing through by expenditure so that budgets are uniquely described by $p^0 = (p^0, 1)$ and $p' = (p', 1)$.

DEFINITION: Given any price p^0 not previously observed we define the set of bundles that *support* p^0 by:

$$S(p^0) = \{x^0 : (p^i, x^i), i = 0, \ldots, n, \text{ satisfies GARP and } p^0 x^0 = 1\}.$$

As before the requirement that $p^0 x^0 = 1$ is only a normalization.

We can now describe the set of budgets "revealed preferred" or "revealed worse" than a given budget by:

$$RW(p^0) = \{p : \text{for all } x \text{ in} S(p), 1 \overset{\geq}{=} p^0 x^i \text{ for some } p^i P p,$$
$$\text{or } 1 > p^0 x^i \text{ for some } p^i R p\},$$

$$RP(p') = \{p : \text{for all } x' \text{ in } S(p'), 1 \overset{\geq}{=} p x^i \text{ for some } p^i P p'$$
$$\text{or } 1 > p x^i \text{ for some } p^i R x'\}.$$

Of course these definitions could also be stated as:

$$RW(p^0) = \{p : \text{for all } x \text{ in} S(p), 1 \overset{\geq}{=} p^0 x^i \text{ for some } x^i P x,$$
$$\text{or } 1 > p^0 x^i \text{ for some } x^i R x\},$$

$$RP(p') = \{p : \text{for all } x' \text{ in } S(p'), 1 \overset{\geq}{=} p x^i \text{ for some } x^i P x'$$
$$\text{or } 1 > p x^i \text{ for some } x^i R x'\}.$$

Or even more succinctly:

$$RW(p^0) = \{p : \text{ for some } x \text{ in } S(p), p^0 R p\},$$

$$RP(p') = \{p : \text{ for some } x' \text{ in } S(p'), p P p'\}.$$

We can now state the dual versions of Facts 2 and 4. The proofs are completely analogous and are left to the reader.

FACT 8.   *A bundle x^0 is in $S(p^0)$ if and only if it satisfies the following system of linear inequalities:*

$$p^0 x^0 = 1, \tag{1}$$
$$p^i x^i \overset{\leq}{=} p^i x^0 \qquad \text{for all } p^i \text{ such that } p^0 R p^i, \tag{2}$$
$$p^i x^i < p^i x^0 \qquad \text{for all } p^i \text{ such that } p^0 P p^i.$$

FACT 9.   *A budget p' is in $RP(p^0)$ if and only if there does not exist an $x^0 \overset{\geq}{=} 0$ that satisfies the following system of linear inequalities:*

$$p^0 x^0 = 1, \tag{1}$$
$$p^i x^i \overset{\leq}{=} p^i x^0 \qquad \text{for all } p^i \text{ such that } p^0 R p^i, \tag{2}$$
$$p^i x^i < p^i x^0 \qquad \text{for all } p^i \text{ such that } p^0 P p^i,$$
$$p^j x^j \overset{\leq}{=} p^j x^0 \qquad \text{for all } p^j \text{ such that } p' R p^j, \tag{3}$$
$$p^j x^j < p^j x^0 \qquad \text{for all } p^j \text{ such that } p' P p^j.$$

Of course the dual versions of Facts 3, 5, and 6 are also true. The statement and proofs of these are left to the reader as well.

Another type of comparison that is often useful is to be able to compare bundles with budgets and vice versa. For example if we are given a direct and an associated normalized indirect utility function, $u(x)$ and $v(p)$, we could consider:

(1) All budgets p preferred to a bundle x^0:

$$PP(x^0) = \{p : v(p) > u(x^0)\}.$$

(2) All budgets p worse than a bundle x^0:

$$PW(x^0) = \{p : v(p) < u(x^0)\}.$$

(3) All bundles x preferred to a budget p^0:

$$XP(p^0) = \{x : u(x) > v(p^0)\}.$$

(4) All bundles x worse than a budget p^0:

$$XW(p^0) = \{x : u(x) < v(p^0)\}.$$

Each of these constructs has its "revealed preferred" and "revealed worse" analogy:

(1) All budgets p revealed preferred to a bundle x^0:

$$PRP(x^0) = \{p : \text{ for all } x \text{ in } S(p), xPx^0\}.$$

(2) All budgets p revealed worse than a bundle x^0:

$$PRW(x^0) = \{p : \text{ for all } p^0 \text{ in } S(x^0), \text{ and all } x \text{ in } S(p), x^0Px\}.$$

(3) All bundles x revealed preferred to a budget p^0:

$$XRP(p^0) = \{x : \text{ for all } p \text{ in } S(x), \text{ and all } x^0 \text{ in } S(p^0), xPx^0\}.$$

(4) All bundles x revealed worse than a budget p^0:

$$XRW(p^0) = \{x : \text{ for all } x^0 \text{ in } S(p^0), x^0Px\}.$$

If we want to verify whether p' is in $PRP(x^0)$, etc. we simply have to write down the associated system of linear inequalities following the general model of Facts 2 and 4. In cases (2) and (4) above, these systems involve unknown p's and unknown x's and are therefore somewhat involved. Cases (1) and (4) on the other hand are rather simple. We record this fact for future reference.

FACT 10.

$$PRP(x^0) = \{p : 1 > px^i \text{ for some } x^i R x^0 \text{ or } 1 \overset{\geq}{=} px^i \text{ for some } x^i P x^0\},$$

$$XRW(p^0) = \{x : 1 > p^0 x^i \text{ for some } x^i R x \text{ or } 1 \overset{\geq}{=} px^i \text{ for some } x^i P x\}.$$

7.4 Extrapolation: forecasting demanded bundles

Suppose that we have observed choices $(p^i, x^i), i = 1, \ldots, n$, and that we are given some new budget $(p^0, 1)$ which has not been previously observed. What choice will the consumer make if his choice is to be consistent with the preferences revealed by his previous behavior? What is the best "overestimate" of the demanded bundle at p^0?

It turns out that we have already answered this question: it is simply the set of bundles that support the budget p^0, namely $S(p^0)$. For $S(p^0)$ is by definition all of the bundles of goods x^0 which make the data $(p^i, x^i), i = 0, \ldots, n$, consistent with GARP. It is therefore the tightest overestimate of the demand correspondence at p^0: every bundle in $S(p^0)$ *could* be a chosen bundle at p^0 and any bundle outside of $S(p^0)$ could never be chosen. Figure 4 gives a simple example of $S(p^0)$.

In an analogous manner $S(x^0)$ gives us the tightest overestimate of the *inverse* demand correspondence.

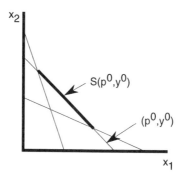

Figure 4. Determining $S(p^0, y^0)$.

7.5 Recoverability: bounding a specific utility function

It is often desirable to know not only whether some bundle is preferred to some other bundle, but by *how much* one bundle is preferred to another.

Now of course, there is no unique answer to this question: demand theory is completely ordinal in nature and there is no unique cardinal representation of utility. On the other hand it is a common practice to use certain specific cardinalizations of utility in measuring economic welfare.

One particularly useful cardinalization is Samuelson's "money metric" utility function (Samuelson (1979)). For reasons that will become apparent, I prefer to call this function the direct income compensation function. We can define it in two equivalent ways:

$$m(p, x^0) = \inf px$$

$$\text{such that } x \text{ is in } P(x^0)$$

where $P(x^0) = \{x : u(x) > u(x^0)\}$ or,

$$m(p, x^0) = e(p, u(x^0)).$$

In the latter definition $e(p, u)$ is the expenditure function and $u(x)$ is the associated utility function. It is obvious from this latter definition that $m(p, x^0)$ behaves like an expenditure function with respect to p. It is also straightforward to show that for fixed p, $m(p, x^0)$ behaves like a *utility* function with respect to x^0: since the expenditure function is always increasing in utility, $m(p, x^0)$ is a monotonic transformation of a utility function and is therefore itself a utility function.

The direct income compensation function can be used to describe at least two measures of "how much" one configuration (p^0, x^0) is preferred to another configuration (p', x'), namely Hicks' compensating and equivalent variations:

$$C = m(p', x') - m(p', x^0),$$
$$E = m(p^0, x') - m(p^0, x^0).$$

Since $m(p^0, x)$ and $m(p', x)$ are each utility functions that represent the same preferences, C and E must always have the same sign, but they generally will have different magnitudes.

Let us accept for the moment that $m(p, x)$ is a reasonable cardinalization of utility. The question that then arises is how we might measure it. If we are given a parametric form for the utility function or expenditure function it is always possible to compute $m(p, x)$ directly. However, in the spirit of the nonparametric approach to demand analysis we ask how we might compare functions that provide bounds on $m(p, x)$ that are consistent with a finite set of observed demands $(p^i, x^i), i = 1, \ldots, n$.

In Section 2 we described the best inner and outer approximations to $P(x^0)$. It is natural to define the upper and lower bounds on the compensation function by:

$$m^+(p, x^0) = \inf px$$

such that x is in $RP(x^0)$,

$$m^-(p, x^0) = \inf px$$

such that x is in $NRW(x^0)$.

I refer to these as the *overcompensation* and the *undercompensation* functions respectively.

FACT 11. *Let m^+ and m^- be defined as above. Then*

(i)$m^+(p^0, x) \gtreqless m(p^0, x) \gtreqless m^-(p^0, x)$ *for all* p^0, x.
(ii)$x^i Rx^i$ *implies* $m^+(p^0, x^i) \gtreqless m^+(p^0, x)$. *If* $x^i Rx^j$ *and* x^j *is chosen at some price* p^j, *then* $m^-(p^0, x^i) \gtreqless m^-(p^0, x^j)$.

Proof. (i) Follows from Fact 5. (ii) Follows from Fact 7. ∎

Fact 11 shows that: (i) $m^+(p, x)$ and $m^-(p, x)$ do bound the compensation function, and (ii) they are themselves utility functions that respect the revealed preference ordering.

Thus the overcompensation and undercompensation functions provide theoretically ideal bounds to the compensation function. The problem with these two functions is that they are rather difficult to compute in practice. Recall that Fact 4 gave us a way to verify whether any given bundle x was an element of $RP(x^0)$ or $RW(x^0)$. However, I do not currently have any *explicit* description of these two sets of the sort suitable for mathematical programming techniques. So instead I have proceeded by defining two approximations to the overcompensation and undercompensation functions. These two approximations do provide bounds, but they are just not the theoretically tightest bounds. We turn now to a description of these approximations.

Let us define the convex, monotonic hull of $\{x^i : x^i Rx^0\}$:

$$CM(x^0) = \text{interior of convex hull of } \{x : x \gtreqless x^i, x^i Rx^0\}.$$

FACT 12. $RP(x^0) \supset CM(x^0)$ *for all* x^0.*

Proof. Let x be a point in $CM(x^0)$ and let p be any price vector that supports x. Then I claim $px > px^i$ for some $x^i Rx^0$. For if not, p would

* Vicki Knoblauch, "A Tight Upper Bound on the Money Metric Utility Function," *American Economic Review*, **82**, 3 (June 1992), 660–663, subsequently showed that $RP(x^0) = CM(x^0)$. This implies that the "approximate" overcompensation function does, in fact, provide the theoretically tightest bounds to compensation function.

separate x from $CM(x^0)$, a contradiction. Since xRx^i, x^iRx^0 we have that x is in $RP(x^0)$. ∎

Then we can define the *approximate overcompensation function* by:

$$am^+(p, x^0) = \inf px$$

$$\text{such that } x \text{ is in } CM(x^0).$$

Since $CM(x^0)$ is a convex polytope whose vertices are precisely those x^iRx^0, we can also describe this minimization problem by:

$$am^+(p, x^0) = \min px^i, \qquad \text{such that } x^iRx^0.$$

Note that this function is quite simple to compute. Nevertheless, this approximate overcompensation function does share some desirable properties with the true overcompensation function.

FACT 13.

$$am^+(p, x) \overset{\geq}{=} m^+(p, x) \overset{\geq}{=} m(p, x). \tag{1}$$

$$x^0Rx \text{ implies } am^+(p, x^0) \overset{\geq}{=} am^+(p, x). \tag{2}$$

There exists a convex monotonic preference order $\overset{\geq}{\sim}$ such that

$$am^+(p, x^0) = m(p, x^0) \text{ for all } x^0. \tag{3}$$

Proof. The first two parts are obvious. The third is rather detailed. First we define the order and verify that it works; then we establish its properties.

Let $x\overset{\geq}{\sim}x'$ if and only if $am^+(p, x) \overset{\geq}{=} am^+(p, x')$. Let us show that the compensation function that goes along with this order is in fact equal to $am^+(p, x)$.
Let px^* solve:

$$px^* = m(p, \bar{x}) = \min px$$

$$\text{such that } am^+(p, x) \overset{\geq}{=} am^+(p, \bar{x})$$

and let $p\tilde{x}$ solve

$$p\tilde{x} = am^+(p, x^*) \overset{\geq}{=} am^+, \qquad \text{such that } x^iR\bar{x}.$$

Now $\tilde{x}R\bar{x}$ so property (2) shows that $am^+(p, \tilde{x}) \overset{\geq}{=} am^+(p, \bar{x})$. Hence $\tilde{x}$ is feasible for the first problem and therefore $px^* \overset{\leq}{=} p\tilde{x}$.

On the other hand

$$px^* \overset{\geq}{=} am^+(p, x^*) \overset{\geq}{=} am^+(p, \bar{x}) = p\tilde{x}.$$

Next we examine the properties of the preference ordering $\overset{\sim}{\gtrsim}$.

(a) $\{x : am^+(p, x) \overset{\geq}{=} k\}$ is convex. To prove this, we suppose $am^+(p, x') \overset{\geq}{=} k$ and $am^+(p, x'') \overset{\geq}{=} k$. Let

$$A = \{x^i : x^i R x'\}.$$
$$B = \{x^i : x^i R x''\},$$
$$C = \{x^i : x^i R(tx' + (1-t)x'')\} \qquad \text{for some } t \text{ such that } 0 \overset{\leq}{=} t \overset{\leq}{=} 1.$$

I claim that if x^i is in C, then x^i is in $A \cup B$. For to say x^i is in C is to say that there exists a finite sequence such that:

$$p^i x^i \overset{\geq}{=} p^i x^r,$$
$$p^r x^r \overset{\geq}{=} p^r x^s,$$
$$p^l x^l \overset{\geq}{=} p^l (tx' + (l_t)x'').$$

From the last inequality it is easy to show that either $p^l x^l \overset{\geq}{=} p^l x'$ or $p^l x^l \overset{\geq}{=} p^l x''$, which establishes the claim. Now, since $C \subset A \cup B$, we have:

$$k \overset{\leq}{=} \min_{x \text{ in } A \cup B} px \overset{\leq}{=} \min_{x \text{ in } C} px = am^+(p, tx' + (1-t)x'').$$

(b) If $x' \overset{\geq}{=} x^0$, then $am^+(p, x') \overset{\geq}{=} am^+(p, x^0)$. This follows since $\{x^i : x^i R x'\} \subset \{x^i : x^i R x^0\}$. ∎

Thus $am^+(p^0, x)$ is a utility function that bounds the compensation function and the bound is uniformly tight in the sense that there exists a "nice" preference ordering that actually generates $am^+(p^0, x)$ as its compensation function.

However it must be pointed out that this ordering typically exhibits regions of satiation, and is in general discontinuous. An example is given in Figure 5. Here all the points in the shaded regions are assigned $am^+(p^0, x) = p^0 x^1$. The approximate overcompensation function increases linearly as one moves out the ray tx, and then is constant, and then jumps discontinuously.

We now turn to the problem of computing an approximation to the undercompensation function. The basic trick here is to get an "inner bound" to $RW(x^0)$ by elimination the nonconvexities shown in Figure 3. We define this inner bound by:

$$IRW(x_0) = \left\{x : \text{ for all } p^0 \text{ in } S(x^0), x^0 R X^i, x^i \neq x^0 \text{ and } p^i x^i \overset{\geq}{=} p^i x\right\}.$$

The crucial difference between $RW(x^0)$ and $IRW(x^0)$ is the requirement that $x^i \neq x^0$. This is made clear in Figure 3. The complement of $IRW(x^0)$, $NIRW(x^0)$, is then given by:

$$NIRW(x^0) =$$
$$\{x : p^i x > p^i x^i \text{ for some } x^i \neq x^0 \text{ such that } x^0 R x^i \text{ for all } p^0 \text{ in } S(x^0)\}.$$

This is simply a set of points defined by a finite number of linear inequalities. Hence there is no problem in computing the "approximate undercompensation function":

$$am^-(p^0, \bar{x}) = \inf p^0 x$$
$$\text{such that } x \text{ is in} NIRW(\bar{x}).$$

This also shares some desirable features with the true undercompensation function:

FACT 14.

$$m(p, x) \overset{\geq}{=} m^-(p, x) \overset{\geq}{=} am^-(p, x), \tag{1}$$
$$x^0 R x^j \text{ implies } am^-(p, x^0) \overset{\geq}{=} am^-(p, x^j).$$

Proof. Left to the reader. ∎

Thus $am^-(p, x)$ bounds the true undercompensation function and it respects the revealed preference ordering, although it does not provide the theoretically ideal bound.

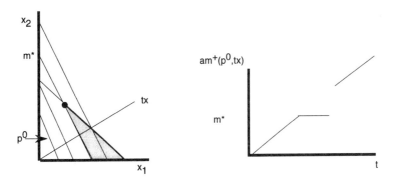

Figure 5. Graph of the approximate overcompensation function.

7.6 Recoverability: bounding a specific indirect utility function

It is natural to extend the results of the last section to indirect utility comparisons. The function one wishes to bound is the *indirect income compensation* function

$$\mu(q; p, y) \equiv e(q, v(p, y))$$

where $e(q, u)$ is the expenditure function and $v(p, y)$ is the indirect utility function.[4] An equivalent way to define $\mu(q; p, y)$ is:

$$\mu(q; p, y) = \inf qx$$

such that x is in $XP(p, y) = \{x : u(x) > v(p, y)\}$.

Applying the approach of the last section, it appears natural to define the *indirect overcompensation function* and the *indirect undercompensation function* by:

$$\mu^+(q; p, y) = \inf qx$$

such that x is in $XRP(p, y)$,

$$\mu^-(q; p, y) = \inf qx$$

such that x is in $NXRW(p, y)$

Recall that $XRP(p, y)$ consists of all bundles revealed preferred to the budget (p, y), and $NXRW(p, y)$ consists of all bundles not revealed worse than the budget (p, y); formal definitions were given in Section 3.

It is by now straightforward to verify the following fact:

FACT 15.   *The indirect over and under compensation functions have the following properties:*

$$\mu^-(q : p, y) \overset{\leq}{=} \mu(q; p, y) \overset{\leq}{=} \mu^+(q; p, y). \tag{i}$$

$$(p^0, y^0) R(p', y') \text{ implies } \mu^-(q; p^0, y^0) \overset{\geq}{=} \mu^-(q; p', y'). \tag{ii}$$

If (p^0, y^0) is the budget for some observed choice then

$$\mu^+(q; p^0, y^0) \overset{\geq}{=} \mu^+(q; p', y').$$

Let us now consider the computability of μ^+ and μ^-. As before, we can verify whether any given x' is an element of $XRP(p, y)$ by solving a set of

---

[4] The indirect compensation function was first discussed by McKenzie (1956). It has been extensively treated by Hurwicz and Uzawa (1971).

linear inequalities; however it seems difficult to get an explicit description of the sort necessary for mathematical programming.

I therefore suggest the following approximation to μ^+:

$$u\mu^+(q;p,y) - am^+(q,x^i)$$

$$\text{if } (p,y) = (p^i, y^i) \text{ for some observed } (p^t, y^i),$$

$$= \max qx$$

$$\text{such that } x \text{ is in } S(p,y) \text{ otherwise.}$$

That is, if (p,y) is observed, we use the value of the approximate overcompensation function. Otherwise, we adopt the most conservative estimate and set $a\mu^+(q;p,y)$ equal to the maximum expenditure over all bundles in the "overestimate" of the demand correspondence. This clearly gives an upper bound on the true overcompensation function.

The indirect undercompensation function is, on the other hand, quite simple to compute. Since Fact 10 gives an explicit description of $XRW(p,y)$, as the solution set to a system of linear inequalities, we can simply compute $\mu^-(q;p,y)$ by solving a small linear program. An illustration of $XRW(p,y)$ and $\mu(q;p,y)$ is given in Figure 6.

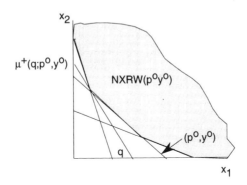

Figure 6. The indirect overcompensation function.

7.7 Some applications

The algorithms described in the previous sections have been assembled in a package of FORTRAN subroutines available from the author. Here I will briefly describe some computational experience with these routines.[5]

[5] Diewert and Parkan (1978) discuss their computational experience with some alternative nonparametric techniques.

First let us consider the issue of testing demand data for consistency with preference maximization. I have applied the routines of Section 1 to several sets of aggregate consumption data. In each case the aggregate consumption data was consistent with GARP: that is, it could have been generated by a single neoclassical "representative consumer." At first glance this may seem somewhat surprising given the negative theoretical results of Sonnenschein (1973) and Debreu (1974). However, upon reflection, it is not difficult to understand why this occurs.[6]

Most existing sets of aggregate consumption data are post-war data, and this period has been characterized by small changes in relative prices and large changes in income. Hence, each year has been revealed preferred to the previous years in the sense that it has typically been possible in a given year to purchase the consumption bundles of each of the previous years. Hence no "revealed preference" cycles can occur and the data are consistent with the maximization hypothesis. This observation implies that those studies which have rejected the preference maximization using conventional parametric techniques are rejecting only their particular choice of parametric form.

Given that a set of aggregate consumption data are consistent with preference maximization, we can compute the over- and undercompensation functions described in Sections 5 and 6. One can use these functions to provide some interesting bounds on cost of living indices.

Let (p^i, y^i) be a budget in year i and (p^0, y^0) be a budget in the base year. Then the *true cost of living index* is defined by:

$$i = \frac{\mu(p^0; p^i, y^i)}{y^0}.$$

The true cost of living index measures how much money one would need in the base year to be as well off as one was in the comparison year expressed as a fraction of base year expenditure. In order to calculate i one needs the indirect income compensation function which is equivalent to requiring complete knowledge of the individual preference ordering over some range.

However, we can use the results of Section 6 to compute upper and lower bounds on i that are consistent with any finite set of data. Table I presents the results of such a computation using U.S. aggregate consumption data by nine categories from 1947-78.

Note the tightness of the bounds. Typically the overestimate is within 15 per cent of the underestimate which allows for a fairly tight estimate of the true cost of living. However, the accuracy of the table is slightly misleading in the following sense.

Given only the information contained in the two observations (p^0, y^0) and (p', y') it is possible to construct the classical bounds depicted in Figure

---

[6] For another independent recent application of revealed preference methodology to aggregate data see Landsburg (1981).

TABLE I

UPPER AND LOWER BOUND ON TRUE COST OF LIVING INDEX[a]
(CLASSICAL BOUNDS IN PARENTHESES)

Year	Upper Bound	Lower Bound
1947	.2496	.1841
1948	.2666	.2004
1949	.2715	.2024
1950	.2906	.2113
1951	.3107	.2237
1952	.3246	.2401
1953	.3409	.2548
1954	.3497	.2634
1955	.3744	.2886
1956	.3905	.3013
1957	.4096	.3172
1958	.4205	.3324
1959	.4500	.3596
1960	.4682	.3779
1961	.4806	.3903
1962	.5082	.4208
1963	.5342	.4499
1964	.5707	.4865
1965	.6119	.5342
1966	.6581	.5864
1967	.6906	.6089
1968	.7524	.6809
1969	.8089	.7406
1970	.8553	.8104
1971	.9174	.8906
1972	1.0000	1.0000
1973	1.0960	1.0409
1974	1.1900	1.0478 (0.9496)
1975	1.2994	1.0623 (1.0466)
1976	2.4354	1.1615
1977	1.5767	1.2764
1978	1.7330	1.4404

[a] Data are U.S. consumption data by 9 categories from the NBER Time Series Database (Tables 2.3 and 2.4). The goods are motor vehicles, furniture, other durables, food, clothing, gasoline and oil, housing, transportation, and other services.

7. Improvements in these bounds are possible only when some budget set from another sample observation intersects the budget set given by (p', y') as in Figure 8.

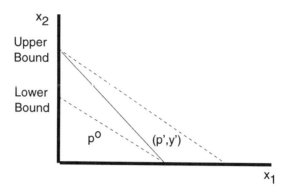

Figure 7. Classical upper bounds and lower bounds.

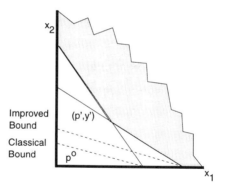

Figure 8. Improved upper bounds and lower bounds.

Given the nature of the data, these intersections are quite rare, and in fact only occur for two years 1974 and 1975. Again, the lack of variation in the price data limits the power of these methods in this case. However, the techniques proposed here do provide an improvement on the classical bounds when sufficient variation in price data is present.

7.8 Summary

We have shown how the nonparametric techniques of revealed preference analysis can be used to: (1) test a finite amount of data for consistency with preference maximization model; (2) construct a nicely behaved utility function capable of rationalizing a finite amount of demand data; (3) compare previously unobserved consumption bundles and budgets with respect to their ordinal rankings; (4) compute cardinal bounds on the direct and indirect compensation functions; and (5) compute estimates of the direct and indirect demand correspondence consistent with previously observed demand data.

7.9 Appendix I: a proof of Afriat's theorem

In this appendix we give a proof of Afriat's theorem. The proof we give is based on earlier proofs by Afriat (1976) and Diewert (1973), but is somewhat more constructive. In fact we will exhibit an algorithm which will actually compute a utility function which rationalizes any given finite amount of data. It turns out that it is convenient to first describe the algorithm to do this computation and then verify that it works in the course of the proof of Afriat's theorem.

The algorithm that we describe below makes use of a subroutine which calculates a maximal element of a finite set with respect to some binary relation.

Let us recall the following definition.

DEFINITION: An element x^m of a set S is maximal with respect to a binary relation B if $x^i B x^m$ implies $x^m B x^i$.

If x^m is a maximal element then either there is nothing that is ranked ahead of it or the only things that are "ahead" of it are things that are indifferent to it.

If we have a finite set with a reflexive and transitive binary relation then there is always at least one maximal element; the following algorithm shows us how to find it. (See Sen (1970), p. 11.)

ALGORITHM 2.   *Finding a maximal element.*

Input: a reflexive and transitive binary relation B defined on a finite set $S = (x^1, \ldots, x^n)$ indexed by $I = (1, \ldots, n)$.
Output: an index m where $x^i B x^m$ implies $x^m B x^i$.
1. Set $m = 1, b^0 = x^1$.
2. For each $i = 1, \ldots, n$ if $x^i B b^{i-1}$ set $b^i = x^i$, and $m = i$. Otherwise set $b^i = b^{i-1}$.

We will let $\max(I)$ be a routine that performs Algorithm 2; that is, given a set S indexed by I, $\max(I)$ returns the index of a maximal element in S.

It is perhaps not immediately obvious that Algorithm 2 works. Hence we provide the following proof.

FACT 15.   *The output of Algorithm 2 is the index of a maximal element of S.*

Proof. First we note that by the transitivity and reflexivity of B, $b^n B b^j$ for all $j = 0, \ldots, n$. Also note that $x^m = b^n$.

Now suppose we are given some $x^i B x^m$; i.e. $x^i B b^n$. We must show that $b^n B x^i$. First we observe that since $x^i B b^n$, and $b^n B b^{i-1}$, then $x^i B b^{i-1}$. Line 2 of the algorithm then implies $b^i = x^i$. But then $b^n B b^i = x^i$ gives $b^n B x^i$ as required.

We note that the revealed preference relation R is transitive and reflexive, so Algorithm 2 will therefore correctly compute a maximal element. We can now present an algorithm which calculates numbers that satisfy the Afriat inequalities:

ALGORITHM 3.   *Constructing the Afriat numbers.*

Input: A set of demand observations $(p^i, x^i), i = 1, \ldots, n$ and the revealed preference relation R that satisfy GARP.

Output: A set of numbers $U^i, \lambda^i > 0, i = 1, \ldots, n$ that satisfy the Afriat inequalities.

1. $I = \{1, \ldots, n\}, B = \emptyset$.
2. Let $m = \max(I)$.
3. Set $E = \{i \text{ in } I : x^i R x^m\}$. If $B = \emptyset$, set $U^m = \lambda^m = 1$ and go to 6. Otherwise go to 4.
4. Set $U^m = \min_{i \in E} \min_{j \in B} \min\{U^j + \lambda^j p^j (x^i - x^j), U^j\}$.
5. Set $\lambda^m = \max_{i \in E} \max_{j \in B} \max\{(U^j - U^m)/p^i (x^i - x^j), U^j, 1\}$.
6. Set $U^i = U^m, \lambda^i = \lambda^m$ for all $i \in E$.
7. Set $I = I \backslash E, B = B \cup E$. If $I = \emptyset$, stop. Otherwise, go to 2.

It is not at all obvious that Algorithm 3 does in fact compute numbers that satisfy the Afriat inequalities: however that fact will be verified in the proof of Afriat's theorem.

AFRIAT'S THEOREM.   *The following conditions are equivalent:*

(1) There exists a nonsatiated utility function that rationalizes the data.

(2) The data satisfies GARP: if $x^i R x^j$, then $p^j x^j \leqq p^j x^i$.

(3) There exist numbers $U^i, \lambda^i > 0$ such that $U^i \leqq U^j + \lambda^j p^j (x^i - x^j)$ for $i, j = 1, \ldots, n$.

(4) There exists a nonsatiated, continuous, concave, monotonic utility function that rationalizes the data.

Proof. (1) $\Rightarrow$ (2). Let $u(x)$ rationalize the data. If $p^i x^i \geqq p^i x^j$ then $u(x^i) \geqq u(x^j)$ by definition so that $x^i R^0 x^j$ implies $u(x^i) \geqq u(x^j)$. If $p^i x^i > p^i x^j$ so that $x^i P^0 x^j$, then I claim that $u(x^i) > u(x^j)$. If not, then $u(x^i) = u(x^j)$. But by local nonsatiation there is then an $\hat{x}$ such that $p^i x^i > p^i \hat{x}$ and $u(\hat{x}) > u(x^i)$. But then $u(x)$ could not rationalize the data point (p^i, x^i). Hence $x^i P^0 x^j$ implies $u(x^i) > u(x^j)$, and GARP follows.

(2) $\Rightarrow$ (3). In order to prove this we need to verify that Algorithm 3 works; i.e., that the numbers it calculates do indeed satisfy the Afriat inequalities.

At each pass through the algorithm a set of indices of "equivalent" elements, E, is removed from I and added to B, a set of indices of "better" elements. We will show that after step 6 is executed, the U's and the λ's at that stage satisfy the Afriat inequalities for all the U's and λ's calculated up to that. That is, we will verify the following three statements:

$$U^i \leqq U^j + \lambda^j p^j (x^i - x^j) \qquad \text{for all } j \text{ in } B \text{ and all } i \text{ in } E, \qquad (a)$$

$$U^j \leqq U^i + \lambda^i p^i (x^j - x^i) \qquad \text{for all } j \text{ in } B \text{ and all } i \text{ in } E, \qquad (b)$$

$$U^i \leqq U^j + \lambda^j p^j (x^i - x^j) \qquad \text{for all } i, j \text{ in } E. \qquad (c)$$

Proof of (a): By step 4 of the algorithm:

$$U^i = U^m \leqq U^j + \lambda^j p^j (x^i - x^j) \qquad \text{for all } j \text{ in } B \text{ and all } i \text{ in E.}$$

Proof of (b): First note that when the algorithm correctly executes statement 5, $p^i(x^j - x^i) > 0$, for all j in B. If not, $x^i R x^j$ for some j in B. But then i would have been moved into B before j was moved into B.

Hence, the division is well defined and

$$\lambda^i = \lambda^m \geqq \frac{U^j - U^i}{p^i (x^j - x^i)} \qquad \text{for all } j \text{ in } B \text{ and all } i \text{ in } E.$$

Cross multiplying:

$$\lambda^i p^i (x^j - x^i) \geqq U^j - U^i \qquad \text{for all } j \text{ in } B \text{ and all } i \text{ in } E$$

which proves (b).

Proof of (c): First note that i, j in E implies $p^j(x^i - x^j) > 0$. If not $x^j P^0 x^i$, giving a violation of GARP. Now for all i and j in E:

$$U^i = U^j \qquad \text{and} \qquad \lambda^j = \lambda^m > 0$$

so

$$U^i \leqq U^j + \lambda^j p^j (x^i - x^j).$$

(3)$\Rightarrow$(4). We define the function $U(x)$ by

$$U(x) = \min_i \left\{ U^i + \lambda^i p^i (x - x^i) \right\}.$$

It is clear from the definition that this piecewise linear function has the stated properties. Hence we only need to verify that it rationalizes the data.

First we note that $U(x^i) = U^i$ for all $i = 1, \ldots, n$. For suppose the minimum is attained at x^m; then

$$U(x^i) = U^m + \lambda^m p^m (x^m - x^i) \leqq U^i$$

since $\lambda^m p^m (x^i - x^i) = 0$. But if this inequality were ever strict we would violate one of the Afriat inequalities.

Now suppose we are given some x such that $p^j x^j \geqq p^j x$. We must show that $U(x^j) \geqq U(x)$. This follows directly from the following set of inequalities:

$$U(x) = \min_i \left\{ U^i + \lambda^i p^i (x - x^i) \right\}$$
$$\leqq U^j + \lambda^j p^j (x - x^j)$$
$$\leqq U^j = U(x^j)$$

since $\lambda^j p^j (x - x^j) \leqq 0$.

(4) $\Rightarrow$ (1). This is obvious.

It is worthwhile giving a somewhat more heuristic argument for Afriat's Theorem, which more directly exhibits the meaning of the Afriat inequalities. Suppose that we have a differentiable concave utility function that rationalizes some data $(p^i, x^i), i = 1, \ldots, n$. Then concavity implies

$$u(x^i) \leqq u(x^j) + Du(x^j)(x^i - x^j)$$

and utility maximization implies

$$Du(x^j) = \lambda^j p^j.$$

Putting these together we see that the Afriat conditions are a necessary condition for utility maximization in this differentiable framework. To motivate the sufficiency result we simply note that by concavity we have n *overestimates* of the utility at some point x since

$$u(x) \leqq u(x^i) + \lambda^i p^i (x - x^i) \qquad \text{for } i = 1, \ldots, n.$$

Hence the minimum of the right hand side over all observation i – the lower envelope – should give us a reasonable measure of the utility of x.

This interpretation of the U^i's as utility levels and the λ^i's as the marginal utilities of income was first suggested by Afriat (1967) and further elucidated by Diewert and Parkan (1978). Varian (1981), has used this sort of argument to derive finite necessary and sufficient conditions for a number of specializations of the utility maximization model.

Finally we give a proof of one last fact concerning Afriat's construction that was stated without proof at one point in the text. If x^i is not revealed preferred to x^j, then it is intuitively plausible that there is a nice utility function that rationalizes the data for which $u(x^j) \geqq u(x^i)$. This is verified in the next statement.

FACT 16.   *If not $x^i R x^j$, then there is a nonsatiated, continuous, concave, monotonic utility function that rationalizes the data for which $u(x^j) \gtreqless u(x^i)$.*

Proof. Simply ensure that $\max(I)$ returns the index j before the index i. Line 4 of Algorithm 3 then implies that $u(x^i) \gtreqless u(x^j)$.

7.10 Appendix II: computing the transitive closure

The following discussion concerning the computation of the transitive closure of a relation is taken from Aho and Ullman (1972), which in turn is based on Warshall (1962). Their results are very slightly generalized in a way that is useful in some other applications (Varian (1981)).

$$M = \begin{bmatrix} 1 & 1 & 1 & 0 \\ 0 & 1 & 1 & 0 \\ 0 & 0 & 1 & 1 \\ 0 & 0 & 0 & 1 \end{bmatrix}$$

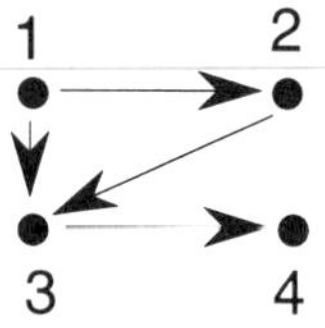

Figure 9. The M matrix and the graph it represents.

Let M be an n by n matrix representing a binary relation; i.e. $m_{ij} = 1$ if $x^i R^0 x^j$ and $m_{ij} = 0$ otherwise. We can also think of M as representing a directed graph as in Figure 9: there is an arrow from vertex i to vertex j if and only if $m_{ij} = 1$. It is this interpretation that gives rise – somewhat indirectly – to Warshall's algorithm.

Suppose now that we have an arbitrary directed graph and some associated cost function c_{ij} where $c_{ij} \gtreqless 0$ measures the cost of transporting one unit of a good directly from vertex i to vertex j. If vertex i and vertex j are not directly connected c_{ij} is by definition infinite. Now although the cost of moving i to j *directly* is given by c_{ij}, the *cheapest* cost of moving i to j may be much less. Warshall's algorithm is concerned with calculating the least cost of moving from any vertex to any other vertex. We denote the magnitude of this least cost by $\bar{c}_{ij}$.

I claim that if we can solve this "least cost problem" we can easily solve the "transitive closure" problem. We just create a cost matrix C where

$$c_{ij} = \begin{cases} 1 & \text{if } m_{ij} = 1, \\ \infty & \text{if } m_{ij} = 0. \end{cases}$$

Now we run C through Warshall's algorithm to compute the least cost matrix $(\bar{c}_{ij})$. Then if $\bar{c}_{ij} = l < \infty$ we know that there is some path of length l that connects vertex i with vertex j. Hence a method to solve the least cost problem gives us a method to solve the transitive closure problem.

ALGORITHM 4. *Minimum cost of paths in a graph.*

Input: c_{ij} = cost of moving from node i to node j; $c_{ij} \geq 0$.
Output: $\bar{c}_{ij}$ = minimum cost of moving from node i to node j.
(1) Set $k = 1$.
(2) For all i and j, if $c_{ij} \geq c_{jk} + c_{kj}$ set $c_{ij} = c_{ik} + c_{kj}$.
(3) If $k < n$, let $k = k + 1$ and go to 2. If $k = n$, set $\bar{c}_{ij} = c_{ij}$ for all i and j.

It is not at all obvious that Algorithm 4 does indeed compute the minimum cost of moving from i to j for all i and j. But the following argument shows that it works.

FACT 17. *Let $(i, l, \ldots, m, j)$ be a path from i to j. Then $\bar{c}_{ij} \leq c_{il} + \ldots + c_{mj}$.*

Proof. Consider the algorithm when it has completed step (2). We will show that c_{ij}, is the cost of the cheapest path from i to j that passes through no intermediate vertex with index greater than k. This is certainly true for $k = 1$, and we suppose it to be true for $k - 1$.
    Let $(i, l, \ldots, m, j)$ be a path from i to j that passes through no intermediate vertex with index greater than k. If it does not pass through vertex k we are done. If it does pass through k, we can suppose it only passes through once, since removing a cycle cannot increase the cost. By the induction hypothesis c_{ik} is the cheapest path from i to k with no intermediate vertex greater than $k - 1$ and similarly for c_{kj}. Since step (2) of the algorithm ensures $c_{ij} \leq c_{ik} + c_{kj}$, we are done. ∎

Note that step (2) of the algorithm will be executed n^3 times; thus we can compute the transitive closure of a relation in n^3 computer additions and comparisons. Of course, if we are using Warshall's algorithm only to compute the transitive closure of a relation we can improve a bit on that bound. Consider for example the following FORTRAN subroutine which computes the transitive closure of a relation represented by the matrix M.

ALGORITHM 5. *Computing the transitive closure.*

Input: $M(I, J) = 1$ if $p^i x^i \geq p^i x^j$, 0 otherwise. N = number of observations; nobs = maximum number of observations.

Output: $M(I, J) = I i f x^i R x^j$, 0 otherwise.

```
SUBROUTINE TCLSR (M, N)
DIMENSION M(nobs, nobs)
DO 30 K = 1, N
DO 20 I = 1, N
DO 10 J = 1, N
IF (M(I, K) .EQ. 0 .OR. M(K, J) .EQ. 0) GO TO 10
M(I,J)= 1
10 CONTINUE
20 CONTINUE
30 CONTINUE
RETURN
END
```

This clearly computes the transitive closure by a straightforward modification of the argument given in Fact 17.

References

Afriat, S. (1967) "The Construction of a Utility Function from Expenditure Data," *International Economic Review*, **8**, 67–77.

Afriat, S. (1972) "The Theory of International Comparison of Real Income and Prices," in *International Comparisons of Prices and Output*, D. J. Daly, ed. New York: National Bureau of Economic Research.

Afriat, S. (1973) "On a System of Inequalities on Demand Analysis: An Extension of the Classical Method," *International Economic Review*, **14**, 460–472.

Afriat, S. (1976) *The Combinatorial Theory of Demand*. London: Input-Output Publishing Company.

Afriat, S. (1977) *The Price Index*. London: Cambridge University Press.

Aho, A., and J. Ullman (1972) *The Theory of Parsing, Translation, and Compiling, Volume 1: Parsing*. Englewood Cliffs, New Jersey: Prentice-Hall, Inc..

Debreu, G. (1974) "Excess Demand Functions," *Journal of Mathematical Economics*, **1**, 15–22.

Diewert, E. (1973) "Afriat and Revealed Preference Theory," *Review of Economic Studies*, **40**, 419–426.

Diewert, E., and C. Parkan (1978) "Test for Consistency of Consumer Data and Nonparametric Index Numbers," University of British Columbia, W.P. 78-27.

Dobell, A. (1965) "A Comment on A. Y. C. Koo's 'An Empirical Test of Revealed Preference Theory'," *Economctrica*, **33**, 451–455.

Hanoch, G., and M. Rothschild (1972) "Testing the Assumptions of Production Theory: A Nonparametric Approach," *Journal of Political Economy*, **80**, 256–275.

Houthakker, H. (1950) "Revealed Preference and the Utility Function," *Economica*, **17**, 159–174.

Hurwicz, L., and H. Uzawa (1971) "On the Integrability of Demand Functions," in *Preference Utility and Demand*, ed.   J. S. Chipman, et al.. New York: Harcourt, Brace, Jovanovich.

Koo, A. (1963) "An Empirical Test of Revealed Preference Theory," *Econometrica*, **31**, 646–664.

Koo, A. (1965) "Reply," *Econometrica*, **32**, 456–458.

Koo, A. (1971) "Revealed Preference – A Structural Analysis," *Econometrica*, **39**, 89–98.

Landsburg, S. (1981) "Taste Change in the United Kingdom 1900-1955," *Journal of Political Economy*, **89**, 92–104.

Little, J. (1979) "Indirect Preferences," *Journal of Economic Theory*, **20**, 182–193.

McKenzie, L. (1956) "Demand Theory Without a Utility Index," *Review of Economic Studies*, **24**, 185–189.

Munroe, L. (1971) "Efficient Determination of the Transitive Closure of a Directed Graph," *Information Processing Letters*, **1**, 56–58.

Richter, M. (1966) "Revealed Preference Theory," *Econometrica*, **34**, 635–645.

Richter, M. (1979) "Duality and Rationality," *Journal of Economic Theory*, **20**, 131–181.

Sakai, Y. (1978) "Revealed Favorability, Indirect Utility, and Direct Utility," *Journal of Economic Theory*, **5**, 113–129.

Samuelson, P. (1948) "Consumption Theory in Terms of Revealed Preference," *Economica*, **15**, 243–253.

Samuelson, P. (1979) "Complementarity," *Journal of Economic Literature*, **7**, 1255–1289.

Sen, A. (1970) *Collective Choice and Social Welfare*, Holden-Day.

Sonnenschein, H. (1973) "Do Walras' Identity and Continuity Characterize the Class of Community Excess Demand Functions?," *Journal of Economic Theory*, **6**, 345-354.

Uebe, G. (1972) "A Note on Anthony Y. C. Koo, 'Revealed Preference – A Structural Analysis'," *Econometrica*, **40**, 771–772.

Varian, H. (1981) "Nonparametric Tests of Models of Investment Behavior," University of Michigan, CREST Working Paper.

Warshall, S. (1962) "A Theorem on Boolean Matrices," *Journal of the American Association of Computing Machinery*, **9**, 11-12.

Chapter 8

THE NONPARAMETRIC APPROACH
TO PRODUCTION ANALYSIS

This paper shows how to test firm demand and supply data for consistency with profit maximization and cost minimization models; test for special restrictions on technology such as constant returns to scale, homotheticity, and separability; recover estimates of the underlying technology; and forecast firm behavior in new situations without making any assumptions concerning the parametric form of underlying production technology.

The neoclassical theory of production postulates that firms maximize profits (and minimize costs) subject to certain technological constraints. In the empirical analysis of production data one is led to ask four sorts of questions concerning this model.

1. Consistency? When is some given data consistent with the profit maximization or cost minimization models?

2. Restriction of Form? When do the technological constraints have particular forms?

3. Recoverability? How can we recover the underlying technological constraints from observed behavior?

4. Extrapolation? Given observed behavior in some economic environments how can we forecast behavior in other environments?

This work was financed by the Guggenheim Memorial Foundation and the National Science Foundation while I was visiting at Nuffield College, Oxford University. I wish to thank the Foundations for their support and Nuffield College for its hospitality. I also wish to thank Angus Deaton and the referees of this journal for many helpful comments on earlier versions of this paper.

The conventional analysis of these questions proceeds by first postulating a parametric form for the production function (or some equivalent parametric representation of the technology) and then using standard statistical techniques to estimate the unknown parameters from the observed data. This procedure suffers from the defect that the maintained hypothesis of parametric form can never be directly tested: it must be taken on faith.

In this paper I describe an alternative *nonparametric* approach to production analysis based on the work of Afriat (1972), Hanoch and Rothschild (1972), and Diewert and Parkan (1979). (Analogous work in consumer demand analysis has been presented by Afriat (1967, 1973, 1976, 1977), Diewert (1973), Diewert and Parkan (1978), and Varian (1982a, 1982b).) In this nonparametric approach one can answer each of the four sorts of question described above without any maintained hypotheses of functional form.

The most direct precursors of this paper are the papers of Afriat (1972), Diewert and Parkan (1978), and Hanoch and Rothschild (1972). Indeed, the first few sections of this paper consist primarily of a review of their earlier work. The contribution of these sections lies in the explicit statements and the unified treatment of the results, rather than the novelty of the results per se. Nevertheless since later sections build on these results in fundamental ways, it seems appropriate for both expositional and pedagogic reasons to include these sections.[1]

Section 1 considers necessary and sufficient conditions for observed firm behavior to be consistent with the cost minimization model. Section 2 asks the same question for the profit maximization model. Sections 3 and 4 consider necessary and sufficient conditions for observed behavior to be consistent with constant-returns-to-scale and homothetic technologies, while Section 5 considers tests for a variety of specifications for separable technologies.

Sections 6 and 7 consider how one might recover underlying technological information in a variety of formats, while Sections 8 and 9 consider how one might forecast firm behavior in new economic situations. Section 10 provides a brief discussion of noncompetitive environments and Section 11 consists of a short summary.

8.1 Testing for consistency with cost minimization

Suppose we are given some data on firm behavior; in particular we suppose we observe *outputs* y^i associated with *factor demands* $\mathbf{x}^i$ and *factor prices* $\mathbf{w}^i$ for $i = 1, \ldots, n$. Here we suppose output to be a scalar and $\mathbf{w}^i$ and

---

[1] A closely related approach to production analysis involves the estimation of "frontier production functions." On this topic see the recent symposium by Aigner and Schmidt (1980).

$\mathbf{x}^i$ to be nonnegative k-vectors for $i = 1, \ldots, n$. We will refer to the list $(\mathbf{w}^i, \mathbf{x}^i, y^i)$, $i = 1, \ldots, n$, as the *observed behavior* or the *data* associated with the form in question.

We will find it convenient to describe the technologically feasible choices of the firm in several ways. The most general of these is the *input requirement set* $V(y)$ which consists of all input vectors $\mathbf{x}$ that can produce at least y units of output. Given some data $(\mathbf{w}^i, \mathbf{x}^i, y^i)$, $i = 1, \ldots, n$, we can ask whether there exists any family of input requirement sets $\{V(y)\}$ at all that make sense of this data.

More precisely, we will say a family of input requirement sets *c-rationalizes* the data if $\mathbf{x}^i$ solves the problem:

$$\min_x \mathbf{w}^i \mathbf{x}$$

$$\text{subject to } \mathbf{x} \text{ is in } V(y^i)$$

for each $i = 1, \ldots, n$. Equivalently, a family of input requirement sets c-rationalizes the data if

$$\mathbf{w}^i \mathbf{x}^i \leq \mathbf{w}^i \mathbf{x} \qquad \text{for all } \mathbf{x} \text{ in } V(y^i).$$

(The "c" in c-rationalizes stands for "cost." Later on we will introduce p-rationalizes where "p" stands for "profit." Where the meaning is clear from the context we will often drop the prefix and just write "rationalizes.")[2]

Since $V(y)$ contains all $\mathbf{x}$ that produce at least y units of output, the family of input requirement sets $\{V(y)\}$ must be "nested" in the following sense:

Nested.   *If $\mathbf{x}$ is in $V(y)$ and $y \geq y'$, then $\mathbf{x}$ is in $V(y')$.*

If we do not have an assumption like this we could trivially rationalize the data by $V(y^i) = \{\mathbf{x}^i\}$ for $i = 1, \ldots, n$ and $V(y) = \emptyset$ otherwise. We will say an input requirement set is *positive monotonic* if $\mathbf{x}$ in $V(y)$ and $\mathbf{x}' \geq \mathbf{x}$ implies $\mathbf{x}'$ is in $V(y)$. This is essentially the property of free disposal.

THEOREM 1.   *The following conditions are equivalent: (1) There exists a family of nested input requirement sets $\{V(y)\}$ that c-rationalizes the data. (2) If $y^j \geq y^i$ then $\mathbf{w}^i \mathbf{x}^j \geq \mathbf{w}^i \mathbf{x}^i$ for all i and j. (3) There exists a*

---

[2] In Sections 1 through 9 we will only consider models where firms take the prices of goods to be parametrically given, i.e., they behave "competitively." A firm that behaves as a monopolist in its output market might behave competitively in its factor markets; thus we desire tests for both (competitive) profit maximization and (competitive) cost minimization.

family of nontrivial, closed, convex, positive monotonic input requirement sets that c-rationalize the data.

Proof. (1) $\Longrightarrow$ (2) Suppose that $\{V(y)\}$ is a family of nested input requirement sets that rationalize the data. Then if $y^j \geq y^i$ nestedness implies $\mathbf{x}^j$ is in $V(y^i)$. Since $V(y^i)$ rationalizes the data, $\mathbf{w}^i\mathbf{x}^j \geq \mathbf{w}^i\mathbf{x}^i$.

(2) $\Longrightarrow$ (3) Define $V(y)$ to be the convex positive monotonic hull[3] of the $\mathbf{x}^i$ such that $y^i \geq y$. That is:

$$V(y) - \text{com}^{\,l}\,\{\mathbf{x}^j : y^j \geq y\}.$$

If there are no $y^i \geq y$ then let $V(y) = \emptyset$.

I claim that this family of input requirement sets rationalizes the data. We must show that for any $\mathbf{x}^i$, $\mathbf{w}^i\mathbf{x}^i \leq \mathbf{w}^i\mathbf{x}$ for all $\mathbf{x}$ in $V(y^i)$. Since $V(y^i)$ is a convex polytope we need only demonstrate this for the vertices of $V(y^i)$. But the vertices of $V(y^i)$ are some subset of $\{\mathbf{x}^j : y^j \geq y^i\}$. These $\mathbf{x}^j$'s satisfy the relevant inequality by condition (2) of the theorem.

Finally we note that by construction $V(y)$ is nested, closed, convex, and monotonic for each y.

(3) $\Longrightarrow$ (1) Since (3) is stronger than (1) it trivially implies (1). (This sort of statement will be omitted in subsequent proofs.) ∎

Theorem 1 is a straightforward generalization of a construction proposed by Hanoch and Rothschild (1972, pp. 259–260, 266–267). I believe that my statement emphasizes a bit more clearly the relationship between the necessity and sufficiency of condition (2): if the data were generated by cost minimization for *any* family of input requirement sets it must satisfy condition (2) and if any data satisfy condition (2) it can be rationalized by a "nice" family of input requirement sets. In particular it is clear from Theorem 1 that the maintained hypotheses that the "true" input requirement sets are closed, convex, and monotonic cannot be rejected by any data that satisfy condition (2). So if the data can be rationalized by any technology at all, it can be rationalized by a nice technology. Clearly any condition as powerful as (2) deserves a name, so I propose to call it WACM: the Weak Axiom of Cost Minimization.[4]

---

[3] Given any set of points in $\mathbf{R}^n$ $\{\mathbf{z}^i\}$ the *convex positive monotonic hull*, $\text{com}^+\{\mathbf{z}^i\}$, is defined to be the convex hull of $\{\mathbf{z}^i + \mathbf{e}^i\}$ for all $\mathbf{e}^i \geq 0$. The convex *negative monotonic hull*, $\text{com}^-\{\mathbf{z}^i\}$ is the convex hull of $\{\mathbf{z}^i + \mathbf{e}^i\}$ for $\mathbf{e}^i \leq 0$.

[4] Diewert and Parkan (1978) also establish versions of Theorem 1 as well as Theorems 3 and 6, below. all of which are generalizations of Hanoch and Rothschild (1972) and Afriat (1972) results. Diewert and Parkan also describe several very interesting nonparametric tests which can be performed when either prices or quantities are not observed. In this paper we limit ourselves to the case where both sets of data are observed. Typically one can generalize the tests described here to the case where part of the data is not observed by asking whether prices or quantities exist which satisfy the given inequalities.

Instead of considering a set theoretic construction like input requirement sets, we might consider a more traditional construct such as a *production function*. In this framework the definition of "rationalizes" becomes:

DEFINITION.   *A production function c-rationalizes the observed behavior* $(\mathbf{w}^i, \mathbf{x}^i, y^i)$ *if* $(f(\mathbf{x}^i) = y^i$ *and* $f(\mathbf{x}) \geq f(\mathbf{x}^i))$ *implies* $\mathbf{w}^i \mathbf{x} \geq \mathbf{w}^i \mathbf{x}^i$ *for* $i = 1, \ldots, n$. *That is,* $\mathbf{x}^i$ *minimizes costs over all bundles that can produce at least* y^i.

Just as in the case of the input requirement sets it is useful to impose a small regularity condition on the production function in order to eliminate some perverse case. The condition we will impose here is that $f(\mathbf{x})$ is to be a continuous function of $\mathbf{x}$. With this proviso the following theorem goes through.

THEOREM 2.   *The following conditions are equivalent: (1) There exists a continuous production function that rationalizes the data. (2) If* $y^j \leq y^i$ *then* $\mathbf{w}^j x^j \leq \mathbf{w}^j \mathbf{x}^i$ *and if* $y^j < y^i$ *then* $\mathbf{w}^j \mathbf{x}^j < \mathbf{w}^j \mathbf{x}^i$. *(3) There exist numbers* $u^i > 0$ *and* $\lambda^i > 0$ *with* $y^i > y^j$ *implying* $u^i > u^j$ *such that* $u^i \leq u^j + \lambda^j \mathbf{w}^j (\mathbf{x}^i - \mathbf{x}^j)$, *all i and j. (4) There exists a continuous, monotonic and quasiconcave production function that rationalizes the data.*

Proof. (1) $\Longrightarrow$ (2) If $y^j = f(\mathbf{x}^j) \geq f(\mathbf{x}^i) = y^i$ we clearly have $\mathbf{w}^i \mathbf{x}^j \geq \mathbf{w}^i \mathbf{x}^i$ by definition of "rationalizes." If $f(\mathbf{x}^j) > f(\mathbf{x}^i)$, then by continuity we can find a θ, $0 < \theta < 1$, so that $f(\theta \mathbf{x}^j) > f(\mathbf{x}^i)$. If the equality case held above so that $\mathbf{w}^i \mathbf{x}^j = \mathbf{w}^i \mathbf{x}^i$, we would now get $\mathbf{w}^i \theta \mathbf{x}^j < \mathbf{w}^i \mathbf{x}^i$ which would contradict the rationalization hypothesis.

(2) $\Longrightarrow$ (3) The proof of Afriat's theorem in Varian (1982a) can be used to show that the numbers u^i and λ^i exist. A careful inspection of the proof demonstrates that $y^j < y^i$ implies $u^j < u^i$.

(3) $\Longrightarrow$ (4) Construct a plot of u' vs. y^i and connect the dots; call the resulting function $g(u)$. Note that since $y^j < y^i$ implies $u^j < u^i$, the function $g(u)$ will be strictly increasing. Now define

$$u(x) = \min_i \{u^i + \lambda^i \mathbf{w}^i (x - x^i)\},$$

$$f(x) = g(u(x)).$$

This function is clearly continuous and monotonic. Since it is a monotonic transformation of a concave function it is quasiconcave. It remains to show that it rationalizes the data.

First we show $f(\mathbf{x}^i) = y^i$. We have

$$u(\mathbf{x}^i) = u^m + \lambda^m \mathbf{w}^m (\mathbf{x}^i - \mathbf{x}^m) \leq u^i$$

If the inequality were strict we would violate one of the inequalities in (3). Since $g(u^i) = y^i$ by construction the statement is proved.

Next we show that if $y^i = f(\mathbf{x}^i) \leq f(\mathbf{x})$ we have $\mathbf{w}^i\mathbf{x}^i \leq \mathbf{w}^i\mathbf{x}$. Equivalently we show that $\mathbf{w}^i\mathbf{x}^i > \mathbf{w}^i\mathbf{x}$ implies $f(\mathbf{x}^i) > f(\mathbf{x})$. Note that $\mathbf{w}^i\mathbf{x}^i > \mathbf{w}^i\mathbf{x}$ implies $u(\mathbf{x}) \leq u^j + \lambda^j\mathbf{w}^j(\mathbf{x} - \mathbf{x}^i) < u^i$. Hence $f(\mathbf{x}) = g(u(\mathbf{x})) < g(u^i) = f(\mathbf{x}^i)$.

(4) $\Longrightarrow$ (1) This is obvious. ∎

If we were willing to assume that the underlying production function were differentiable and concave then Theorem 2 would be immediate. For concavity implies

$$f(\mathbf{x}^j) \leq f(\mathbf{x}^i) + Df(\mathbf{x}^i)(\mathbf{x}^j - \mathbf{x}^i)$$

and cost minimization implies

$$Df(\mathbf{x}^i) = \lambda^i\mathbf{w}^i.$$

Putting these together gives us the inequality in (3) with $u^i = y^i$. Note that λ^i can be interpreted as the reciprocal of marginal cost at observation i.

It seems natural to refer to condition (2) of this Theorem as SACM—the Strong Axiom of Cost Minimization.

Hanoch and Rothschild also constructed a production function to rationalize observed data but their construction is quite different.

8.2 Testing for consistency with profit maximization

For this exercise we generalize our framework a bit and let the observed data consist of *price vectors* $\mathbf{p}^i \geq 0$ and net output vectors $\mathbf{y}^i$. That is $\mathbf{y}^i = (y_1^i, \ldots, y_k^i)$ is a vector where y_j^i is the (signed) net output of good j—hence positive components of $\mathbf{y}^i$ are net outputs and negative components are net inputs. This sign convention implies that profits at observation i are simply the inner product $\mathbf{p}^i\mathbf{y}^i$. The (hypothetical) set of feasible net output vectors is known as the *producion set*, typically denoted by $\mathbf{Y}$. We say $\mathbf{Y}$ is *negative monotonic* if $\mathbf{y}$ in $\mathbf{Y}$ and $\mathbf{y}' \leq \mathbf{y}$ implies $\mathbf{y}'$ is in $\mathbf{Y}$. This is essentially a free disposal hypothesis.

DEFINITION.   *A production set* $\mathbf{Y}$ *p-rationalizes the observed behavior* $(\mathbf{p}^i, \mathbf{y}^i)$ *if* $\mathbf{p}^i\mathbf{y}^i \geq \mathbf{p}^i\mathbf{y}$ *for all* $\mathbf{y}$ *in* $\mathbf{Y}$ *for* $i = 1, \ldots, n$.

Presumably a production set $\mathbf{Y}$ must contain at least the points $y^i, \ldots, y^n$ since they are, after all, observed.

THEOREM 3.   *The following conditions are equivalent: (1) There exists a production set that p-rationalizes the data. (2)* $\mathbf{p}^i \mathbf{y}^i \geq \mathbf{p}^i \mathbf{y}^j$ *for* $i, j = 1, \ldots, n$. *(3) There exists a closed, convex, negative monotonic production set that p-rationalizes the data.*

Proof. (1) $\Longrightarrow$ (2) Immediate.

(2) $\Longrightarrow$ (3) Let $Y = \text{com}^-\{\mathbf{y}^i\}$.[5] I claim that this rationalizes the data. For let $y = \sum_{j=1}^{n} = t^j(\mathbf{y}^j + \mathbf{e}^j)$, with $\mathbf{e}^j \leq 0$. By condition (2) $t^j \mathbf{p}^i(\mathbf{y}^j + \mathbf{e}^j) \leq t^j \mathbf{p}^i \mathbf{y}^i$ for all i and j. Summing over j we have:

$$\mathbf{p}^i \sum_{j=1}^{n} t^j(\mathbf{y}^j + \mathbf{e}^j) = \mathbf{p}^i \mathbf{y}^i \leq \mathbf{p}^i \mathbf{y}^i$$

as required. ∎

Theorem 3 is of course well known. Samuelson (1947) made considerable use of the fact that condition (2) is a necessary consequence of profit maximization and Hanoch and Rothschild (1972) point out the sufficiency of this condition. Again it lacks a name; I suggest we call it WAPM for Weak Axiom of Profit Maximization.

In the case where we have only a single output Theorem 3 takes an especially convenient form. For purposes of this theorem let us revert to our earlier notation where y represents the (scalar) measure of output and p represents its (scalar) price.

THEOREM 4.   *The following conditions are equivalent: (1) There exists a production function that p-rationalizes the data. (2)* $y^j \leq y^i + (\mathbf{w}^i/p^i)(\mathbf{x}^j - \mathbf{x}^i)$ *for* $i, j = 1, \ldots, n$. *(3) There exists a continuous, concave, monotonic production function that p-rationalizes the data.*

Proof. (1) $\Longrightarrow$ (2) In the single output case SAPM takes the form:

$$p^i y^i - \mathbf{w}^i \mathbf{x}^i \geq p^i y^j - \mathbf{w}^i \mathbf{x}^j \qquad (i, j = 1, \ldots, n)$$

This can be rearranged to give (2).

(2) $\Longrightarrow$ (3) Define the function

$$f(\mathbf{x}) = \min_i \{y^i + (\mathbf{w}^i/p^i)(\mathbf{x} - \mathbf{x}^i)\}.$$

This is clearly continuous, concave, and monotonic, so we only need show that it rationalizes the data. For any $\mathbf{x}$ have:

$$p^j f(\mathbf{x}) - \mathbf{w}^j \mathbf{x} \leq p^j y^j + p^j(\mathbf{w}^j/p^j)(\mathbf{x} - \mathbf{x}^j) - \mathbf{w}^j \mathbf{x}$$
$$= p^j y^j - \mathbf{w}^j \mathbf{x}^j$$

---

[5] Recall that $\text{com}^-\{\mathbf{z}^i\}$ = convex hull of $\{\mathbf{z}^i + \mathbf{e}^i : \mathbf{e}^i \leq \mathbf{0}\}$.

which shows the profits at $(y^j, \mathbf{x}^j)$ are at least as great as the profits at $f(\mathbf{x})$. ∎

Note the similarity of condition (2) in the above theorem with condition (3) in Theorem 2. There $1/\lambda^i$ had the interpretation of marginal cost at observation i. If the price p^i is observed then price equals marginal cost, and we get conditions (2) above.

8.3 Testing for constant returns to scale

We will say that constant returns to scale prevails when a production function is homogeneous of degree 1 ($f(t\mathbf{x}) = tf(\mathbf{x})$ for all $t > 0$) or when a production set is a cone ($\mathbf{y}$ in $\mathbf{Y}$ implies $t\mathbf{y}$ is in $\mathbf{Y}$ for all $t > 0$).
   In this section it is convenient to work with normalized prices defined by $\mathbf{v}^i = \mathbf{w}^i / \mathbf{w}^i \mathbf{x}^i$. Of course this imposes no extra restrictions; it only makes for simpler formulas.

THEOREM 5.   *The following conditions are equivalent: (1) There exists a homogeneous production function that c-rationalizes the data. (2) $\mathbf{v}^j \mathbf{x}^i \geq y^i / y^j$ for all i and j. (3) There exists a homogeneous, continuous, concave monotonic production function that c-rationalizes the data.*

Proof. Suppose $f(x)$ is a homogeneous function that rationalizes the data. Then

$$1 = f(\mathbf{x}^i / y^i)$$

so

$$y^j = y^j f(\mathbf{x}^i / y^i) = f(y^j \mathbf{x}^i / y^i).$$

Since $y^j \mathbf{x}^i / y^i$ is a feasible way to produce y^j it must cost at least as much as $\mathbf{x}^j$ costs, so

$$\mathbf{v}^j (y^j \mathbf{x}^i / y^i) \geq \mathbf{v}^j \mathbf{x}^j = 1$$

or

$$\mathbf{v}^j \mathbf{x}^i \geq y^i / y^j.$$

   (3) Let $f(\mathbf{x}) = \min_j \{ y^j \mathbf{v}^j \mathbf{x} \}$. This is clearly homogeneous, continuous, monotonic, and concave. We only need to show that it rationalizes the data. First we note that $f(\mathbf{x}^i) = y^i$, for

$$f(\mathbf{x}^i) = \min_j \{ y^j \mathbf{v}^j \mathbf{x}^i \} = y^m \mathbf{v}^m \mathbf{x}^i \leq y^i \mathbf{v}^i \mathbf{x}^i = y^i.$$

If the inequality were ever strict we would violate condition (2). Now suppose we have

$$y^i = f(\mathbf{x}^i) \leq f(\mathbf{x}) = \min_j \{ y^j \mathbf{v}^\times \} \leq y^i \mathbf{v}^i \mathbf{x}.$$

Hence $y^i \leq y^i \mathbf{v}^i \mathbf{x}$ or $1 \leq \mathbf{v}^i \mathbf{x}$. Recalling the normalization this becomes $\mathbf{v}^i \mathbf{x}^i \leq \mathbf{v}^i \mathbf{x}$ which shows that $f(\mathbf{x})$ rationalizes the data. ∎

THEOREM 6. *The following conditions are equivalent: (1) There exists a conical production set* $\mathbf{Y}$ *that p-rationalizes the data. (2)* $0 = \mathbf{p}^i \mathbf{y}^i \geq \mathbf{p}^i \mathbf{y}^j$ *for all* $i, j = 1, \ldots, n$. *(3) There exists a closed convex conical, negative monotonic production set that p-rationalizes the data.*

Proof. Left to the reader. ∎

Hanoch and Rothschild (1972) state Theorem 6. They do not state or prove Theorem 5, but it follows rather quickly from their section B, p. 273. Afriat (1972), Theorem 5.1 establishes basically the same result.

8.4 Testing for homotheticity

We say that a function $f(\mathbf{x})$ is homothetic if it is a monotonic transform of a homogeneous function. That is $f(\mathbf{x}) = g(h(\mathbf{x}))$ where $h(\mathbf{x})$ is homogeneous of degree 1 and $g(h)$ is a monotonic function. The concept of homotheticity only makes sense for a single output production function, at least as we define the concept here. (Generalizations that allow for multiple outputs are known; see Hall (1978).)

THEOREM 7. *The following conditions are equivalent: (1) There exists a homothetic production function that c-rationalizes the data. (2) There exist numbers* a^i *which are increasing in* y^i *in the sense that* $y^i > y^j$ *implies* $a^i > a^j$ *such that* $\mathbf{v}^j \mathbf{x}^i \geq a^i / a^j$. *(3) There exists a continuous, quasiconcave monotonic homothetic production function* $g(h(\mathbf{x}))$ *that c-rationalizes the data with* $h(\mathbf{x})$ *being a concave function.*

Proof. (1) $\Longrightarrow$ (2) Let $g(h(\mathbf{x}))$ be a homothetic production function that rationalizes the data. Then $g^{-1}(y)$ is well defined since g is monotonic, so we can define $a^i = g^{-1}(y^i)$. Clearly the data $(\mathbf{w}^i, \mathbf{x}^i, a^i)$, $i = 1, \ldots, n$, should be consistent with constant returns to scale; applying Theorem 5 gives us the result.
    (2) $\Longrightarrow$ (3) As in Theorem 5, define

$$a(\mathbf{x}) = \min_j \{a^j \mathbf{v}^j \mathbf{x}\}.$$

As before $a(\mathbf{x})$ is a homogeneous concave production function that rationalizes the data. Since $a^i = a(\mathbf{x}^i)$ and a^i is increasing in y^i, we can construct a monotonic transform that maps $a(\mathbf{x})$ into output. ∎

Hanoch and Rothschild state condition (2) (section VI.B) and note that it can be tested by a linear program with n unknowns and n^2 constraints. They observe that this may in some cases be computationally infeasible. However if the data were generated by profit maximization it is not necessary to solve a linear program at all, as our next theorem shows.* (Note: in this theorem we assume that the output price p^i has been normalized by $\mathbf{w}^i\mathbf{x}^i$ as well as the input prices.)

THEOREM 8.   *The following conditions are necessary for the existence of a homothetic production function that p-rationalizes the data. (1) The data satisfy WAPM and in addition there exist numbers $\phi^i > 0$, $i = 1, \ldots, n$, such that $\phi^i \leq \phi^j \mathbf{v}^j \mathbf{x}^i$ $(i, j = 1, \ldots, n)$. (2) The data satisfy WAPM and in addition for all strings $(i, j, \ldots, l)$ we have*

$$(\mathbf{v}^i\mathbf{x}^j)(\mathbf{v}^j\mathbf{x}^k)\cdots(\mathbf{v}^l\mathbf{x}^i) \geq 1.$$

Proof. Let $g(h(\mathbf{x}))$ be the homothetic production function that rationalizes the data with $h(\mathbf{x})$ homogeneous. Then $(\mathbf{w}^i, \mathbf{x}^i, h(\mathbf{x}^i))$ must satisfy the homogeneity conditions given in Theorem 5, condition (2). Setting $\phi^i = h(\mathbf{x}^i)$ gives the result.

(1) $\implies$ (2) This can be established by appealing to Afriat (1981) or Varian (1982a), Theorem 2. ∎

The condition (2)—called HAPM for Homothetic Axiom of Profit Maximization—is quite simple to test in practice. See, for example, Varian (1982b) or Afriat (1981).

8.5 Testing for separability

Let us now partition the inputs to a production function into two subvectors $(\mathbf{x}, \mathbf{z})$ and partition the factor price vectors $(\mathbf{w}, \mathbf{v})$ in the same manner. We say that a production function $f(\mathbf{x}, \mathbf{z})$ is weakly separable in the $\mathbf{z}$ factors if there exists a "subproduction function," $h(\mathbf{z})$, and an "aggregator function," $g(\mathbf{x}, h)$, such that

$$f(\mathbf{x}, \mathbf{z}) \equiv g(\mathbf{x}, h(\mathbf{z})).$$

We require $g(\mathbf{x}, h)$ to be strictly increasing in h and $h(\mathbf{z})$ to be continuous in z to avoid some perverse cases. For an encyclopedic discussion of separability, see Blackorby, Primont, and Russell (1979).

---

* In the published version of this work, it was erroneously claimed that the conditions stated in Theorems 8 and 9 were necessary and sufficient. This error was noted and corrected in Houtman, M., *Nonparametric Consumer and Producer Analysis*, Dissertation 95-32, Thesis Rijksuniversiteit Limburg Maastricht, 1995.

In order to state the next theorem we need to introduce some terminology from the revealed preference approach to consumer theory.

Let $(\mathbf{v}^i, \mathbf{z}^i)$, $i = 1, \ldots, n$, be some observed choices. Then we say: (i) $\mathbf{z}^i$ is *directly revealed preferred* to $\mathbf{z}^j (\mathbf{z}^i R^0 \mathbf{z}^j)$ if $\mathbf{v}^i \mathbf{z}^i \geq \mathbf{v}^i \mathbf{z}^j$; (ii) $\mathbf{z}^i$ is *revealed preferred* to $\mathbf{z}^j (\mathbf{z}^i R \mathbf{z}^j)$ if there is some sequence of observations such that $\mathbf{z}^i R^0 \mathbf{z}^k, \mathbf{z}^k R^0 \mathbf{z}^m, \ldots, \mathbf{z}^n R^0 \mathbf{z}^j$; (iii) the data satisfy the *Generalized Axiom of Revealed Preference* (GARP) if $\mathbf{z}^i R \mathbf{z}^j$ implies $\mathbf{v}^j \mathbf{z}^j \leq \mathbf{v}^j \mathbf{z}^i$.

For further discussion of these concepts, including discussion of how one tests GARP in practice, see Varian (1982a, 1982b).

THEOREM 9. *The following conditions are necessary for the existence of a separable production function that p-rationalizes the data. (1) The data satisfy WAPM and the subdata* $(\mathbf{v}^i, \mathbf{z}^i)$ *satisfy GARP. (2) The data satisfy WAPM and there exist numbers* $\phi^i, \lambda^i > 0$, $i = 1, \ldots, n$, *such that* $\phi^i \leq \phi^j + \lambda^j \mathbf{v}^j (\mathbf{z}^i - \mathbf{z}^j)$ *for* $i, j = 1, \ldots, n$.

Proof. We need to show that $\mathbf{v}^i \mathbf{z}^i > \mathbf{v}^i \mathbf{z}^j$ implies $h(\mathbf{z}^i) > h(\mathbf{z}^j)$. Suppose not so that $h(\mathbf{z}^j) \leq h(\mathbf{z}^i)$ and $\mathbf{v}^i \mathbf{z}^i > \mathbf{v}^i \mathbf{z}^j$. Then $f(\mathbf{x}^i, \mathbf{z}^j) = g(\mathbf{x}^i, h(\mathbf{z}^j)) \geq g(\mathbf{x}^i, h(\mathbf{z}^i)) = f(\mathbf{x}^i, \mathbf{z}^i)$ so total output is at least as big as $(\mathbf{x}^i, \mathbf{z}^j)$ than at $(\mathbf{x}^i, \mathbf{z}^i)$ and total costs are lower, contradicting profit maximization. $(1) \Longrightarrow (2)$ This follows from Afriat's theorem (Varian (1982a).) ∎

Note that condition (2) can be checked quite simply by using Warshall's algorithm as described in Varian (1982a, 1982b).

In the literature one often finds references to the concept of "Hicksian separability" (Hicks (1956), Diewert (1978)). This concept refers to the fact that when the sub-price vector $\mathbf{v}^i$ moves proportionally to some fixed base price vector $(\mathbf{v}^i = t^i \mathbf{v}^0$ for some scalar $t^i > 0$ for $i = 1, \ldots, n)$ we can find a "composite commodity"; that is, we can aggregate all of the components of the $\mathbf{z}$ bundle into one "composite good." The standard treatment of "functional separability" (the concept defined above) does not seem to be directly related to the Hicksian case. However in our framework the Hicksian case is a simple corollary to the above Theorem.

THEOREM 10. *Suppose that the subfactor prices* $\mathbf{v}^i$ *are all proportional to some fixed price vector* $\mathbf{v}^0$ *so that* $\mathbf{v}^i = t^i \mathbf{v}^0$ *for some scalars* t^i, $i = 1, \ldots, n$. *Suppose further that the data can be p-rationalized by some production function. Then the data can be rationalized by a separable production function* $g(\mathbf{x}, h(\mathbf{z}))$ *where* $h(\mathbf{z}) = \mathbf{v}^0 \mathbf{z}$.

Proof. We show that condition (3) of Theorem 9 is satisfied in this case. Simply choose $\phi^i = \mathbf{v}^0 \mathbf{z}^i$ and $\lambda^i = 1/t^i$. For this choice

$$\phi^i = \mathbf{v}^0 \mathbf{z}^i = \mathbf{v}^0 \mathbf{z}^j + \frac{1}{t^j} t^j \mathbf{v}^0 (\mathbf{z}^i - \mathbf{z}^j) = \phi^j + \lambda^j \mathbf{v}^j (\mathbf{z}^i - \mathbf{z}^j)$$

so Theorem 9 applies. ∎

One might also consider the concept of *additive separability*. In this case we require that the production function can be decomposed *additively* so that

$$f(\mathbf{x}, \mathbf{z}) = g(\mathbf{x}) + h(\mathbf{z}).$$

Theorem 11 covers this situation.

THEOREM 11.   *The following statements are equivalent: (1) The data can be p-rationalized by $g(\mathbf{x}) + h(\mathbf{z})$. (2) There exist numbers (g^i, h^i), $i = 1, \ldots, n$, such that sets of data $(\mathbf{w}^i, \mathbf{x}^i, g^i)$, $(\mathbf{v}^i, \mathbf{z}^i, h^i)$, $i = 1, \ldots, n$, each satisfy WAPM and $y^i = g^i + h^i$. (3) There exist numbers (g^i, h^i), $i = 1, \ldots, n$, such that*

$$g^i \leq g^j + (\mathbf{w}^j/p^j)(\mathbf{x}^i - \mathbf{x}^j),$$
$$h^i \leq h^j + (\mathbf{v}^j/p^j)(\mathbf{z}^i - \mathbf{z}^j),$$
$$y^i = g^i + h^i,$$

for $i = 1, \ldots, n$. (4) The data can be p-rationalized by the sum of two continuous, monotonic concave subproduction functions.

Proof. (1) $\Longrightarrow$ (2) It is clear that if $p(g(\mathbf{x}) + h(\mathbf{z})) - \mathbf{wx} - \mathbf{vz}$ is maximized, then $pg(\mathbf{x}) - \mathbf{wz}$ and $ph(\mathbf{z}) - \mathbf{vz}$ must be maximized. But then the data $(\mathbf{w}^i, \mathbf{x}^i, g^i)$ and $(\mathbf{v}^i, \mathbf{z}^i, h^i)$ must satisfy WAPM.
   (2) $\Longrightarrow$ (3) Apply Theorems 3 and 4.
   (3) $\Longrightarrow$ (4) Define

$$g(\mathbf{x}) = \min_i \{g^i + (\mathbf{w}^i/p^i)(x - \mathbf{x}^i)\},$$
$$h(\mathbf{z}) = \min_i \{h^i + (\mathbf{v}^i/p^i)(z - \mathbf{z}^i)\}.$$

Then

$$p^i(g(\mathbf{x}) + h(\mathbf{z})) - \mathbf{w}^i\mathbf{x} - \mathbf{v}^i\mathbf{z}$$
$$\leq (p^i g^i + \mathbf{w}^i\mathbf{x} - \mathbf{w}^i\mathbf{x}^i) + (p^i h^i + \mathbf{v}^i\mathbf{z} - \mathbf{v}^i\mathbf{z}^i) - \mathbf{w}^i\mathbf{x} - \mathbf{v}^i\mathbf{z}$$
$$= p^i(g^i + h^i) - \mathbf{w}^i\mathbf{x}^i - \mathbf{v}^i\mathbf{z}^i$$
$$= py^i - \mathbf{w}^i\mathbf{x}^i - \mathbf{v}^i\mathbf{z}^i \qquad \blacksquare$$

8.6 Recovering technological information from cost minimizing behavior

Suppose that we have some data on observed behavior $(\mathbf{w}^i, \mathbf{x}^i, y^i)$, $i = 1, \ldots, n$, that satisfy WACM and are therefore consistent with the cost minimization model. We have shown in Section 1 how one can construct a *possible* family of input requirement sets that rationalize this behavior. Of course this choice is not unique; typically there will be many input requirement sets that will be consistent with a finite number of observations on economic behavior. But can we "bound" the technological possibilities in any way?

It turns out that we *can* bound the possibilities in a satisfactory way. More precisely, given observed behavior we can construct two families of input requirement sets $VI(y)$ and $VO(y)$ that provide the tightest inner and outer bounds on the underlying constraints in the following sense: *any* $V(y)$ *consistent with the observed behavior (and certain other regularity conditions) must satisfy* $VI(y) \subset V(y) \subset VO(y)$.

Actually we have already encountered the construction of the inner bound to $V(y)$; it is simply the construction given in Section 1; that is:

$$VI(y) = \begin{cases} \text{com}^+\{\mathbf{x}^i \colon y^i \geq y\} & \text{if such a } y^i \text{ exists,} \\ \emptyset & \text{otherwise.} \end{cases}$$

We have already noted in Theorem 1 that $VI(y)$ does rationalize the data. As Hanoch and Rothschild (1972) observe, any $V(y)$ that rationalizes the data must contain $VI(y)$. In the following results $\mathbf{y}_m$ is the largest observed output.

THEOREM 12.   *The following statements are true: (1)* $\{VI(y)\}$ *c-rationalizes the data. (2) Let* $V(y)$ *be a family of closed convex monotonic input requirement sets that rationalize the data. Then* $V(y) \supset VI(y)$ *for all* $y \leq y^m$. *(3) Let* $S(y)$ *be a closed convex positive monotonic input requirement set which is strictly contained in* $VI(y)$. *Then* $S(y)$ *cannot rationalize the data.*

Proof. (1) This was proved in Theorem 1.

(2) Since the $V(y)$ are nested $y^i \geq y$ implies $\mathbf{x}^i$ is in $V(y)$. Since by hypothesis $V(y)$ is convex and monotonic, $V(y) \supset \text{com}^+\{\mathbf{x}^i \colon y^i \geq y\} = VI(y)$.

(3) In order to be a legitimate input requirement set $S(y)$ must contain $\{\mathbf{x}^i \colon y^i \geq y\}$. But $VI(y)$ is the smallest closed convex positively monotonic set that contains these points. ∎

The outer bound is also rather straightforward to construct. We define

$$VO(y) = \{x \colon \mathbf{w}^i \mathbf{x} \geq \mathbf{w}^i \mathbf{x}^i \text{ for all } y^i \leq y\}.$$

Diewert and Parkan (1978) observe that this construction gives an outer bound to the true input requirement set; this observation is formalized in the next theorem.

THEOREM 13.   *The following statements are true: (1)* $\{VO(y)\}$ *c-rationalizes the data. (2) If* $\{V(y)\}$ *is a family of input requirement sets that rationalize the data, then* $VO(y) \supset V(y)$ *for* $y \leq y^m$. *(3) If* $S(y)$ *is an input requirement set that strictly contains* $VO(y)$, *then* $S(y)$ *cannot c-rationalize the data.*

Proof. (1) First we note that $\mathbf{x}^j$ is in $VO(y^j)$. If not there is some $y^i \leq y^j$ such that $\mathbf{w}^i \mathbf{x}^j < \mathbf{w}^i \mathbf{x}^i$. But this contradicts WACM.

Secondly, let $\mathbf{x}$ be any element of $VO(y^i)$. Then by construction $\mathbf{w}^i \mathbf{x} \geq \mathbf{w}^i \mathbf{x}^i$ for all $y^i \leq y^j$ so in particular $\mathbf{w}^j \mathbf{x} \geq \mathbf{w}^j \mathbf{x}^j$. Hence $VO(y^i)$ rationalizes the observed behavior.

(2) Let $\{V(y)\}$ be any family of input requirement sets that rationalize the observed behavior. Let $\mathbf{x}$ be an element of $V(y^j)$. Suppose that $\mathbf{x}$ is not in $VO(y^j)$; this means that there is some $y^i \leq y^j$ such that $\mathbf{w}^i \mathbf{x} < \mathbf{w}^i \mathbf{x}^i$. Since $y^i \leq y^j$, and $\mathbf{x}$ is in $V(y^j)$, nestedness implies $\mathbf{x}$ is in $V(y^i)$. But the hypothesis of c-rationalizes then implies $\mathbf{w}^i \mathbf{x} \geq \mathbf{w}^i \mathbf{x}^i$. This contradiction establishes the result.

(3) Let $\mathbf{x}$ be in $S(y)$ but not in $VO(y)$. Then by construction $\mathbf{w}^i \mathbf{x} < \mathbf{w}^i \mathbf{x}^i$ for some $y^i \geq y$. Then $S(y)$ cannot c-rationalize the data. ∎

Theorems 12 and 13 show that $VI(y)$ and $VO(y)$ are the tightest inner and outer bounds on the true input requirement sets. In this sense they completely recover all of the information available in the observed behavior.

An illustration of $VI(y)$ and $VO(y)$ is given in Figure 1.

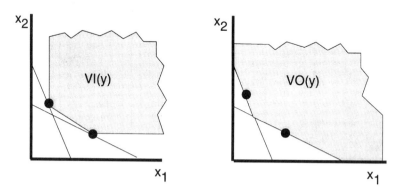

Figures 1. $VI(y)$ and $VO(y)$.

We suppose that the two factor demands $\mathbf{x}^1$ and $\mathbf{x}^2$ are observed at the indicated prices and that they produce the same level of output, y. Then $VI(y)$ will be the monotonic convex hull, as illustrated, and $VO(y)$ will be all combinations of factors that cost at least as much as $\mathbf{x}^1$ and $\mathbf{x}^2$.

To see how $VI(y)$ and $VO(y)$ can be calculated in general, let us suppose that we are given some previously unobserved factor bundle $\mathbf{x}$. How can we tell whether it is sufficient to produce some level of output y?

First we apply Theorem 12 to see if $\mathbf{x}$ can be expressed as a convex combination of $\{\mathbf{x}^i + \mathbf{e} : y^i \geq y\}$ where $\mathbf{e} \geq \mathbf{0}$. The easiest way to do this is to see if we can find a hyperplane that separates $\mathbf{x}$ from $VI(y)$. This is equivalent to the following question: *does there exist* $\mathbf{w} \geq 0$, $\mathbf{w} \neq 0$ *such that* $\mathbf{w}\mathbf{x} \leq \mathbf{w}\mathbf{x}^i$ *for all* $\mathbf{x}^i$ *for which* $y^i \geq y$? The most straightforward way to answer this question is to set up the linear program:

$$S = \max \mathbf{w}\mathbf{x}$$
$$\text{subject to} \quad \mathbf{w}(\mathbf{x} - \mathbf{x}^i) \quad \leq \quad 0, \quad y^i \geq y,$$
$$\mathbf{w}\mathbf{x} \quad \leq \quad 100,$$
$$\mathbf{w} \quad \geq \quad 0.$$

If the maximized value $S = 100$ then there is a nontrivial $\mathbf{w}$ that satisfies the inequalities and therefore $\mathbf{x}$ is *not* in the interior of $VI(y)$.[6] If $S = 0$ then $\mathbf{x}$ cannot be separated from the $\mathbf{x}^i$'s so $\mathbf{x}$ is in $VI(y)$.

If $\mathbf{x}$ is in $VI(y)$ we are done—this means $\mathbf{x}$ is feasible to produce y for any convex monotonic technology consistent with the observed behavior. If $\mathbf{x}$ is not in $VI(y)$ we proceed to the next stage and see if $\mathbf{x}$ is in $VO(y)$. This is merely a matter of checking whether $\mathbf{w}^i\mathbf{x} < \mathbf{w}^i\mathbf{x}^i$ for some $y^i \leq y$ If we do find such a situation we know that $\mathbf{x}$ is not even capable of producing y^i, much less the larger amount y. Of course checking the above conditions is quite straightforward.

We can also use $VI(y)$ and $VO(y)$ to construct bounds on the true production function. We can define the *overproduction function* $f^+(\mathbf{x})$ and the *underproduction function* $f^-(\mathbf{x})$ by:

$$f^+(\mathbf{x}) = \max\{y : \mathbf{x} \in VI(y)\},$$
$$f^-(\mathbf{x}) = \max\{y : \mathbf{x} \in VO(y)\}.$$

Since $VI(y) \subset V(y) \subset VO(y)$ we have $f^+(\mathbf{x}) \geq f(\mathbf{x}) \geq f^-(\mathbf{x})$.

In other applications such as benefit cost calculations we may wish to estimate the costs involved in providing some new level of output. By definition the "true" cost function is related to the "true" technology by

$$c(\mathbf{w}, y) = \min \mathbf{w}\mathbf{x}$$
$$\text{subject to} \quad \mathbf{x} \text{ is in } V(y).$$

We can bound this true cost function by the *overcost* and the *undercost* functions:

$$c^+(\mathbf{w}, y) = \min \mathbf{w}\mathbf{x}$$
$$\text{subject to } \mathbf{x} \text{ is in } VI(y);$$

$$c^-(\mathbf{w}, y) = \min \mathbf{w}\mathbf{x}$$
$$\text{subject to } \mathbf{x} \text{ is in } VO(y).$$

---

[6] The case where $\mathbf{x}$ is on the boundary of $I(y)$ must be handled separately.

The actual calculation of the overcost and the undercost functions is fairly straightforward. $VI(y)$ is a convex polytope whose vertices are defined by $\{\mathbf{x}^i \colon y^i \geq y\}$. Hence the minimum of the linear function $\mathbf{w} \cdot \mathbf{x}$ is achieved at a vertex so we can write:

$$c^+(\mathbf{w}, y) = \min \mathbf{w}\mathbf{x}^i$$
$$\text{subject to} \qquad y^i \geq y.$$

This is of course trivial to compute.

The undercost function is given by the following linear program:

$$c^-(\mathbf{w}, y) = \min \mathbf{w}\mathbf{x}$$
$$\text{subject to} \quad \mathbf{w}^i\mathbf{x} \; \geq \; \mathbf{w}^i x^i \text{ for } y^i \leq y$$
$$\mathbf{x} \; \geq \; 0$$

This is quite simple to solve in practice.

8.7 Recovering technological information from profit maximizing behavior

Let us now revert to the notation where $\mathbf{y}$ measures net output vectors and $\mathbf{p}$ measures the price vector. We are given data $(\mathbf{p}^i, \mathbf{y}^i)$, $i = 1, \ldots, n$, and want to recover estimates of the true production set. We can apply the same logic as in the last section to define

$$YI = \text{com}^-\{\mathbf{y}^i\},$$
$$YO = \{\mathbf{y} \colon \mathbf{p}^i \mathbf{y} \leq \mathbf{p}^i \mathbf{y}^i \text{ for } i = 1, \ldots, n\}^.$$

THEOREM 14.   *The following statements are true: (1) YI p-rationalizes the data. (2) If Y is a convex negative monotonic production set that p-rationalizes the data, then $Y \supset YI$. (3) If Z is a convex negative monotonic production set strictly contained in YI, then Z cannot p-rationalize the data.*

Proof. Statement (1) has already been proved in part (3) of Theorem 3. Statements (2) and (3) are immediate from the definition. ∎

THEOREM 15.   *The following statements are true: (1) YO p-rationalizes the data. (2) If Y is a production set that p-rationalizes the data, then $YO \supset Y$. (3) If Z strictly contains YO, then Z cannot p-rationalize the data.*

Proof. (1) Let $\mathbf{y}$ be in YO. Then by construction $\mathbf{p}^i \mathbf{y} \leq \mathbf{p}^i \mathbf{y}^i$, $i = 1, \ldots, n$, so YO rationalizes the data.

(2) If Y rationalizes the data then for any $\mathbf{y}$ in Y $\mathbf{p}^i\mathbf{y} \leq \mathbf{p}^i\mathbf{y}^i$, $i = 1, \ldots, n$. Hence $\mathbf{y}$ is in YO.

(3) Obvious. ∎

Just as in Section 6 we can define the overprofit and underprofit functions by:

$$\pi^+(\mathbf{p}) = \max \mathbf{py}$$

$$\text{subject to } \mathbf{y} \text{ in } YO;$$

$$\pi^-(\mathbf{p}) = \max \mathbf{py}$$

$$\text{subject to } \mathbf{y} \text{ in } YI.$$

It is straightforward to show that these bound the true profit function and that they can be easily computed. As before $\pi^-(\mathbf{p})$ is just the maximum of $\mathbf{py}^i$ over the observed $\mathbf{y}^i$'s and $\pi^+(\mathbf{p})$ can be found by solving a small linear program.

Diewert and Parkan (1978) have also described a construction similar to that of YO and YI.

8.8 Forecasting firm behavior from cost data

Suppose as usual we observe cost data $(\mathbf{w}^i, \mathbf{x}^i, y^i)$, $i = 1, \ldots, n$. Suppose now that some new factor price vector $\mathbf{w}^0$ is proposed. How will the firm behave? That is, what factor demands will it choose to produce at any level of output y^0?

Of course we cannot hope to get an *exact* estimate of this factor demand. But we would like to be able to describe a range of choices, in fact, the widest range of choices consistent with the previously observed behavior.

The crucial observation is to note that all that is necessary for the new demanded bundle $\mathbf{x}^0$ is that the data $(\mathbf{w}^i, \mathbf{x}^i, y^i)$, $i = 0, \ldots, n$, must satisfy WACM. That is, if we add $\mathbf{w}^0$ and y^0 to the original data, then the set of possible demands $\mathbf{x}^0$ are just those bundles that make the data consistent with WACM. For if this expanded data set is consistent with WACM then Theorem 1 tells us that a nice technology exists that rationalizes the data; and if the expanded data set is not consistent with WACM then no technology can rationalize the data.

To make this explicit we just define the set of bundles $\mathbf{x}^0$ that *support* $(\mathbf{w}^0, y^0)$ by:

$$S(\mathbf{w}^0, y^0) = \{\mathbf{x}^0 \colon (\mathbf{w}^i, \mathbf{x}^i, y^i), \quad i = 0, \ldots, n, \text{ satisfy WACM}\}.$$

Or even more explicitly we let $S(\mathbf{w}^0, y^0)$ be the set of solutions to the following linear equations:

$$\mathbf{w}^0\mathbf{x}^0 \leq \mathbf{w}^0\mathbf{x}^i \qquad \text{for all } y^i \geq y^0,$$

$$\mathbf{w}^i\mathbf{x}^i \leq \mathbf{w}^i\mathbf{x}^0 \qquad \text{for all } y^0 \geq y^i.$$

THEOREM 16. *If x^0 is in $S(w^0, y^0)$ then there is a technology that c-rationalizes (w^i, x^i, y^i), $i = 0, \ldots, n$, and for which x^0 is a cost minimizing choice at w^0. If x^0 is not in $S(w^0, y^0)$, then no such technology exists.*

Proof. Left to the reader. ∎

8.9 Forecasting firm behavior from profit data

Suppose now that we observe net output choices (p^i, y^i), $i = 1, \ldots, n$. We can apply the same trick to forecast net supply at some new p^0. Define:

$$S(p^0) = \{y^0 : (p^i, y^i), \quad i = 0, \ldots, n, \text{ satisfies WAPM}\}.$$

Or, explicitly, $S(p^0)$ is the set of solutions to the following linear equations:

$$p^0 y^0 \geq p^0 y^i$$
$$p^i y^i \geq p^i y^0.$$

THEOREM 17. *If y^0 is in $S(p^0)$ then there exists a technology that p-rationalizes (p^i, y^i), $i = 0, \ldots, n$, and for which y^0 is a profit maximizing choice at w^0. If y^0 is not in $S(p^0)$ then no such technology exists.*

Proof. Left to the reader. ∎

8.10 Imperfect competition

Suppose that we observe some data (p^i, w^i, x^i, y^i), $i = 1, \ldots, w$, that we suspect might be generated by some sort of monopolistic behavior. How can we test this hypothesis?

The only new feature that is added is the concept of a *subjective demand function*. Presumably the firm is maximizing profits given its understanding of the relationship between its output choice and the market price of its product.

Let us write p_e^{ij} for the price that the firm would expect to prevail in observation i if it produced output y^j. Then the hypothesis of profit maximizing behavior implies that:

$$p^i y^i - w^i x^i \geq p_e^{ij} y^j - w^i x^j \qquad (i, j = 1, \ldots, w).$$

I propose that we call this condition the Monopolistic Axiom of Profit Maximization (MAPM). The question of whether we can rationalize the observed behavior by a model of monopolistic profit maximization then reduces to the question of whether we can find prices (p_e^{ij}) that satisfy the above inequalities.

We can incorporate further restrictions on these expected prices if we wish. For example we might impose the condition:

$$(p^i - p_e^{ij})(y^i - y^j) \leq 0$$

which requires that the subjective demand function be downward sloping.

Another interesting hypothesis is that the subjective demand function coincides with the observed demand relationship so that $p_e^{ij} = p^j$.

A third hypothesis is that the subjective demand function is linear in output so that:

$$p_e^{ij} = p^i + \alpha(y^j - y^i)$$

If there are additional exogenous factors $\mathbf{Z}$ that shift the subjective demand function we can write

$$p_e^{ij} = \mathbf{p}^i + \alpha(y^j - y^i) + \beta\mathbf{Z}$$

In each of the above cases we can append these demand specifications to MAPM and ask whether there exists any configuration of the unknown parameters that can rationalize the observed behavior.

8.11 Summary

We have presented finite computationally feasible techniques to answer the four sorts of questions described in the introduction. Building on the work of Hanoch and Rothschild (1972), Afriat (1972), Diewert and Parkan (1978), and Varian (1982a, 1982b), we have shown how one can: 1. test data for consistency with the competitive cost minimization and profit maximization models; 2. test for restricted forms of the technology such as constant returns to scale, homotheticity, weak separability and additive separability; 3. recover the tightest inner and outer estimates of the input requirement sets, the production sets, the production functions, the cost functions, and the profit functions; 4. forecast bounds on factor demand and output supply behavior for new price configurations; 5. test data for consistency with models of imperfectly competitive behavior.

References

Afriat, S. (1967) "The Construction of a Utility Function from Expenditure Data," *International Economic Review*, **8**, 67–77.

Afriat, S. (1972) "Efficiency Estimates of Production Functions," *International Economic Review*, **13**, 568–598.

Afriat, S. (1973) "On a System of Inequalities on Demand Analysis: An Extension of the Classical Method," *International Economic Review*, **14**, 460–472.

Afriat, S. (1976) *The Combinatorial Theory of Demand*. London: Input-Output Publishing Company.

Afriat, S. (1977) *The Price Index*. London: Cambridge University Press.

Afriat, S. (1981) "On the Constructability of Consistent Price Indices Between Several Periods Simultaneously," in *Essays in the Theory and Measurement of Consumer Behavior*, ed. A. Deaton. Cambridge: Cambridge University Press.

Aigner, D. and P. Schmidt (1980) "Specification and Estimation of Frontier Production Functions, Profit and Cost Functions," *Journal of Econometrics*, **13**.

Blackorby, C., D. Primont, R. Russell (1979) *Duality, Separability, and Functional Structure: Theory and Economic Applications*. Amsterdam: North-Holland.

Diewert, E. (1973) "Afriat and Revealed Preference Theory," *Review of Economic Studies*, **40**, 419–426.

Diewert, E. (1978) "Hicks' Aggregation Theorem and the Existence of a Real Value Added Function," in *Production Economics: A Dual Approach to Theory and Applications*, ed. M. Fuss and D. McFadden. Amsterdam: North-Holland.

Diewert, E., C. Parkan (1978) "Test for Consistency of Consumer Data and Nonparametric Index Numbers," University of British Columbia, Working Paper 78-27.

Diewert, E., C. Parkan (1979) "Linear Programming Tests of Regularity Conditions for Production Functions," University of British Columbia.

Fuss, M., D. McFadden (1978) *Production Economics: A Dual Approach to Theory and Applications*. Amsterdam: North-Holland.

Hall, R (1978) "The Specification of Technology with Several Kinds of Output," in *Production Economics: A Dual Approach to Theory and Applications*, ed. M. Fuss and D. McFadden. Amsterdam: North-Holland.

Hanoch, G., M. Rothschild (1972) "Testing the Assumptions of Production Theory: A Nonparametric Approach," *Journal of Political Economy*, **80**, 256–275.

Hicks J. (1956) *A Revision of Demand Theory.* Oxford: Oxford University Press.

Samuelson, P. (1947) *Foundations of Economic Analysis.* Cambridge, MA: Harvard University Press.

Varian, H. (1982a) "The Nonparametric Approach to Demand Analysis," *Econometrica*, **50**, 945–974.

Varian, H. (1982b) "Nonparametric Tests of Consumer Behavior," *Review of Economic Studies*, **50**, 99–110.

Chapter 9

A BAYESIAN APPROACH TO
REAL ESTATE ASSESSMENT

Real estate assessors are required by law to estimate current market value on all taxable properties in their districts each year. For even moderate-sized districts this is a huge task. In recent years, this burden has been somewhat alleviated by the application of regression techniques to the appraisal process; see Gustafson (1967), Hinshaw (1968), Jancsek (1972), and Pendleton (1965). The assessor's office of San Mateo, California, for example, routinely assesses single-family homes by applying a formula estimated from data on previous sales using ordinary least squares procedures (OLSQ).

The purpose of this study is to investigate this problem from the Bayesian viewpoint, emphasizing the ways in which loss minimizing estimators and prior information can lead to more appropriate methods of mechanized appraisal.

9.1 The loss function approach

In this study, we will be concerned entirely with appraisal of single-family homes. In this case, the goal of the assessor is to estimate the current market value of a house, given the values of certain characteristics of the house such as total living area, number of bedrooms, etc. If the appraiser's estimate is denoted by y_e and the actual value is y_a certain losses are incurred, denoted by $L(y_e, y_a)$.

In general, these losses could arise from various causes, for example private costs versus social costs. However, for this study, we will consider only

Research performed under the auspices of the Center for Real Estate and Urban Economics, University of California, Berkeley, California. An earlier version of this paper was presented to the Western Economic Association meeting, Santa Clara, California, August 1972. I would like to thank Arnold Zellner for his kind help and encouragement in writing this paper. Helpful suggestions were also made by Darius Gaskins. Of course any errors remain the sole responsibility of the author.

losses accruing to the assessor's office. If the assessor's office underestimates the value of a house, the loss is equal to the amount of the underestimate. If the office overestimates the value of the house, the California homeowner has two recourses: he can (1) complain to the assessor's office, confer with them and attempt to convince them that his home was overassessed; or (2) present an appeal to the Assessment Board of Equalization, which evalu ates evidence presented by both sides as to the correct assessment. (Other states have similar appeal processes.)

Both of these are lengthy procedures which incur considerable expense for both parties. If the assessor's office loses the case, it not only loses the amount of the overassessment but also the costs involved in the appeal procedure.

If the case is won, the county must still pay the court costs involved. In cases involving substantial assessment error, the losses may amount to a considerable fraction of the tax. Therefore, the assessors would want to choose an estimate for home value that would minimize the total expected loss.

It is well known that if the loss function is quadratic, that is

$$L(y_e, y_a) = a(y_e - y_a)^2$$

the loss minimizing estimate is just the expected value of y_a. However, in the situation under consideration, a quadratic loss function seems inappropriate in that it assigns the same loss to overestimates as to equal underestimates.

But by virtue of the above considerations it is clear that the assessor's loss function should be asymmetric. The following features may be noted:

(1) The loss function should be linear for large negative errors.

(2) The loss function should be increasing for positive errors at a greater than linear rate.

(3) Even if court costs are constant, the probability of a complaint being submitted increases with the magnitude of the overestimate, and thus the loss function should increase monotonically for positive errors.

For the purposes of exposition I have chosen the following asymmetric loss function:

$$L(y_e, y_a) = b \exp[a(y_e - y_a)] - c(y_e - y_a) - b. \qquad (1)$$

This function, which I call the *linex* loss function (for linear-exponential), has many appealing properties: (1) for $c = 1$, $b = a^{-1}$ it has a minimum loss of 0 for $y_e = y_a$; (2) it has exponential losses for large overestimates and linear losses for large underestimates; (3) parameters can be chosen to provide a variety of asymmetric effects; and (4) it combines readily with a normal probability distribution. The shape of L is depicted in fig. 1 for various values of the parameters a and b.

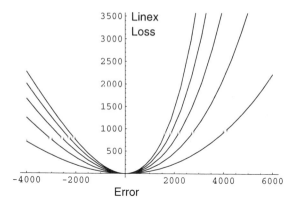

Figure 1. Plot of linex loss function.

The estimation of the correct parameters for the assessor's loss function would require considerable information about the probability of a complaint arising, the probability of a complaint winning a reversal, and the magnitude of the court costs involved. However, it can be seen that $a = 0.0004$, $b = 2500$, $c = 1$ gives values that are not unreasonable and will be adequate for purposes of this study.

Given the loss function L, and a probability distribution $p(y_a)$ on y_a, expected losses can be expressed by the following:

$$E[L] = \int_{-\infty}^{\infty} L(y_e, y_a)p(y_a)dy_a \qquad (2)$$

Solving this integral gives us expected loss as a function of y_e:

$$E(L) = f(y_e). \qquad (3)$$

Solving (3) for the value of y_e that minimizes expected loss gives us our loss minimizing estimate.

9.2 The particular model

It is commonly assumed that the selling price of a house is a linear function of the characteristics of that house plus an error term. Given a sample of previous sales of houses and their characteristics, we can formulate the following regression model:

$$y = X\beta + \epsilon \qquad (4)$$

where y is a m vector of selling prices, X is a k by m matrix of observed characteristics, β is a k vector of parameters, and ϵ is an m vector of error terms, assumed to be distributed $N(0, \sigma^2 I)$.

Under these assumptions, if we have diffuse prior information about the value of β and σ, Bayesian methods can be used to show that, given a new observation of a house with unobserved value y_a and characteristics x_a, y_a has a t-distribution with mean $x_a \beta_d$ and variance

$$v_d = \frac{\nu s_d^2}{\nu - 2}[1 + x_a(X'X)^{-1}x_a'],$$

where β_d is the OLSQ estimate of β, s_d^2 is the OLSQ estimate of σ^2 and $\nu = n - k$ [Zellner (1971), pp. 73-74]. (This result is similar to the classical OLSQ result concerning the predictive distribution [Johnson (1972), p. 154].)

With large samples of previous sales, the t-distribution can be well approximated by a normal distribution of mean x_a^d and variance v_d. Under this assumption of normality and the particular loss function we have chosen, we can derive the loss minimizing estimator of y_a, which is done in the Appendix.

The result is:

$$y_e = x_a \beta_d - \frac{a v_d}{2} + a^{-1} \ln \frac{c}{ba}. \tag{5}$$

This estimate has an appealing intuitive interpretation. As can be seen in fig. 1 small values of a correspond to a small degree of asymmetry. Thus for no asymmetry, y_e coincides with the usual estimate; as the degree of asymmetry rises, positive errors will incur higher and higher losses, causing the OLSQ estimator to be biased downwards in compensation. Also, if our regression is highly accurate, s_d^2 will be small; as the accuracy of the regression falls, there is a higher probability of large positive errors, again causing the OLSQ estimate to be compensated downwards. Finally, if a house has "average" characteristics, the quadratic term $x_a(X'X)^{-1}x_a'$ will be small and the correction factor will be low; for "unusual" houses, the equation "gives them the benefit of the doubt" and applies a large correction.

The positive term, on the other hand, tends to counteract the negative correction factor as the ratio c/b rises. This ratio indicates the relative magnitudes of the losses from over and underestimates.

9.3 The data

The data for this study consist of 168 observed sales of single-family homes in a middle-sized California town in 1965. In a previous study using these data, Jancsek (1972) found the following nine variables to be good predictors of selling price: (1) lot width, (2) view (1 = average or above average view, 0 = below average view), (3) age, (4) number of bedrooms, (5) quality class (see State Board of Equalization (1968)), (6) total living area, (7) flatwork cost (patios, driveways, etc.), (8) fence cost, (9) a constant term.

The sample was split into two groups: the first, consisting of 125 observations, was used in estimation and the second, consisting of 43 observations, was used for projection and comparison purposes.

9.4 Regression results

The regression coefficients, standard errors, and standard error of the regression are summarized in table 1, column 1. The R^2 for this regression was 0.85 which would indicate that the equation would have reasonable predictive ability.

Table 1
Estimation Results

Variable	1 OLSQ	2 Non-data-based prior	3 Non-data-based Bayesian reg.	4 Data-based prior	5 Data-based Bayesian reg.
Lot width	33.11 (20.30)	50.00	41.55 (31.18)	98.08 (31.16)	53.88 (15.97)
View	1879.27 (433.21)	2000.00	1939.64 (665.25)	2405.24 (828.87)	2109.04 (379.04)
Effective years	−175.34 (27.11)	−200.00	−187.67 (41.64)	−139.22 (48.21)	−173.50 (23.02)
Number of bedrooms	−722.48 (32.35)	1000.00	138.76 (496.74)	−12.04 (741.66)	−608.90 (289.63)
Quality class	2000.54 (33.61)	2000.00	2002.73 (516.17)	2454.36 (626.19)	2119.04 (285.23)
Total living area	7.95 (0.78)	10.00	8.98 (1.20)	6.12 (1.56)	7.33 (0.67)
Flatwork cost	5.05 (1.29)	5.00	5.03 (1.98)	4.52 (3.50)	4.48 (1.18)
Fence cost	3.89 (1.80)	2.00	2.94 (2.80)	−0.31 (5.78)	3.51 (1.72)
Constant	1356.11 (1840.49)	1000.00	1178.05 (2826.29)	−4413.44 (4016.91)	161.53 (1641.28)
Standard error	1827.16		3993.47	2081.64	1889.34

Since we based our derivation of the loss minimizing estimate on the assumption of normality of the errors, it is important to examine the residual behavior to verify this assumption. A cumulative normal plot of the residuals indicates that normality is not a bad approximation for these data. The comparative results concerning loss minimization will be deferred to a later section.

9.5 A prior probability distribution

When preparing to estimate the model represented by (4), we often have prior information involving the parameter β. For example, such prior information could be of the following types:

(1) Appraisal rules of thumb. – Most appraisers have developed ideas about the relative importance of various factors in determining home value. In our model, for example, we would expect total living area to be more important than fence cost, and the coefficient for total living area ought to be positive. If pressed, an appraiser might even be able to quantify his subjective beliefs about such factors, in so far as he could make statements such as: "I believe that an extra square foot of floor space would, on the average, be worth twice as much as an extra dollar spent on fence costs. However, my estimate is rather imprecise." Suitably formulated, such statements can be used to construct a subjective prior probability distribution on the parameters.

(2) Previous experience. – If similar models have been successfully applied in other communities, their estimations can be used to construct prior probability distributions. Thus the estimates of β for community A can serve as a general guideline for community B while the actual data for community B can serve to pinpoint the estimates more precisely.

(3) Past estimates. – Market conditions continually change and hence it is important to continually revise estimates of β by incorporating new data. However, since market conditions may change relatively slowly, we may believe that the β to be estimated for 1972 will probably be similar to the β estimated in 1971. We can incorporate this belief into our estimation procedure by using the estimated in 1971 in the prior probability distribution when estimating β for 1972.

Assuming then, that we do have a prior probability distribution of β representing our beliefs, how do we incorporate it into our analysis?

If $p(\beta, X, y)$ is the joint probability density function for our parameter β and the random variables X and y, we can factor it in two ways:

$$p(\beta, X, y) = p(\beta|X, y)p(X, y) = p(X, Y|\beta)p(\beta$$

Thus,

$$p(\beta|X, y) \propto p(\beta)p(x, y|\beta).$$

The posterior probability density function of β given the data (X, y) is proportional to the product of the prior probability density of β and the likelihood function. This is of course Bayes' formula. Since the integral of $p(\beta|X, y)$ must be 1, this proportionality completely determines the posterior probability distribution.

For the purposes of our analysis we will assume that (β, σ^2) has a Normal-gamma prior probability distribution. That is:

$$p(\beta|\sigma) \propto \frac{1}{\sigma^k} \exp\left[-\frac{1}{2\sigma^2}(\beta - b)'N(\beta - b)\right]$$

$$p(\sigma) \propto \frac{1}{\sigma^{v+1}} \exp\left[-\frac{vs^2}{2\sigma^2}\right] \qquad v = n - p, \quad p = \text{rank}(N).$$

Here the parameters of these prior distributions are just (b, N) and (s^2, v). Further, let $p - \text{rank}(N)$.

Suppose we are given data (X, y), where X is $k \times n$ and y is $1 \times n$. Then define:

$$b_d = (X'X)^{-1}X'y$$
$$N_d = X'X$$
$$p_d = \text{rank}(N_d)$$
$$v_d = n - p_d$$
$$s_d^2 = \frac{1}{v_d}(y - Xb_d)'(y - Xb_d)$$

It is well known (see for example Raiffa and Schlaifer (1961), p. 343, or Zellner (1971), pp. 70-72) that in this case, the posterior probability distribution is again Normal-gamma with parameters:

$$N_p = N_d + N$$
$$b_p = N_p^{-1}(N_db_d + Nb)$$
$$p_p = \text{rank}(N_p)$$
$$v_p = p_d + v + p - p_p + v_d$$
$$s_p^2 = \frac{1}{v_p}\left[(v_dp_d + b_d'N_db_d) + (y'y - b_p'N_pb_p)\right]$$

Since we have a normal distribution on β, we will again have a t-distribution on y_d which, exactly as before, we will approximate as a normal distribution. If the loss function is of the linex form, the derivation of the loss minimizing estimate goes through exactly as before yielding:

$$y_d = x_db_p - \frac{av_p}{2} + a^{-1}\ln\frac{c}{ba}.$$

9.6 Construction of the prior and results

For the purpose of this exposition, I experimented with two prior distributions. One was a data-based prior using the aforementioned 43 cases to represent another "prior" observation of the sample; the other was non-data-based, relying on an intuitive notion of relative importance of the variables in determining the value of a house.

9.7 The non-data-based prior

Examining table 1, column 1, the coefficients appear reasonable, with the exception of the coefficient on bedrooms which is negative, rather than having the positive effect one would expect. This situation arises frequently in this type of analysis; for example, Hinshaw cites an equation with negative signs on the number of bathrooms, fence cost, air conditioning, etc. These effects are probably due to misspecification of the model; for example, (1) the linear form may be incorrect, (2) there may be left out variables, especially concerning neighborhood effects, and (3) there is often considerable multi-collinearity in the right-hand variables. However, if we want to use the linear functional form and are restricted to this set of data, this negative sign is irrelevant for prediction.

For the purposes of this example, we will deliberately "mis-specify" the prior so as to examine the effect of this on the loss-minimizing estimator. We then ask the following question: "What is the best loss minimizing estimate of β given that β has the 'right' signs?"

I chose 1000 as the prior mean for bedrooms in table 1, column 3. I let $s_p = 2460$, and $N = N_d$, the cross-product matrix from the data. The resulting posterior means of β are summarized in table 1, column 4. Notice that the posterior mean for the bedroom coefficient is indeed positive; however, this "right" sign has resulted in a rather large increase in the standard error of the regression. Thus the predictive ability of this regression is undoubtedly poorer than OLSQ.

9.8 The data-based prior

Assume that the 43 cases used for testing purposes in fact come from another sample – perhaps another community, or last year's sample. We can run a regression on these variables which influences our beliefs about the significance of the various parameters. When we encounter the new sample of 125 houses, we wish to use our previous estimations as a prior.

These results are summarized in table 1, columns 4 and 5.

Here the standard error has risen only slightly, while most of the coefficients remain similar, with the exception of the constant. It appears that the posterior distribution may be an improvement over the prior.

9.9 Comparative results and conclusions

Table 2 presents the average linex loss incurred and standard deviation of the loss when the estimation methods discussed are used to assess the aforementioned sample of 43 houses. The linex estimator with data-based prior gives the lowest average loss. One would expect this, since it completely utilizes the information in the entire 168 observations and applies the optimal correction factor. The next best is the diffuse linex estimate (this can also be regarded as an OLSQ regression combined with the correction factor). The three "uncorrected" regressions all give higher average losses than the loss minimizing estimators.

An interesting effect occurs with the non-data-based prior. Since this prior was deliberately misspecified, the Bayesian regression does quite poorly with average loss 13 times worse than with the best method. However, when the loss minimizing correction term is applied, the estimates performance improves substantially.

The example worked through in this paper illustrates the feasibility of Bayesian and decision theoretic assessment. The average loss resulting from the loss minimizing Bayesian regression is only 72% of the loss resulting from ordinary least squares. In monetary terms, this could result in a substantial amount of savings.

The next step would be to repeat the type of work done here on a larger scale with an eye towards more realism in the parameter choices. For example: the actual loss function appropriate for the assessor's office could be estimated; other sets of independent variables could be used; and one could experiment with other functional forms.

Table 2
Loss minimization results

| Method | | Average | Standard |
Prior	Correction	linex loss	deviation
(1) Data-based	Linex	718.0	1367.0
(2) Diffuse (OLSQ)	Linex	790.0	1578.0
(3) Data-based	Quadratic	901.0	1922.0
(4) Diffuse (OLSQ)	Quadratic	999.0	2161.0
(5) Non-data-based	Linex	1278.0	2822.0
(6) Non-data-based	Quadratic	9351.0	14965.0

The estimate is of the form $x_a\beta+$ correction. If correction $= 0$ this estimate minimizes quadratic loss, if correction $= -av_d/2$ the estimate minimizes linex loss. The estimate of β depends on the type of prior used.

The loss function was:

$$L(x) = 2500 \exp(0.0004x) - x - 2500$$

where x is the error in the estimation; i.e., $x = y_e - y_a$.

9.10 Appendix. Derivation of the loss minimizing estimate

We assume the distribution of y_a to be $N(u, v)$. Letting r denote the error, $x = y_e - y_a$, we have a loss function of the form:

$$L(x) = b \exp[ax] - cx - b.$$

The distribution of x is easily seen to be $N(y_e - u, v)$. Letting $d = y_e - u$ and dropping the constant we can express expected loss by:

$$E[L] = \frac{b}{\sqrt{2\pi v}} \int_{-\infty}^{\infty} \exp\left[ax - \frac{(x-d)^2}{2v}\right] dx - \frac{c}{\sqrt{2\pi v}} \times \int_{-\infty}^{\infty} \exp\left[-\frac{(x-d)^2}{2v}\right] dx. \tag{1}$$

The second integral is simply the mean of the distribution, namely d. As for the first we note that:

$$ax - \frac{(x-d)^2}{2v} = \frac{2vax - (x^2 - 2xd + d^2)}{2v}$$
$$= \frac{-x^2 + (2d + 2va)x - d^2}{2v}.$$

Completing the square, we have:

$$ax - \frac{(x-d)^2}{2v} = \frac{-[x - (d_v a)]^2 + (d + va)^2 - d^2}{2v}$$
$$= \frac{-[x - (d + va)]^2 + 2vad + v^2 a^2}{2v}$$
$$= \frac{-[x - (d + va)]^2}{2v} + a\left(d + \frac{va}{2}\right).$$

Substituting this into (1), simplifying and bringing the constant term outside the integral we have:

$$E(L) = \frac{b}{\sqrt{2\pi v}} \exp\left[a\left(d + \frac{va}{2}\right)\right] \times \int_{-\infty}^{\infty} \exp\left[-\frac{(x - (d + va))^2}{2v}\right] dx - cd.$$

The integral conveniently cancels out, leaving:

$$E(L) = b \exp\left[a\left(d + \frac{va}{2}\right)\right] - cd. \tag{2}$$

Taking the derivative of (2) with respect to y_e and equating to 0 gives:

$$ba \exp\left[a\left(d + \frac{va}{2}\right)\right] - c = 0$$

$$\exp\left[a\left(d + \frac{va}{2}\right)\right] = \frac{c}{ba}$$

$$a\left(d + \frac{va}{2}\right) = \ln\frac{c}{ba}$$

$$d = a^{-1}\ln\frac{c}{ba} - \frac{va}{2}.$$

Substituting for d and rearranging:

$$y_e = u + a^{-1}\ln\frac{c}{ba} - \frac{va}{2}.$$

In the regression model, u is simply $x_a\beta_d$ and v is v_d, so the optimal estimator is:

$$y_e = x_a\beta_d + a^{-1}\ln\frac{c}{ba} - \frac{v_d a}{2}.$$

References

Robert Gustafson (1967) "EDP and the appraiser," Delivered at the 35th Annual Conference of the National Association of Tax Administrators, San Francisco.

Andrew J. Hinshaw (1968) "The assessor and computerization of data," *Assessor's Journal*, **3**, 1.

Joel Jancsek (1972) "Property tax assessment applications of multiple regression analysis in California," Technical Report No. 4, University of California, Center for Real Estate.

J. Johnston (1972) *Econometric methods, 2nd Ed.* New York: McGraw-Hill.

William C. Pendleton (1965) "Statistical inference in appraisal and assessment procedures," *The Appraisal Journal.*

H. Raiffa and R. Schlaifer (1961) "Applied statistical decision theory," Division of Research, Graduate School of Business Administration, Harvard University.

State Board of Equalization (1968) "Residential building costs," Sacramento, California.

Arnold Zellner (1971) *An introduction to Bayesian inference in econometrics.* New York: John Wiley.

Chapter 10

NONPARAMETRIC ANALYSIS OF OPTIMIZING BEHAVIOR WITH MEASUREMENT ERROR

We consider how one might test observed behavior for consistency with optimizing behavior in the presence of measurement error. We derive an appropriate test statistic and examine a specific case study involving cost minimization behavior by electric utility plants.

In several earlier papers listed in the references I have described methods for testing observed economic behavior for consistency with optimizing models. These tests have built on the work of Afriat (1967), (1972), (1976), Diewert (1973), Diewert and Parkan (1978), (1980) and Hanoch and Rothschild (1972). A defect of the methods proposed in these works is that there it seems difficult to incorporate measurement error into the analysis. The data are assumed to be observed without error, so that the tests are "all or nothing:" either the data satisfy the optimization hypothesis or they don't.

Despite this stringent nature of the tests, they may well be worth doing. Indeed, if some data pass such a test *without* resorting to any specification of measurement error one might feel more confident than usual about the veracity of the null hypothesis. (Or perhaps feel more dubious than usual about the power of the data to reveal violations of the null hypothesis.)

However, it seems that if some data fail the tests, but only by a small amount, we might well be tempted to attribute this failure to measurement error, left out variables, or other sorts of stochastic influences rather than to reject the hypothesis outright. The problem here of course is to give formal content to the phrase "only a small amount."

That is the goal of this paper. In the following sections I offer a general method that is, in principle, capable of measuring the magnitude of departure from the underlying model of optimizing behavior. I am able to interpret this procedure in terms of the classical statistical framework of hypothesis testing, and I provide an actual case study to illustrate the feasibility of the method.

10.1 Stochastic considerations in nonparametric analysis

The nonparametric tests mentioned above usually take the form of asking whether there exists a solution to a certain set of linear inequalities. For example, suppose that we have n observations on the output (y_i) the factor prices (w_i) and the factor demands (x_i) for a particular firm. It is shown in Varian (1984) that the following "Weak Axiom of Cost Minimization" (WACM) is a necessary and sufficient condition for the observed behavior of the firm to be compatible with cost minimizing behavior:

$$w_i x_i \leq w_i x_j \text{ for all } y_i \leq y_j$$

This condition is quite simple to test in practice, but it may be a bit more difficult to interpret. If the data do not satisfy WACM, what are we to do? The answer seems to depend on the *magnitude* of the violation. If the data fail to satisfy WACM by only a small amount, then we might well be tempted to attribute this violation to measurement error and accept the hypothesis of cost minimization.

The problem here is to give specific content to the words "magnitude of the violation" and if possible to phrase the discussion in the formal language of statistical hypothesis testing. I will describe my progress towards achieving these goals.

Let us suppose that the observed demand for factor k in observation i, x_{ik}, is related to the "true" factor demand z_{ik} in the following way:

$$x_{ik} = z_{ik} + \epsilon_{ik} \quad i = 1, \ldots, n \quad k = 1, \ldots, m$$

where ϵ_{ik} is a random error term. We will suppose that this error term ϵ_{ik} is IID $N(0, \sigma^2)$. Of course other stochastic specifications are possible; but this choice is a convenient one for discussion.[1]

The null hypothesis that I wish to consider can be stated as:

H0: the data (w_i, z_i, y_i) satisfy WACM.

It is convenient to think of the matrix of observations (x_{ik}) as a vector with mn components which we will denote by X. Thus the nonnegative orthant of R^{mn} is the set of all possible data. The set of data consistent with the null hypothesis is then that subset H of R^{mn} that satisfies WACM. The observed choices, X, is not an element of this set, but under the null hypothesis, the true choices, Z, is an element of H. The situation is depicted in Figure 1.

---

[1]   In most applications, an assumption of proportional measurement error is often more appropriate. This is in fact the specification that we use in the empirical work presented below.

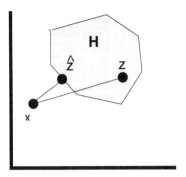

Figure 1. Non-parametric test.

How can we conveniently test this null hypothesis? There are several approaches that one might consider. The first way we might consider is somewhat Bayesian in flavor. Since $z_{ik} = x_{ik} - \epsilon_{ik}$ we might regard z_{ik} as a Normal random variable with mean x_{ik} and variance σ^2. The vector Z can then be thought of as multivariate normal with some probability density $f(Z)$. We can integrate the density over the region H to compute the probability that the null hypothesis actually holds.

There are three sorts of problems with this approach that I can see. First, this procedure is not in the spirit of classical statistical hypothesis testing, since we generally want to consider the distribution of the observed data given that the null hypothesis is true, not the distribution of the true data given the observations. Secondly, the test may be computationally quite demanding, especially since it may need to be performed for several different values of σ^2. Thirdly, it does not generalize in a convenient way to other sorts of nonparametric tests.

For example, if we are given observations on a consumer's choices (x_i) when facing prices (p_i), a necessary and sufficient condition for the data to be consistent with maximizing behavior is that there exist positive numbers (U_i, λ_i) that satisfy the following system of inequalities:

$$U_i \leq U_j + \lambda_j p_j (x_i - x_j) \quad i,j = 1,\ldots,n$$

Thus in the case of consumer maximization, the region H will be all data sets for which these inequalities have a positive solution. This may be rather difficult to calculate, much less to integrate over.

For these reasons I have adopted a different approach. There are two arguments that lead to the same test procedure, which we will examine in the following two sections.

10.2 A chi-squared test

Suppose that we could somehow observe the true data, (z_{ik}). Then since $\epsilon_{ik} = z_{ik} - x_{ik}$, we could compute the "test statistic:"

$$T = \sum_{i=1}^{n} \sum_{k=1}^{m} (z_{ik} - x_{ik})^2 / \sigma^2$$

Under the null hypothesis $H0$, this "statistic" has a chi-squared distribution. Thus we can find a critical value C for any desired level of significance, α. If $T > C$ we would reject the null hypothesis.

The problem is of course that the "statistic" T is not observable. However, it turns out that we can calculate an observable *lower bound* on T that will still allow us to apply the above testing method. Consider the following quadratic programming problem:

$$S = \min \sum_{i=1}^{n} \sum_{k=1}^{m} (\zeta_{ik} - x_{ik})^2 / \sigma^2$$

$$\text{s.t. } w_i \zeta_i \leq w_i \zeta_j \text{ for } y_i \leq y_j$$

Under the null hypothesis, the "true data" (w_i, z_i, y_i) satisfy the constraint. Hence the minimum of the sum of squares S must be no larger than the "test statistic" T.

Thus if we reject $H0$ whenever $S > C$, we are certain that in fact $T > C$, and thus we have *at least* the desired level of significance. That is, the probability of rejecting $H0$ when it is true will be less that α. In this sense, the test is very conservative.

The basic trick in the above method is using the mathematical programming problem to derive a bound on the unobserved random variable. The exact stochastic specification and the distributional assumptions were chosen in order to present a specific example and are not critical to the structure of the test. The choice of specification in these nonparametric methods rests on the tradeoff between generality and computability here just as it does in all statistical work.[1]

Although I believe the hypothesis test described above is in the spirit of classical hypothesis testing, it is comforting to note that it is also quite sensible. We are simply asking for the minimal perturbation of the data that satisfies $WACM$. If the minimal perturbation is small relative to the amount of noise thought to be present in the data then it seems reasonable to accept the null hypothesis.

---

[1] This idea has been used before in the statistics literature. The classic upper and lower bounds on the Durbin-Watson statistic were calculated by using just this form of bounding argument.

One particularly nice feature of the test outlined above is that it can handle "nuisance parameters" quite easily. For example, in the case of the utility maximization problem described above the programming problem becomes:

$$S = \min \sum_{i=1}^{n} \sum_{k=1}^{m} (\zeta_{ik} - x_{ik})^2 / \sigma^2$$

$$\text{s.t. } A_i \leq A_j + b_j p_j (\zeta_i - \zeta_j) \quad i, j = 1, \ldots, n$$

This time the minimization takes place over the variables (ζ_{ik}, A_i, b_i). Under the null hypothesis, there is a set of variables (z_i, U_i, λ_i) that satisfies the constraints, so the answer to this minimization problem will be an appropriate bound to the desired test statistic. It appears that it would be quite difficult, if not impossible, to analyze this problem by the integration technique mentioned earlier.

A further advantage of the method is that it actually constructs the a perturbation of the data that satisfies cost minimization. If we want to go on to calculate bounds on the underlying technology, or to forecast demand behavior as described in Varian (1984), we can use this constructed technology. The integration approach described above lacks this feature.

There is a nice geometric interpretation of the proposed test that is depicted in Figure 1. Here the Euclidean distance between X and Z is a sum of squared residuals, and this distance in obviously bounded by the minimal distance from X to H.

However, despite these observations, there are some unpleasant features of the proposed test. The major difficulty is the fact that one needs to specify a known variance.[2] However, the fact that one must postulate a value for this parameter does not make the undertaking entirely arbitrary. For example one could use estimates of the error variance derived from parametric fits, or from knowledge about how the variables were actually measured. In any event, it seems that postulating one parameter, an indication of how noisy the investigator believes the data to be, is much less objectionable than the common practice of postulating an entire functional form. It must be remembered that the usual estimates of error variances are correct only under the maintained hypothesis of the specified functional form; and this maintained hypothesis is often arbitrary.

Even if we are not able to estimate the error variance as in parametric models, we can still derive bounds on the error variance that is necessary in order to reject the maintained hypothesis of maximizing behavior. Let us consider this point in more detail.

As above, let C be the critical value for our proposed test, and let S be the value of our objective function. Then by inspection of the objective

---

[2] If there are several observed choices at each price it may be possible to actually estimate the variance. However, this type of data is rather rare.

function, $S = R/\sigma^2$, where σ^2 is the "true" variance of the error term and R is the sum of squared residuals. We are proposing to reject the null hypothesis when $S > C$ which means when $\sigma^2 < R/C$. Let us refer to the $\bar{\sigma}^2 = R/C$ as the *critical value* of σ^2, and let $\bar{\sigma}$ be its square root. Note that $\bar{\sigma}$ is easily computable once we have solved the quadratic programming problem.

The critical value, $\bar{\sigma}$, measures what the standard error of the data would have to be for us to consider the rejection of the maximization hypothesis to be a statistically significant rejection. If $\bar{\sigma}$ is much smaller than our prior opinions concerning the precision with which these data have been measured we may well want to accept the maximization hypothesis.

10.3 A constrained maximum likelihood approach

Another approach to the sort of test described above is through the method of constrained maximum likelihood. Given some observations (x_{ik}) and the specification of a normal error term we can write the log-likelihood function:

$$\log L = mn \log(2\pi)/2 - mn \log\sigma - \sum_{i=1}^{n}\sum_{k=1}^{m}(z_{ik} - x_{ik})^2/2\sigma^2$$

We think of (z_{ik}) and σ^2 as unknown parameters to be estimated. Under the null hypothesis, $Z = (z_{ik})$ is an element of the set H, so we can consider the *constrained* maximum likelihood estimates derived by maximizing the likelihood over the set H. It is easy to see that this gives us as our estimator for (z_{ik}) the values that solve the quadratic programming problem described above. Let these values be denoted by $(\hat{z}_{ik})$. The associated estimator for σ^2 is:

$$\hat{\sigma}^2 = \sum_{i=1}^{n}\sum_{k=1}^{m}(\hat{z}_{ik} - x_{ik})^2/mn$$

Thus the "fitted values" $(\hat{z}_{ik})$ are a (constrained) maximum likelihood estimate of the true unknown values. However, I doubt if one can establish any useful statistical properties for these estimates. After all, we are estimating one more parameter that we have observations. The only thing that allows our estimates to be identified at all is the constraint.

However, the statistic $\hat{\sigma}^2$ can be used for hypothesis testing purposes. As before we simply note that:

$$mn\hat{\sigma}^2/\sigma^2 = R$$

is no larger than a chi-squared variable with mn degrees of freedom. Hence if we reject the null hypothesis that Z is in H whenever $R > C$ we are guaranteed a test of *at least* the desired level of significance.

Rearranging the test condition, we have:

$$\sigma^2 < mn\hat{\sigma}^2/C = R/C$$

which is exactly the test condition given earlier. If our prior beliefs about σ are less than R/C, we should reject the optimization hypothesis. Otherwise, it should not be rejected.

10.4 A comparison with parametric methods

The diagram in Figure 1 can be used to establish a nice link with standard parametric estimation techniques in models with optimizing behavior. Suppose that we have some parametric form for the underlying technology which we can use to derive functional forms for the factor demand for factor k at observation i as a function of the factor prices, output levels, and an unknown vector of parameters β. We denote this factor demand by $g_k(w_i, y_i, \beta)$.

Then under the null hypothesis of optimizing behavior and known parametric form, the true data, (z_{ik}), will satisfy the parametric relationship:

$$z_{ik} = g_k(w_i, y_i, \beta) \quad i = 1, \ldots, n \quad k = 1, \ldots, m$$

If there are b unknown parameters, the set of all Z that satisfy this relationship will be a b dimensional manifold in R^{mn} which we denote by M. Since Z satisfies the optimization conditions by construction, the manifold M must be a subset of the set H. This relationship is depicted in Figure 2.

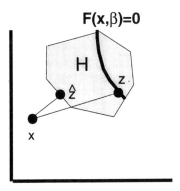

Figure 2. Relationship with a parametric test.

The usual approach to constrained parametric estimation involves maximizing the likelihood function over the manifold M. This simply means that we find some fitted values (z_{ik}) in M that maximize the likelihood function. The associated values of β are the maximum likelihood estimates of the unknown parameters. The maximum likelihood estimate for σ^2 is just the sum of squared residuals divided by mn.

These estimates are entirely analogous to the nonparametric estimates given above. The only difference is that we are maximizing the likelihood over the mn dimensional set H rather than the b dimensional manifold M. Despite this resemblance in method, the statistical properties of the estimators may be quite different. I suspect that the major differences arise because the dimension of the manifold M stays fixed as the number of observations increases while the dimension of H keeps changing.

Let us use R_p to denote the minimal sum of squared residuals for the parametric estimate, and R_n the minimal sum of squared residuals for the nonparametric estimate. The ratio R_n/R_p is, in some sense, a measure of the "goodness of fit" of the parametric model, conditional on the optimization hypothesis. If the perturbation of the data necessary to satisfy the optimization hypothesis in the presence of a specific parametric form is very large relative to the perturbation necessary to satisfy optimization alone, we might not find the parametric hypothesis very convincing.

Of course again we need to ask "large relative to what?" I have not yet come up with a satisfactory answer to that question, and until someone does we will simply have to make do with an intuitive notion of what magnitudes are plausible.

10.5 A case study

In order to examine the feasibility of the methods described above I undertook a case study involving data on California electric power generation. The data in question were obtained from Woo (1982) and are discussed in detail in his Chapter 4. The data consist of 18 time series observations from 1960-1979 on the factor inputs and output of 2 electric power generation plants.[1] The factors used in this study are labor, fuel, and capital.

We first checked the plants for consistency with the cost minimization hypothesis. We found that the observed behavior *violated* the WACM inequalities. The natural questions is: by how much were the inequalities violated?

To answer this question we solved up the quadratic programming problem described above. Each program involved 54 variables (3 factors, 18 observations) and around 200 constraints. The actual program solved was different from that described above in that we postulated a proportional measurement error rather than an additive one. Since the factor demands

---

[1] Woo's original data set contained two observations in which the cost of capital variable was negative. These observations were discarded.

were measured in very different units this seemed like a much more plausible specification.

Specifically, we assumed that the true demand was related to the observed demand in the following way:

$$z_{ik} = x_{ik}(1 + \epsilon_{ik})$$

where ϵ_{ik} is an IID Normal disturbance with mean zero and constant variance. This leads to an objective function of the form:

$$\sum_{i=1}^{m}\sum_{k=1}^{n}(z_{ik}/x_{ik} - 1)^2$$

The quadratic programming problem was solved by a quadratic programming package called MINOS by Murtagh and Saunders (1977). We found the cost of each quadratic programming problem was around \$2.00 during normal priority on the University of Michigan computer system, an Amdahl 5860 running MTS. The result of these calculations are presented in Tables 1 and 2.

We will describe the data in Table 1 since the story in Table 2 is much the same. Columns 2-4 give the observed output and input levels while columns 5-7 give the per cent "residuals" that would make the observed firm choices consistent with WACM and minimize the sum of squared deviations. The value SSR, the sum of squared residuals, is given for each factor and overall, as well as the square root of the overall SSR divided by the number of observations. The latter variable may be thought of as something like a standard error so we have denoted it by SE.

There are several interesting things about the "fit" described in Table 1. Note for example the size of the perturbations for the different factors. One would imagine that the labor cost component of these electric power plants would be the easiest to measure, with the fuel costs a close second. The most difficult factor to measure is certainly the capital stock. Indeed, when we look at the sum of squared residuals for each factor we find that they conform to this expected pattern.[2]

Secondly note how small the perturbations are. The largest perturbation is in the period 8 capital stock, and this is only about 4.4 per cent. These perturbations seem to be quite small relative to my beliefs about the size of the measurement error associated with these data.

---

[2] Of course if the analyst thought that there were extreme differences in the degree of measurement error across the factors of production he would presumably modify the null hypothesis of equal percentage error variance. This seems to me to be analogous to the problem of heteroskedasticity in ordinary regression analysis. Just as in the case of ordinary least squares, we can minimize a *weighted* sum of squares if this problem is felt to be a serious one. In most cases, I doubt that it is.

We can be more precise about this statement. Following the discussion in Section 1, we have computed the critical value of σ outlined there. The 95% critical value of a chi- squared variable with 54 degrees of freedom is about 44. This implies that $\bar{\sigma}$ is .0005. This means that one would have to believe the data were measured with a standard error of *less than* .05 per cent in order to reject the null hypothesis of cost minimization. This seems a substantially smaller measurement error than anyone would be likely to attribute to these data. On this ground I am willing to accept the hypothesis of cost minimization.

How does these data fare when confronted with standard sorts of parametric methods? To answer this question I found the minimal perturbation of the data to satisfy factor demands derived from Cobb-Douglas and CES production functions. The fit is described in Table 3. Note that in the Cobb-Douglas case the sum of squared residuals is over 500 times as large as the perturbation needed to satisfy minimization alone! The CES case fares somewhat better, with a SSR only 50 times as large as that needed in the nonparametric case. Even so this perturbation seems quite large. The conclusion seems to be that the data are consistent with cost minimization – but not Cobb-Douglas or CES cost minimization.

10.6 Objections and replies

After describing the above method, I have often encountered various objections to it. In this section I will describe several of the most common objections and my replies.

1. *You have specified error terms only on the quantity terms; the price terms may also be measured with error.*

I agree. It would be desirable to incorporate error terms on the prices as well. However, note that the resulting programming problem would then have nonlinear constraints and thus be considerably more difficult to solve. Furthermore, note that standard regression methods typically specify that regressors are nonstochastic. If one is estimating conditional factor demand equations, this means that price and output variables are hypothesized to be measured without error, and only factor demands themselves are assumed to be measured with error – exactly as specified here.

2. *Simply because you fail to reject the null hypothesis doesn't mean that the data were generated by optimization.*

Of course not. If we fail to reject the null hypothesis then we have simply stated that the observed departures from the model are not extremely unlikely given the null hypothesis. That is exactly what is done in ordinary statistical hypothesis testing.

3. *It would be useful to have a measure of the power of this test.*

Absolutely. But of course the power of a test *depends* on the specific alternative hypothesis. Given some reasonable alternative and the distribution of the errors it would be possible to compute the probability that the proposed test would be satisfied. This would almost certainly have to be done by Monte Carlo methods, since I see little hope of an analytic solution. However, by way of comparison, let me note that it is quite rare that one sees power reported in parametric econometric studies.

4. *The fact that one needs to specify the error variance effectively renders this approach worthless.*

I think not. Rather than speculate idly on this point, it is worth considering the particular example presented above. Does anyone really believe that the factor demand data described in Table 1 has a standard error of less than .05 per cent? If not, the procedures outlined above indicate that the departures from cost minimizing behavior depicted in that table are not statistically significant. This seems to me to be a perfectly satisfactory statement. Furthermore, specifying the likely magnitude of the measurement error seems to me to be much *less difficult* a task than specifying a plausible functional form for a production function, as is required in the conventional approach.

5. *It is difficult to argue that we know enough to specify the way disturbances enter the demand equations and can specify a parametric form of the distribution while at the same time arguing that we do not know enough to specify the form for the demand system.*

I find the specification of a Normal error term much less difficult than the specification of a particular parametric form for technology or demand. In any event parametric studies usually require a specification of *both* the functional form of the demand relationship and the parametric form of the distribution.

6. *What is the relationship of this approach to the literature on frontier estimation and envelope analysis?*

In this paper I have specified the error term as a measurement error on the measured factor demands, since in my opinion these are the variables that are the most poorly measured in this sort of study. However, one could consider alternative approaches in a nonparametric context as well.

For example, suppose that we thought that the output levels (y_i) were underestimates of the "true" output frontier levels (y_i^*). That is,

$$y_i = y_i^* + \epsilon_i \qquad i = 1, \ldots, n$$

where $\epsilon_i \leq 0$. In this case we might find a minimal perturbation of the observations that would satisfy WACM, while respecting the sign restriction on the perturbations implied by the nonpositivity of the error term. Under the null hypothesis this would be a lower bound on the actual perturbation and all the analysis of this paper applies.

10.7 Summary

I have shown how one can extend the nonparametric methods described in the introduction to cases involving measurement error. The logic of the approach involves asking for the minimal perturbation of the data that satisfies the inequality relations implied by the underlying theory. This sort of test can be given an interpretation consistent with the classical theory of statistical hypothesis testing. Furthermore, the methods are practical from the computational perspective and can be applied in a wide variety of stochastic specifications.

References

Afriat, S. (1967), "The Construction of a Utility Function from Expenditure Data", *International Economic Review* , **8**, 67-77.

Afriat, S. (1972), "Efficiency Estimation of Production Functions", *International Economic Review* , **13**, 568-598.

Afriat, S. (1976), *The Combinatorial Theory of Demand*, Input-Output Publishing Company, London.

Diewert, E. (1973), "Afriat and Revealed Preference Theory", *Review of Economic Studies*, **40**, 419-426.

Diewert, E. and C. Parkan (1978), "Tests for Consistency of Consumer Data and Nonparametric Index Numbers", University of British Columbia Working Paper 78-27.

Diewert, E. and C. Parkan (1980), "Linear Programming Tests of Regularity Conditions for Production Functions", University of British Columbia. To appear in *Quantitative Studies on Production and Prices* , W. Eichhorn, K. Henn, K. Neumann, R. Shepherd (eds), Physica-Verlag.

Hanoch, G. and M. Rothschild (1972), "Testing the Assumptions of Production Theory", *Journal of Political Economy*, **80**, 256-275.

Murtagh, B. and M. Saunders, (1977), *MINOS: A Large Scale Nonlinear Programming System (For Problems with Linear Constraints)*, Department of Operations Research, Stanford University, Technical Report SOL 77-9.

Varian, H. (1982a), "Nonparametric Methods in Demand Analysis", *Economics Letters*, **9**, 23-29.

Varian, H. (1982b), "The Nonparametric Approach to Demand Analysis", *Econometrica*, **50**, 4, 945-973.

Varian, H. (1982c), "Trois Evaluations de l'Impact 'Social' d'un Changement de Prix", *Cahiers du Seminar d'Économétrie*, No. 24.

Varian, H. (1983a), "Nonparametric Tests of Consumer Behavior", *Review of Economic Studies*, 99-110.

Varian, H. (1983c), "Nonparametric Tests of Models of Investor Behavior", *Journal of Financial and Quantitative Analysis*, **18**, 3, 269-278.

Varian, H. (1984), "The Nonparametric Approach to Production Analysis", *Econometrica*, **52**, 3, 549-597 .

Woo, C. (1982), "The Nonparametric Approach to Production Analysis: a Case Study on a Regulated Electric Utility", Ph. D. Thesis, University of California at Davis.

Table 1
Alamitos

Year	Actual Fuel	Actual Labor	Actual Capital	Residual times 100	Residual times 100	Residual times 100
1	24150	55.00	33.27	0.01	0.00	0.00
2	26624	67.00	63.24	.00	0.00	0.00
3	50010	81.00	95.12	.00	0.00	0.00
4	48608	67.00	90.39	.00	0.00	0.00
5	56676	98.00	86.48	4.37	−0.15	1.94
6	52526	126.00	119.28	−4.00	−0.20	−2.68
7	88855	132.00	141.67	−1.03	−0.03	−0.53
8	97145	139.00	137.03	−6.32	−0.55	−4.42
9	95378	141.00	130.55	−3.23	−0.10	−2.74
10	98783	161.00	135.12	3.29	−0.12	−1.65
11	91613	158.00	128.72	0.49	0.24	−1.82
12	92427	156.00	122.53	−0.36	0.13	3.20
13	83392	154.00	116.54	.00	0.00	0.00
14	90072	149.00	111.56	.00	0.00	0.00
17	77048	140.00	99.49	.00	0.00	0.00
18	101445	143.00	94.59	2.63	0.30	3.81
19	88150	147.00	90.22	.00	0.00	0.00
20	111575	148.00	86.13	5.58	0.18	1.47
SSR				0.0136	0.0001	0.0710
SE				0.0275	0.0018	0.0199

Overall SSR = 0.0208   Overall SE = 0.0196   Critical value $\bar{\sigma} = 0.0005$

Table 2
Pittsburg

Year	Actual Fuel	Actual Labor	Actual Capital	Residual times 100	Residual times 100	Residual times 100
1	52336	100.00	110.22	0.57	0.01	0.40
2	76601	135.00	138.15	.00	0.00	0.00
3	70065	135.00	131.62	−4.80	−0.12	−2.92
4	63000	129.00	125.07	.00	0.00	.00
5	69602	129.00	116.44	0.96	0.03	0.52
6	55398	134.00	110.25	2.32	−1.62	−4.75
7	70906	127.00	104.78	3.86	0.09	1.85
8	52797	132.00	99.67	3.41	1.62	3.77
9	61286	133.00	94.15	.00	0.00	0.00
10	37792	139.00	89.42	.00	0.00	0.00
11	44233	152.00	85.16	.00	0.00	0.00
12	47155	157.00	81.08	.00	0.00	0.00
13	108952	163.00	146.41	−1.01	−0.03	−0.21
14	84772	170.00	145.69	.00	0.00	.00
17	105566	185.00	150.17	0.67	0.47	2.51
18	105935	199.00	155.81	0.37	−0.47	−2.39
19	82745	204.00	150.76	.00	0.00	.00
20	86842	209.00	142.48	.00	−0.00	.00
SSR				0.0058	0.0006	0.0061
SE				0.0179	.0056	0.0184

Overall SSR = 0.0125 Overall SE = 0.0152 Critical value $\overline{\sigma} = 0.0002$

Table 3
Comparison with Parametric Method

Plant	SSR Cobb–Douglas	SSR CES	SSR Nonparametric
Alamitos	12.359	1.0697	.0208
Pittsburg	6.444	.8704	.0125

Chapter 11

GOODNESS-OF-FIT IN OPTIMIZING MODELS

Conventional econometric tests of optimizing models typically involve embedding the optimizing model in a parametric specification and then examining the parametric restrictions imposed by the optimization hypothesis. The optimization hypothesis is rejected if the estimated parameters are significantly different, in the statistical sense, from the values implied by optimization. I argue that a more fruitful approach to testing optimizing behavior is to measure the departure from optimization using the estimated objective function, and see whether this departure is significant in an economic sense. I discuss procedures for doing this that can be used in several sorts of optimizing models, and give a detailed illustration in the case of aggregate demand estimation.

Much of economics rests on the principle of optimizing behavior. Firms are assumed to minimize costs and maximize profits; consumers are assumed to maximize utility, and so on. In the last several years, standard techniques have been developed to test these models of optimizing behavior. Suppose, for example, that we are attempting to test the hypothesis that a time series of observations on factor choices by a firm can be viewed as cost-minimizing behavior. A common approach would be to pick a parametric form for the underlying cost or production function, derive the associated set of factor demand functions, and then see if the estimated parameters satisfy the restrictions imposed by the model of cost minimization.

Similarly, if one wanted to test a set of data on consumer choices for consistency with utility maximization behavior, one would first specify a function form for the utility function, derive the associated set of utility-maximizing demand functions, estimate the parameters of these demand functions using the consumer choice data, and then see if these estimated parameters satisfy the restrictions imposed by the model of utility maximization.

In my view, these procedures are not very good ways to test models of optimizing behavior for two distinct reasons. First, there is often no need

I would like to thank Wei Li for programming assistance and Eduardo Ley for proofreading. This work was supported in part by the National Science Foundation. This paper was prepared for the conference on *Parametric and Nonparametric Approaches to Frontier Analysis*, held at the University of North Carolina, September 29–October 1, 1988.

to embed the optimizing model in a parametric framework. I argue below that it is perfectly possible to test reasonably complex models of optimization behavior without having to use parametric specifications. Second, testing parametric restrictions by using classical significance tests involve an overly restrictive sense of "significance." What matters for most purposes in economics is not whether a consumer's violation of the optimizing model is *statistically* significant, but whether it is *economically* significant. And the economic significance of a departure from optimizing behavior has nothing to do with whether or not estimated parameters pass or fail a test of statistical significance.

Hence the conventional methods are lacking in two senses: first, they have an excess reliance on parametric forms, and second, they test for statistically significant violations of optimization rather than economically significant violations. Let us examine each of these points in more detail.

11.1 Nonparametric tests of optimizing behavior

Suppose that we observe a set of price vectors, p^t, and net output vectors, y^t, for $t = 1, \ldots, T$ and want to test the hypothesis of period-by-period profit maximization. Then a necessary condition for these data to be consistent with profit maximization is that the following inequalities are satisfied:

$$p^t y^t \geq p^t y^s$$

for all pairs of observations s and t. These inequalities simply say that the profit from the observed choices must be at least as large as the profits from any other feasible choice. Varian (1984b) refers to this as the Weak Axiom of Profit Maximization (WAPM). Similar inequalities have been examined by several other authors including Afriat (1972) and Samuelson (1947).

It can also be shown that WAPM is a *sufficient* condition for profit maximization in the sense that any set of data that satisfies WAPM can be used to construct a "nice" production set that could have generated the observed behavior as optimizing behavior. See Varian (1984b) for details.

Hence a sensible test of optimizing behavior in this context is simply to see if the observed prices and net output vectors satisfy the inequalities implied by WAPM. If the data violate the inequalities then we can reject the model of optimizing behavior.

Suppose that we observe a set of data (w^t, x^t, y^t) for $t = 1, \ldots, T$, were w^t is a vector of factor prices, x^t is a vector of factor demands, and y^t is a (scalar) measure of output. We might be interested in testing the hypothesis that the firm that generated this data was minimizing the cost of producing the observed output.

If the firm is minimizing costs, it must satisfy the following set of inequalities

$$w^t x^t \leq w^t x^s \quad \text{for all } y^s \geq y^t.$$

These inequalities require that the cost of the observed production plan must be no greater than the cost of any other production plan that produces at least as much output. Varian (1984b) calls this the Weak Axiom of Cost Minimization (WACM).[1]

Again, this condition is necessary and sufficient for cost-minimizing behavior in the sense that if some data satisfy WACM then it is possible to construct a production set that would generate the observed choices as cost minimizing choices. It is very easy to apply this test to observed choices to see if they violate the inequalities; no appeal to parametric methods is required.

Finally, suppose that we observe some price vectors p^t and quantity vectors x^t, for $t = 1, \ldots, T$ and want to test the hypothesis that these data were generated by a utility maximizing consumer. Define the revealed preference relation R by $x^t R x^s$ if and only if there is some sequence of observations $x^r \ldots x^u$ such that $p^t x^t \geq p^t x^r, \ldots, p^u x^u \geq p^u x^s$. Then a set of data is consistent with the model of utility maximization if and only if it satisfies the Generalized Axiom of Revealed Preference (GARP),

$$x^t R x^s \text{ implies } p^s x^s \leq p^s x^t.$$

Again, this condition is easily tested; see Varian (1982a) for details.

Given that each of these classical models of optimizing behavior is easily tested by simply checking a set of inequalities, why do the conventional procedures use complicated statistical measures? Certainly the inequalities described above have been in the literature a long time. See Samuelson (1938), Afriat (1967), Diewert and Parkan (1985) and others.[2]

One explanation is that economists are simply not used to thinking about the implications of optimizing models for a finite set of observations. It is more natural for economists, perhaps, to think of the outcome of optimization to be an entire demand or supply *function*.

Another, perhaps more important explanation, is that the nonparametric tests described above are "sharp" tests: either the data pass the test *exactly*, or they don't. If the data don't satisfy the tests, the optimizing model is rejected: the tests do not allow for an "error term."

There have been some attempts to deal with this problem of the overly sharp nature of nonparametric tests. Banker and Maindiratta (1988) suggest finding the largest set of observations consistent with optimization.

---

[1] See Varian (1984b) for a discussion of the literature on this sort of test, which includes contributions from Samuelson (1947), Hanoch and Rothschild (1972) and Afriat (1972).

[2] For more recent work in nonparametric analysis of consumption behavior see Browning (1984), Bronars (1987), Deaton (1987) Green and Srivastava (1985), (1986), Houtman and Maks (1987), Landsburg (1981), Manser and McDonald (1988), and Varian (1982a), (1982b), (1984b), (1985), (1988).

Varian (1985) suggests finding the set of data that is nearest to the observed data in some appropriate norm.

Conventional statistical test *do* allow for an error term. To test the hypothesis that some relationship holds among some estimated parameters, we ask whether the value of some test statistic is likely or unlikely according to the sampling distribution of the parameters. Roughly speaking, the optimization model is rejected if the observed value of the test statistic is unlikely.

The problem with this procedure, in my view, is that it has little to do with the *economic* significance of the violation. For example, optimization of some particular parametric form may imply that two parameters should sum to one. If we test this hypothesis and reject it, we must reject the optimizing model. But what are we rejecting? Exact optimization implies that the two parameters must sum to *exactly* one. But *exact* optimization isn't a very interesting hypothesis. It is very unlikely that firms *exactly* maximize profits or minimize costs; it is even more unlikely that consumers *exactly* maximize utility. It is especially unlikely that consumers maximize some arbitrary parametric approximation to utility.

What we usually care about is whether optimization is a *reasonable* way to describe some behavior. For most purposes, "nearly optimizing behavior" is just as good as "optimizing" behavior.[3]

The conventional parametric tests miss this distinction: given enough data, we can always reject non-optimizing behavior, even if it is "nearly optimizing behavior." The value of the test statistic will typically give no clue as to whether the economic agent under examination is nearly optimizing or grossly non-optimizing.[4]

11.2 Goodness of fit measures

An alternative approach to testing optimizing behavior is to ask how large the violations of relevant inequalities are in terms of a reasonable *economic* norm. For example, suppose that we observe some violations of the Strong Axiom of Profit Maximization. That is, we observe a pair of observations s and t for which

$$p^t y^t < p^t y^s.$$

---

[3] See Akerlof and Yellen (1985) and Cochrane (1989) for interesting discussions of nearly optimizing behavior.

[4] A similar point is made by McCloskey (1985), (1989) in a somewhat different context. McCloskey points out that significance testing, as commonly used in economics, does not provide an appropriate measure of the "importance" of a variable in a regression. But McCloskey's critique applies more broadly; most statistical tests measure violations of a hypothesis in terms of the sampling distribution of the test statistic, and this is rarely a useful measure of the *importance* of the violation.

This inequality says that the firm could make more profit by choosing y^s when in fact it chose y^t. In this case, a reasonable measure of the magnitude of the violation of profit maximizing behavior is

$$r^{ts} - \frac{p^t(y^s - y^t)}{p^t y^t} = \frac{p^t y^s}{p^t y^t} - 1.$$

This is simply the percent *extra* profit that the firm could have made at the prices p^t if it had chosen the production vector y^s, rather than the production vector y^t.

The numbers r^{ts} should be interpreted as "residuals" appropriate for examining the optimization model. The best way to present these residuals might be to list the observations and indicate next to each one the magnitude of the foregone profit. Or, one might want to look at the average value of the foregone profit, or the largest value of the foregone profit. Any of these numbers would be a reasonable way to measure how "close" the observed behavior comes to profit maximizing behavior.

The case of cost minimization is almost the same. If we have a violation of WACM, we have two observations t and s such that

$$w^t x^t > w^t x^s \text{ for some } y^s \geq y^t.$$

In this case

$$\frac{w^t(x^t - x^s)}{w^t x^t} = 1 - \frac{w^t x^s}{w^t x^t}$$

is a reasonable measure of the departure from cost minimization. This number simply measures how much the firm could have saved if it had chosen x^s rather than x^t when it faced factor prices w^t. Again, one might choose the average value or the maximum value of this index as a measure of the degree of violation of maximization.

If these numbers are small then it seems reasonable to think of the firm under consideration as being "more-or-less" an optimizing firm.[5] True, it isn't exactly optimizing, but *exactly* optimizing behavior isn't a very plausible hypothesis to begin with.

In addition, the distribution of these measures of profit maximization or cost minimization may be of considerable interest themselves. Suppose, for example, that we are examining the case of profit maximization using data on a single firm, and we find that most violations of WAPM indicate that the firm would be better off at time t making a choice that was made at some later date. This suggests that technological progress or learning-by-doing may be involved: the more profitable choices weren't made at time t because they weren't feasible.

---

[5] How small is small? In general this depends on the problem at hand. The "magic number" of significance tests, 5%, is probably a reasonable choice.

Or suppose that we are examining cross-sectional data and we find that most of the violations of WAPM involve a single firm. This might be taken as evidence that this firm really doesn't have access to the same technology as the others. The *pattern* of violations can tell us a lot about what is going on in the data.

11.3 Consumer choice

The description of a reasonable measure of goodness-of-fit in the case of consumer choice is somewhat more involved. We follow the suggestion of Afriat (1967).

Afriat's measure is calculated in the following manner. For a given set of numbers (e^t), $t = 1, \ldots, T$, with $0 \le e^t \le 1$, define an extension of the standard direct revealed preference relation by

$$x^t \; R_e^0 \; x^s \text{ if and only if } e^t p^t x^t \ge p^t x^s.$$

If $e^t = 1$ this is the standard direct revealed preference relation; if $e^t = 0$ the relation is vacuous in the sense that observation t cannot be revealed preferred to any other observation. As e^t varies from 1 to 0 the number of observations revealed preferred to other observations monotonically decreases.

We refer to e^t as the *Afriat efficiency index* for observation t. It can be thought of as how much less the potential expenditure on a bundle x^s has to be before we will consider it worse than the observed choice x^t. If e^t is .90, for example, we will only count bundles whose cost is less than 90% of an observed choice as being revealed worse than that choice. Said another way: if e^t is .90 and x^s would cost only 5% less than x^t, we would not consider this a significant enough difference to conclude that x^t was preferred by the consumer to x^s. We are allowing the consumer a "margin of error" of $(1 - e^t)$.

Given an arbitrary set of data (p^t, x^t), let us choose a set of efficiency indices (e^t) that are as close as possible to 1 in some norm. If the data satisfy the revealed preference conditions exactly, then we can choose $e^t = 1$ for all $t = 1, \ldots, T$. If we choose $e^t = 0$ for all $t = 1, \ldots, T$, then the data vacuously satisfy the revealed preference conditions, since no observation is revealed preferred to any other. Thus for any reasonable norm, there will be some set of (e^t) that are as close as possible to 1 that will summarize "how close" the observed choices are to maximizing choices.

In Afriat's (1967) original treatment of this idea, he considered choosing a single e that applied to all observations, rather than a different e^t for each observation. The advantage of Afriat's original proposal is that it is much easier to compute a single index e than the multiple indices (e^t).

Houtman and Maks (1987) suggest the following binary search. Start with $e = 1$ and test for violations of revealed preference using Warshall's algorithm as described in Varian (1982a). If the data fail to satisfy the strong axiom, try $e = 1/2$. If $e = 1/2$ doesn't work, try $e = 1/4$. If $e = 1/2$ *does* work, try $e = 3/4$, and so on. After n revealed preference tests, you are within $1/2^n$ of the actual efficiency index.

Computing the set of efficiency indices that are as close as possible to 1 in some norm is substantially more difficult. If we choose a quadratic norm, for example, we would have so solve a problem such as:

$$F = \min_{(e^t)} \sum_{t=1}^{T} (e^t - 1)^2 \tag{11.1}$$

subject to the constraint that the revealed preference relation R_e satisfies the Generalized Axiom of Revealed Preference. This approach is significantly more demanding from a computational perspective.

11.4 A characterization of the efficiency indices

There is a characterization of the set of (e^t) that minimize some norm that will be useful in what follows. In order to describe it, we need some formal definitions.

As above, define the relation R_e^0 by $x^t \; R_e^0 \; x$ iff $e^t p^t x^t \geq p^t x$, and let R_e be the transitive closure of this relation. Then define $GARP_e$ to mean

$$x^s \; R_e \; x^t \text{ implies } e^t p^t x^t \leq p^t x^s.$$

If $e^t = 1$ for all t then this reduces to the standard definition of GARP.

Here is another way to state this definition: if some data (p^t, x^t, e^t) satisfy $GARP_e$, then

$$\text{for all } x^s \; R_e \; x^t \text{ we have } e^t p^t x^t \leq p^t x^s.$$

This statement can be written as

$$e^t \leq \frac{p^t x^s}{p^t x^t} \text{ for all } x^s \; R_e \; x^t.$$

If we attempt to choose a set of (e^t) that are on the average as close as possible to 1, then this inequality will typically be binding for *some* observation s so we have:

$$e^t = \min_{x^s R_e x^t} \frac{p^t x^s}{p^t x^t}. \tag{11.2}$$

Note that this is not really an "operational" way to determine e^t, since e^t is implicitly involved in the relation R_e. Nevertheless, the characterization is still useful, as we shall see shortly.

11.5 Parametric methods in production analysis

We have seen how to compute measures of goodness-of-fit for nonparametric methods to test models of profit maximization, cost minimization,
and utility maximization. However, the same methods can be used in a
parametric context.

Consider first the case of profit maximization. Let p^t be the price of
output and w^t the vector of factor prices in observation t. Let y^t be the
(scalar) output and x^t the vector of factor inputs in observation t. Suppose
that we estimate some parametric production function $y = f(x, \beta)$ where
β is a vector of parameters. Given an estimate of the parameters, $\hat{\beta}$, we
can calculate the maximal profits at each observation t, $\pi(p^t, w^t, \hat{\beta})$. We
can then compare the maximal profits from the estimated technology to
the actual profits:

$$\pi(p^t, \hat{\beta}) - (p^t y^t - w^t x^t).$$

The magnitude of this number measures the degree to which the observed
choice behavior at observation t fails to maximize the *estimated* production
function. Hence, it is a measure of how closely the observed production
function comes to approximating profit-maximizing behavior.

If we are interested in cost minimizing behavior, we would simply estimate the cost function implied by some parametric production function,
$c(w^t, y^t, \hat{\beta})$. The deviation from cost minimization is given by

$$w^t x^t - c(w^t, y^t, \hat{\beta}).$$

This is the difference between the actual costs incurred and the minimal
costs, conditional on the assumption that the true technology is of the
particular parametric form described by $f(x, \hat{\beta})$.

11.6 Parametric methods for consumption analysis

Suppose that one is willing to postulate that some observed demand behavior was generated by the maximization of a particular parametric utility
function $u(x, \beta)$, where β is a vector of parameters.

Given a parametric utility function $u(x, \beta)$, we can define the associated
money metric utility function, $m(p, x, \beta)$ by

$$m(p, x, \beta) = \min_{y} \ py$$

$$\text{s.t. } u(y, \beta) \geq u(x, \beta).$$

In words, the money metric utility function measures the minimum expenditure at prices p the consumer would need to be as well off as he would

be consuming the bundle x. For more on the money metric utility function see Samuelson (1974), King (1982), and Varian (1984a).

In terms of the money metric utility function an index of the degree of violation of utility maximizing behavior could be given by

$$i^t = \frac{m(p^t, x^t, \beta)}{p^t x^t}.$$

This index is closely related to the Afriat efficiency index. We can see this by writing i^t as:

$$i^t = \min_{u(x,\beta) \geq u(x^t,\beta)} \frac{p^t x}{p^t x^t}.$$

Note the similarity with equation 11.2; the only difference is that e^t uses the partial order over consumption bundles given by the revealed preference relation, while i^t uses the total order over consumption bundles given by the utility function.

This sort of money metric index is a very natural measure of how close the observed consumer choices come to maximizing a particular utility function $u(x,\beta)$. I suggest that it is a useful statistic to report as a goodness-of-fit measure in models of demand estimation.

As with most measures of goodness-of-fit, we can also use the money metric measure as a criterion to estimate the parameters in question. A natural estimate is to find that value of β that minimizes the degree of violation of maximizing behavior as measured by the values of the indices i^t. For example, one could try to minimize the sum of squares,

$$\sum_{t=1}^{T} (i^t)^2.$$

I believe that this sort of estimator has several desirable properties.

First, it uses a sensible *economic* norm for goodness-of-fit. Conventional estimators of demand parameters use the sum-of-squared errors of the observed and predicted quantities demand, or some variant on this. But this has little *economic* content; a large difference between predicted and observed demand can easily be consistent with a small difference in utility. This is depicted in Figure 1. Here the observed choice is far from the predicted choice in Euclidean distance, but quite close in terms of money metric utility. The model is a bad fit in terms of Euclidean distance, but a good fit in the sense that the consumer isn't that far from maximizing behavior in terms of money metric utility.

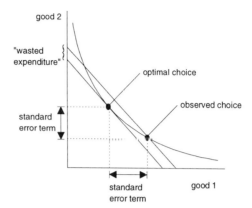

Figure 1. This is a good fit in terms of money metric utility although it is a bad fit in terms of the usual error terms.

Second, the minimized value of the objective function gives a meaningful economic measure of how close the observed choices are to maximizing choice for the particular parametric form involved. If the average value of e^t is .95, then it is meaningful to say that the observed choice behavior was 95 percent as efficient as maximizing behavior.

Third, the mechanics of the estimation problem may be much simpler than they are using the conventional approach. Economic theory imposes the restriction that a money metric utility function must be an increasing, linearly homogeneous, and concave function of prices. These constraints are not terribly difficult to impose on the maximization problem. By contrast theory implies that a system of demand equations must have a symmetric negative semidefinite Slutsky substitution matrix. Imposing this restriction involves imposing nonlinear cross-equation restrictions on a system of equations. In general this is a difficult thing to do.

Fourth, this same method can easily be applied to estimation of production relationships. If one starts with a null hypothesis of cost minimization, say, then it makes sense to measure the goodness-of-fit of estimation procedure by comparing the actual costs to the minimum costs implied by the estimated parameters. If it is thought that errors in optimization are a significant component of the error term, then it can make sense to estimate the parameters by choosing parameter estimates that minimize the difference between the observed costs and the minimum costs.

11.7 An example

In order to examine the money metric goodness-of-fit measure described in the last section, I tried an experiment using U.S. aggregate consumption data. The data were taken from the Citibank economic database and consisted of aggregate consumption of durables, nondurables, and services from 1947 to 1987.

Like most aggregate consumption data, these figures satisfy the Generalized Axiom of Revealed Preference. This is due to the fact that during the post-war period, most developed economies have experienced reasonably steady real growth: each year has generally been revealed preferred to the previous year and the data trivially satisfy the revealed preference restrictions. Hence the aggregate demand data are consistent with the maximization of utility of a representative consumer.

However, it may be of interest to ask how well common parametric forms of utility functions do in describing these data. It is typically the case that one can reject the restrictions imposed by maximization using parametric forms such as the translog utility function; see, for example, Christensen, Jorgenson and Lau (1975). But how large are these violations in terms of the *economic* norm described in the last section? In order to answer this question, I estimated the parameters of a Cobb-Douglas utility function and measured the goodness-of-fit using the money metric measure.

The Cobb-Douglas utility function is a convenient parametric form since it has a minimal number of parameters and it automatically satisfy the maximization restrictions. This means that our estimated goodness-of-fit measure will generally be an upper bound on the goodness-of-fit using a more flexible function form. For example, the Cobb-Douglas utility function is a special case of the translog utility function. Thus the "best fitting" Cobb-Douglas function will have at least as good a fit, in terms of our money-metric measure, as the best fitting translog function.

I estimated the parameters of a Cobb-Douglas utility system using three different techniques. The first technique was simply to take the average expenditure share of each good. The second technique was to estimate the regression $x_i = a_i e / p_i$, where e is the total expenditure on the three goods. I used Zellner's seemingly unrelated regression technique and imposed the normalization that $a_1 + a_2 + a_3 = 1$. (Estimating the three equations separately gave almost the same estimates.) The third technique was to determine the values of the parameters that maximized the goodness-of-fit, as measured by difference between the money metric utility and the actual expenditure. The first two methods are straightforward, but a description of the third method may be in order.

Let us derive the money metric utility function associated with the Cobb-Douglas utility function $u(x_1, x_2, x_3) = x_1^{a_1} x_2^{a_2} x_3^{a_3}$. For algebraic convenience we impose the normalization that the exponents sum to 1. The money metric utility function is defined to be the amount of money that it takes as some prices (p_1, p_2, p_3) to choose an optimal bundle that has the same utility as the bundle (x_1, x_2, x_3).

If we let m be the necessary amount of money, we have the equation

$$x_1^{a_1} x_2^{a_2} x_3^{a_3} = \left(\frac{a_1 m}{p_1}\right)^{a_1} \left(\frac{a_2 m}{p_2}\right)^{a_2} \left(\frac{a_3 m}{p_3}\right)^{a_3}$$

Solving for m we have

$$m(p, x) = a_1^{-a_1} a_2^{-a_2} a_3^{-a_3} (p_1 x_1)^{a_1} (p_2 x_2)^{a_2} (p_3 x_2)^{a_3} \qquad (11.3)$$

(For a different derivation, see Varian (1984a), page 129.) Taking logs, we can write this equation as

$$\ln m(p, x) = -a_1 \ln a_1 - a_2 \ln a_2 - a_3 \ln a_3 + a_1 \ln p_1 x_1 + a_2 \ln p_2 x_2 + a_3 \ln p_3 x_3. \qquad (11.4)$$

We suppose that the log of the actual expenditure in period t, $\ln e^t$, is equal to the log of the expenditure minimizing amount, $\ln m(p^t, x^t)$, plus an error term representing the optimization error. Using equation (11.4), we have

$$\ln e^t = -a_1 \ln a_1 - a_2 \ln a_2 - a_3 \ln a_3 + a_1 \ln p_1^t x_1^t + a_2 \ln p_2^t x_2^t + a_3 \ln p_3^t x_3^t + \epsilon^t.$$

I estimated this equation using the nonlinear least squares routine in MicroTSP, imposing the restriction that $a_1 + a_2 + a_3 = 1$. The results from the three estimation methods are in Table 1.

Table 1			
Estimated Parameter Values			
Method	a_1	a_2	a_3
Expenditure shares	0.152	0.461	0.387
Regression	0.129	0.358	0.413
Nonlinear Least Squares	0.150	0.472	0.378

The first thing to observe is that the three methods give somewhat different answers. This is simply a consequence of the fact that the estimates which "fit the data best" depend on what measure of goodness-of-fit you use. The regression estimates that minimizes the sum of squared deviations from the observed demands will not in general be the same as the estimates that minimize the squared difference between money metric utility and actual expenditure.

It is surprising that the expenditure share method and the money metric method give very similar estimates, especially since the expenditure share estimate involves a system of equations while the money metric estimation involves only a single equation. Of course, ultimately it is a single sum-of-squares that is minimized in the regression technique, so perhaps this is not so surprising after all.

The computed values of the money metric utility function for each of the different parameters are given in Table 2, along with the percentage difference between money metric utility and the actual expenditure for each of the three different estimation methods.

Note that these percent differences are very small, at least for the expenditure share estimates and the NLS estimates. Using the expenditure share methods the largest difference is 7.4%, and the majority of the differences are less than one percent. The average difference is 2%. This suggests that the observed aggregate demand behavior is not very different from optimizing behavior, at least when measured in units of "wasted expenditure."[6]

Similar results hold for the nonlinear least squares estimates. Here the average value of the error is only 1.9%. The regression estimates do much poorer, resulting in an average error of about 5%.

It is worth noting that the residuals in all of the estimates are positive in each observation; this is as it should be if the optimizing model is to make any sense since the minimum expenditure to achieve a given level of utility must always be less than an arbitrary expenditure.

A closer examination of the index shows the limitations of the Cobb-Douglas functional form. The Cobb-Douglas form requires that expenditure shares remain constant, while the data clearly show that the share of services in expenditure has significantly increased. Obviously, a more flexible functional form would be appropriate for these data.

To the extent that a more flexible functional form would fit the data better than the Cobb-Douglas form, our goodness-of-fit measure should be regarded as an upper bound on "wasted expenditure." If the average "wasted expenditure" in the Cobb-Douglas case is less than 2%, it would be even less if we used a more flexible functional form.

References

Afriat, S. (1967) "The Construction of a Utility Function from Expenditure Data," *International Economic Review*, **8**, 67–77.

---

[6] Cochrane (1989) independently adopted a similar approach to examining tests of intertemporal consumption models. He finds that the deviation of actual consumption from the optimal intertemporal allocation of consumption is on the order of 30 cents per month—a remarkably small number. Cochrane also discusses the distinction between statistical significance and economic significance in much the same terms as I do.

Afriat, S. (1972) "Efficiency Estimates of Production Functions," *International Economic Review*, **8**, 568–598.

Akerlof, G. and J. Yellen (1985) "Can Small Deviations from Rationality Make Significant Differences to Economic Equilibria?," *American Economic Review*, **75**, 708–720.

Banker, R. and A. Maindiratta (1988) "Nonparametric Analysis of Technical and Allocative Efficiencies in Production," *Econometrica*, **56**, 1315-1332.

Bronars, S. (1987) "The Power of Nonparametric Tests," *Econometrica*, **55**, 3, 693–698.

Browning, M. (1984) "A Non-Parametric Test of the Life-Cycle Rational Expectations Hypothesis," *International Economic Review*, **30**, 979–992.

Christensen, L., Jorgensen, D. and Lau, L. (1975) "Transcendental Logarithmic Utility Functions," *American Economic Review*, **65**, 367–383.

Cochrane, J. (1989) "The Sensitivity of Tests of Intertemporal Allocation of Consumption to Near-Rational Alternatives," *American Economic Review*, **79**, 319–337.

Deaton, A. (1987) "Life-cycle models of consumption: is the evidence consistent with the theory?," in *Advances in Econometrics — Fifth World Congress, volume II*, ed. T. Bewley. Cambridge, England: Cambridge University Press.

Diewert, E. and C. Parkan (1985) "Tests for Consistency of Consumer Data and Nonparametric Index Numbers," *Journal of Econometrics*, **30**, 127–147.

Green, R. and S. Srivastava (1985) "Risk Aversion and Arbitrage," *Journal of Finance*, **40**, 1, 257–268.

Green, R. and S. Srivastava (1986) "Expected Utility Maximization and Demand Behavior," *Journal of Economic Theory*, **38**, 2, 313–323.

Hanoch, G. and Rothschild, M. (1972) "Testing the Assumptions of Production Theory: a Nonparametric Approach," *Journal of Political Economy*, **8**, 256–272.

Houtman, M. and J. Maks (1987) "The Existence of Homothetic Utility Functions Generating Dutch Consumer Data," University of Groningen.

King, M. (1982) "Welfare Analysis of Tax Reforms Using Household Data," *Journal of Public Economics*, **21**, 183–214.

Landsburg, S. (1981) "Taste Change in the United Kingdom, 1900–1955," *Journal of Political Economy*, **89**, 92–104.

Manser, M. and R. McDonald (1988) "An Analysis of Substitution Bias in Measuring Inflation, 1959–85," *Econometrica*, **56**, 909–930.

McCloskey, D. (1985) "The Loss Function Has Been Mislaid: The Rhetoric of Significance Tests," *American Economic Review*, **75**, 201–205.

McCloskey, D. (1989) "Formalism In Economics, Rhetorically Speaking," *Ricerche Economniche*, **43**, 57–75.

Samuelson, P. (1938) "A Note on the Pure Theory of Consumer Behavior," *Economica*, **5**, 61–71.

Samuelson, P. (1947) *Foundations of Economic Analysis*. Camridge, MA: Harvard University Press.

Samuelson, P. (1974) "Complementarity: an Essay on the 40th Anniversary of the Hicks-Allen Revolution in Demand Theory," *Journal of Economic Literature*, **12**, 4, 1255–1289.

Varian, H. (1982a) "The Nonparametric Approach to Demand Analysis," *Econometrica*, **50**, 4, 945–972.

Varian, H. (1982b) "Nonparametric Test of Models of Consumer Behavior," *Review of Economic Studies*, **50**, 99–110.

Varian, H. (1984a) *Microeconomic Analysis*. New York: W. W. Norton & Co.

Varian, H. (1984b) "The Nonparametric Approach to Production Analysis," *Econometrica*, **52**, 3, 579–597.

Varian, H. (1985) "Nonparametric Analysis of Optimizing Behavior with Measurement Error," *Journal of Econometrics*, **30**, 445–458.

Varian, H. (1988) "Revealed Preference with a Subset of Goods," *Journal of Economic Theory*, **46**, 179–185.

	**Table 2**
	Comparison of estimation techniques
Year	Actual expenditure	Shares m_1	Regress m_2	NLS m_3	Shares $1 - m_1/e$	Regress $1 - m_2/e$	NLS $1 - m_3/e$
1947	3855	3568	3117	3600	0.074	0.191	0.066
1948	4462	4132	3609	4169	0.074	0.191	0.066
1949	4470	4235	3755	4265	0.053	0.160	0.046
1950	4876	4637	4129	4666	0.049	0.153	0.043
1951	5534	5249	4658	5286	0.052	0.158	0.045
1952	5872	5634	5057	5670	0.041	0.139	0.034
1953	6257	6088	5543	6120	0.027	0.114	0.022
1954	6576	6444	5924	6474	0.020	0.099	0.015
1955	7285	7149	6585	7177	0.019	0.096	0.015
1956	7816	7713	7163	7740	0.013	0.084	0.010
1957	8537	8441	7867	8469	0.011	0.079	0.008
1958	9048	8979	8436	9006	0.008	0.068	0.005
1959	9939	9881	9318	9904	0.006	0.063	0.004
1960	10560	10525	10002	10545	0.003	0.053	0.001
1961	11019	10996	10517	11014	0.002	0.046	0.000
1962	11933	11915	11423	11930	0.002	0.043	0.000
1963	12785	12767	12290	12777	0.001	0.039	0.001
1964	13914	13894	13414	13901	0.001	0.036	0.001
1965	15350	15319	14793	15325	0.002	0.036	0.002
1966	17163	17135	16550	17143	0.002	0.036	0.001
1967	18581	18554	18038	18555	0.001	0.029	0.001
1968	21431	21380	20804	21376	0.002	0.029	0.003
1969	24340	24282	23729	24272	0.002	0.025	0.003
1970	27471	27389	26961	27372	0.003	0.019	0.004
1971	31294	31124	30829	31082	0.005	0.015	0.007
1972	35846	35591	35382	35531	0.007	0.013	0.009
1973	42530	42374	41812	42341	0.004	0.017	0.004
1974	50710	50507	49743	50503	0.004	0.019	0.004
1975	61383	61131	60316	61113	0.004	0.017	0.004
1976	72478	72090	71506	72012	0.005	0.013	0.006
1977	85701	85969	84889	84822	0.009	0.009	0.010
1978	102261	101237	101465	101043	0.010	0.008	0.012
1979	124104	122988	123047	122804	0.009	0.009	0.010
1980	148952	146795	148177	146525	0.014	0.005	0.016
1981	180406	177153	179803	176757	0.018	0.003	0.020
1982	205088	199545	204941	198908	0.027	0.001	0.030
1983	232873	255046	232866	224161	0.034	0.000	0.037
1984	263642	253883	263598	252772	0.037	0.000	0.041
1985	294808	282220	294461	279813	0.046	0.001	0.051
1986	322488	304152	321354	302408	0.057	0.004	0.062
1987	358848	331047	351875	329083	0.064	0.006	0.070
				Mean	0.020	0.052	0.019

Chapter 12

A MODEL OF SALES

I present a model in which firms randomize the price at which they offer their product in an attempt to price discriminate between informed and uninformed consumers. This price randomization can be interpreted as "sales."

Economists have belatedly come to recognize that the "law of one price" is no law at all. Most retail markets are instead characterized by a rather large degree of price dispersion. The challenge to economic theory is to describe how such price dispersion can persist in markets where at least some consumers behave in a rational manner. Starting with the seminal paper of George Stigler, a number of economic theorists have proposed models to describe this phenomenon of equilibrium price dispersion. See, for example, Gerard Butters, John Pratt, David Wise, and Richard Zeckhauser, Michael Rothschild, Steven Salop, Salop and Joseph Stiglitz (1977), Yuval Shilony, Stiglitz, and Louis Wilde and Alan Schwartz.

Most of the models of price dispersion referred to above are concerned with analyzing "spatial" price dispersion; that is, a situation where several stores contemporaneously offer an identical item at different prices. A nice example of such a model is the "bargains and ripoffs" paper of Salop and Stiglitz (1977). They consider a market with two kinds of consumers; the "informed" consumers know the entire distribution of offered prices, while the "uninformed" consumers know nothing about the distribution of prices. Hence the informed consumers always go to a low-priced store, while the uninformed consumers shop at random. The stores have identical U-shaped cost curves and behave as monopolistically competitive price setters. Salop and Stiglitz show that for some parameter configurations, the market equilibrium takes a form where some fraction of the stores sell at the competitive price (minimum average cost) and some fraction sell at a higher price. The high-price stores' clientele consists only of uninformed consumers, but there is a sufficiently large number of them to keep the stores in business.

Research support by the National Science Foundation and the Guggenheim Memorial Foundation is gratefully acknowledged. Helpful comments were received from James Adams, Paul Courant, Vincent Crawford, and John Panzar. Research assistance was provided by Todd Lanski. Corrections from "Errata: A Model of Sales," *American Economic Review*, 71 (3), June 1980, 517, have been incorporated.

In the Salop and Stiglitz model – as in all the models of spatial price dispersion – some stores are supposed to *persistently* sell their product at a lower price than other stores. If consumers can learn from experience, this persistence of price dispersion seems rather implausible.

An alternative type of price dispersion might be called "temporal" price dispersion. In a market exhibiting temporal price dispersion, we would see each store varying its price over time. At any moment, a cross section of the market would exhibit price dispersion; but because of the intentional fluctuations in price, consumers cannot learn by experience about stores that consisltently have low prices, and hence price dispersion may be expected to persist.

One does not have to look far to find the real world analog of such behavior. It is common to observe retail markets where stores deliberately change their prices over time – that is, where stores have *sales*. A casual glance at the daily newspaper indicates that such behavior is very common. A high percentage of advertising seems to be directed at informing people of limited duration sales of food, clothing, and appliances.

Given the prevalence of sales as a form of retailing, it is surprising that so little attention has been paid to sales in the literature of economic theory. In fact, I know of no work in economic theory that *explicitly* examines the rationale of price dispersion by means of sales.[1] However, the work of Shilony does provide an implicit rationale for the use of sales as a marketing device. Shilony examines an oligopolistic market where consumers can purchase costlessly from neighborhood stores, but incur a "search cost" if they venture to more distant stores in search of a lower price. He shows that no Nash equilibrium exists in pure pricing strategies. On the other hand, Shilony does establish the existence of an equilibrium mixed strategy – that is, a strategy where firms randomize their prices. Such a strategy could be interpreted as stores having randomly chosen sales.

In this paper, I explicitly address the question of sales equilibria. The model may be regarded as a combination of the Salop-Stiglitz and the Shilony models described above. As in the Salop-Stiglitz model, it will be assumed that there are informed and uninformed consumers. As in the Shilony model, I will allow for the possibility of randomized pricing strategies by stores. I will be interested in characterizing the equilibrium behavior in such markets.

In the model to be described below, firms engage in sales behavior in an attempt to price discriminate between informed and uninformed customers. This is of course only one aspect of real world sales behavior. Other reasons for sales behavior might include inventory costs, cyclical fluctuations in costs or demand, loss leader behavior, advertising behavior, and so on. The theoretical examination of these motives is left for future work.

---

[1]   Salop and Stiglitz' 1976 paper is concerned with "spatial" price dispersion rather than temporal price dispersion.

12.1 The model

Let us suppose there is a large number of consumers who each desire to purchase, at most, one unit of some good. The maximum price any consumer will pay for the good – a consumer's reservation price – will be denoted by r. Consumers come in two types, informed and uninformed.[2] Uninformed consumers shop for the item by choosing a store at random; if the price of the item in that store is less than r, the consumer purchases it. Informed consumers, on the other hand, know the whole distribution of prices, and in particular they know the lowest available price at any time. Hence, they go to the store with the lowest price and purchase the item there.

One might think of a model where stores advertise their sale prices in the weekly newspaper. Informed consumers read the newspaper and uninformed consumers do not. Let $I > 0$ be the number of informed consumers, and $M > 0$ the number of uninformed consumers. Let n be the number of stores, and let $U = M/n$ be the number of uninformed consumers per store.

Each store has a density function $f(p)$ which indicates the probability with which it charges each price p. In its choice of this pricing strategy, each firm takes as given the pricing strategies chosen by the other firms and the demand behavior of the consumers. Only the case of a symmetric equilibrium will be examined, where each firm chooses the same pricing strategy.[3]

Each week, each store randomly chooses a price according to its density function $f(p)$. A store succeeds in its sale if it turns out to have the lowest price of the n prices being offered. In this case the store will get $I + U$ customers. If a store fails to have the lowest price, it will get only its share of uninformed customers, namely U. If two or more stores charge the lowest price, it will be considered a tie, and the low-price stores will each get an equal share of the informed customers.

Finally the stores are characterized by identical, strictly declining average cost curves.[4] The cost curve of a representative firm will be denoted by $c(q)$. It will be assumed that entry occurs until (expected) profits are driven to zero. Thus we will be examining a symmetric monopolistically competitive equilibrium in pricing strategies.

---

[2] For now, the uninformed-informed distinction is exogenously given. The decision to become informed or uninformed will be examined in Section III.

[3] Some justification for this symmetry assumption is given by Proposition 9 in the Appendix.

[4] The motivation for this assumption is the casual observation that retail stores are characterized by fixed costs of rent and sales force, plus constant variable costs – the wholesale cost – of the item being sold.

12.2 The analysis

The maximum number of customers a store can get is $I+U$. Let $p^* = c(I+U)/(I+U)$ be the average cost associated with this number of customers.

PROPOSITION 1. $f(p) = 0$ *for* $p > r$ *or* $p < p^*$.

Proof. No price above the reservation price will be charged since there is zero demand at any such price. No price less that p will be charged since only negative profits can result from such a price.

PROPOSITION 2.   *There is no symmetric equilibrium where all stores charge the same price.*

Proof. Suppose that all stores were charging a single price with $r \overset{\geq}{=} p > p^*$. Then a slight cut in price by one of the stores would capture all of the informed market, and thus make a positive profit. If all stores were charging p^*, each would get an equal share of the market and thus be making negative profits.

Proposition 2 is simply a variant of the well-known argument that declining average cost curves and "competitive" behavior are incompatible. I therefore concentrate on establishing the nature of a price-randomizing solution. Recall that p is a *point mass* of a probability density function f if there is positive probability concentrated at p.

PROPOSITION 3.   *There are no point masses in the equilibrium pricing strategies.*[5]

Proof. The intuition of this argument is seen to be quite straightforward. If some price p were charged with positive probability, there would be a positive probability of a tie at p.

If a deviant store charged a slightly lower price, $p - \epsilon$, with the same probability with which the other stores charged p, it would lose profits on order ϵ, but gain a fixed positive amount of profits when the other stores tied. Thus for small ϵ its profits would be positive, contradicting the assumption of equilibrium.

Let us proceed to a detailed formulation of this argument. First note that p can never be charged with positive probability, for when p is the lowest price charged, profits are zero, and if there is a tie at p, profits are negative. Suppose then that $p > p^*$ is charged with positive probability.

The number of points of positive mass in any probability distribution must be countable so we can find an arbitrarily small ϵ such that $p - \epsilon$

---

[5] Proposition 9 in the Appendix provides a partial converse to this assertion.

is charged with probability 0. Consider what happens if we charge $p - \epsilon$ with the probability with which we used to charge p, and charge p with probability 0. The increase in profits will be

$$Pr(P_i > p - \epsilon \text{ all } i, P_i \neq p \text{ any } i)((p - \epsilon)(I + U) - c(I + U))$$
$$-Pr(P_i > p \text{ all } i)(p(I + U) - c(I + U))$$
$$+Pr(p_i < p - \epsilon \text{ some } i)((p - \epsilon)U - c(U))$$
$$Pr(P_i < p \text{ some } i)(pU - c(U))$$
$$+ \sum_{k=2}^{n} Pr(P_i \geq p - \epsilon \text{ all } i, P_i = p \text{ for } k \text{ stores})$$
$$((p - \epsilon)(I + U) - c(I + U))$$
$$- \sum_{k=2}^{n} Pr(P_i > p \text{ all } i, P_i = p \text{ for } k \text{ stores})$$
$$(p(U + I/k) - c(U + I/k))$$

As ϵ approaches zero, the sum of the first four terms approaches zero, while the sum of the last two terms remains a positive number. Hence for small ϵ profits are positive, contradicting the assumption of an equilibrium strategy.

Proposition 3 expresses the essential difference between models of spatial price dispersion and models of temporal price dispersion. Most models of spatial price dispersion, such as the Salop-Stiglitz model or the Wilde-Schwartz model, have equilibria with specific prices being charged with positive probability mass. The above argument shows that such strategies cannot be profit-maximizing Nash behavior in a temporal randomizing model.

Since there are no point masses in the equilibrium density, the cumulative distribution function will be a continuous function on (p^*, r). Let $F(p)$ be the cumulative distribution function for $f(p)$; thus $f(p) = F'(p)$ almost everywhere.

We can now construct the expected profit function for a representative store. When a store charges price p, exactly two events are relevant. It may be that p is the smallest price being charged, in which case, the given store gets all of the informed customers. This event happens only if all the other stores charge prices higher than p, an event which has probability $(1 - F(p))^{n-1}$. On the other hand, there may be some store with a lower price, in which case the store in question only gets its share of the uninformed customers. This event happens with probability $1 - (1 - F(p))^{n-1}$. (By Proposition 3 we can neglect the probability of any ties.) Hence the expected profit of a representative store is

$$\int_{p^*}^{r} \left\{ \pi_s(p)(1 - F(p))^{n-1} + \pi_f(p) \left[1 - (1 - F(p))^{n-1}\right] \right\} f(p) dp$$

where

$$\pi_s(p) = p(U + I) - c(U + I)$$
$$\pi_f(p) = pU - c(U)$$

The maximization problem of the firm is to choose the density function $f(p)$ so as to maximize expected profits subject to the constraints:

$$f(p) \geq 0; \qquad \int_{p^*}^{r} f(p) dp = 1$$

It is clear that all prices that are charged with positive density must yield the same expected profit; for if some price yields a greater profit than some other price it would pay to increase the frequency with which the more profitable price were charged. Since we require zero profits due to free entry, this common level of profit must be zero.[6] This argument yields

PROPOSITION 4.   *If $f(p) > 0$, then*

$$\pi_s(p)(1 - F(p))^{n-1} + \pi_f(p) \left[1 - (1 - F(p))^{n-1}\right] = 0$$

(Of course, Proposition 4 also follows directly from the application of the Kuhn-Tucker theorem to the specified maximization problem.) Rearranging this equation, we have a formula for the equilibrium cumulative distribution function:

$$1 - F(p) = \left(\frac{\pi_f(p)}{\pi_f(p) - \pi_s(p)} \right)^{\frac{1}{n-1}}$$

Note that the denominator of this fraction is negative for any p between p^* and r. Hence the numerator must be negative so that profits in the event of failure are definitely negative. The construction of $(1 - F(p))^{n-1}$ is illustrated in Figure 1. At each p where $f(p) > 0$ we can construct $\pi_f(p)$ and $\pi_s(p)$ as illustrated and take the relevant ratio. Proposition 4 gives us an explicit expression for the equilibrium distribution function at those values of p where $f(p) > 0$. If this is to be a legitimate candidate for a cumulative distribution function, it should be an increasing function of p. This is easy to verify:

---

[6] One can also formulate the model with a fixed number of firms. In this case, expected profits must be equal to $\Pi_f(r)$.

PROPOSITION 5. $\pi_f(p)/(\pi_f(p) - \pi_s(p))$ *is strictly decreasing in p.*

Proof. Taking the derivative it suffices to show that

$$(\pi_f(p) - \pi_s(p))\, U - \pi_f(p)(-I) < 0$$

Using the definitions of π_f and π_s this can be rearranged to yield

$$\frac{c(I + U)}{I + U} < \frac{c(U)}{U}$$

which is obvious since average cost has been assumed to strictly decrease.

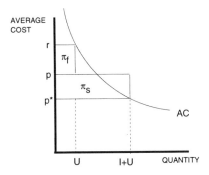

Figure 1. Graphical determination of $\pi_s(p)$ and $\pi_f(p)$.

Of course, Proposition 4 characterizes the equilibrium density function only for those prices where $f(p) > 0$. In order to fully characterize the equilibrium behavior, we need to establish which prices are charged with positive density.

First, it is clear that prices close to p^* must be charged with positive density:

PROPOSITION 6. $F(p^* + \epsilon) > 0$ *for any* $\epsilon > 0$.

Proof. If not, some store could charge $p^* + \epsilon/2$, and thereby undercut the rest of the market and make positive profits.

Similarly we can characterize the behavior of $f(p)$ near its upper limit.

PROPOSITION 7. $F(r - \epsilon) < 1$ *for any* $\epsilon > 0$

Proof.[7] Suppose not, and let $\hat{p} < r$ be the highest price that is ever charged so that $F(\hat{p}) = 1$. When p is charged, the store will only get the uninformed

---

[7] A heuristic proof is presented here and a more rigorous proof in the Appendix. The same holds true for Proposition 8.

customers since with probability 1 some other store will be charging a lower price. Since the store must get zero expected profits at each price charged, we must have $\hat{p}U - c(U) = 0$. But then $rU - c(U) > 0$, so charging r with probability 1 could make a positive profit.

Propositions 6 and 7 show that prices near p^* and r are charged with positive density. It is now easy to show:

PROPOSITION 8.   *There is no gap* (p_1, p_2) *where* $f(p) \equiv 0$.

Proof. If not, let $p_1 < \hat{p} < p_2$ Now $\hat{p}$ succeeds in being the lowest price in exactly the same circumstances that p_1 succeeds in being the lowest price; namely, when all other prices are greater than p_2. Similarly, $\hat{p}$ fails to be the lowest price when some store charges a price less than p_1, in which case p_1, also fails to be the lowest price. But in each circumstance, since $\hat{p} > p_1$, $\hat{p}$ will make larger profits than p_1. Since p_1, must make zero profits, this shows that charging $\hat{p}$ with probability 1 will make positive profits.

We now have a complete characterization of the equilibrium density: $f(p) > 0$ for all p in (p^*, r) and $f(p) = F'(p)$, where

$$F(p) = 1 - \left(\frac{\pi_f(p)}{\pi_f(p) - \pi_s(p)} \right)^{\frac{1}{n-1}} \tag{1}$$

We can also solve for the endogenous variables n and p^*. First, note that if a store charges r, it only gets the uninformed customers, and profits must therefore satisfy $\pi_f(r) = 0$. Similarly, if a store charges p^* it gets all the informed customers with probability 1 so $\pi_s(p^*) = 0$. These two equations can be used to determine n and p^*.

As an example, let us compute the equilibrium density when the cost function has fixed cost $k > 0$ and zero marginal cost. Then

$$\pi_s(p) = p(I + U) - k \tag{2}$$

$$\pi_f(p) = pU - k \tag{3}$$

Since $\pi_f(r) = 0$, and $U = M/n$

$$rM/n - k = 0 \tag{4}$$

or

$$n = rM/k \tag{5}$$

Thus

$$U = M/n = k/r \tag{6}$$

Since $\pi_s(p^*) = 0$ we have

$$p^* \left(I + \frac{k}{r} \right) - k = 0$$

or

$$p^* = \frac{k}{I + k/r} \tag{7}$$

The equilibrium distribution function can be found by substituting (2) and (3) into (1). We have

$$F(p) = 1 - \left(\frac{k - pU}{pI}\right)^{\frac{1}{n-1}} \tag{8}$$

Substituting from (6) and rearranging, we find

$$F(p) = 1 - [(k/I)(1/p - 1/r)]^{\frac{1}{n-1}} \tag{9}$$

The equilibrium density function is found by differentiating (9):

$$f(p) = F'(p) \tag{10}$$
$$= \frac{(k/I)^{\frac{1}{n-1}}}{n-1} \frac{(1/p - 1/r)^{\frac{1}{n-1} - 1}}{p^2}$$

Let

$$m = 1 - \frac{1}{n-1} = \frac{n-2}{n-1} = \frac{rM - 2k}{rM - k} \tag{11}$$

Then $f(p)$ can be written as

$$f(p) = \frac{k(k/I)^{1-m}}{(rM - k)} \frac{1}{p^{2-m}(1 - p/r)^m} \tag{12}$$

If n is reasonably large, m will be approximately 1, so $f(p)$ will be proportional to

$$\frac{1}{p(1 - p/r)} \tag{13}$$

This density is illustrated in Figure 2. Note that stores tend to charge extreme prices with higher probability than they charge intermediate prices. This seems intuitively plausible; a store would like to discriminate in its pricing and charge informed customers p^* (to keep their business) and charge uninformed customers r (to exploit their surplus). Since they are required to sell to all consumers at the same price this tendency shows up in the U-shaped density of prices.

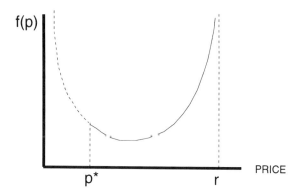

Figure 2. Graph of $f(p) = 1/p(1 - p/r)$.

The relevant part of the density is of course that part between p^* and r. Referring to equation (7) we see that if fixed costs are small, or the number of informed consumers is large, p^* will be small. Hence low prices will be charged a high percentage of the time. In some sense the market will be more competitive. On the other hand, the influence of the uninformed consumers is never entirely absent, since high prices will always be charged for some fraction of the time.

It is of interest to calculate the average price paid by the informed and the uninformed consumers under the equilibrium price density. The average price the uninformed consumers pay is simply:

$$\bar{p} = \int_{p^*}^{r} pf(p)dp$$

If we integrate this by parts we have

$$\bar{p} = r - \int_{p^*}^{r} F(p)dp$$

Substituting from (9)

$$\bar{p} = p^* + \left(\frac{k}{I}\right)^{\frac{1}{n-1}} \int_{p^*}^{r} \left(\frac{1}{p} - \frac{1}{r}\right)^{\frac{1}{n-1}} dp \tag{14}$$

There seems to be no simple expression for the integral in (14). However in the duopoly case (where $n = 2$) the expression becomes rather trivial. Suppose for example that we have $r = 1$, $M = 2$, $I = 1$, $k = 1$. Then by (5) we have $n = 2$, and by (7), $p^* = .5$. Substituting into (14),

$$\bar{p} = .5 + \int_{.5}^{1} \left(\frac{1}{p} - 1\right) dp = -\ln .5 \simeq .69 \tag{15}$$

Let us denote the price paid by the informed customers by p_{min}. Then the density function of p_{min} is just

$$f_{min}(p) = n(1 - F(p))^{n-1}f(p)$$

Substituting from (9)

$$f_{min}(p) = \frac{nk}{I}(1/p - 1/r)f(p)$$

Thus, using (5)

$$\bar{p}_{min} = \frac{nk}{I} \int_{p^*}^{r} p(1/p - 1/r)f(p)dp$$

$$= \frac{M}{I}(r - \bar{p}) \qquad (16)$$

For the example given above, $\bar{p}_{min} = .62$.

Table 1 presents the results of the comparative statics computations. The signs are for the most part as expected. The response of price to an increase in the number of uninformed consumers is particularly interesting. It can be shown that both the average price and the minimum price increase with M, which means both the informed and the uninformed consumers consumers pay more as the number of uninformed consumers increases, demonstrating the detrimental externalities that noneconomizing behavior can impose.[8]

Table 1 – Summary of Comparative Statics

	k	I	M	r	λ
p^*	+	−	0	+	−
n	−	0	+	+	−
$F(p)$	?	+	−	−	+
$\bar{p}$	?	−	+	+	−
$\bar{p}_{min}$	?	?	+	?	?

Note: K = fixed costs, I = number of informed consumers, M = number of uniformed consumers, r = reservation prices, and λ = fraction of informed consumers: $\lambda = I/(I + M)$.

[8] See Morgan, John and Martin Sefton, "A Model of Sales: Comment," Woodrow Wilson School, Princeton University.

12.3 Does it pay to be informed?

The model presented above takes the informed and uninformed consumers as exogenously given. However, the decision to become informed or uninformed can easily be made endogenous. Following the Salop-Stiglitz example, let us now suppose that it is possible to become fully informed about the available prices in the market by paying a fixed cost c. We think of this as the cost involved in reading newspaper advertisements, processing the information, and so on. Further, suppose that there are two types of consumers: one group has "search costs" c_2 and the other has search costs c_1, with $c_2 \geq c_1$.

The decision to be informed or uninformed now depends on the "full price" one pays to purchase the product in question. An uninformed person pays $\bar{p}$ on the average while an informed person pays $p_{min} + c_i$, $i = 1, 2$. In order for the equilibrium to be a full equilibrium, neither the informed, nor the uninformed group should find it in their interest to change their behavior.

For example, suppose $c_2 > c_1 = 0$. Then the low-cost consumers will always be informed. If the high-cost customers also find it in their interest to be informed no equilibrium will exist.[9] It is in the interest of the high-cost consumers to remain uninformed if $\bar{p} < \bar{p}_{min} + c_2$. Using the results of (15) and (16), this reduces to $\bar{p} < k(1 - \bar{p}/r)/I + c_2$, or $\bar{p}/r < (k + c_2 I)/(k + rI)$. If c_2 is greater than r, for example, this condition will certainly be satisfied.

12.4 Some suggestive evidence

The prediction of a J-shaped distribution of prices is quite dramatic, and it is worth looking at some data to see if this holds true in practice. To do so, I examined the advertised prices for 19-inch color TVs in the *Ann Arbor News* from July 1, 1977 to July 7, 1978. Each week there were at least two full-page ads for appliances from two major competitors; the most heavily advertised 19-inch color TV was the RCA XL-100. The advertised price ranged from a low of $294 to a high of the "regular price" of $377. There was no particular trend or seasonal pattern to the prices.

---

[9] If all consumers are informed, only the lowest-price store will have any customers, and there can be only one price charged in equilibrium. But this is impossible by Proposition 2.

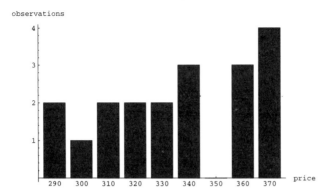

Figure 3. Frequency of advertised prices of RCS XL-100 color TVs during 1977-78.

Figure 3 depicts the frequency of advertised prices in $10 ranges. I think that it is not unreasonable to view this frequency distribution as J-shaped. Note that the "regular price" of $377 was advertised on four occasions. If one assumes that the TV was sold at the regular price when not advertised, there would be a total of 33 observations at the $377 price, which would certainly qualify as a J-shaped distribution.

12.5 Summary

I have shown how stores may find it in their interest to randomize prices in an attempt to price discriminate between informed and uninformed consumers, and have solved explicitly for the resulting monopolistically competitive equilibrium in randomized pricing strategies.

The form of the resulting pricing strategy as given in Figure 2 does not seem out of line with commonly observed retailing behavior. Large retailing chains such as Sears and Roebuck and Montgomery Ward sell appliances at their regular price much of the time, but often have sales when the price is reduced by as much as 25 percent. However, we rarely observe them selling an appliance at an intermediate price. Although this casual empiricism can hardly be conclusive, it suggests that the features of the model described here may have some relevance in explaining real world retailing behavior.

12.6 Appendix

PROPOSITION 7. $F(r - \epsilon) < 1$ *for any* $\epsilon > 0$

Proof. If not, let $\hat{p} < r$ satisfy $F(\hat{p}) = 1$ and let (p^i) be a sequence of prices with $f(p^i) > 0$ and $(p^i) \to \hat{p}$. Clearly $F(p^i) \to 1$, so

$$1 = 1 - \left(\frac{\pi_f(\hat{p})}{\pi_f(\hat{p}) - \pi_s(\hat{p})} \right)^{\frac{1}{n-1}}$$

Hence $\pi_f(\hat{p}) = 0$ or $\hat{p}U - c(U) = 0$ But then $rU - c(U) > 0$, so a store charging r with probability 1 would make a positive profit.

PROPOSITION 8.   *There is no gap* (p_1, p_2) *where* $f(p) \equiv 0$.

Proof. If not, let (p_1, p_2) be the largest such gap and let (p^i) and (p^j) be sequences of prices in the support of f converging to p_1 and p_2, respectively. Then, $\lim F(p^i) = \lim F(p^j)$ since F is continuous, which implies

$$\frac{\pi_f(p_1)}{\pi_f(p_1) - \pi_s(p_1)} = \frac{\pi_f(p_2)}{\pi_f(p_2) - \pi_s(p_2)}$$

According to Proposition 5 this is impossible unless $p_1 = p_2$.

PROPOSITION 9.   *If each store's optimal strategy involves zero probability of a tie, and* $f(p) > 0$ *for all* $p^* \overset{\leq}{=} p < r$, *then each store must choose the same strategy.*

Proof. Let $F_i(p)$ be the optimal strategy for store $i = 1, \ldots, n$. Then by the reasoning of Proposition 4, stores k and j must satisfy the equations

$$\pi_s(p)8_{i \neq j}(1 - F_i(p))^{n-1} = -\pi_f(p)8_{i \neq j}\left[1 - (1 - F_i(p))^{n-1}\right]$$
$$\pi_s(p)8_{i \neq k}(1 - F_i(p))^{n-1} = -\pi_f(p)8_{i \neq k}\left[1 - (1 - F_i(p))^{n-1}\right]$$

Dividing one equation into the other, we have

$$\frac{(1 - F_k(p))^{n-1}}{(1 - F_j(p))^{n-1}} = \frac{1 - (1 - F_k(p))^{n-1}}{1 - (1 - F_j(p))^{n-1}}$$

which implies $F_j(p) = F_k(p)$.

References

G. Butters (1977) "Equilibrium Distribution of Sales and Advertising Prices," *Rev. Econ. Stud*, **44**, 465–91.

J Pratt, D. Wise, and R. Zeckhauser (1979) "Price Variations in Almost Competitive Markets," *Quart. J. Econ.*, **93**, 189–211.

M. Rothschild (1973) "Models of Markets with Imperfect Information: A Survey," *J. Polit. Econ.*, **81**, 1283–308.

S. Salop (1977) "The Noisy Monopolist: Imperfect Information, Price Dispersion and Price Discrimination," *Rev. Econ. Stud*, **44**, 393–406.

S. Salop and J. Stiglitz (1976) "A Theory of Sales," mimeo., Stanford Univ..

S. Salop and J. Stiglitz (1977) "Bargains and Ripoffs: A Model of Monopolistically Competitive Price Dispersion," *Rev. Econ. Stud*, **44**, 493–510.

Y. Shilony (1977) "Mixed Pricing in Oligopoly," *J. Econ. Theory*, **14**, 373–88.

G. Stigler (1961) "The Economics of Information," *J. Polit. Econ.*, **69**, 213–25.

J. Stiglitz (1979) "Equilibrium in Product Markets with Imperfect Information," *Amer. Econ. Rev. Proc.*, **69**, 339–45.

L. Wilde and A. Schwartz (1979) "Equilibrium Comparison Shopping," *Rev. Econ. Stud*, **46**, 543–54.

Chapter 13

PRICE DISCRIMINATION
AND SOCIAL WELFARE

I derive conditions under which price discrimination increases or decreases social welfare. In general this will depend on whether price discrimination increases or decreases output.

The effect on social welfare of third-degree price discrimination was first investigated by Joan Robinson (1933). Richard Schmalensee (1981) has recently reexamined this question and presented several new results. In particular, he noted that a *necessary* condition for price discrimination to increase social welfare – defined as consumers' plus producers' surplus – is that output increase.

Schmalensee established this result only in the case of independent demands and constant marginal costs. However, it turns out to be true in much more general circumstances. In this paper I show how simple methods from duality theory can be used to establish this result and several other new results on the welfare effect of price discrimination.

13.1 A reservation price model

Before proceeding to an examination of price discrimination in a general context, it is worth pausing to consider the special case of a reservation price model. I will describe the model in the context of discrimination by age – as in senior citizen discounts or youth discounts – but several other interpretations are possible. Assume that we have a set of consumers of different ages, and that one unit will be demanded by the consumers of age

This research was supported in part by the National Science Foundation. I thank Richard Schmalensee, Louis Phlips, Andreu Mas-Collel, and an anonymous referee for helpful comments on an earlier draft.

a if the price facing these consumers, $p(a)$, is less than or equal to $r(a)$, the reservation price of these consumers. Suppose that the slope of $r(a)$ is of one sign, which without loss of generality we take to be negative. For simplicity, it is assumed that costs are zero, or equivalently, that constant marginal costs are incorporated into the definition of $r(a)$.

Suppose first that the monopolist must choose one price p_0 that will apply to all consumers. Then the maximization problem facing the monopolist is to chose a_0 to solve:

$$\max r(a_0)a_0.$$

Now suppose that the monopolist is allowed to price discriminate; that is, he can choose critical ages a_1, a_2 and prices p_1, p_2 such that the consumers younger than a_1 face price p_1 and consumers between a_1 and a_2 face price p_2 . The problem facing the monopolist now is to solve:

$$\max r(a_1)a_1 + r(a_2)(a_2 - a_1).$$

In this model it is easy to see that consumers' plus producers' surplus is given by the area below the reservation price function, as depicted in Figure 1. Thus the total welfare rises when price discrimination is allowed if and only if total output goes up. And, as shown below, output must always rise in this sort of model.

FACT 1. *If $r(a)$ is a decreasing function, then output and thus welfare must increase when price discrimination is allowed.*

Proof. Assume not so that $a_0 > a_2$ and thus: $-r(a_0)a_1 \geq -r(a_2)a_1$. By profit maximization: $r(a_0)a_0 > r(a_2)a_2$. Adding these two inequalities together, and adding $r(a_1)a_1$ to each side of the resulting inequality gives

$$r(a_1)a_1 + r(a_0)(a_0 - a_1) > r(a_1)a_1 + r(a_2)(a_2 - a_1),$$

which contradicts profit maximization.

This result easily generalizes to the choice of many regimes of price discrimination as well: allowing more price discrimination always increases output and welfare. As the number of prices increases to infinity, we converge to perfect price discrimination and thus maximal social welfare.

In this model we have a very simple story about price discrimination: price discrimination always increases output and an increase in output is always associated with an increase in welfare. But the reservation price model is a very special sort of demand structure and it is worth investigating whether these results carry over to more general demand specifications. As Schmalensee shows in general, output and welfare may increase or decrease when price discrimination is allowed, although an increase in output remains a necessary condition for welfare increase. This result provides an observable criterion for when welfare has gone down under price discrimination, but how can we recognize those circumstances in which welfare has increased? I provide some answers to this question and related questions below.

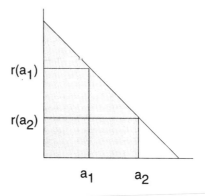

Figure 1. Surplus in reservation price model

13.2 Quasilinear utility and consumers' surplus

I want to continue to use the classical measure of consumers' plus producers' surplus, and the most general preference structure for which that is possible is that of quasilinear utility, which is also known as the case of "constant marginal utility of income." For this class of preferences it is well known that not only does consumer's surplus serve as a legitimate measure of individual welfare, but also that the individual consumers' utility functions can be added up to form a social utility function, so that aggregate *consumers'* surplus is also meaningful. For a discussion of consumers' surplus and indirect utility, see my 1984 book (ch. 7). These observations imply that we can treat the aggregate demand function as though it were generated by a representative consumer with an indirect utility function of the form:

$$V(\mathbf{p}, y) = v(\mathbf{p}) + y.$$

The aggregate consumer's income, y, is composed of some exogenous income which we take to be zero and the profits of the firm. Thus the appropriate form of the social objective function becomes:

$$V(\mathbf{p}, y) = v(\mathbf{p}) + \pi(\mathbf{p}).$$

By Roy's law the demand for good i is given by the negative of the derivative of $v(\mathbf{p})$ with respect to p_i – since the marginal utility of income is one. Thus the integral of demand is just $v(\mathbf{p})$. It follows that the above expression is nothing but the classical welfare measure of consumers' plus producers' surplus.

As a general principle, it is easier to differentiate to find demands than to integrate to find surplus; thus starting with the properties of the indirect utility function rather than the demand functions tends to simplify most problems in applied welfare economics. The most important property for our purposes concerns the curvature of the indirect utility function. The indirect utility function is always a quasiconvex function of prices, but in the case of quasi-linear utility, it is not hard to show that it is in fact a *convex* function of prices. (Proof: the expenditure function is $e(\mathbf{p}, u) = u - v(\mathbf{p})$ and it is necessarily a concave function of prices.)

13.3 Upper and lower bounds on welfare change

I turn now to the welfare effects of price discrimination for demand structures generated by quasi-linear utility. I start by describing a general result about such demands which can then be specialized in a number of ways. Consider an initial set of prices $\mathbf{p}^0$ and a final set of prices $\mathbf{p}^1$, and let $c(\mathbf{x}(\mathbf{p}^0))$ and $c(\mathbf{x}(\mathbf{p}^1))$ denote the total costs of production at the two different output levels associated with the price vectors $\mathbf{p}^0$ and $\mathbf{p}^1$. Let $\Delta\mathbf{x}$ denote the vector of changes in demand (i.e., $\Delta\mathbf{x} = \mathbf{x}(\mathbf{p}^1) - \mathbf{x}(\mathbf{p}^0)$), and let Δc denote the change in the total costs of production.

FACT 2.   *The change in welfare, ΔW, satisfies the following bounds:*

$$\mathbf{p}^0\Delta\mathbf{x} - \Delta c \geq \Delta W \geq \mathbf{p}^1\Delta\mathbf{x} - \Delta c.$$

Proof. Since the indirect utility function is a convex function of prices, we have:

$$v(\mathbf{p}^0) \geq v(\mathbf{p_1}) + \mathbf{D}v(\mathbf{p}^1)(\mathbf{p}^0 - \mathbf{p}^1)$$

where $\mathbf{D}v(\mathbf{p})$ stands for the gradient of $v(\mathbf{p})$. Using Roy's law, and rearranging:

$$\mathbf{x}(\mathbf{p}^1)(\mathbf{p}^0 - \mathbf{p}^1) \geq v(\mathbf{p}^1) - v(\mathbf{p}^0) = \Delta v.$$

The change in profits is given by

$$\mathbf{x}(\mathbf{p}^1)\mathbf{p}^1 - \mathbf{x}(\mathbf{p}^0)\mathbf{p}^0 - \Delta c = \Delta\pi.$$

Adding these expressions together we have

$$\left[\mathbf{x}(\mathbf{p}^1) - \mathbf{x}(\mathbf{p}^0)\right]\mathbf{p}^0 - \Delta c = \mathbf{p}^0\Delta\mathbf{x} - \Delta c \geq \Delta v + \Delta\pi = \Delta W.$$

The other bound can be derived in a similar manner.

Now think of the n goods as being one good sold in n different markets and produced at constant marginal cost. I want to compare a uniform pricing policy to a policy of price discrimination. Making the necessary substitutions in the bounds given in Fact 2, we have the following:

FACT 3.   *Let* $\mathbf{p}^0 = (p_0, \ldots, p_0), \mathbf{p}^1 = (p_1, \ldots, p_n)$ *and let* c *be the constant level of marginal costs. Then the bounds on welfare change become*

$$(p_0 - c) \sum_{i=1}^{n} \Delta x_i \geq \Delta W \geq \sum_{i=1}^{n} (p_i - c) \Delta x_i.$$

Note that the upper bound in Fact 3 immediately gives Schmalensee's result that an increase in output is a necessary condition for welfare to increase. The lower bound in Fact 3 was not discussed by Schmalensee. It implies that if the profitability of the new output exceeds the profitability of the old output, valued at the new prices, then welfare must have risen at the discriminatory equilibrium. This is basically a revealed preference relationship. Both of these facts hold in complete generality, for independent and dependent demands, as long as one is willing to assume quasilinear utility; that is, that aggregate consumers' surplus serves as an acceptable welfare measure. The bounds have a simple geometric interpretation in the case of a single demand curve which is given in Figure 2. However, it is worth emphasizing that these results are purely statements about demand and utility functions and hold for arbitrary configurations of prices. The fact that the prices are chosen by a profit-maximizing monopolist has not been used in their derivation.

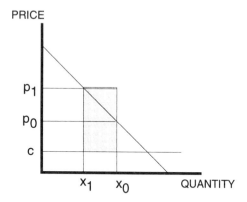

Figure 2. Bounds on welfare change in single market

13.4 Bounds on welfare change with optimal price discrimination

I now ask what results can be derived that use the conditions implied by *profit-maximizing* price discrimination. Let us specialize the notation above to consider only three prices, the initial price p_0 that is charged in both markets, and the final prices p_1 and p_2 that are profit-maximizing prices in their respective markets. We also continue to suppose that the good is produced at constant marginal cost c.

Fact 3 holds for all prices and all demand structures. If we consider only profit-maximizing prices and restrict ourselves to the textbook case of independent demands, we can apply the standard marginal revenue equals marginal cost formulas to find:

FACT 4.   *If demand functions are independent, welfare is bounded by*

$$\frac{c[\Delta x_1 + \Delta x_2]}{\epsilon_0 - 1} \geq \Delta W \geq \frac{c\Delta X_1}{\epsilon_1 - 1} + \frac{c\Delta x_2}{\epsilon_2 - 1},$$

where ϵ_0, ϵ_1, ϵ_2 are the (absolute values of the) respective elasticities of demand, evaluated at p_0, p_1, and p_2.

This result may be of use if one has estimates of the elasticities of demand in the various submarkets. However the independent demand case is rather restrictive. Profit maximization alone yields the following sufficient condition for a welfare increase.

FACT 5.   *A sufficient condition for welfare to increase under profit-maximizing price discrimination is that*

$$(p_0 - c)[x_1(p_0, p_0) + x_2(p_0, p_0)] > (p_1 - c)x_1(p_0, p_0) + (p_2 - c)x_2(p_0, p_0).$$

Proof. By profit maximization at (p_1, p_2) we have

$$(p_1 - c)x_1(p_1, p_2) + (p_2 - c)x_2(p_1, p_2) \geq (p_0 - c)x_1(p_0, p_0) + (p_0 - c)x_2(p_0, p_0).$$

Combining this with the hypothesis and rearranging, we have $(p_1 - c)\Delta x_1 + (p_2 - c)\Delta x_2 > 0$. By Fact 3 this yields a welfare increase.

The interesting thing about Fact 5 is that it only involves a condition on the nondiscriminatory levels of output. If you can forecast the prices that would be charged under discrimination and those prices satisfy the condition given in Fact 5, you can be assured that welfare will rise when discrimination is allowed.

It might be worthwhile to give an example of how these bounds can be used to verify that a welfare increase or decrease has occurred. The simplest example is the case of linear demands described by Schmalensee. If both markets are served in the single price regime, then it is easy to show by direct calculation that total output with discrimination is the same as in the single price regime. Hence, as noted by Schmalensee, welfare must decline when discrimination is allowed.

However, suppose we are in a situation where market 2 is not served in the single price regime. Then when discrimination is allowed, $p_1 = p_0$,

$\Delta x_1 = 0$, and $\Delta x_2 > 0$. By Fact 3 welfare must increase. Note also that in this situation the sufficient condition given in Fact 5 is satisfied as an equality.[1]

Thus Fact 3 verifies that welfare will increase when price discrimination is allowed in the linear demand case if a new market is served. However, Fact 3 also shows that for *arbitrary* independent demands, welfare goes up if a new market is served when price discrimination is allowed. The argument is simply that of the above paragraph: $\Delta x_1 = 0$ and $\Delta x_2 > 0$, so welfare must increase. These examples give some intuition for the case where both markets are served in both the discriminatory and nondiscriminatory regimes as in Figure 4. What is needed for welfare to increase when price discrimination is allowed is that one of the markets has small demand over the price range where the other market has large demand.

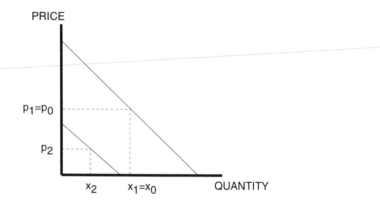

Figure 3. Increase in welfare (boundary case)

Another test case for the bounds is the reservation price model described in Section 1. Here we should think of each consumer as being a different market with demand function $x_a(p)$. If there are a_0 consumers purchasing the good in the single-price regime and $a_2 > a_0$ under price discrimination, then we know that $\Delta x_a = 0$ for $a \le a_0$ and $\Delta x_a = 1$ for $a_2 \ge a > a_0$, which by Fact 3 implies welfare must increase when discrimination is allowed.

The bounds can also be used to show that marginal cost pricing and perfect price discrimination are welfare optima in the reservation price model. For if price equals marginal cost, the upper bound on welfare change is zero. And if each consumer is being charged his reservation price, then Δx_a is either 0 or -1 which implies the upper bound is nonpositive.

---

[1] Of course, total output rises as well. The reader might wonder what is wrong with the "direct calculation" mentioned above. The problem is that what economists call "linear" demand curves are not really linear functions; instead they have the form: $Q = \max\{A - BP, 0\}$.

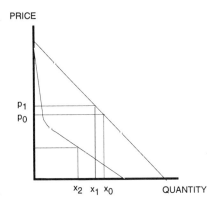

Figure 4. Increase in welfare (interior case)

The welfare bounds given above take a nice form if we are willing to make curvature assumptions on the demand functions. Let us restrict ourselves to the case of independent demands and focus on the market for good 1. Then the argument of Fact 2 implies that the welfare effect of a price change of good 1 is bounded by $(p_0 - c)\Delta x_1 \geq \Delta W \geq (p_1 - c)\Delta x_1$. Suppose that the demand for good 1 is a concave function of its own price. Then we have $\Delta x_1 \geq x_1'(P_1)(p_1 - p_0)$. Combining these two inequalities we have $\Delta W_1 \geq (p_1 - c)x_1'(p_1)[p_1 - p_0]$. The first-order conditions for profit maximization imply that $(p_1 - c)x_1'(p_1) + x_1(p_1) = 0$. Substituting we have $\Delta W_1 \geq x_1(p_1)(p_0 - p_1)$. If both markets have concave demand curves we can write:

$$\Delta W \geq x_1(p_1)(p_0 - p_1) + x_2(p_2)(p_0 - p_2)$$
$$= p_0[x_1(p_1) + x_2(p_2)] - [p_1 x_1(p_1) + p_2 x_2(p_2)].$$

Add and subtract $(p_0 - c)[x_1(p_0) + x_2(p_0)] - c[x_1(p_1) + x_2(p_2)]$ to get $\Delta W \geq (p_0 - c)\Delta x - \Delta \pi$, where Δx is the total change in output and $\Delta \pi$ is the total change in profits. Thus the change in welfare is at least as large as the change in profit valued at the old prices minus the change in actual profit. Or, to put it another way, $\Delta x > \Delta \pi/(p_0 - c)$ is a sufficient condition for welfare to increase when price discrimination is allowed if all demand curves are independent and concave. Combining this with Fact 3 we can conclude:

FACT 6. *If all demand curves are independent and concave the welfare bounds can be written as*

$$(p_0 - c)\Delta x \geq \Delta W \geq (p_0 - c)\Delta x - \Delta \pi.$$

Note that Facts 5 and 6 use profit maximization at p_1 and p_2, but do **not** use profit maximization at p_0. Thus these results are independent of firm behavior at the nondiscriminatory equilibrium.

If the demand curves are concave and convex (i.e., linear), then the inequality in Fact 6 shows that $0 \geq \Delta W \geq -\Delta \pi$. Stephen Layson (1988) uses a geometric argument to show that $\Delta \pi = -2\Delta W$.

13.5 More general cost structures

The above results were all derived in the case of constant marginal cost but they can be partially extended to the case of increasing marginal costs; that is, the case of a convex cost function. By the standard convexity inequality:

$$\mathbf{Dc}\left(\mathbf{x}(\mathbf{p}^1)\right) \Delta \mathbf{x} \geq \Delta c \geq \mathbf{Dc}\left(\mathbf{x}(\mathbf{p}^0)\right) \Delta \mathbf{x}.$$

Combining this with the inequality given in Fact 2 we have

$$\left[p^0 - Dc\left(x(p^0)\right)\right] \Delta x > \left[p^1 - Dc\left(x(p^1)\right)\right] \Delta x.$$

Again, these are general bounds which hold for all pairs of price vectors p^0 and p^1 as well as for arbitrary convex cost functions, in particular the cost function can be a function of the vector of outputs rather than just the total output. Thus the bounds can be useful in more general contexts. For example, they give a simple proof of the optimality of marginal cost pricing in the presence of convex costs: if $\mathbf{p}^0 = \mathbf{Dc}(\mathbf{x}(\mathbf{p}^0))$ then any movement from $\mathbf{p}^0$ must decrease social welfare. If costs depend only on total output, denoted by x_0 and x_1, and $\mathbf{p}^0$ is a vector of constant prices p_0 as above, we can write these bounds as

$$[p_0 - c'(x_0)] \sum_{i=1}^{n} \Delta X_i \geq \Delta W \geq \sum_{i=1}^{n} [p_i - c'(x_1)] \Delta x_i.$$

Thus in the case of increasing marginal costs, Schmalensee's proposition still holds: price must be greater than marginal cost at the nondiscriminatory price, so an increase in output is still a necessary condition for welfare to increase.

References

Layson, S. (1988) "Third-Degree Price Discrimination, Welfare, and Profits: A Geometrical Analysis," *American Economic Review*, **78**, 1131-32.

Robinson, J. (1933) *Economics of Imperfect Competition*. London: Macmillan.

Schmalensee, R. (1981) "Output and Welfare Implications of Monopolistic Third-Degree Price Discrimination," *American Economic Review*, **71**, 242–47.

Varian, H. (1984) *Microeconomic Analysis, 2d ed.* New York: W. W. Norton.

Chapter 14

DIVERGENCE OF OPINION
IN COMPLETE MARKETS: A NOTE

We consider an Arrow-Debreu model with agents who have different subjective probabilities. In general, asset prices will depend only on aggregate consumption and the distribution of subjective probabilities in each state of nature. If all agents have identical preferences then an asset with "more dispersed" subjective probabilities will have a lower price than an asset with less dispersed subjective probabilities if risk aversion does not decline too rapidly. It seems that this condition is likely to be met in practice, so that increased dispersion of beliefs will generally be associated with reduced asset prices in a given Arrow-Debreu equilibrium.

There have been several recent investigations concerning the effect of heterogeneous probability beliefs on asset prices. Most of these investigations have taken place in the context of CAPM-like mean-variance models; see, for example, Lintner (1969), Miller (1977), Williams (1977), Jarrow (1980), and Mayshar (1983).

Comparatively little has been done in the analysis of differences of opinion in an Arrow-Debreu contingent claims context. Rubinstein (1976), Breeden and Litzenberger (1978), and Breeden (1979) have presented nice analyses of asset price determination in an Arrow-Debreu model, but most of their results have assumed commonly held probability beliefs.

In this paper we analyze the impact of divergence of opinion on asset prices in an Arrow-Debreu economy. The results serve to generalize the findings of Rubinstein and Breeden-Litzenberger to the case of different probability beliefs. Among the results we establish are:

This research was supported in part by the National Science Foundation. I wish to thank Ted Bergstrom and Larry Blume for helpful comments.

1. In equilibrium, asset prices depend only on aggregate consumption and the distribution of subjective probability beliefs.

2. Asset values are an increasing function of any one individual's probability beliefs.

3. An increase in the "spread" of the probability beliefs of investors may increase or decrease equilibrium asset values depending on the value of a parameter of the utility function. However, the most likely effect is to decrease the asset values.

These results are especially interesting in light of the recent empirical work of Cragg and Malkiel (1982). They studied the relationship between ex post return and various measures of risk for common stocks and found that the measure of risk that performed best in their analysis was a measure of divergence of opinion about the asset returns. This seems like an interesting empirical finding in search of a model. This paper is an attempt to provide such a model.

14.1 The Arrow-Debreu model

Suppose that there are n investors indexed by $i = 1, \ldots, n$. There are S states of nature indexed by $s = 1, \ldots, S$. Investor i has a von Neumann-Morgenstern utility function for consumption in state s denoted by $u_i(c_{is})$. This function is assumed to be strictly increasing and strictly concave in consumption. We assume that there are given endowments of consumption in state s by consumer i which we denote by $\bar{c}_{is}$. Each consumer has a subjective probability distribution over the states of nature. We let π_{is} denote consumer i's probability that state s will occur. We assume that there are a set of Arrow-Debreu securities that pay off one unit of consumption if and only if a given state of nature occurs. We let p_s denote the price of an Arrow-Debreu security that pays off in state s.

Each consumer chooses a portfolio of Arrow-Debreu securities by solving the following maximization problem:

$$\max \sum_{s=1}^{S} \pi_{is} u_i(c_{is}$$

$$\text{subject to} \sum_{s=1}^{S} p_s c_{is} = \sum_{s=1}^{S} p_s \bar{c}_{is}.$$

We assume that final consumption in each state of nature is nonnegative, but the net position in each Arrow-Debreu security for a given individual may be positive or negative. Thus, there are no short sales restrictions of any sort. We will suppose that the standard conditions are satisfied so that an Arrow-Debreu equilibrium will exist. Note that this implies that each agent behaves strictly as a price-taker. In particular, agents do not acquire any information from market prices about other agents' probability beliefs; they behave purely as passive expected utility maximizers. Thus, the standard first-order conditions apply, which we note here for reference.

$$\pi_{is} u_i'(c_{is}) = \lambda_i p_s \tag{1}$$

Under standard assumptions, the pattern of consumption across states of nature in an Arrow-Debreu equilibrium will be Pareto-efficient. Similarly, all Pareto-efficient allocations of consumption can be supported as Arrow-Debreu equilibria. The results below are phrased in terms of an Arrow-Debreu equilibrium, but given these standard theorems of welfare economics, they can also be viewed as statements about Pareto-efficient risk bearing.

14.2 Asset valuation in the Arrow-Debreu model

Any asset can be valued in terms of the Arrow-Debreu prices. For example, let an asset have a payoff of x_s, in state of nature s. Then its equilibrium value must be:

$$v_x = \sum_{s=1}^{S} p_s x_s$$

Following the lines of Rubinstein (1976), we can write this sum as:

$$v_x = \sum_{s=1}^{S} \frac{p_s}{\pi_{is}} x_s \pi_{is} = E_i \frac{p}{\pi_i} x$$

where E_i is the expectation with respect to agent i's subjective probability distribution. Using the covariance identity, this term can be rewritten as:

$$v_x = \text{cov}\left(\frac{p}{\pi_i}, x\right) + E_i x E_i \frac{p}{\pi_i}$$

where cov_i is the covariance with respect to agent i's probability distribution and symbols without the s subscript are random variables. Using the definition of expectation,

$$E_i \frac{p}{\pi_i} = \sum_{s=1}^{S} \frac{p_s}{\pi_{is}} \pi_{is} = \sum_{s=1}^{S} p_s$$

This sum is simply the value today of a certain payoff of one dollar next period. That is, it is the reciprocal of the risk-free rate of return, R_F.

Substituting from the first-order conditions for individual optimization, we now have:

$$v_x = \text{cov}_i(u_i'(c_{is}), x_s)/\lambda_i + \frac{E_i x}{R_F}$$

This formula states that in equilibrium an asset's value is the sum of its discounted expected return and its risk premium – its covariance with individual consumption. Denoting the risk measure by γ_i, we have the final form for the asset valuation formula:

$$v_x = \gamma_i + \frac{E_i x}{R_F}$$

In this expression v_x, x_s, and R_F are publicly observable while γ_i and $E_i x$ differ from person to person. Thus, the subjective beliefs of the agents about an asset's "risk" and "return" cannot vary across individuals in an arbitrary way, but must satisfy the equilibrium pricing relation given above. This relation places restrictions on how the individual perceptions of risk and return relate to each other; if an agent tells us his or her beliefs about the expected return on an asset, then we can use the equilibrium pricing relationship to solve for the risk premium as a function of the publicly observable variables v_x and R_F. Note that the risk premium depends on the covariance between marginal utility and the asset payoffs. Since marginal utility is a decreasing function of consumption, assets whose payoffs are positively correlated with individual i's consumption will have a negative risk premium for that individual, while assets that are negatively correlated will have a positive risk premium for that individual.

When the economic agents have homogeneous beliefs, we can go further. Following Rubinstein (1976) and Breeden and Litzenberger (1978), we proceed to examine the individual first-order conditions in more detail. We write these conditions as:

$$\frac{u_i'(c_{is})}{\lambda_i} = \frac{p_s}{\pi_s}$$

The left-hand side of this expression is a decreasing function of consumption, so it has an inverse, $f_i(\cdot)$. Applying this inverse to each side of the expression and summing over the consumers, we have:

$$c_s = \sum_{i=1}^{n} c_{is} = \sum_{i=1}^{n} f_i\left(\frac{p_s}{\pi_s}\right)$$

The right-hand side of this expression is decreasing in p_s/π_s, so it has an inverse, $F(\cdot)$. Applying this inverse, we have:

$$\frac{p_s}{\pi_s} = F(c_s)$$

Substituting into the asset valuation formula, we have:

$$v_x = \text{cov}(F(c), x) + \frac{Ex}{R_F}$$

Thus, when all agents have common probability beliefs, the risk premium depends on the covariance of the asset payoffs with a decreasing function of *aggregate* consumption. This insight can be further generalized in two directions. Rubinstein (1976) shows that if consumption and asset payoffs are bivariate normally distributed then the risk premium can be expressed in terms of the covariance with aggregate consumption alone, not just a nonlinear function of aggregate consumption. Breeden (1979) shows that the same thing happens in a continuous time model. (Both of these simplifications can be applied to the γ_i term in the earlier valuation formula as well.)

However, when probability beliefs are heterogeneous such simplifications do not appear to be possible. Breeden and Litzenberger (1978) observe that agents need only agree on the probability of occurrence of various levels of aggregate consumption; but other than this result, there is not much that is known.

Referring to the original expression for asset values, $v_x = \sum p_x x_s$, we see that if we can isolate the effect of divergence of probability beliefs on Arrow-Debreu prices, we will have determined the effect on all asset values. In the next section, we will see how this might be done.

14.3 Heterogeneous probability beliefs

In equilibrium each consumer maximizes expected utility as given above. Hence, optimal consumption must satisfy the first-order conditions given in Equation (1).

Since $u_i'(c_{is})$ is a strictly decreasing function, it has an inverse $f_i(\cdot)$. Thus, we can write:

$$c_{is} = f_i(\lambda_i p_s / \pi_{is}) \tag{2}$$

(Note that the definition of $f_i(\cdot)$ is slightly different than before.) Summing over all investors, we have:

$$\sum_{i=1}^{n} c_{is} = c_s = \sum_{i=1}^{n} f_i(\lambda_i p_s / \pi_{is}) \tag{3}$$

For fixed values of (π_{is}) and (λ_i), the right-hand side of this expression is a strictly decreasing function of p_s. Hence, it has an inverse $F(\cdot, \pi_{1s}, \ldots, \pi_{ns})$. Applying this function to each side of this expression, we have:

$$F(c_s, \pi_{1s}, \ldots, \pi_{ns}) = p_s \tag{4}$$

In any given Arrow-Debreu equilibrium, the values of the λ_i terms are determined. Hence, the above equation implies that the equilibrium-contingent commodity prices are solely a function of *aggregate* consumption in each state and the distribution of beliefs about that state. Recording this fact for future reference, we note the following:

FACT 1. *In equilibrium the Arrow-Debreu price for consumption in state s depends only on aggregate consumption in that state and the distributions of subjective probabilities that the state will occur. The Arrow Debreu price is a decreasing function of consumption in state s and an increasing function of π_{is} for each $i = 1, \ldots, n$.*

Proof. Only the last sentence remains to be proved. That the prices are decreasing in consumption is obvious from the definition of F. In order to prove the second part, we consider Equation (3). Hold aggregate consumption and the λ_i terms fixed in this equation and increase π_{is}. Then p_s must increase to maintain the equality. Q.E.D.

The first part of this fact is a generalization of Theorem 1 in Breeden and Litzenberger (1978), alluded to earlier. Extending their discussion to this model, we note that two states of nature that have the same aggregate consumption and the same distribution of probability beliefs have the same Arrow-Debreu prices; thus, a set of Arrow-Debreu securities need only distinguish states with different values of aggregate consumption and different probability beliefs in order to support a given efficient pattern of consumption.

We now consider the impact of a change in the "spread" of the probability beliefs on asset prices. Consider two states of nature with the same value of aggregate consumption but with different probability beliefs. Suppose that the "average" probability over the investors is constant across the two states, but the "divergence of opinion" is higher in one state than the other. Which Arrow-Debreu price will be larger?

Intuition provides conflicting answers. One might argue that divergence of opinion about an asset's payoffs makes the asset seem more risky. Hence, divergence of opinion will decrease the value of an asset. On the other hand, one can argue that the market price is determined by the optimists, so that increasing the divergence of opinion is likely to increase an asset's price. Several of the CAPM-type models mentioned in the introduction support this latter view.

In order to develop some intuition, we might consider a simple reservation price model. Suppose that each consumer is limited to purchasing at most one unit of a given asset in fixed supply, and let the reservation prices differ across consumers. Then the simple supply-demand diagram depicted in Figure 1 gives us the equilibrium price.

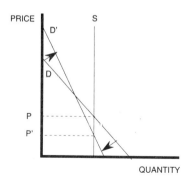

Figure 1. Effect of increase in dispersion of tastes.

Now suppose that the reservation prices become more dispersed; i.e., the pessimists think that the asset is worth less and the optimists think that it is worth more. This will tend to rotate the demand curve clockwise about the average reservation price. Hence, the equilibrium price of the asset will increase or decrease as the supply of the asset is to the right or left of the pivot point.

Even in this simple model, an increase in the diversity of opinion has an ambiguous effect on asset prices. Thus, it seems unlikely that a definitive result is available in more general cases. However, the additional structure provided by the state-independent von Neumann-Morgenstern utility functions does allow us to isolate the relevant parameter of the utility function that determines the effect of diversity on asset prices in a given equilibrium.

14.4 The effect of diversity of opinion

Let us consider a fixed equilibrium and a particular state. We will assume that all consumers have the same von Neumann-Morgenstern utility function $u(c_{is})$ with associated Arrow-Pratt measure of absolute risk aversion $r(c)$. We also introduce the *weighted* probabilities q_{is} for $i = 1, \ldots, n$ defined by:

$$q_{is} = \pi_{is}/\lambda_i$$

In general, wealthier consumers will have lower marginal utilities of income so that their subjective probability beliefs will have a higher weight in the above expression. Using this notation we can rewrite Equation (3) as:

$$c_s = \sum_{i=1}^{n} f(p_s/q_{is}) \tag{5}$$

We now note the following:

FACT 2.   *The function $f(p_s/q_{is})$ is an increasing function of q_{is}. It is a concave or convex function of q_{is} as $r'(c)$ is greater than or less than $-r^2$.*

Proof. Suppose that $r'(c) > -r^2$. Then it is a straightforward calculation to show that:

$$\frac{u'u'''}{u''u''} < 2$$

Using the fact that $f(u'(c)) \equiv c$, we can derive expressions for the derivatives of f in terms of the derivatives of u:

$$f' = 1/u''$$
$$f'' = -u'''/(u'')^3$$

These expressions in turn can be used to calculate the following derivatives:

$$\frac{\partial f}{\partial q_{is}} = -f'(p_s/q_{is})p_s/q_{is}^2 > 0$$

$$\frac{\partial^2 f}{\partial q_{is}^2} = \frac{p_s}{u''q_{is}^3}\left[2 - \frac{u'u'''}{u''u''}\right]$$

Combining this last expression with the first inequality, we have the result. Q.E.D.

The fact that $f(p_s/q_{is})$ has a definite curvature allows us to use the standard techniques of Rothschild-Stiglitz (1970) to determine the effect of diversity of opinion on asset prices.

FACT 3.   *If $f(p_s/q_{is})$ is an increasing concave (convex) function of q_{is} then a mean-preserving spread across the population in q_{is} must decrease (increase) the equilibrium value of p_s.*

Proof. Refer to Equation (5). Since $f(p_s/q_{is})$ is a concave function of q_{is}, a mean-preserving spread in the distribution of q_{is} will decrease the value of the sum. If c is to remain fixed, this means that p_s must decrease. Q.E.D.

Note that this fact holds only for a "cross-sectional" comparison of asset prices in a fixed equilibrium. Thus, if we have two states s and t with the same aggregate consumption but more dispersed beliefs in s than in t in the sense that the distribution of weighted beliefs in s is a mean-preserving spread of the one in t, then the Arrow-Debreu price for consumption in s will be less than the Arrow-Debreu price for consumption in t.

Facts 2 and 3 taken together indicate that the crucial determinant effect of dispersion of opinion on asset prices is whether risk aversion declines "too rapidly." However, this condition in itself is not terribly transparent. There is an equivalent expression for the condition in terms of the Arrow-Pratt measure of relative risk aversion.

FACT 4.   Let $\rho(c) = r(c)c$ be the coefficient of relative risk aversion. Then $r'(c) > -r^2$ if and only if the consumption elasticity of relative risk aversion is greater than $1 - \rho$. That is, $\rho'c/\rho > 1 - \rho$.

Proof. Differentiating $\rho = rc$, we have:

$$\rho' = r + r'c$$

Thus, $r' > r^2$ can be expressed as:

$$\frac{\rho' - r}{c} > -\frac{\rho^2}{c^2}$$

which reduces to:

$$rc - \rho'c < \rho^2$$

or

$$\rho - \rho^2 < \rho'c$$
$$1 - \rho < \frac{\rho'c}{\rho}. \qquad\qquad Q.E.D.$$

Thus, if we consider the family of constant relative risk averse utility functions, we see that the condition will be satisfied when $\rho > 1$. Since the empirical evidence indicates that ρ is at least 2, it seems that equilibrium asset prices should generally decrease with an increase in diversity of opinion.

It is an easy calculation to check other commonly used functional forms. For example, quadratic utility and constant absolute risk aversion each imply $f(p_s/q_{is})$ is a concave function of q_{is}. Thus, asset prices will decrease with an increase in diversity of opinion in both of these cases.

The most convenient general class of expected utility functions is the HARA, or linear risk tolerance class defined by:

$$-\frac{u'(c)}{u''(c)} = a + bc$$

FACT 5.   If the representative utility function is of the HARA class, then increasing the dispersion of opinion will decrease asset prices if and only if $b < 1$.

Proof. By Fact 2 and direct computation. Q.E.D.

14.5 An example with constant relative risk aversion

The family of constant relative risk averse utility functions provides a nice example. Here the first-order conditions for utility maximization have the form:

$$\pi_{is} c_{is}^{-\rho} = \lambda_i p_s$$

Solving for c_{is}, we have:

$$c_{is} = \left(\frac{\lambda_i}{\pi_{is}} \right)^{-1/\rho} p_s^{-1/\rho}$$

Summing this over $i = 1, \ldots, n$ and rearranging, we have:

$$p_s^{1/\rho} c_s = \sum_{i-1}^{n} (\pi_{is} \lambda_i)^{1/\rho}$$

For $\rho > 1$ the right-hand side of this expression is a concave function of π_{is}/λ_i, so that a mean-preserving spread of $\pi_{is}/\lambda_i = q_{is}$ across individuals will decrease the right-hand side. Hence, p_s must decrease to maintain the equality.

Finally, let us consider the general condition given in Fact 2. We might well ask when this condition is met with equality. That is, for what von Neumann-Morgenstern utility function is $r'(c) = r(c)^2$? It is not difficult to verify that $u(c) = \ln c$ is the essentially unique solution to this differential equation. Thus, logarithmic utility is the borderline case not only in the class of constant relative risk averse utility functions, but also in the class of *all* utility functions. As long as risk aversion declines less rapidly than it does in the case of logarithmic utility, an increase in the diversity of opinion will be associated with decreased asset prices.

References

D. Breeden (1979) "An Intertemporal Asset Pricing Model with Stochastic Consumption and Investment Opportunities," *Journal of Financial Economics*, **7**, 265–96.

D. Breeden and R. Litzenberger (1978) "Prices of State-Contingent Claims Implicit in Option Prices," *Journal of Business*, **51**, 621–51.

J. Cragg and B. Malkiel (1982) *Expectations and the Structure of Share Prices*. Chicago: University of Chicago Press.

R. Jarrow (1980) "Heterogeneous Expectations, Restrictions on Short Sales, and Equilibrium Asset Prices," *Journal of Finance*, **35**, 1105–13.

J. Lintner (1969) "The Aggregation of Investors' Diverse Judgments and Preferences in Purely Competitive Markets," *Journal of Financial and Quantitative Analysis*, **4**, 347–400.

J. Mayshar (1983) "On Divergence of Opinion and Imperfections in Capital Markets," *American Economic Review*, **73**, 114–28.

Edward M. Miller (1977) "Risk, Uncertainty, and Divergence of Opinion," *Journal of Finance*, **32**, 1151–68.

M. Rubinstein (1976) "The Valuation of Uncertain Income Streams and the Pricing of Options," *Bell Journal of Economics*, **7**, 407–25.

M. Rothschild and J. Stiglitz (1970) "Increasing Risk I: A Definition," *Journal of Economic Theory*, **2**, 225–43.

J. Williams (1977) "Capital Asset Prices with Heterogeneous Beliefs," *Journal of Financial Economics*, **5**, 219–39.

Chapter 15

DIFFERENCES OF OPINION
AND THE VOLUME OF TRADE

Agents trade because of differences in endowments, tastes and beliefs. In the standard models of finance beliefs are assumed to be identical across agents so that trade is due only to differences in endowments and tastes. In this paper I investigate trade due to different beliefs. Differences in equilibrium beliefs may be due to different opinions (i.e., prior probabilities) or different information (i.e., different values of the likelihood function). Using modified versions of a mean-variance model due to Grossman and an Arrow-Debreu model due to Milgrom-Stokey I argue that differences in information will not in general cause trade. Rather it is only differences in opinion that generate stock market volume. I then go on to examine the effect of different opinions on asset prices. I show that if tastes are identical, and if risk tolerance does not grow too rapidly, then assets that have more dispersed opinions will, other things being equal, have lower prices and a greater volume of trade. In general the effect of differences of opinion on asset prices will depend on the curvature of asset demand functions with respect to the opinions of the agents.

The standard models of financial markets such as the Sharpe-Lintner mean variance model or the Rubinstein-Breeden-Litzenberger contingent consumption model both assume more-or-less homogeneous probability beliefs.[1]

This work was supported by the National Science Foundation. I wish to thank Sudipto Bhattacharya, Fisher Black, Robert Holbrook, Jeff MacKie-Mason, Dale Morse, Paul Milgrom, Tom Russell, Duane Seppi, Sarab Seth, Joseph Swierzbinski, and Jean Tirole for helpful discussions and references.

---

[1] More precisely, the mean variance model requires that agents agree on the mean returns and covariance matrix of the assets; the contingent consumption model requires that agents agree on the probability of occurrence of different levels of aggregate consumption.

There has been some work on extending the mean-variance model to allow for differences in beliefs across agents; see Jarrow (1980), Lintner (1969), Mayshar (1983), and Williams (1977). Differences in beliefs in contingent commodities models have received much less attention. The major references are Rubinstein (1975), (1976), Breeden-Litzenberger (1978), Hakansson-Kunkel-Ohlson (1982) and Milgrom-Stokey (1982).

Cragg and Malkiel (1982) have done some empirical work concerning the effect of the diversity of beliefs on asset prices. According to them:

> "We found that the best single risk measure available for each company was the extent to which different forecasters were not in agreement about that company's future growth ... [These results] suggest that the variance of analysts' forecasts may represent the most effective risk proxy available ..." Cragg and Malkiel (1982, p.4).

The strong empirical relationship between dispersion of forecasts and share performance found by Cragg and Malkiel suggests that it is appropriate to examine more deeply the theoretical relationship between dispersion of beliefs and asset prices.

One issue that must be faced at the outset is how there can be any differences of belief in equilibrium. Several authors have argued that differences in beliefs that are due solely to differences in information should tend to be eliminated in equilibrium. I briefly discuss this literature in Section 1 and argue that to explain observed trading volumes, one must allow for differences in *opinions*—that is, differences in beliefs that are not shared by other agents, even when they are known to other agents. Equilibrium models that allow for both differences in opinions and differences in information are explored in Sections 2–5.

In Sections 2–4 I study a simple mean-variance model with differential information of the sort examined by Grossman (1976), (1978). I generalize Grossman's model to allow for different prior probabilities and for two periods of trade and find that even when the equilibrium prices reflect all available information, the volume of trade is determined entirely by the differences of opinion. In Section 5 I examine an Arrow-Debreu contingent consumption model of the sort studied by Milgrom and Stokey (1982). A similar result emerges there: prices are determined by information, but the pattern of trade is determined by the differences in opinion.

Having established the importance of differences of opinion for trade, I then examine some of its consequences for asset market equilibrium in Sections 6–10. In the context of an Arrow-Debreu equilibrium I show that if risk aversion does not decrease too rapidly, then assets with more dispersed opinion will have lower prices, other things being equal. If risk aversion does decrease too rapidly, then more dispersion of opinion will be associated with higher prices.[2] Under general conditions assets with more dispersion of opinion will have more equilibrium trade, other things being equal.

It is important to understand that the results in Sections 6–10 involve comparisons of asset prices and trading volumes in a single Arrow-Debreu equilibrium; they are emphatically *not* comparative statics results about how an equilibrium price changes as the overall dispersion of opinion changes. Rather they are *comparative asset pricing* results that compare the prices of two different assets in the *same* equilibrium. These results are analogous to those in standard asset pricing models that compare the equilibrium relationship between the prices of assets and various characteristics of the assets such as their betas, the covariance with aggregate consumption, and so on. We have simply added a new characteristic of assets, namely, the dispersion of opinion.

Since the results describe the relationship between the *equilibrium* price and volume of trade in assets and the *equilibrium* probability beliefs about those assets, they are independent of the exact model of how equilibrium beliefs are formed. As long as one admits that probability beliefs may differ in equilibrium, the results in Sections 6–10 of this paper describe how those differences in belief will be related to asset prices, regardless of precisely *why* these beliefs differ.

15.1 No trade theorems

The main results of this paper described in Sections 6–10 are independent of the exact model of why equilibrium beliefs may differ. However, it is worthwhile investigating conditions in which equilibrium probability beliefs differ and agents actually trade on the basis of these different beliefs, since a number of authors have shown that in a speculative market composed of fully rational agents with identical priors there will be no trade in equilibrium. The basic structure of the argument has been summarized by Tirole (1982):

> "Consider a purely speculative market (i.e., a market where the aggregate monetary gain is zero and insurance plays no role). Assume that it is common knowledge that traders are risk averse, rational, have the same prior and that the market clears. Then it is also common knowledge that a trader's expected monetary gain given his information must be positive in order for him to be willing to trade. The market clearing condition then requires that no trader expect a monetary gain from his trade." Tirole (1982, p.1164).

Put in more familiar terms, if one agent has information that induces him to want to trade at the current asset price, then other rational agents would

---

[2] The meaning of "too rapidly" is made precise below.

be unwilling to trade with him, because they realize that he must have superior information. Papers that explore this kind of No Trade Theorem in a variety of contexts include Rubinstein (1975), Bhattacharya (1976), Hakannsson, Kunkel and Ohlson (1982), and Milgrom and Stokey (1982).

Hence, if we to are examine models with different equilibrium beliefs and non-zero trading volume, we must consider models that lack one of the necessary hypotheses for the No Trade Theorems described above. Tirole (1982, p. 1167) describes the possibilities: (1) there may be some risk loving or irrational traders; (2) insurance and diversification considerations may play a significant role; or (3) agents may have different prior beliefs.

The first option is compelling on grounds of casual empiricism; clearly *some* participants in speculative markets behave in apparently irrational ways. Black (1986) explores some of the implications of this observation. It has sometimes been argued that introducing a "fringe" of irrational traders into traditional models will not significantly alter the analysis of these models, since the irrational traders will only introduce a non-systematic "error term" on top of the traditional results. However, if the rational traders know that irrational traders are present in a market they would rationally attempt to exploit them. *The introduction of irrational traders will, in general, alter the behavior of the rational players and thereby change the nature of the equilibrium.* The problem with pursuing this approach lies in deciding what kinds of irrational behavior are plausible. Some interesting leads are being examined in this area, but, as yet, little progress has been made.

The second way to get around the No Trade Theorems is the route that most of the literature in finance has taken. All trade in speculative markets is taken to be due to differences in endowments and risk aversion, and observed portfolio holdings are taken to be the outcome of pure "hedging" rather than "speculation" per se.

However, attributing all trade to hedging seems implausible empirically and doesn't really get around the No Trade Theorems. Suppose that agents do have different risk aversion and different endowments, so that there is some gain from trade on these characteristics. After a single round of trading based on hedging and insurance considerations, there is no further reason to trade when new information arrives for exactly the same reasons described by Tirole: in a market of rational individuals there would be no one to trade with. Trading on the arrival of new information can only arise if agents *interpret* the information differently—i.e., if the information affects their posterior beliefs differently. This point will be explored in greater detail below.

This leaves us with the third option: different prior beliefs. This is the motive force for trade that we will explore in this paper. If differences in prior beliefs can generate trade, then these differences in belief can not be due to *information* as such, but rather can only be pure differences in *opinion*. Let us consider the difference between information and opinion more closely.

The distinction between what counts as differences in information and differences of opinion must lie in the eyes of the beholder. According to Bayesian decision theory, a rational agent will combine his prior probability beliefs and his likelihood function via Bayes' law to determine his posterior probability beliefs. If I convey a probability belief to another agent and he updates his posterior just as though this probability belief were objective evidence, then he has interpreted my probability beliefs as information: he has accepted my beliefs as being *credible*. If he doesn't update his posterior at all, then he has interpreted my beliefs as opinion—he has interpreted my beliefs as being noncredible. The extent that one agent's beliefs are capable of influencing another agent's beliefs determines to what extent one agent conveys information or opinion to the others. We will refer to an agent's belief about what fraction of other agents' beliefs are opinion and what fraction is information as the first agent's beliefs about the *credibility* of the other agents' views.

One hardly needs to consider speculative markets to encounter this distinction. In any kind of human communication it is necessary for one party to determine how credible the other's "information" is. When is someone really conveying information and when is he just conveying his opinion? How much weight should I attach to another individual's pronouncements?

The same sort of question arises in financial markets. If a firm introduces a new product which I find attractive, but the stock market value of the firm falls, what am I to conclude? How much of the price fall is due to superior information of others, and how much is due to differences in opinion? What credibility should we attach to market price movements? As we will see below, the nature of the market equilibrium will depend crucially on the degree of credibility that agents' attach to the "information" conveyed by the market price.

Allowing for differences of opinion in this sense can be viewed as allowing for a certain kind of irrational agents. If each agent truly believed that all other agents were rational, doesn't that mean that each agent would accept the other agents' beliefs as being due solely to different information? If I "weight" another agent's beliefs differently than hard evidence, doesn't this mean that I view the other agent as having some degree of irrational behavior? Harsanyi (1983), for example, has argued that under certain conditions fully rational agents must have the same prior beliefs. According to this view, having different priors—differences of opinion—is tantamount to irrationality in some cases. However, Harsanyi's discussion certainly allows that there also exist cases where rational people can agree to disagree at least with respect to prior probability beliefs.[3]

---

[3] Aumann's (1976) famous paper on this topic establishes only that rational individuals with *identical* priors and likelihoods who communicate their posteriors cannot disagree.

I prefer to remain agnostic on this issue. It seems to me that agents do have different beliefs in practice, and that they do have different degrees of credibility. This is enough to generate equilibrium trade, and nothing in particular hinges on whether we want to call this "rational" or "irrational," at least for the purposes of this paper.

15.2 A mean-variance model

We first consider a simplified version of a model of the sort studied by Grossman (1976), (1978). There are two assets, one with an unknown payoff and one with a certain payoff. We let v denote the unknown value of the risky asset next period. For simplicity we assume that the certain asset has a zero rate of return.

Each investor i has a subjective prior distribution for the value of the risky asset which we take to be Normally distributed with mean v_i and precision α.[4]

We assume that investor i has a constant absolute risk tolerance utility function with coefficient of risk tolerance τ.[5] For simplicity we assume for now that all agents have the same risk tolerance; this assumption will be relaxed in Section 3. It can be shown that the demand function for the risky asset for each agent will have the linear form

$$D_i = \frac{\tau[E_i(v) - P]}{\text{var}_i(v)} \tag{15.1}$$

where $E_i(v)$ is the expected value of v in the opinion of agent i, $\text{var}_i(v) = 1/\alpha$ is the variance v in the opinion of agent i, and P is the market price. Thus the demand function for agent i is

$$D_i = \tau\alpha[v_i - P]. \tag{15.2}$$

Each agent has a supply S_i of the risky asset, and we suppose that the price P adjusts so as to equate aggregate demand and supply which yields an equilibrium price of

$$P^* = \overline{v} - \overline{S}/\tau\alpha \tag{15.3}$$

where bars over a variable denote the arithmetic mean of that variable across the agents.

---

[4] The precision of a random variable is the reciprocal of the variance.

[5] Risk tolerance is given by $-u'(c)/u''(c)$; it is the reciprocal of the Arrow-Pratt measure of absolute risk aversion. For a discussion of the Arrow-Pratt measure see Varian (1984).

Inserting this into the demand function of agent i we find the equilibrium demand for the risky asset to be

$$D_i^* = \tau\alpha[v_i - \bar{v}] + \bar{S}. \qquad (15.4)$$

Note that each agent's equilibrium demand depends on the deviation of his opinion from the average opinion.

Up until now, the trade has been due entirely to differences in opinion. Now suppose that some information arrives that allows each agent to improve his estimate of the value of the asset. In particular, we suppose that each agent i observes a signal V_i where

$$V_i = v + \epsilon_i \qquad (15.5)$$

and ϵ_i is IID Normal with mean zero and precision ω. Each agent will have a different piece of information about the value of the asset, but all agents will have information of the same precision. Of course the information set of agent i is not limited to just this piece of information; he or she will also use the market price in forming a final estimate of the value of the asset.

Given the n observations (V_i) an omniscient observer could calculate the sample mean

$$\bar{V} = \sum_{i=1}^{n} \frac{V_i}{n} \qquad (15.6)$$

which will have a Normal distribution with mean v and precision $\beta = n\omega$. In this model the equilibrium price turns out to be fully revealing, so that each agent will be able to calculate $\bar{V}$ in equilibrium.

Being good Bayesians, each investor will then form a posterior distribution for the value of the risky asset by combining his prior and his sample information in accord with Bayes' law. Given the distributional assumptions we have made, the posterior distribution of investor i will be Normal with precision of $\gamma = \alpha + n\omega$ and mean of

$$\frac{\alpha}{\gamma}v_i + \frac{\beta}{\gamma}\bar{V}. \qquad (15.7)$$

Using the assumption of constant absolute risk tolerance, the demand for the risky asset will have the linear form

$$D_i = \frac{\tau[E(v|I_i) - P]}{\text{var}(v|I_i)} \qquad (15.8)$$

where $E(v|I_i)$ is the expected value of the asset conditional on the information set of agent i, $\text{var}(v|I_i)$ is the variance of the asset conditional on i's information, and P is the market price.

Inserting the expressions for the expected value and the variance given in equation (15.7) in equation (15.8), the demand of agent i reduces to

$$D_i = \tau[\alpha v_i + \beta \overline{V} - \gamma P]. \tag{15.9}$$

We suppose that the market price P adjusts so as to equate aggregate demand and supply which gives us a post-information equilibrium price of

$$\hat{P} = \frac{\alpha \overline{v} + \beta \overline{V} - \overline{S}/\tau}{\gamma} \tag{15.10}$$

where, as before, bars over a variable denote the mean across the population.

Let us consider the information structure in this market more closely. Suppose that all agents agree on the value of the *information*, (V_i), observed by the other agents but disagree about the value of the other agents' opinions, (v_i). Then knowing the average prior mean, $\overline{v}$, would not lead any agent to revise his own posterior mean, but knowing the average *information* $\overline{V}$ would induce an agent to change his posterior mean. That is, each agent would agree that $\overline{V}$ would be a superior estimate of the true value of the asset compared to any agent's individual information V_i. The distinction being drawn here is the distinction between the other agents' *opinions*—which do not change a given agent's beliefs—and other agents' pieces of *information*—which do change a given agent's beliefs.

But, if each consumer knows the value of the coefficients in the aggregate demand function, he or she can estimate $\overline{V}$ from the observed equilibrium price and the formula:

$$\overline{V} = \frac{\overline{S}/\tau + \gamma \hat{P} - \alpha \overline{v}}{\beta}. \tag{15.11}$$

As in the original Grossman (1976) model, the equilibrium price aggregates all of the information in the economy and thus provides a superior estimate of the "true" expected value of the asset.

In Grossman's original paper all agents had the same prior beliefs but different tastes. In that paper he argues for the rational expectations equilibrium by appealing to a long run equilibrium where agents can tabulate the empirical distribution of the $(\hat{P}, \overline{V})$ pairs and thus infer $\overline{V}$ from observations of $\hat{P}$. The agents do not have to know the structure of the model, but only the reduced form relationship between $\hat{P}$ and $\overline{V}$.

This sort of argument does not work here. For if the events were repeated a large number of times the different prior beliefs would tend to converge to identical posterior beliefs. Instead it appears that we must assume that agents have some understanding of the structure of the model and are able to disentangle the information contained in the market price directly rather than to simply use a reduced form model. It appears that a model with different prior opinions demands even more "rational expectations" than does Grossman's model.

Luckily this is not the case. For we have an extra feature not present in the original Grossman model. We have assumed that the agents can observe an equilibrium price prior to the arrival of the information. And certainly the *change* in the equilibrium price when new information arrives should reveal more about the new information than simply the *level* of the equilibrium price. In particular, if we rearrange expressions (15.3) and (15.10) which characterize the pre-information and post-information equilibrium prices, we have

$$\alpha P^* = \alpha \overline{v} - \overline{S}/\tau \tag{15.12}$$

$$\gamma \hat{P} = \alpha \overline{v} + \beta \overline{V} - \overline{S}/\tau. \tag{15.13}$$

These equations can be solved for $\overline{V}$ to yield:

$$\overline{V} = \frac{\gamma \hat{P} - \alpha P^*}{\beta}. \tag{15.14}$$

Using the definitions of the precisions, $\beta = n\omega$, and $\gamma = \alpha + n\omega$, this expression can be rewritten as

$$\overline{V} = \hat{P} + \frac{\alpha}{n\omega}(\hat{P} - P^*). \tag{15.15}$$

Thus if the agents are able to observe the *change* in the equilibrium prices when information arrives, they only need to know the precisions α and ω in order to estimate the aggregate information. The number ω/α is the ratio of the precision of the likelihood to the precision of the prior opinion, and can be thought of as a measure of credibility. A credible agent gives a larger weight to the evidence than to his opinions; therefore the ratio ω/α should be large. If all agents believe that all agents are very credible— or that there is a very large number of not-so-credible agents—then the market price will essentially be equal to $\overline{V}$, the average information in the population.

If agents perceive the other agents' beliefs as not being particularly credible in the sense that ω/α is small then they will attempt to use the change in the equilibrium price, appropriately weighted, to try to sort out the "information" from the "opinion".[6]

---

[6] Milgrom and Stokey (1982) also make use of the change in equilibrium prices to convey information. We will examine their model in shortly. I would like to thank Sarab Seth for suggesting that a similar approach would be useful in the mean-variance context considered here.

Inserting the "rational expectations" estimate of $\overline{V}$ into the demand function for agent i and simplifying we have the equilibrium demand of agent i:

$$D_i = \tau\alpha(v_i - \overline{v}) + \overline{S} \tag{15.16}$$

Note the interesting feature of this expression: all of the information variables have dropped out—an agent's trade in equilibrium is determined solely by the deviation of his or her opinion from the average opinion.

The size of agent i's position in the risky asset depends positively on his risk tolerance, τ, and on his *prior* precision, α. This latter point is somewhat surprising. The sample precision of $\beta = n\omega$ may be much larger than the prior precision α, and one might have thought that for large n it would swamp the prior precision. Nevertheless the equilibrium demand for the risky asset is exactly the same as if the agent had no sample information at all! An agent's posterior *beliefs* may be dominated by the sample information but his *trades* will depend only on the prior information. The explanation of this seeming paradox is that the market price adjusts to reveal all information in the economy and thus eliminates the value of the sample information to any one agent. Trade can only occur when people are different; and in this model the only difference that people have are in their prior opinions.

Note that the equilibrium demand for each agent in the post-information equilibrium is exactly the same as in the pre-information equilibrium. The arrival of the information will have zero impact on the volume of trade. This is because each agent is able to extract the same information from the market price. The only differences among the agents are the differences in their prior opinions, and trade on the differences in opinions has already taken place. Thus there is nothing left to trade on when the information arrives.

Of course the equilibrium *price* will respond to arrival of information; if $\overline{V}$ is large in some particular realization then the market price will be large. Indeed, the price responds in such a way as to perfectly offset the desire to trade. But it has to be that way in a fully revealing equilibrium—if the price reveals all information, there is nothing left to be revealed by the volume of trade. Thus the volume of trade cannot depend in any independent way on the information signals received by the agents.[7]

These observations become even more striking if we consider what happens as the information becomes more and more precise, relative to the prior. According to equation (15.10) as n goes to infinity, for example, the precision of the information goes to infinity, and the equilibrium post-information price becomes $\overline{V}$. Thus as the sample information becomes

---

[7] Of course this model leads directly to the Grossman paradox as well: if the market price reveals all information, why does anyone bother to acquire information? Various resolutions of this paradox can be found in Grossman and Stiglitz (1980), Hellwig (1980), and Diamond and Verrecchia (1981).

more and more informative, the price of the asset approaches its average perceived value: the post-information equilibrium price reflects all available information. Nevertheless, the equilibrium trade of each agent, as given in equation (15.16), is entirely determined by the initial dispersion of opinion and remains unaffected by a change in the accuracy of the information. When information is very informative the equilibrium price is determined almost entirely by the information, while the equilibrium trade is determined entirely by the differences in opinion.

What are the implications of opinion differences for the volume of trade? Agent i's net trade in the risky asset is

$$T_i = \tau\alpha(v_i - \bar{v}) - (S_i - \bar{S}) \tag{15.17}$$

so that the equilibrium volume depends on both the differences in opinions and the differences in endowments. Suppose for simplicity that each agent has an identical endowment $\bar{S}$ of the risky asset. Then the net trade of agent i is simply $T_i = \tau\alpha(v_i - \bar{v})$ and the overall volume of trade is given by:

$$\sum_{i=1}^{n} \tau\alpha|v_i - \bar{v}|/2 \tag{15.18}$$

which clearly depends only on the dispersion of opinion. An increase in the dispersion of opinion, as measured by the sum of the absolute deviations of the priors, will necessarily increase the volume of trade, regardless of the private information received by the market participants.

15.3 Different tastes

In Grossman's original model all agents had identical priors but different risk tolerances; the equilibrium volume was therefore due solely to the differences in tastes. In the model above the agents all have the same tastes, but different prior opinions, and the equilibrium volume depends only on the differences of opinion. What if agents have different tastes and different opinions?

Letting τ_i denote the risk tolerance of agent i, the pre-information price is determined by solving:

$$\sum_{i=1}^{n} \tau_i\alpha[v_i - P] = \sum_{i=1}^{n} S_i \tag{15.19}$$

and the post equilibrium price is determined by solving:

$$\sum_{i=1}^{n} \tau_i[\alpha v_i + \beta\bar{V} - \gamma P] = \sum_{i=1}^{n} S_i. \tag{15.20}$$

Subtracting equation (15.19) from (15.20) and solving for $\overline{V}$, we find that the rational expectations estimate of $\overline{V}$ is exactly the same that given in equation (15.15):

$$\overline{V} = \frac{\gamma \hat{P} - \alpha P^*}{\beta} = \hat{P} + \frac{\alpha}{n\omega}(\hat{P} - P^*). \tag{15.21}$$

The agents do not need to know anything about the taste differences in the population to estimate $\overline{V}$, as long as they can observe the pre information and post-information prices. Everything hinges on the magnitude of "credibility" of the market price, as determined by α relative to $n\omega$.

Using this estimate of $\overline{V}$ it can be shown that the equilibrium trade of agent i is:

$$D_i = \tau_i \alpha \left(v_i - \sum_{j=1}^{n} w_j v_j \right) + w_i S \tag{15.22}$$

where

$$w_i = \frac{\tau_i}{\sum_{j=1}^{n} \tau_j}.$$

The volume of trade still depends on the deviation of agents opinion from the average opinion, but now it is a weighted average rather than the simple average we had before.

15.4 Differences in interpretation

The no-trade result may appear to fly in the face of common sense; certainly the arrival of new information in real markets may contribute to volume. It seems that this view is held by those who have examined the empirical determinants of the volume of trade. For example:

> "One reason to suggest a relationship between changes in price and transactions volume is that both are related to the type and flow of information in the market. New information can simultaneously spur trading and lead to new equilibrium prices." Karpoff (1985)

Casual empiricism (i.e., the nightly news) suggests that volume does react to new information. Empirical work by Epps and Epps (1976), Tauchen and Pitts (1983), Harris (1983) and others suggest that volume is highly correlated with the absolute value of the price change for daily stock returns. How can we reconcile this observation with the model described above?

One assumption of the above model was that all agents interpreted the information in the same way. That is, all agents agree that the observation of V_i contributed to their posterior estimate of v in the same way. For some kinds of information this may be plausible; but for other types it may be quite implausible. If OPEC were to break up tomorrow would everyone agree on the impact of this event on all asset prices? When Apple introduces a new computer line does everyone agree on the impact of this product on the market value of Apple stock?

We might model this by distinguishing between the *arrival* of the information and the *interpretation* of the information. Let Y_i be a random variable denoting the "magnitude" of a piece of information, and let $V_i = \delta_i Y_i$ be agent i's estimate of the impact of this information on the mean value of the risky asset. That is, agent i views $\delta_i Y_i$ as a signal about the value of the risky asset in the sense that he believes the model

$$V_i = \delta_i Y_i = v + \epsilon_i. \tag{15.23}$$

All agents agree on the magnitude of the information Y_i but the "interpretation" of the information, δ_i, differs from agent to agent. That is, each agent i has a potentially different belief, δ_i, about how the information Y_i will affect the equilibrium value of the asset.

Let us assume that the interpretations, (δ_i), and the observations, (Y_i), are distributed independently across the set of agents so that $\overline{V} = \overline{\delta}\,\overline{Y}$. Substituting this into equation (15.15) and solving for $\overline{Y}$ yields

$$\overline{Y} = \frac{\hat{P}}{\overline{\delta}} + \frac{\alpha}{n\omega} \frac{(\hat{P} - P^*)}{\overline{\delta}}. \tag{15.24}$$

Thus as long as the average value of δ is common knowledge, each agent will be able to estimate $\overline{Y}$ from the observed change in equilibrium price. After observing the equilibrium price of the asset, agent i should then revise his own estimate of the expected value of the risky asset to be $\delta_i \overline{Y}$. This leads to an equilibrium demand of the form

$$D_i = \tau[\alpha v_i + \beta \delta_i \overline{Y} - \gamma P]. \tag{15.25}$$

Solving for the post-information equilibrium price we have

$$\hat{P} = \frac{\alpha \overline{v} + \beta \overline{\delta} \overline{Y} - \overline{S}/\tau}{\gamma}. \tag{15.26}$$

Substituting this back into the demand function of agent i and subtracting off his endowment to get his equilibrium net trade, T_i, we have

$$T_i = \tau \left[\alpha(v_i - \overline{v}) + \beta(\delta_i - \overline{\delta})\overline{Y} \right] + (S_i - \overline{S}). \tag{15.27}$$

The interpretation of this equation is rather nice. The equilibrium net trade of an agent depends on the difference in his opinion, his interpretation, and his endowment from the averages of these variables. In this model, the agents can use the market price to estimate whether or not the events have occurred, but then put their own interpretation on the events themselves. In equilibrium the arrival of the information affects the volume of trade, but only through the differences of opinion about how the information should be interpreted, not through the difference in information itself.

15.5 An Arrow-Debreu model

The model described in the first part of this paper is a mean-variance model. However, the ideas described there are robust; we will demonstrate that by considering the same issues in the context of a contingent-consumption model which is a simplification of the model described in Milgrom-Stokey (1980). Let $s = 1, \ldots, S$ index states of nature and $i = 1, \ldots, n$ index the economic agents. Use $\pi_i(s)$ to denote agent i's prior probability belief about the occurrence of state s, and c_{is} to denote agent i's contingent consumption in state s. Finally, let $u_i(c)$ be agent i's von Neumann-Morgenstern utility function and p_s the Arrow-Debreu price for consumption in state s.

We suppose that all agents trade to an equilibrium which will be characterized by the first-order conditions for utility maximization:

$$\pi_i(s)u_i'(c_{is}) = \lambda_i p_s \qquad (15.28)$$

where λ_i is agent i's marginal utility of wealth.

Now suppose that each agent observes a private signal y_i which is a realization of a random variable that affects the probability of occurrence of state s. We suppose that if agent i could observe the signals of all the agents, $y = (y_1, \ldots, y_n)$, he would calculate the probability of occurrence of state s via Bayes' law, and that all agents agree on the form of the likelihood function, which we denote by $\pi(y|s)$.

After each agent observes his private signal, markets are reopened and all agents can revise their contingent consumption plans. Given the new information we would expect that prices of the various states would change. As in the model presented above the agents can take these price changes into account and use them to infer something about what signals the other agents observed. What will the new post-information equilibrium look like?

Given this framework, Milgrom-Stokey establish a remarkable result: there will always be a post-information equilibrium that reveals all the information observed by all the agents, and furthermore, the new equilibrium involves no trade by any agent.[8]

The proof is simply to consider what happens if the price of state s consumption changes to $\hat{p}_s = \pi(y|s)p_s$. In this case, each agent can extract the likelihood function $\pi(y|s)$ by dividing the post-information price by the pre-information price and use this likelihood to revise his or her prior probability via Bayes' law. The resulting equilibrium is characterized by the first-order conditions:

$$\pi_i(s|y)u_i'(c_{is}) = \frac{\pi(y|s)\pi_i(s)}{\pi_i(y)}u_i'(c_{is}) = \frac{\lambda_i}{\pi_i(y)}\pi(y|s)p_s = \hat{\lambda}_i\hat{p}_s \qquad (15.29)$$

---

[8] Related insights can be found in Marshall (1974), Rubinstein (1975), Bhattacharya (1976), Hakansson, Kunkel and Ohlson (1982) and Verrecchia (1981).

where $\hat{\lambda}_i = \lambda_i/\pi_i(y)$. Since the new prices, $(\hat{p}_s)$, the new beliefs $(\pi_i(s|y))$, and the original consumption levels, (c_{is}), satisfy the appropriate first-order conditions, we do indeed have an equilibrium in the post-information market that involves no trade due to the arrival of the information.

As before, one could question the assumption of a common likelihood function. If agents have different opinions about the effect of a given piece of information on the probability of occurrence of a state of nature, the Milgrom-Stokey result need no longer hold. Arrival of new information will in general cause agents to trade in this case, but only because agents *interpret* the information differently, not because it is different information.

This observation can be sharpened; Milgrom-Stokey show that if everyone has the same likelihood function there will always exist an equilibrium which is fully revealing and which involves no trade. But there is a partial converse: if there is no trade after information is revealed, then all agents must have essentially the same likelihood function and equilibrium will be fully revealing. So the relationship between differences of opinions and the volume of trade is an if-and-only-if relationship—common opinions about how information affects state probabilities means zero volume, and zero volume means essentially common opinions.

This proposition is a small extension of arguments given by Rubinstein (1975, Nonspeculation Condition), Milgrom-Stokey (1982, Theorem 3), and Hakansson, Kunkel and Ohlson (1982, Lemma 2). However, it seems worthwhile to give a brief exposition of the result.

Following Hakansson, Kunkel and Ohlson (1982), we will say that likelihood functions are *essentially homogeneous* if

$$\pi_i(y_i, \hat{p}|s) = k_i(y_i, \hat{p})\pi_1(y_i, \hat{p}|s)$$

for all $i = 1, \ldots, n$. If two likelihood functions are essentially homogeneous, then Bayes' law implies that they will generate the same posterior probabilities, since the $k_i(y_i, \hat{p})$ terms will cancel out from the numerator and the denominator. Thus agents that have essentially homogeneous likelihood functions will make the same inferences from the information they observe.

THEOREM 1. *Let (c_{is}, p_s) be an equilibrium before the information y is revealed and let $(c_{is}, \hat{p}_s)$ be a no-trade equilibrium after y_i is revealed to each agent. Then the value of each agent's likelihood function is given by:*

$$\pi_i(y_i, \hat{p}|s) = k_i(y_i, \hat{p})\frac{\hat{p}_s}{p_s}$$

so that agents' likelihood functions must be essentially homogeneous.

Proof. Choose two states, s and t. Since the economy is in equilibrium before and after the information is revealed, we must have:

$$\frac{\pi_i(s)u_i'(c_{is})}{\pi_i(t)u_i'(c_{it})} = \frac{p_s}{p_t}$$

and

$$\frac{\pi_i(s|y_i,\hat{p})u_i'(c_{is})}{\pi_i(t|y_i,\hat{p})u_i'(c_{it})} = \frac{\hat{p}_s}{\hat{p}_t}.$$

By Bayes' law we can write the latter expression as:

$$\frac{\pi_i(y_i,\hat{p}|s)\pi_i(s)u_i'(c_{is})}{\pi_i(y_i,\hat{p}|t)\pi_i(t)u_i'(c_{it})} = \frac{\hat{p}_s}{\hat{p}_t}.$$

Dividing by the first equation gives:

$$\frac{\pi_i(y_i,\hat{p}|s)}{\pi_i(y_i,\hat{p}|t)} = \frac{\hat{p}_s/p_s}{\hat{p}_t/p_t}.$$

This implies that:

$$\pi_i(y_i,\hat{p}|s) = k_i(y_i,\hat{p})\frac{\hat{p}_s}{p_s}$$

for all s as required. ∎

As indicated above, this result is essentially a corollary to Theorem 3 in Milgrom-Stokey (1982). However, the focus is different; Milgrom-Stokey show that if all agents have the same likelihood function, then in a post-information, no trade equilibrium, each agent's posterior probability must depend only on the post-information prices and be independent of his private signal. We show something a bit different: that *if* there is no trade in a post-information equilibrium, then all agents must have essentially the same likelihood value, and the equilibrium price change must reveal this common likelihood value. Hakansson, Kunkel and Ohlson (1982) have essentially the same result in a somewhat different setting while Bhattacharya (1976) has shown that this result is closely related to Rubinstein's (1975) Nonspeculation Condition.

15.6 The effect of differences of opinion on asset prices

The results of the last section suggest that the volume of trade in an Arrow-Debreu model is due primarily to the differences of opinion. In a one period model, these can be differences of opinion about the prior probabilities; in a two period model, trade requires differences of opinion about likelihood functions—that is, the interpretation of information.

How far can this insight be pushed? If two assets are otherwise identical but one has "more diverse" beliefs, which asset will have the larger volume of trade? Which asset will have the higher price? It is important to note that these questions can be addressed independently of the particular model of information transfer. For the questions are phrased in terms of *equilibrium* differences in beliefs; they are questions about comparative asset pricing, not about comparative statics.

Varian (1985a) has described some results concerning relative pricing in this framework; here we review these results and consider the implications for the volume of trade. In this section we will consider only the case of identical utility functions; the case of different utility functions will be considered in Sections 9 and 10.

Letting $f(\cdot)$ be the inverse of $u'(\cdot)$ we can write the Arrow-Debreu first-order conditions in equation (15.28) as:

$$c_{is} = f(\lambda_i p_s / \pi_i(s))$$

where $\pi_i(s)$ is now interpreted as either a prior or a posterior probability. Let us define $q_{is} = \pi_i(s)/\lambda_i$ to be a "weighted" probability for agent i. In general we would expect wealthier agents to have lower marginal utilities of wealth in equilibrium so that their beliefs will get a higher weight in the q_{is} expression. (It is easy to show that if two agents have the same probability beliefs and the same utility function, the wealthier one will have a lower marginal utility of wealth.)

Then we can sum the first-order conditions across the agents to derive an expression for aggregate consumption in state s:

$$C_s = \sum_{i=1}^{n} c_{is} = \sum_{i=1}^{n} f(p_s/q_{is}).$$

THEOREM 2. *The function $f(p_s/q_{is})$ is always an increasing function of q_{is}. It will be a concave (convex) function of q_{is} as the derivative of risk tolerance is less (greater) than 1.*

Proof. The first part of the theorem is proved in Varian (1985a). The same paper shows that $f(p_s/q_{is})$ will be concave in q_{is} iff $r'(c) > -r(c)^2$ where $r(c) = -u''(c)/u'(c)$ is the Arrow-Pratt measure of absolute risk aversion. This condition can be rearranged to give:

$$-\frac{r'(c)}{r(c)^2} = \frac{d}{dc}\left(\frac{1}{r(c)}\right) < 1$$

which establishes the second statement. ∎

It is easy to check that the derivative of risk tolerance for a logarithmic utility is precisely one, so we can conclude that $f(p_s/q_{is})$ will be a concave function of q_{is} when risk tolerance increases less rapidly than it does in the case of logarithmic utility. This seems like a very natural assumption.

Following Varian (1985a) we now consider two different states, s and t, such that $C_s = C_t$, but the probability beliefs for state t are a mean preserving spread of the probability beliefs for state s in the sense of Roth-schild-Stiglitz (1970). It follows from the strict concavity of $f(\cdot)$ that:

$$\sum_{i=1}^{n} f(p_s/q_{it}) < \sum_{i=1}^{n} f(p_s/q_{is}) = C_s = C_t = \sum_{i=1}^{n} f(p_t/q_{it})$$

and therefore $p_t < p_s$.

This argument proves:

THEOREM 3. *Consider two Arrow-Debreu assets that pay off in states with the same level of aggregate consumption. Then if all agents have identical tastes and risk tolerance does not increase too rapidly, the asset with the more dispersion of weighted probability beliefs will have the lower equilibrium price.*

Thus increased dispersion of beliefs should be associated with lower prices in equilibrium. It is important to understand that this is *not* a comparative statics statement. We are not examining two different equilibria. Rather we are examining two different assets in a *given* equilibrium. Theorem 3 followed solely from the first-order conditions and the assumption about risk tolerance; it is therefore compatible with any model of how equilibrium beliefs are formed. Equilibrium beliefs could be due to differences in likelihoods, non-rational behavior, or whatever, as long as the first-order conditions for an Arrow-Debreu equilibrium hold.

15.7 The effect of differences of opinion on volume

In order to get a result concerning the relative volume of trade in different assets we must refine the meaning of "other things being equal" and use a more restrictive notion of "increased dispersion of opinion." Since the final volume of trade depends on the pattern of initial endowments across the agents we will further assume that assets s and t have the same pattern of initial endowments: $\bar{c}_{is} = \bar{c}_{it}$ for all $i = 1, \ldots, n$.

In a given equilibrium and state s, let D_s be the set of net demanders—those agents for whom $f(p_s/q_{is}) > \bar{c}_{is}$—and let S_s be the set of net suppliers, defined in a similar manner. Since the amount bought equals the amount sold in equilibrium, we can express the volume of trade in state s by

$$V_s = \sum_{i \in D_s} [f(p_s/q_{is}) - \bar{c}_{is}] = \sum_{i \in S_s} [\bar{c}_{is} - f(p_s/q_{is})].$$

Now consider two states, s and t, and suppose that all of the agents who purchase asset s feel that state t is at least as likely as state s, and that all agents who sell asset s feel that t is less likely that s. That is:

$$q_{it} \geq q_{is} \quad \text{for all } i \in D_s$$
$$q_{it} \leq q_{is} \quad \text{for all } i \in S_s.$$

Informally, we are assuming that all of the net demanders for state s securities are even more optimistic about state t occurring than they are about state s occurring and all of the net suppliers of state s securities are even more pessimistic about state t occurring than they are about state s occurring. Thus there is certainly more dispersion of equilibrium beliefs about state t than about state s.

THEOREM 4.   *If all of the net demanders in state s are more optimistic about state t occurring than state s occurring and all of the net suppliers in state s are more pessimistic about state t occurring than state s occurring, then the volume of trade in state t must be higher than the volume of trade in state s.*

Proof. Suppose first that $p_t > p_s$, and let agent i be a net supplier of asset s in equilibrium. By the hypothesis of the theorem, $q_{it} < q_{is}$. The function $f(p_s/q_{is})$ is increasing in q_{is} and decreasing in p_s by Theorem 2, so we have that

$$f(p_s/q_{is}) > f(p_t/q_{it}).$$

Since $\bar{c}_{is} = \bar{c}_{it}$ by assumption we have

$$\bar{c}_{is} - f(p_s/q_{is}) < \bar{c}_{it} - f(p_t/q_{it}).$$

Summing over the net suppliers shows that $V_s < V_t$.

Now suppose that $p_t < p_s$. Then let agent i be a net *demander* of asset s in equilibrium. By exactly the same argument, we have

$$f(p_s/q_{is}) - \bar{c}_{is} > f(p_t/q_{it}) - \bar{c}_{it}.$$

Summing shows that $V_t > V_s$, as required. ∎

It is worth observing that this argument does not depend on agents having identical tastes or on the earlier assumption about risk tolerance: it is true in complete generality. Furthermore, the argument holds for the unweighted beliefs, $\pi_i(s)$, as well as the weighted beliefs, q_{is}. In fact, the argument has a very simple graphical proof which is depicted in Figure 15.1a. The assumption that all net demanders become more optimistic implies that the aggregate demand curve shifts to the right and the assumption that all net suppliers become more pessimistic implies that the aggregate net supply curve shifts to the right. Hence the volume of trade must increase, as shown in Figure 1.[9]

---

[9] The fact that Theorem 4 has an elementary graphical argument was pointed out to me by Duanne Seppi.

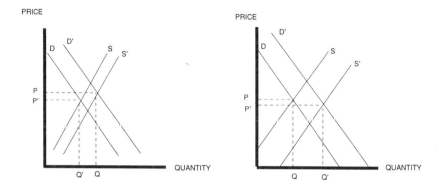

Figure 1. (a) An increase in the dispersion of beliefs of both demanders and suppliers must increase volume. (b) If the buyers become more optimistic and the equilibrium price decreases, then the volume must increase, regardless of what happens to the beliefs of suppliers.

However, this particular kind of increase in the dispersion of opinion is rather special. We can get a different result using a weaker definition of an increase in the dispersion of belief. In particular, let us consider a mean preserving spread that does not decrease q_{is} for any agent who is a net purchaser of the asset. That is, we assume that the mean preserving spread in beliefs is such that:

$$q_{it} \geq q_{is} \quad \text{for all } i \text{ such that } c_{is} > \bar{c}_{is}.$$

Let us also assume that the derivative of risk tolerance is less than 1, so that $f(p_s/q_{is})$ is concave. Then we have the situation illustrated in Figure 2. Here we have plotted the weighted probabilities q_{is} on the horizontal axis, and $c_{is} = f(p_s/q_{is})$ on the vertical axis. When we consider the movement from q_{is} to q_{it} we see that:

$$f(p_s/q_{is}) \leq f(p_s/q_{it}) < f(p_t/q_{it})$$

for all net purchasers of the asset where the first inequality follows from the monotonicity of $f(\cdot)$ and the second from the fact that $p_t < p_s$ which we established in Theorem 3. Since all of the net purchasers of the asset are now buying more, the net sellers of the asset must be selling more, and the volume of the trade is therefore larger. The volume of trade has increased for two reasons: each net purchaser wants to buy more at the same price, and the price decrease makes him or her want to buy even more again.

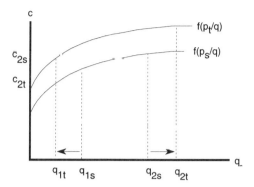

Figure 2. A mean preserving spread in weighted beliefs increases volume.

This can also be demonstrated using the supply and demand graph in Figure 1. If the demand increases and the equilibrium price decreases, then it follows that the equilibrium volume must be larger, as shown in Figure 1b. This result holds regardless of the change in the beliefs of the sellers of the asset, although it must be the case that on the average their beliefs have become more pessimistic.

If it appears obvious that making buyers more optimistic will increase the volume of trade, it might be worth considering the case where $f(\cdot)$ is a *convex* function of q_{is}. For example, take constant relative risk averse utility functions with $\rho < 1$. Then increasing the dispersion of opinion will *increase* asset prices, so the two effects described above work in opposite directions and the volume of trade can go either way. We give an algebraic example of this below.

An example can also be constructed using the supply and demand framework in Figure 1. Simply imagine the case where the demand curve shifts to the right as illustrated in Figure 1b, but the supply curve shifts far enough to the left so that the equilibrium price rises and the equilibrium transactions decrease.

15.8 Constant relative risk aversion

The case of constant relative risk averse utility functions, $u(c_{is}) = c_{is}^{1-\rho}/(1-\rho)$, serves as a convenient example of the above discussion. The first-order conditions take the form:

$$c_{is}^{\rho} = \frac{\lambda_i p_s}{\pi_{is}}$$

Straightforward but tedious calculations show that the equilibrium value of λ_i is given by:

$$\lambda_i = \left(\frac{\sum_{s=1}^{S} p_s^{\frac{\rho-1}{\rho}} \pi_{is}^{\frac{1}{\rho}}}{m_i} \right)^\rho$$

where m_i is agent i's equilibrium wealth. As indicated earlier, λ_i is a decreasing function of equilibrium wealth. If $\rho = 1$, λ_i is simply $1/m_i$.

Letting $q_i = \pi_{is}/\lambda_i$ the first-order conditions may be rewritten as:

$$c_{is}^{-\rho} = \frac{p_s}{q_{is}}$$

so that

$$c_{is} = \left(\frac{q_{is}}{p_s} \right)^{\frac{1}{\rho}}.$$

This in turn implies

$$C_s = \sum_{j=1}^{n} \left(\frac{q_{js}}{p_s} \right)^{\frac{1}{\rho}}$$

and

$$p_s = C_s^{-\rho} \left(\sum_{j=1}^{n} q_{js}^{\frac{1}{\rho}} \right)^\rho.$$

This function gives us the explicit equilibrium relationship between aggregate consumption, probability beliefs, and equilibrium prices. Inserting this into the first equation, we see that the equilibrium demand of agent i takes the form

$$c_{is} = w_{is} C_s$$

where

$$w_{is} = \frac{q_{is}^{\frac{1}{\rho}}}{\sum_{j=1}^{n} q_{js}^{\frac{1}{\rho}}}.$$

Thus the equilibrium demand of agent i is completely determined by his weighted probability, relative to the weighted probabilities of the other agents.

We can use this expression to present the example promised above. Suppose that $\rho = .5$, $C_s = C_t = 1$ and (q_{is}) and (q_{it}) are as given in Table 1. Note that in state s all agents have the same value of q_{is} so that any mean-preserving change in the equilibrium beliefs about state s will be a mean preserving spread. In the case illustrated in the table, both of the net demanders have the same probability beliefs about state t as state s while one of the net suppliers is more optimistic and one is more pessimistic about state s as compared to state t.

Using the formula given above it is straightforward to calculate the net trades (x_{is}) and (x_{it}). We find that state s has a volume of .200 and state t

has a volume of .190. Even though the dispersion of opinion has increased, and no net purchaser has become more pessimistic, the volume of trade has decreased. This is not of course a violation of Theorem 4, since one of the net demanders of the Arrow-Debreu security is more optimistic about state t than about state s. Nevertheless, the example is somewhat surprising since it shows that without the curvature assumption on demands somewhat perverse results can arise.

Table 1. Example of decreased volume of trade

	q_{is}	q_{it}	$\overline{c}_{is}$	x_{is}	x_{it}
1	.250	.200	.300	−.050	−.143
2	.250	.300	.400	−.150	−.047
3	.250	.250	.100	.150	.145
4	.250	.250	.200	.050	.045

15.9 Different tastes and different opinions

Here we discuss the general case where tastes differ across the agents. Letting $f_i(\cdot)$ be the inverse of agent i's marginal utility function, and following the derivation in Section 5 we have:

$$C_s = \sum_{i=1}^{n} f_i(p_s/q_{is}).$$

For fixed values of $(q_{1s}, \ldots, q_{ns})$, $f_i(\cdot)$ is a decreasing function of p_s. Thus we can invert it to get $p_s = F(C_s, q_s)$ where $q_s = (q_{1s}, \ldots, q_{ns})$. It is easy to show, following Varian (1985a), that $F(C_s, q_s)$ is a decreasing function of C_s and an increasing function of q_{is} in a given Arrow-Debreu equilibrium. What about the curvature of $F(C_s, q_s)$? The results of Varian (1988) show that increasing risk tolerance (i.e., decreasing absolute risk aversion) implies that $F(C_s, q_s)$ is a convex function of C_s. With some more effort we can show:

THEOREM 5. *If risk tolerance increases less rapidly than in the case of logarithmic utility, $F(C_s, q_s)$ will be a quasiconcave function of q_s.*

Proof. Fix C at $\overline{C}$, say, and consider three different sets of prices and weighted probabilities such that:

$$\sum_{i=1}^{n} f_i(p''/q_i'') = \sum_{i=1}^{n} f_i(p'/q_i') = \sum_{i=1}^{n} f_i(p/q_i) = \overline{C}$$

where $q_i'' = tq_i + (1 - t)q_i'$.

In order to establish quasiconcavity, we need to show that:

$$F(C, q'') \geq \min\{F(C, q), F(C, q')\}$$

or, equivalently, that

$$p'' \geq \min\{p, p'\}.$$

Without loss of generality let $p = \min\{p, p'\}$.

The assumption that risk tolerance does not increase too rapidly implies that $f_i(p/q)$ is concave in q. This implies that

$$f_i(p/q_i'') \geq t f_i(p/q_i) + (1 - t) f_i(p/q_i').$$

By the negative monotonicity of $f_i(p/q_i)$ in p and the assumption that $p' \geq p$ we have:

$$t f_i(p/q_i) + (1 - t) f_i(p/q_i') \geq t f_i(p/q_i) + (1 - t) f_i(p'/q_i').$$

Putting these two inequalities together and summing we have:

$$\sum_{i=1}^{n} f_i(p/q_i'') \geq t \sum_{i=1}^{n} f_i(p/q_i) + (1 - t) \sum_{i=1}^{n} f_i(p'/q_i')$$
$$= t\overline{C} + (1 - t)\overline{C} = \overline{C}$$
$$= \sum_{i=1}^{n} f_i(p''/q_i'').$$

It follows that $p \leq p''$, as was to be shown. ∎

This result suggests that even if preferences are different, there is a tendency for divergence of opinion to lead to lower asset prices. Consider Figure 3 where we have illustrated a level set of $F(C, q_1, q_2)$. In this example we have two states of nature with the same value of aggregate consumption and state prices but different weighted subjective probabilities, (q_1, q_2) and (q_1', q_2'). As established above, the upper contour set is convex and monotonic. Therefore, if we take a weighted average of (q_1, q_2) and (q_1', q_2') to get (q_1'', q_2''), the equilibrium value of p'' must increase. In this sense, taking an average of "extreme" distributions of beliefs will tend to increase state prices.

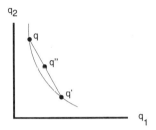

Figure 3. Averaging beliefs will tend to lead to lower asset prices.

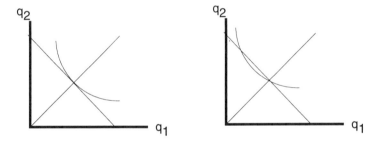

Figure 4. A mean preserving spread with identical tastes (a) and different tastes (b)

It is instructive to consider this geometry when the tastes are identical. In Figure 4a we have illustrated a typical level set of $F(C, q_1, q_2)$. We can also describe this level set implicitly as the set of all (q_1, q_2) such that:

$$C = f(p/q_1) + f(p/q_2)$$

where p and C are fixed.

Consider the slope of this level set along the diagonal, where $q_1 = q_2$. Since $f(p/q_i)$ is independent of i along the diagonal, the slope of the level set must be -1. Thus if we take a "spread" in (q_1, q_2) away from the diagonal that preserves the mean of (q_1, q_2) we are moving along a 45 degree line and must therefore move to a lower level set. At any other point on the curve a mean preserving spread will necessarily move us to a lower level set, as illustrated.

Now consider the general case with different utilities as depicted in Figure 4b. Here the level curve does not necessarily have slope of -1 at the diagonal so that a spread in beliefs may easily move us to a higher level set.

15.10 Moving from homogeneous to diverse beliefs

The geometric analysis of the last section can be used to describe another sense in which increases in the dispersion of opinion will tend to lower asset prices. Consider Figure 4 once again. It is true that the level curve may not have a slope of -1 at the diagonal, but we can compute its slope easily enough. The level curve is defined by the identity

$$f_1(p/q_1) + f_2(p/q_2) = C.$$

Totally differentiating this expression gives us

$$-f_1'(p/q_1)\frac{p}{q_1^2}dq_1 - f_2'(p/q_2)\frac{p}{q_2^2}dq_2 = 0.$$

Now use the facts that $f_i' = 1/u_i''$ and $u_i' = p/q_i$ to write

$$\left(-\frac{u_1'(c_1)}{u_1''(c_1)}\right)\frac{dq_1}{q_1} + \left(-\frac{u_2'(c_2)}{u_2''(c_2)}\right)\frac{dq_2}{q_2} = 0. \tag{15.30}$$

Using τ_i to represent individual i's risk tolerance, and evaluating this expression where $q_1 = q_2$ we have

$$\tau_1 dq_1 + \tau_2 dq_2 = 0 \tag{15.31}$$

or

$$\frac{dq_2}{dq_1} = -\frac{\tau_1}{\tau_2}. \tag{15.32}$$

This gives us the slope of the level set when the weighted beliefs are the same. A change in (q_1, q_2) that keeps the *weighted* sum in equation (15.31) constant represents an increase in the dispersion of beliefs which preserves the *weighted* mean. By the convexity of the level set, any such change must reduce the state price, starting from equal weighted beliefs.

   In this expression an agent's beliefs are weighted by both his marginal utility of wealth and his risk tolerance. Generally speaking, the beliefs of wealthy and risk tolerant agents will have a larger weight in the above expression. Thus an increase in the dispersion of those agents' beliefs will have a larger impact than an increase of the dispersion of beliefs of poorer and more risk averse agents, as one might expect.

   This result can also be stated in terms of the absolute beliefs rather than the weighted beliefs. By definition of q_i, we have that $dq_i/q_i = d\pi_i/\pi_i$ since the λ_i terms will cancel from the numerator and denominator. Thus if we evaluate (15.30) at a state where $\pi_1 = \pi_2$, we have:

$$\tau_1 d\pi_1 + \tau_2 d\pi_2 = 0. \tag{15.33}$$

In this expression the risk tolerances τ_1 and τ_2 are evaluated at a different level of consumption than before—the consumption in the state associated with homogeneous probabilities rather than homogeneous weighted probabilities.

Since the upper contour set is convex in (π_1, π_2) space as well as in (q_1, q_2) space, any movement along tangent line defined in (15.33) will necessarily decrease the state price. Thus moving from a state with homogeneous beliefs to a state with heterogeneous beliefs but the same level of aggregate consumption will necessarily lower the state price, as long as the *weighted* average of probability beliefs remains constant—where the weights are given by the risk tolerances.

Summarizing the above discussion we have:

THEOREM 6. *Assume that risk tolerance decreases less rapidly than in the case of logarithmic utility. Suppose the agents have homogeneous beliefs about the probability of occurrence of state s. Then if state t has identical aggregate consumption, and identical "weighted mean opinion," $\overline{\pi}$, but more dispersed probability beliefs, it must have a lower state price.*

15.11 Other equilibrium models

The basic analytic tool used in the last few sections is the relationship between a mean preserving spread in opinions and the concavity of the "demand functions". This observation can be applied to a variety of other equilibrium models.

The simplest case is that of a single risky asset. Let v_i be agent i's estimate of the expected value of this asset, and let p be the market price. Suppose that all agents have identical demand functions $D(p, v_i)$ and that the equilibrium price is determined by demand and supply:

$$\sum_{i=1}^{n} D(p, v_i) = S.$$

Suppose that the demand function is a concave function of v_i. Then a mean preserving spread in v_i will decrease the sum of the demands. In order to restore equilibrium, the price must rise. The reverse result holds if the demand function is convex in v_i. These statements, unlike those of the last few sections, *are* comparative statics results since they refer to how the equilibrium values change when opinions become more dispersed, rather than how different asset values compare in a given equilibrium.

So the problem of how an increase in the dispersion of some variable affects equilibrium prices can be reduced to the question of whether demand functions are concave or convex in that variable. How can that be determined? The answer comes from examining the structure of the maximization model that lies behind the demands.

The standard comparative static technique to determine the slope of a demand function with respect to some parameter is to differentiate the first-order conditions. In order to determine the *curvature* of a demand function, it is necessary to take the *second derivative* of the first order conditions which will typically involve the third derivatives of the utility function. In the case investigated in this paper we were able to give a simple interpretation of the conditions for concavity of the demand func tion in terms of how risk tolerance changes as wealth changes. In general these third-order terms are rather messy, but it seems that there is hope of interpreting them in special cases.

Of course in some models one can derive explicit forms for demand functions. For example, a constant relative risk aversion model with a single, Normally distributed asset gives rise to a demand function of the form

$$D_i = \frac{\tau_i[v_i - P]}{\sigma_i^2},$$

where τ_i is agent i's risk tolerance, v_i is his expected value, and σ_i^2 is his variance. In this case, demand is linear in the "weighted beliefs" $\tau_i v_i / \sigma_i^2$, so that a mean-preserving spread in these weighted beliefs will leave asset prices unchanged. However, demand is a *convex* function of the variances, (σ_i^2), so a mean preserving spread in the agents' beliefs about the variance of the risky asset will tend to *increase* the equilibrium price.[10]

Similar conclusions emerge in a CAPM or continuous time model.[11] Since asset demand functions are linear functions of expected values for each agent, the equilibrium prices of assets will simply depend on the average expected values; assets with different degrees of dispersions of opinion will have the same equilibrium prices, other things being equal.

15.12 Summary

In the first part of this paper I examined the distinction between information and opinions and showed that in equilibrium the pattern and volume of trade would be determined by differences of opinion, not differences in information.

In the second part of the paper, I examined a model with pure opinion differences and derived the implications for comparative asset pricing. Maintaining the assumption that risk tolerance decreases, but not too rapidly,

---

[10] For an interesting analysis of an equilibrium in a futures market in which traders have different variances, see Stein (1986).

[11] See the Appendix for a discussion of dispersion of beliefs in a continuous time framework.

I showed that if tastes are identical, asset prices would be decreasing functions of the dispersion of opinion. If tastes are different, asset prices would be quasiconcave function of the vector of weighted probability beliefs, so that averaging beliefs would tend to increase asset prices. The curvature of the demand function is the crucial feature in determining how asset prices relate to different degrees of dispersion of beliefs.

15.13 Appendix: A continuous time model

In this appendix, we examine a continuous time model in which there are heterogeneous beliefs about asset returns. Models of this sort have been extensively investigated by Williams (1977) and Grossman and Shiller (1982), with a somewhat different emphasis. By combining the insights of these authors we can adapt their results to the problem at hand.

Let r_s be the (instantaneous) random return on security s, and let r_0 be the (instantaneous) risk free rate. Suppose that all asset returns and the optimal consumption of each agent follow an Ito process. Then in our notation Grossman and Shiller's equation (11a) takes the form:

$$r_{is} = r_0 + A_i \text{cov}_i(r_s, dc_i/c_i)$$

where r_{is} is agent i's expected return on security s, $\text{cov}_i(r_s, dc_i/c_i)$ is agent i's belief about the covariance of the rate of growth of his consumption and the rate of return on security s, and

$$A_i = -\frac{u_i''(c_i)}{u_i'(c_i)} c_i$$

is agent i's coefficient of *relative* risk aversion. This is simply the first order condition for optimal choice in a continuous time model, combined with Ito's lemma. Using the linearity of the covariance operator, and that fact that c_i is nonstochastic at the time the optimal choice is made we have:

$$r_{is} = r_0 + \frac{1}{\tau_i}\text{cov}_i(r_s, dc_i). \tag{15.34}$$

where $\tau_i = -u'(c_i)/u_i''(c_i)$ is agent i's absolute risk tolerance.

Williams (1977) and Merton (1980) have argued that if security returns follow an Ito process, it is possible to estimate the covariance matrix of security returns arbitrarily accurately in an arbitrarily short time interval. The expected returns of the assets, on the other hand, will always be estimated imprecisely. Thus, following the argument of Williams (1977), we will assume that agents agree about the covariance matrix of the returns, and disagree only in their beliefs about the expected returns. This allows us to drop the subscript i on the covariance term in (15.34) and simply write it as $\text{cov}(c_i, r_s)$.

Cross multiply (15.34), sum over the agents $i = 1, \ldots, n$, and use the linearity of the covariance operator to get:

$$\sum_{i=1}^{n} \tau_i r_{is} = r_0 \sum_{i=1}^{n} \tau_i + \text{cov}(r_s, dC) \tag{15.35}$$

where $dC = \sum_{i=1}^{n} dc_i$ is the change in aggregate consumption.

Now define

$$\gamma_i = \frac{\tau_i}{\sum_{j=1}^{n} \tau_j}$$

and

$$\kappa = \frac{C}{\sum_{j=1}^{n} \tau_j}$$

and rewrite this expression as:

$$\sum_{i=1}^{n} \gamma_i r_{is} = r_0 + \kappa \; \text{cov}(r_s, dC/C). \tag{15.36}$$

In order to interpret this equation, we note that the left hand side is the weighted average of expected returns, where the weight given to agent i's beliefs is proportional to his risk tolerance. The right hand side of the equation is the risk free return plus a constant depending on the average risk tolerance in the economy, times the covariance of the asset return with the rate of growth of aggregate consumption.

This calculation is similar to the derivation of Grossman and Shiller (1982) but with a different interpretation. They take expectations with respect to the set of common information available to the agents at the time their consumption decisions are made. The left hand side of equation (15.36) in their framework is the expected return on security s based on the publicly available information at a given time. In our framework, the left hand side of (15.36) is a weighted average of subjective beliefs about the expected returns.

Following Williams (1977) we have assumed that agents have homogeneous beliefs about the covariance structure of the asset returns, but differ in their expected values for asset returns. The expectations in equation (15.36) are the actual expectations of the agents, based on their own private information and beliefs, not the expectations based on some common information as in Grossman and Shiller.

Equation (15.36) is the analog of Williams (1977) continuous time CAPM with heterogeneous beliefs, but because we use the covariance with consumption rather than the covariance with respect to wealth, the "hedging portfolios" in his equation are not needed here. (See Breeden (1979) for further discussion of why "hedging portfolios" are not needed in general in consumption based pricing models in continuous time.)

For our purposes, the interesting thing about equation (15.36) is what it says about comparative asset pricing. If two securities have the same "consumption beta" then they have to have the same "average expected return." This in turn implies that the pricing of securities is independent of the dispersion of opinion about their expected values. To see this, let v_s be the market value of security s at a specific time and let dv_s be the random change in its value in the next instant. Then since the instantaneous return is given by $r_s = dv_s/v_s$, we can solve (15.36) to get:

$$v_s = \frac{\sum_{i=1}^{n} \gamma_i dv_{is} + \kappa \operatorname{cov}(dC/C, dv_s)}{r_0}.$$

Here dv_{is} is agent i's belief about the expected change in value of asset s. Thus two securities that have the same "consumption beta" and the same *average* expected return must have the same price.

It is interesting to compare this result with equation (15.33). In that equation π_1 and π_2 are the expected returns on the Arrow–Debreu asset under consideration, since it pays zero in all states but one. Theorem 6 established that an increase in dispersion of opinion that keeps the weighted average of opinions constant will decrease the state price. In the continuous time framework examined above, such an increase in dispersion of opinion will leave the state price unchanged.

The insensitivity of asset prices to differences of opinion arise in this framework because of the linearity of the asset demand functions in the expected returns. Since only the first two derivatives of utility enter into the portfolio choice problem, the higher order curvature properties of utility considered earlier will not affect asset prices in equilibrium.

A similar result occurs in a discrete time model, if we are willing to postulate that individuals believe that their optimal consumption in future periods and asset returns will be Normally distributed. Since the algebra is almost the same as that given above, we will only sketch the details.

The first order conditions for utility maximization by individual i will take the form:

$$E_i u_i'(c_i)(r_s - r_0)$$

where E_i stands for expectation with respect to agent i's subjective beliefs about the asset returns. (The expectations are at time 0 for some given time in the future, but we omit the time subscript so as not to clutter the notation.)

Using the standard covariance identity, and rearranging, we can write this as:

$$r_{is} = r_0 - \frac{\operatorname{cov}_i(u_i'(c_i), r_s)}{E_i u'(c_i)}$$

where $r_{is} = E_i r_s$, as before. Assume now that c_i and r_s are perceived as bivariate Normal by investor i. Applying a theorem due to Rubinstein (1975) we have:

$$r_{is} = r_0 + \left(-\frac{E_i u_i''(c_i)}{E_i u_i'(c_i)}\right) \operatorname{cov}_i(c_i, r_s).$$

Letting $\tau_i = -E_i u_i'(c_i)/E_i u''(c_i)$ we can write this as:

$$r_{is} = r_0 + \frac{1}{\tau_i}\operatorname{cov}_i(c_i, r_s). \tag{15.37}$$

This equation is virtually the same as (15.34). If we assume that agents have the same beliefs about the covariance structure of the asset returns, then we can apply the same algebraic manipulations as before gives us:

$$\sum_{i=1}^{n} \gamma_i r_{is} = r_0 + \kappa \; \mathrm{cov}(C, r_s). \tag{15.38}$$

The only difference between (15.36) and (15.38) is that γ_i has a slightly different interpretation in the two equations, and that (15.38) is expressed in levels rather than instantaneous rates of change.

Equations (15.36) and (15.38) are on the verge of being estimable, at least given survey data on expectations and the time series estimates of the covariance between asset returns and aggregate consumption that are beginning to appear. Perhaps the addition of heterogeneous beliefs about asset returns will improve the performance of the empirical estimates of consumption based asset pricing models.

Finally, we consider the volume of trade in this kind of model. If we increase dispersion of opinion in the way described earlier — where the net demanders become more optimistic and the endowments of the two assets across the consumers are the same — and we keep the weighted sum of expected returns constant then it is easy to see that the volume of trade must increase. For an increase in the expected return on an asset must increase net demand for it by an individual, and we have established above that the asset price remains unchanged. Thus the transactions volume in the asset with the more dispersed beliefs must unambiguously be larger.

References

Aumann, R. (1976), "Agreeing to Disagree," *Annals of Statistics*, **4**, pp. 1236–39.

Bhattacharya, S. (1976), "Information Efficiency and Inter-temporal Rates of Return," Sloan School mimeo.

Black, F. (1986), "Noise," *Journal of Finance*, 41, 52–43 .

Breeden, D. and M. g (1978), "Prices of State-Contingent Claims Implicit in Option Prices," *Journal of Business*, **51**, 621–51.

Breeden, D. (1979), "An Intertemporal Asset Pricing Model with Stochastic Consumption and Investment Opportunities," *Journal of Financial Economics*, 7, 265–296.

Cragg, J. and B. Malkiel (1982), *Expectations and the Structure of Share Prices*, University of Chicago Press, Chicago.

Diamond, D. and R. Verrecchia (1981), "Informational Aggregation in a Noisy Rational Expectations Economy," *Journal of Financial Economics*, **9**, 221–235.

Epps, T. and M. Epps (1976), "The Stochastic Dependence of Security Price Changes and Transaction Volumes: Implications for the Mixture of-Distribution Hypothesis," *Econometrica*, **44**, 305–321.

Grossman, S. (1976), "On the Efficiency of Competitive Stock Markets Where Traders Have Diverse Information," *The Journal of Finance*, **31**, 573–585.

Grossman, S. (1977), "The Existence of Futures Markets, Noisy Rational Expectations, and Informational Externalities," *Review of Economic Studies*, **44**, 431–449.

Grossman, S. (1978), "Further Results on the Informational Efficiency of Competitive Stock Markets," *Journal of Economic Theory*, **18**, 81–101.

Grossman, S. and R. Shiller (1982), "Consumption Correlatedness and Risk Measurement in Economies with Non–Traded Assets and Heterogeneous Information," *Journal of Financial Economics*, 10, 195–210.

Grossman, S. and J. Stiglitz (1980), "On the Impossibility of Informationally Efficient Markets," *American Economic Review*, **70**, 393–408.

Hakansson, N., J. Kunkel and J. Ohlson (1982), "Sufficient and Necessary Conditions for Information to have Social Value in Pure Exchange," *Journal of Finance*, **37**, 1169–1181.

Harris, L. (1983), "The Joint Distribution of Speculative Prices and of Daily Trading Volume," University of Southern California Working Paper.

Harsanyi, J. (1983), "Bayesian Decision Theory, Subjective and Objective Probabilities, and Acceptance of Empirical Hypotheses," *Synthese*, **57**, pp. 341–365.

Hellwig, M. (1980), "On the Aggregation of Information in Competitive Markets," *Journal of Economic Theory*, **22**, 477–498.

Jarrow, R. (1980), "Heterogeneous Expectations, Restrictions on Short Sales, and Equilibrium Asset Prices," *Journal of Finance*, **35**, 1105–13.

Karpoff, J. (1985), "The Relationship between Stock Prices and Volume," *Center for the Study of Banking and Financial Markets Digest*, University of Washington, Seattle.

Lintner, J. (1969) "The Aggregation of Investors' Diverse Judgements and Preferences in Purely Competitive Markets," *Journal of Financial and Quantitative Analysis*, **4**, 347–400.

Marshall, J. (1974), "Private Incentives and Public Information," *American Economic Review*, **64**, 373–390.

Mayshar, J. (1983), "On Divergence of Opinion and Imperfections in Capital Markets", *American Economic Review*, **73**, 114–28.

Merton, R. (1980), "On Estimating the Expected Return on the Market," *Journal of Financial Economics*, **8**, 323–361.

Milgrom, P. and N. Stokey (1982), "Information, Trade and Common Knowledge," *Journal of Economic Theory*, **26**, 17–27.

Rothschild, M. and J. Stiglitz (1970), "Increasing Risk I: a Definition," *Journal of Economic Theory*, **2**, 225–243.

Rubinstein, M. (1975), "Security Market Efficiency in an Arrow-Debreu Economy," *American Economic Review*, **65**, 812–824.

Rubinstein, M. (1976), "The Strong Case for the Generalized Logarithmic Utility Model as the Premier Model of Financial Markets," *Journal of Finance*, **31**, 551–571.

Stein, J. (1986), "Real Effects of Futures Speculation: Asymptotically Rational Expectations," *Economica*, **53**, pp. 159–180.

Tauchen, G. and M. Pitts (1983), "The Price Variability–Volume Relationship on Speculative Markets," *Econometrica*, **51**, 485–506.

Tirole, J. (1982), "On the Possibility of Speculation Under Rational Expectations," 50, *Econometrica*, 1163–81.

Varian, H. (1984), *Microeconomic Analysis*, W. W. Norton & Co., New York.

Varian, H. (1985a), "Divergence of Opinion in Complete Markets," *Journal of Finance*, **40**, 1, 309—317.

Varian, H. (1988), "Estimating Risk Aversion from Arrow-Debreu Portfolio Choice," *Econometrica*, **56**, pp. 973–980, July 1988.

Verrecchia, R. (1981), "On the Relationship Between Volume Reaction and the Consensus of Investors: Implications for Interpreting Tests of Information Content," *Journal of Accounting Research*, **19**, 271–283.

Williams, J. (1977), "Capital Asset Prices with Heterogeneous Beliefs," *Journal of Financial Economics*, **5**, 219–39.

Chapter 16

ESTIMATING RISK AVERSION FROM ARROW-DEBREU PORTFOLIO CHOICE

This paper derives necessary and sufficient conditions for Arrow-Debreu choices of contingent consumption to be compatible with the maximization of a state independent expected utility function that exhibits increasing or decreasing absolute risk aversion, or increasing or decreasing relative risk aversion. The conditions can be used to bound different measures of risk aversion based on a single observation of Arrow-Debreu portfolio choice.

The expected utility hypothesis forms the basis for much of our understanding of investor behavior under uncertainty. It is commonly agreed that a well-behaved expected utility function should be an increasing and concave function of wealth, or, equivalently, that its first derivative should be positive and its second derivative should be negative. It is also widely accepted that the Arrow-Pratt measure of absolute risk aversion should be declining with wealth. There is much less agreement about the behavior of the Arrow-Pratt measure of *relative* risk aversion, although some investigators have argued that it should increase with wealth.

In this note I derive necessary and sufficient conditions for choices of contingent consumption across states of nature to satisfy various hypotheses about the behavior of these measures of risk aversion. If the portfolio choice behavior of the consumer is consistent with the conditions I derive, then the conditions can be used to bound the Arrow–Pratt measures of absolute and relative risk aversion. The conditions are derived using methods of the "nonparametric approach" to optimizing behavior introduced by

This research was supported in part by the National Science Foundation. I would like to thank Richard Green for helpful remarks. I am especially grateful to an anonymous referee whose comments significantly improved the statements and proofs of the results.

Afriat (1967) and extended by Diewert (1973), Diewert and Parkan (1978), and Varian (1982), (1983a). Applications of these methods to choice under uncertainty include Dybvig and Ross (1982), Green and Srivastava (1983), and Varian (1983b).

16.1 The maximization problem

Consider an investor who chooses a pattern of consumption across states of nature to solve the following problem.

$$\max \sum_{s=1}^{S} \pi_s u(c_s)$$

$$\text{s.t.} \quad \sum_{s=1}^{S} q_s c_s = \sum_{s=1}^{S} q_s \bar{c}_s \tag{16.1}$$

Here π_s is the probability that state s will occur, $\bar{c}_s$ is the endowment of consumption in state s, and q_s is the price for an Arrow-Debreu contingent commodity that pays off one unit of consumption if state s occurs. We will suppose that $u(c)$ is a strictly increasing, strictly concave, twice differentiable function.

The first-order conditions for this problem are:

$$\pi_s u'(c_s) = \lambda q_s \quad s = 1, \dots, S$$

We can always choose an affine transformation of the expected utility function so that $\lambda = 1$. Thus, we can define $p_s = q_s/\pi_s$ and rewrite the first order conditions as:

$$u'(c_s) = p_s \quad s = 1, \dots, S$$

The ratios of state prices to probabilities are assumed to be observable, so that the numbers (p_s, c_s) for $s = 1, \dots, S$ represent the potentially observable consumption data associated with the choice problem we are studying.

We will say we can *rationalize* this choice behavior if we can find a once differentiable increasing concave function $v(c)$ that satisfies the appropriate first-order conditions. Since the first-order conditions are sufficient conditions for the maximization of a concave function, this will guarantee that (c_s) actually solves the given maximization problem.

Breeden and Litzenberger (1978), Dybvig and Ross (1982) and Green and Srivastava (1983) show that a necessary and sufficient condition for a utility function to exist that rationalizes some choices (p_s, c_s) is that c_s is a decreasing function of p_s. If we number the states of nature so that $c_1 < c_2 < \dots < c_S$ we can express this condition as simply requiring that

$p_1 > p_2 > \ldots > p_S$. From now on we will assume that the states have been numbered in this way and that the observed consumption values satisfy this condition. The question that we pose is: what further conditions must be satisfied if the observed choices are to be compatible with various hypotheses about the behavior of risk aversion?

16.2 Absolute risk aversion

Let $r(c) = -u''(c)/u'(c)$ be the Arrow-Pratt measure of absolute risk aversion. We observe that decreasing (increasing) absolute risk aversion is equivalent to the requirement that $\log u'(c)$ is a convex (concave) function. This follows since

$$\frac{d \log u'(c)}{dc} = \frac{u''(c)}{u'(c)} = -r(c).$$

Differentiating both sides of this identity, and using the assumption that $r'(c) < 0$, we have

$$\frac{d^2 \log u'(c)}{dc^2} = -r'(c) > 0.$$

Since $\log u'(c)$ is a convex function, it must satisfy the following inequalities:

$$\log u'(c_{s+1}) \geq \log u'(c_s) + \frac{d \log u'(c_s)}{dc}[c_{s+1} - c_s] \qquad (16.2)$$

$$\log u'(c_{s-1}) \geq \log u'(c_s) + \frac{d \log u'(c_s)}{dc}[c_{s-1} - c_s] \qquad (16.3)$$

Substituting $p_s = u'(c_s)$, $r(c_s) = -d \log u'(c_s)/dc$, and recalling that $c_{s-1} < c_s < c_{s+1}$, we can rearrange these inequalities to give us the following *Ratio Condition*:

$$\frac{\log p_s - \log p_{s+1}}{c_{s+1} - c_s} \leq r(c_s) \leq \frac{\log p_{s-1} - \log p_s}{c_s - c_{s-1}} \qquad (16.4)$$

The Ratio Condition gives us an observable bound on risk aversion at each choice of contingent consumption. It has a simple geometric interpretation given in Figure 1. Here we have plotted $\log p_s$ versus c_s and connected the dots. (The other constructions in Figure 1 will be explained below.) It follows easily from risk aversion that the resulting piecewise linear function must be downward sloping. The Ratio Condition implies that the slopes of the line segments connecting each dot must be becoming flatter as consumption increases. That is, the piecewise linear function in Figure 1 depicted by the bold line must be a convex function. If risk aversion is increasing then the piecewise linear function must be concave.

Thus the Ratio Condition gives us a *necessary* condition for decreasing absolute risk aversion. However, it turns out that the condition is sufficient as well. That is, if the inequalities defined by the Ratio Condition are satisfied, then it will always be possible to construct an increasing, concave von Neumann-Morgenstern utility function $v(c)$ that exhibits decreasing absolute risk aversion and which generates the choices (c_s) as optimizing choices.

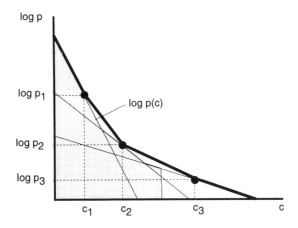

Figure 1. Geometric interpretation of the Ratio Condition.

In order to prove this, let us suppose that the inequalities given in the Ratio Condition can be satisfied so that we can choose a set of numbers (r_s) that satisfies the inequalities

$$\frac{\log p_s - \log p_{s+1}}{c_{s+1} - c_s} \le r_s \le \frac{\log p_{s-1} - \log p_s}{c_s - c_{s-1}} \qquad (16.5)$$

Geometrically, this simply means that we can choose a set of slopes (r_s) that lie between the slopes given by piecewise linear function depicted in Figure 1 at each observation.

Now define the function given by the lower envelope of these lines:

$$\log p(x) = \min_s \{\log p_s - r_s(x - c_s)\}.$$

Since we have assumed that $c_{s-1} < c_s < c_{s+1}$ this function will be differentiable at $x = c_s$ for $s = 1, \ldots, S$, and its derivative will be given by

$$\frac{d \log p(c_s)}{dc} = \frac{p'(c_s)}{p(c_s)} = -r_s.$$

Now define the function

$$v(c) = \int_0^c p(x) \, dx = \int_0^c \exp[\log p(x)] \, dx.$$

This is simply a monotonic transformation of the area under $\log p(x)$, as depicted in Figure 1. We now observe the following:

1. The first derivative of $v(c)$ at c_s is p_s.

2. The second derivative of $v(c)$ at c_s is given by

$$v''(c_s) = p'(c_s) = -r_s p_s < 0.$$

Thus $v(c)$ is a concave function. It follows that the satisfaction of the first-order conditions is a sufficient condition for the observed choices to actually solve the maximization problem given in (16.1). That is, the function $v(c)$ rationalizes the choices (p_s, c_s).

3. The absolute risk aversion of $v(c)$ at c_s is given by

$$r(c_s) = -\frac{v''(c_s)}{v'(c_s)} = r_s,$$

and the numbers (r_s) form a decreasing sequence by construction.

This completes the argument. It follows that the Ratio Conditions are a necessary and sufficient condition for the observed Arrow-Debreu portfolio choices to satisfy decreasing absolute risk aversion. Of course, the entire argument works *mutatis mutandis* for the case of increasing absolute risk aversion.

16.3 Relative risk aversion

Let us turn now to the case of relative risk aversion, given by

$$\rho(c) = -\frac{u''(c)c}{u'(c)}.$$

Essentially the same kind argument works, but there are a few twists, so it is worthwhile spelling out the details.

We first observe that the chain rule gives us

$$\frac{d \log u'(c)}{dc} = \frac{d \log u'(c)}{d \log c} \frac{d \log c}{dc}.$$

Taking the derivatives,

$$\frac{u''(c)}{u'(c)} = \frac{d \log u'(c)}{d \log c} \frac{1}{c}.$$

It follows that

$$\rho(c) = -\frac{d \log u'(c)}{d \log c}. \tag{16.6}$$

Applying the chain rule once more to (16.6), we have

$$\rho'(c) = -\frac{d^2 \log u'(c)}{d(\log c)^2} \frac{d \log c}{dc}.$$

It follows that increasing (decreasing) relative risk aversion is equivalent to $\log u'(c)$ being a concave (convex) function of $\log c$. We will treat the case of increasing relative risk aversion, but the other case simply involves switching around the inequalities.

Concavity implies the following inequalities

$$\log u'(c_{s+1}) \le \log u'(c_s) + \frac{d \log u'(c_s)}{d \log c}[\log c_{s+1} - \log c_s] \tag{16.7}$$

$$\log u'(c_{s-1}) \le \log u'(c_s) + \frac{d \log u'(c_s)}{d \log c}[\log c_{s-1} - \log c_s] \tag{16.8}$$

Manipulation and substitution along the lines of that performed above yields

$$\frac{\log p_{s-1} - \log p_s}{\log c_s - \log c_{s-1}} \le \rho(c_s) \le \frac{\log p_s - \log p_{s+1}}{\log c_{s+1} - \log c_s}. \tag{16.9}$$

We will refer to this as the *Relative Ratio Condition*.

The Relative Ratio Condition has the same geometric interpretation as before if we plot $\log p_s$ against $\log c_s$. And, as before, it is also a sufficient condition: given an increasing series of numbers (ρ_s) that satisfy the relative ratio condition, it is possible to construct a utility function that will generated the observed choices. The construction is given by

$$v(c) = \int_0^c p(x)\, dx.$$

where $\log p(x) = \min_s\{\log p_s - r_s(\log x - \log c_s)\}.$

The demonstration that this construction actually works is left as an exercise for the reader.

16.4 A continuous state space

The conditions given above easily generalize to an economy with a continuum of possible consumption values. Let $p(c)$ be the Arrow–Debreu price for contingent consumption c. From the first-order conditions for maximization, we know that:

$$\log p(c) = \log u'(c)$$

Differentiating twice with respect to c, we have

$$\frac{d^2 \log p(c)}{dc^2} = -r'(c). \tag{16.10}$$

It follows that decreasing absolute risk aversion, for example, implies that $\log p(c)$ is a convex function. Similar conditions can be stated for increasing absolute risk aversion, increasing or decreasing relative risk aversion, and so on.

Equation (16.10) shows that the derivative of $\log p(c)$ gives absolute risk aversion directly, so the bounds given earlier are irrelevant in the case of a continuum of consumption values. Indeed, the ratios given on the left and right-hand sides of (16.4) are simply the definitions of the left and right derivatives of $\log p(c)$ as c_{s-1} and c_{s+1} approach c_s.

16.5 Aggregation across individuals

Up until now the analysis has only applied to a single consumer. However, the conditions easily generalize to aggregate consumption, since curvature is preserved under addition. Suppose, for example, that we have n consumers, each of whom has a concave utility function that exhibits decreasing absolute risk aversion.

Using a superscript to denote consumer i, the lower bound in equation (16.4) implies that

$$\frac{1}{r^i(c_s^i)} [\log p_s - \log p_{s+1}] \le c_{s+1}^i - c_s^i.$$

Summing over all consumers $i = 1, \ldots, n$, letting C_s denote aggregate consumption in state s, and rearranging we have

$$\frac{\log p_s - \log p_{s+1}}{C_{s+1} - C_s} \le \left(\sum_{i=1}^{n} \frac{1}{r^i(c_s^i)} \right)^{-1}.$$

The gives us a lower bound on a particular average of absolute risk aversion, and an upper bound can be derived in a similar manner. It follows by inspection that if every consumer has decreasing absolute risk aversion then the graph of $\log p_s$ against C_s will have to have the same general shape as that depicted in Figure 1; that is, it must be a decreasing, convex function.

References

Afriat, S. (1967) "The Construction of a Utility Function from Expenditure Data," *International Economic Review*, **8**, 67–77.

Breeden, D. and R. Litzenberger (1978) "Prices of State-Contingent Claims Implicit in Option Prices," *Journal of Business*, 621–651.

Diewert, E. (1973) "Afriat and Revealed Preference Theory," *Review of Economic Studies*, **40**, 419–426.

Diewert, E. and C. Parkan (1978) "Tests for Consistency of Consumer Data and Nonparametric Index Numbers," Working Paper 78-27, University of British Columbia.

Dybvig, P. and S. Ross (1982) "Portfolio Efficient Sets," *Econometrica*, 1525–1546.

Green, R. and S. Srivastava (1983) "Preference Restrictions, Asset Returns, and Consumption," mimeo, Carnegie–Mellon University.

Varian, H. (1982) "The Nonparametric Approach to Demand Analysis," *Econometrica*, **50**, 945–973.

Varian, H. (1983a) "Nonparametric Tests of Models of Consumer Behavior," *Review of Economic Studies*, **50**, 99–110.

Varian, H. (1983b) "Nonparametric Tests of Models of Investor Behavior," *Journal of Financial and Quantitative Analysis*, **18**, 269–278.

Chapter 17

SEQUENTIAL CONTRIBUTIONS
TO PUBLIC GOODS

I examine games involving private contributions to a public good and show that less of the public good will be supplied if agents move sequentially than if they move simultaneously. If the agents bid for the right to move first, the agent who values the public good least will win. If each agent chooses the rate at which he will subsidize the other agent's contributions, the subsidies that support the Lindahl allocation are the unique equilibrium outcome. I also describe two related subsidy-setting games that yield Lindahl allocations in n-person games with general utility functions. This paper will appear in the Journal of Public Economics.

Several authors have examined the private provision of public goods in simultaneous-move games. The Nash equilibria in these games turn out to have several surprising and interesting properties. For details see Warr (1983), Cornes-Sandler (1986) and Bergstrom-Blume-Varian (1986). In this paper I investigate games where agents decide on their contributions to a public good sequentially. In this sort of "Stackelberg contribution game" the agent who moves first can credibly commit to his contribution in a way that is not possible in a simultaneous-move game.

Admati-Perry (1991) analyze a game in which agents alternate contributions to joint project. However, in their game the project is either completed or not, and no benefits are generated from a partially completed

This work was supported by the National Science Foundation Grant SES-8800114 and a Fulbright grant. I wish to thank Ted Bergstrom, Joel Guttman, Leif Danziger, Robert McClelland, Ig Horstman, the participants at the Michigan-Western Ontario economic theory workshop and an anonymous referee for their comments and suggestions. I also wish to thank the Santa Fe Institute for their hospitality during the period of this research.

project. In this paper, by contrast, the focus is on the amount of the public good that is provided in the contribution game.

It turns out that the ability to commit to a contribution exacerbates the free rider problem: I show that the total amount of the public good provided in a sequential game is never larger than the amount provided in a simultaneous-move game. Along the way, I establish several other interesting results concerning equilibria in sequential contribution games. In particular, I examine some mechanisms in which agents choose to subsidize the contributions made by other agents, and show that these mechanisms provide simple and natural solutions to the problem of implementing Lindahl equilibria.

17.1 An example with quasilinear utility

It is instructive to start with a simple example with two agents. Each agent i divides his wealth w_i between private consumption, $x_i \geq 0$, and a contribution to a public good, $g_i \geq 0$. The total amount of the public good is $G = g_1 + g_2$.

Each agent's utility function is linear in his private consumption and a concave increasing function of G, so that the utility of agent i is

$$u_i(G) + x_i = u_i(g_1 + g_2) + w_i - g_i.$$

Let $\bar{g}_i$ be the amount of the public good that maximizes agent i's utility when the other agent contributes zero. We call this amount agent i's *standalone contribution*. We say that agent i *likes the public good more than agent j* if $\bar{g}_i > \bar{g}_j$; i.e., if agent i would contribute more to the public good if he were the only contributor.[1] We assume that $w_i > \bar{g}_i$ so that consumption of the private good, x_i, is always strictly positive. This makes it possible to drop w_i, since it is an inessential constant in each agent's utility function.

The reaction function

The reaction functions and Nash equilibria for the simultaneous contribution game are reasonably well known. We sketch the derivation here for purposes of comparison to the sequential case.

First, we derive the reaction function for agent 2. The first-order condition if agent 2 contributes a positive amount to the public good is

$$u_2'(g_1 + g_2) = 1.$$

---

[1] It is easy to show that if one agent's marginal willingness to pay for the public good agent is uniformly larger than the other's, then his standalone contribution will be larger.

Letting $G_2(g_1)$ be agent 2's reaction function, we must have

$$u_2'(g_1 + G_2(g_1)) = 1.$$

Since $\bar{g}_2$ is the amount that agent 2 contributes when $g_1 = 0$, we have:

$$G_2(g_1) = \bar{g}_2 - g_1.$$

This derivation is valid only when agent 2 contributes a positive amount to the public good. Since $g_2 \geq 0$, we must have

$$G_2(g_1) = \max\{\bar{g}_2 - g_1, 0\}.$$

This "kink" in the reaction function is what makes the analysis interesting.

The Nash equilibrium

A Nash equilibrium is a pair of contributions (g_1, g_2) such that

$$g_1 = G_1(g_2)$$
$$g_2 = G_2(g_1).$$

A Nash equilibrium is depicted in Figure 1. In the case depicted, agent 1 likes the public good more than agent 2. In this case agent 1 contributes the entire amount of the public good and agent 2 free rides. If both agents have the same tastes for the public good, the reaction functions overlap and there is a whole range of equilibrium contributions, although there is still a unique equilibrium amount of the public good.

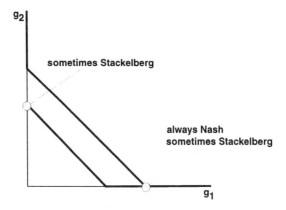

Figure 1. Nash and Stackelberg equilibria. In the Nash equilibrium the player who likes the public good the most contributes everything and the other player free rides. In the Stackelberg equilibrium the first contributor may free ride even if he likes the public good more than the other agent.

The Stackelberg equilibrium

We assume that agent 1 moves first. The utility of agent 1 as a function of his contribution is given by

$$V_1(g_1) = u_1(g_1 + G_2(g_1)) - g_1$$
$$= u_1(g_1 + \max\{\bar{g}_2 - g_1, 0\}) - g_1.$$

We can also write this as

$$V_1(g_1) = \begin{cases} u_1(\bar{g}_2) - g_1 & \text{for } g_1 \leq \bar{g}_2 \\ u_1(g_1) - g_1 & \text{for } g_1 \geq \bar{g}_2. \end{cases}$$

It is clear from Figure 2 that there are two possible optima: either the first agent contributes zero and achieves utility $u_1(\bar{g}_2)$ or he contributes $\bar{g}_1$ and achieves utility $u_1(\bar{g}_1) - \bar{g}_1$.

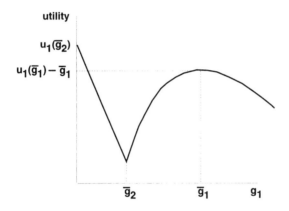

Figure 2. Utility of the first contributor as a function of his gift. In this example, agent 1's optimal choice is to contribute zero, but if the "hump" were higher, he would want to contribute $\bar{g}_1$.

Case 1. *The agent who likes the good least is the first contributor.* In this case the optimal choice by the first player is to contribute zero. This is true since

$$u_1(\bar{g}_2) > u_1(\bar{g}_1) > u_1(\bar{g}_1) - \bar{g}_1.$$

Case 2. *The agent who likes the public good the most is the first contributor.* In this case, either contributor may free ride. The easiest way to see this is by example. Suppose that agent i's utility for the public good is $u_i(G) = a_i \ln G$, so that agent i's standalone contribution is a_i. Then the first contributor will get utility $\ln a_1 - a_1$ or $\ln a_2$, and either of these may be larger. ∎

If the agents have tastes that are very similar, then the first contributor will free ride on the second's contribution. However, if the first agent likes the public good *much* more than the second, then the first agent may prefer to contribute the entire amount of the public good himself.

Referring to Figure 1 we see that there are two possible Stackelberg equilibria: one is the Nash equilibrium, in which the agent who likes the good most contributes everything. The other Stackelberg equilibrium is where the agent who likes the good *least* contributes everything. This equilibrium cannot arise as a Nash equilibrium since the threat to free ride by the agent who likes the public good most is not credible in the simultaneous-move game.

Note that it is always advantageous to move first since there are only two possible outcomes and the first mover gets to pick the one he prefers. Also note that the sum of the utilities is higher at the higher level of the public good. It follows that if you want to ensure that the higher level of the public good is provided, then you should make sure that the person who likes the good *least* moves first.

17.2 Examples

Here we briefly describe two examples of free riding in games involving sequential contributions to public goods. The first is a variation on the Samaritan's dilemma as described by Buchanan (1975), Varian (1982), and Lindbeck (1988). Consider a game between the young generation and the old generation. The old generation has two choices: they can save for their retirement, or they can squander their earnings on their consumption. The young generation likewise has two strategies: they can support the older generation when it retires, or they can let them starve.

A natural assignment of payoffs to these strategies implies that there are two Nash equilibria in this game. In one equilibrium, the older generation expects younger generation to support them and they therefore choose to squander. Given the choice between letting the older generation starve or providing support, the younger generation chooses to provide support. In the other Nash equilibrium, the older generation expects the younger generation not to provide support, and so they prudently choose to save. Since they reach retirement with adequate resources, the younger generation chooses not to support them.

However, only one of these equilibria survives when we take account of the fact that the older generation gets to move first. The unique subgame perfect equilibrium is for the older generation to squander, recognizing that the younger generation will be forced to provide for them in their old age.

Even though the older generation cares more about their consumption than the younger generation does, the older generation still finds it optimal to free ride on the younger generation's contribution.

The second example has to do with reproductive strategy in animals. Males and females normally contribute equal amounts of genetic material to their offspring. However, they often contribute unequally to the care of the offspring. The degree to which males and females provide care for their offspring depends, in part, on the timing of their choices. In mammals, the male is generally the first mover when he fertilizes the eggs of the female. Once the female egg is fertilized the male may well depart, leaving most childcare responsibilities to the female.

In some species of fish, the childcare responsibilities are completely reversed. Among fish, the female is the first mover when she lays the eggs. The male moves second by fertilizing them. At that point the female may well depart, leaving the male to care for the eggs.

Forsyth (1986) describes a particularly interesting case in which there is yet another level of free-riding. There are two types of bluegill sunfish: large "territorial" males and much smaller "satellite" males. The territorial males build nests in order to attract females, while the satellite males hover around the nest built by the territorial male. After a female selects a nest and releases her eggs, the satellite male rushes into the nest and releases its sperm at the same time as the territorial male attempts to fertilize the eggs. The territorial male then has no recourse but to care for the eggs, even though only a fraction of them carry his genetic material, since he is better able to fend off predators than the smaller satellite male. The female bluegill and the satellite male then blithely swim away, free riding on the childcare activities of the territorial male!

17.3 Bidding for the right to move first

Since the first mover always has an advantage in the sequential contribution game, we might consider auctioning off the right to move first. If the first mover likes the public good much more than the second, then he will provide the entire amount of the public good anyway, so it is no advantage to him to be first mover. The advantage to the first mover only arises when the players have similar tastes for the public good. In this case, each player would prefer to move first and free ride on the other's contribution.

Consider, then, the case where agent 1 likes the public good a bit more than agent 2, so that $\overline{g}_1 > \overline{g}_2$, but not so much more as to contribute everything himself. Agent 1 can get utility $u_1(\overline{g}_2)$ by moving first and free riding. If he moves second, he gets utility $u_1(\overline{g}_1) - \overline{g}_1$. The amount that he would be willing to bid to move first, b_1, is therefore

$$b_1 = u_1(\overline{g}_2) - u_1(\overline{g}_1) + \overline{g}_1.$$

We assume that the bids are either thrown away or given to the other agent. Since there are no income effects, it doesn't matter what is done with the bids.

The difference between the bids of the two agents is

$$b_1 - b_2 = [u_1(\bar{g}_2) - u_1(\bar{g}_1)] + [u_2(\bar{g}_2) - u_2(\bar{g}_1)] - [\bar{g}_2 - \bar{g}_1]. \qquad (17.1)$$

It seems plausible to suppose that the agent who values the public good more would be willing to pay more to move first. However, this is exactly wrong! Under our assumptions, the agent who values the public good *least* is willing to pay more for the first-mover position.

To see this, note that concavity of the utility functions gives us the following inequalities:

$$u_1(\bar{g}_2) - u_1(\bar{g}_1) \leq u_1'(\bar{g}_1)[\bar{g}_2 - \bar{g}_1]$$
$$u_2(\bar{g}_2) - u_2(\bar{g}_1) \leq u_2'(\bar{g}_1)[\bar{g}_2 - \bar{g}_1].$$

Substituting these into (17.1) we have

$$b_1 - b_2 \leq [u_1'(\bar{g}_1) + u_2'(\bar{g}_1) - 1](\bar{g}_2 - \bar{g}_1).$$

Since $u_1'(\bar{g}_1) = 1$, this simplifies to

$$b_1 - b_2 \leq u_2'(\bar{g}_2)[\bar{g}_2 - \bar{g}_1] < 0,$$

where the last inequality follows since $\bar{g}_1 > \bar{g}_2$.

It follows that $b_1 < b_2$. That is, the agent who likes the public good the *least* will be willing to pay the *most* in order to move first. As we've seen, this will ensure that the largest amount of the public good will be provided. Essentially each agent is bidding for the right to free ride on the other agent, and it better to free ride on someone who will provide a lot of the public good than someone who will provide only a little.

17.4 Subsidizing the other agent

In the game considered above, one agent is able to commit to a contribution to the public good before the other agent makes his choice. The contribution by the first agent affects the *benefits* that the second agent receives from his contribution. In this section we examine public goods games in which the agents can influence the *cost* to other agents of their contributions. In particular, we examine what will happen if one agent has the opportunity to subsidize the other agent's contributions.

For simplicity we consider the case of identical utilities. As we have seen, the Nash equilibrium amount of the public good, G^n, is determined by the condition

$$u_i'(G^n) = 1,$$

and any set of contributions (g_1^n, g_2^n) such that $g_1^n + g_2^n = G^n$ is a Nash equilibrium.

Suppose that agent 1 offers to subsidize agent 2's contributions at rate s_2. The payoffs to the two agents become

$$u_1(g_1 + g_2) - g_1 - s_2 g_2$$
$$u_2(g_1 + g_2) - (1 - s_2)g_2.$$

Since agent 2 now faces a lower cost of contributing than agent 1, agent 2 will contribute the entire amount of the public good. The amount that agent 2 contributes, $G(s_2)$, is determined by the equation

$$u_2'(G(s_2)) = 1 - s_2.$$

Given our assumption that $u_2(G)$ is strictly concave, $G(s_2)$ will be a continuous increasing function. Agent 1's utility from offering the subsidy rate s_2 is

$$u_1(G(s_2)) - s_2 G(s_2).$$

Originally agent 1 had utility $u_1(G^n) - g_1^n = u_1(G(0)) - g_1^n$. The increase in agent 1's utility from offering the subsidy is

$$u_1(G(s_2)) - u_1(G(0)) + g_1^n - s_2 G(s_2). \tag{17.2}$$

As s_2 approaches zero, this expression converges to $g_1^n \geq 0$. This implies that if agent 1 was initially contributing a positive amount, he would be strictly better off by offering to subsidize agent 2's contribution by a sufficiently small amount. Intuitively, if agent 1 offers a very tiny subsidy to agent 2, agent 2 will end up contributing the entire amount of the public good in the second stage. But a tiny subsidy hardly costs agent 1 anything, which means that each agent will always want to subsidize the other agent's contribution.

Roberts (1987) and Bergstrom (1989) show that if a subsidy on contributions to a public good is financed by an equal lump-sum tax, then each agent prefers that the other agent be subsidized. We have shown that each agent prefers to subsidize the other agent even if he must pay for the subsidy himself. However, the Roberts-Bergstrom result holds for general preferences, while our result only holds for quasilinear preferences.

17.5 Equilibrium subsidies

We have seen that each agent will prefer to subsidize the other agent in our contribution game. Suppose that each agent simultaneously names a rate at which he is willing to subsidize the other agent. Then, given these subsidy rates, the agents play a simultaneous contribution game. What is the equilibrium of this game?

In order to answer this question, we need some facts about the Lindahl allocation in this model. In the case of quasilinear utility there will be a unique amount of the public good that the sum of the utilities. This amount, G^e, satisfies the first-order condition

$$u_1'(G^e) + u_2'(G^e) = 1. \tag{17.3}$$

This is just the familiar condition that maximizes the sum of the marginal willingnesses-to-pay must equal marginal cost.

Suppose that we choose rates s_i^e to support the efficient amount of the public good.

$$\begin{aligned} u_1'(G^e) &= 1 - s_1^e \\ u_2'(G^e) &= 1 - s_2^e, \end{aligned} \tag{17.4}$$

Note that (17.3) and (17.4) together imply

$$s_1^e + s_2^e = 1. \tag{17.5}$$

Equation (17.5) implies that the utility of agent 1 at the Lindahl allocation is

$$u_1(G^e) - (1 - s_1^e)g_1 - s_2^e g_2 = u_1(G^e) - (1 - s_1^e)G^e.$$

Hence $s_2^e = 1 - s_1^e$ is effectively a Lindahl price for agent 1; accordingly, we call (s_1^e, s_2^e) the *Lindahl subsidies*.

Theorem 1.   *The unique subgame perfect equilibrium of the subsidy setting game yields the Lindahl subsidies, and the resulting allocation is the Lindahl allocation.*

Proof. If we have an interior equilibrium in the contribution stage, the amount of the public good must satisfy:

$$\begin{aligned} u_1'(g_1^* + g_2^*) &= 1 - s_1 \\ u_2'(g_1^* + g_2^*) &= 1 - s_2 \end{aligned} \tag{17.6}$$

Suppose that agent 2, say, is not contributing. There is no cost to agent 1 of increasing s_2 up to the point where agent 2 is just on the verge of contributing. We assume that this has been done, which means that (17.6) will apply even in the case of boundary solutions.

If agent 1 increases the subsidy agent 2 faces slightly then agent 2 will do all the contributing, and agent 1 will contribute zero. If we are in equilibrium, such a change cannot benefit agent 1. Using a limiting argument similar to that used to establish equation (17.2) this implies

$$u_1(g_1^* + g_2^*) - (1 - s_1)g_1^* - s_2 g_2^* \geq u_1(g_1^* + g_2^*) - s_2(g_1^* + g_2^*).$$

After simplification, we have

$$g_1^*(s_1 + s_2 - 1) \geq 0. \tag{17.7}$$

Similarly, if agent 1 reduces the subsidy rate that agent 2 faces, then agent 1 will do all the contributing. In equilibrium agent 1 cannot benefit from this change which implies

$$u_1(g_1^* + g_2^*) - (1 - s_1)g_1^* - s_2g_2^* \geq u_1(g_1^* + g_2^*) - (1 - s_1)(g_1^* + g_2^*).$$

Simplification yields

$$g_2^*(s_1 + s_2 - 1) \leq 0. \tag{17.8}$$

The same arguments applied to agent 2 yield

$$g_2^*(s_1 + s_2 - 1) \geq 0 \tag{17.9}$$
$$g_1^*(s_1 + s_2 - 1) \leq 0. \tag{17.10}$$

At least one of (g_1^*, g_2^*) must be nonzero in equilibrium. This observation, together with (17.7)–(17.10), implies $s_1 + s_2 = 1$. It follows from (17.6) that the resulting allocation is the Lindahl allocation. ∎

The intuition behind this result is rather nice: if agent 1 contributes *directly* to the public good, it costs him a dollar for each dollar he contributes. But if he contributes *indirectly*, say by giving a ten percent subsidy, then it costs agent 1 only ten cents for each dollar that agent 2 contributes to the public good. Each agent will continue to subsidize the other until the marginal cost of contributing directly is equal to the marginal cost of contributing indirectly. In the case of identical consumers, this is where each agent gives the other a fifty percent subsidy—which is is the Lindahl price.

Related literature

There is a large literature on designing mechanisms to solve the public goods problem. Groves (1979), Groves-Ledyard (1987), Moore (1991), and Ledyard (1992) provide surveys of various aspects of this literature.

The classic solutions to the free-rider problem are due to Groves-Ledyard (1977), Hurwicz (1979), and Walker (1981). However, the most closely related result to ours is Guttman (1978, 1986). In the first stage of Guttman's game each agent announces a rate at which he will match the other agent's contribution. In the second stage each agent contributes a "flat" amount plus a matching amount tied to the other agent's direct contribution. Guttman argues that the equilibrium of this game is the Pareto efficient amount of the public good.[2] In Guttman's game, the matching contribution goes directly to the public good;   in my game, the subsidy is paid to the other contributor. However, the strategic nature of the two games are similar since each agent is effectively setting a price for the other agent's contribution. Guttman (1986) describes some experimental evidence in his matching game.

More recently, Jackson-Moulin (1992) describe a two-stage bidding game that yields a Lindahl-like allocation in the case of a *discrete* public good. In the first stage of the Jackson-Moulin game, each agent announces the total value of the public good. In the second stage, each agent announces his own valuation. The Jackson-Moulin game implements an efficient allocation in undominated Nash equilibrium, although they offer a variation that implements efficiency in subgame perfect equilibrium.

In Varian (1989b) I describe a subsidy-setting game for implementing Lindahl-like outcomes for completely general externalities problems. The mechanism in Varian (1989b) is more general than the subsidy setting game described here, but it is also more complicated. The nice thing about the subsidy game is that it is very natural.

17.6 General utility functions

I have described several results for public goods problems with two stages in which a price or a quantity is set in the first stage, and further quantity choices are made in the second stage. However, the quasilinear case is very special: do these results generalize to a model with income effects?

Let $u_i(G, x_i)$ be a utility function with G is the level of the public good and x_i is the private consumption of agent i. As before, I assume that utility is a differentiable, strictly concave function.

I first derive the form of the reaction function. Agent 2's maximization problem is

$$\max_{x_2,g_2} u_2(g_1 + g_2, x_2)$$

$$\text{such that } g_2 + x_2 = w_2$$

$$g_2 \geq 0.$$

We can add g_1 to each side of the constraints and use the definition $G = g_1 + g_2$ to rewrite the problem as

$$\max_{x_2,G} u_2(G, x_2)$$

$$\text{such that } G + x_2 = w_2 + g_1$$

$$G \geq g_1.$$

---

[2] Guttman (1978) did not contain a complete proof of this result due to space limitations.

In this problem, agent 2 is choosing the level of the public good, subject to the constraint that the level that he chooses is at least as large as the contribution of agent 1.

Following Bergstrom-Blume-Varian (1986) we note that this problem is a standard consumer demand problem except for the inequality constraint. Let $f_2(w)$ be agent 2's demand function for the public good. It follows from the above remarks that

$$G = g_1 + g_2 = \max\{f_2(w_2 + g_1), g_1\}.$$

Subtracting g_1 from each side of this equation, we have the reaction function

$$G_2(g_1) = \max\{f_2(w_2 + g_1) - g_1, 0\}.$$

According to this reaction function, agent 1 will either contribute zero or the amount of the public good that he would demand if his wealth were $w_1 + g_2$ *minus* the amount contributed by the other agent. The following assumption is quite natural:

Normal goods. Both the public and the private good are strictly normal goods at all levels of wealth.

Given this assumption it is easy to see the general shape of the reaction function. When $g_1 = 0$, agent 2 will contribute $f_2(w_2)$. As g_1 increases, the contribution of agent 2 will decrease, but less than one-for-one. For some g_1^c we may have $f_2(w_2 + g_1^c) = 0$; at this point agent 1 contributes so much that agent 2 chooses to free ride. We call this amount the *complete crowding out* contribution.

We summarize some properties of the reaction function in the following fact, the proof of which follows immediately from the assumption.

Fact 1. *The reaction function $G_2(g_1)$ is a nonincreasing function. It will be strictly decreasing when it is not equal to zero. The function $H(g_1) = g_1 + G_2(g_1)$ is a strictly increasing function.*

As before, we can use this reaction function to calculate the Nash equilibria and the Stackelberg equilibrium. A Nash equilibrium is a solution (g_1^n, g_2^n) to
$$g_1^n = \max\{f_1(w_1 + g_2^n) - g_2^n, 0\}$$
$$g_2^n = \max\{f_2(w_2 + g_1^n) - g_1^n, 0\}.$$
A Stackelberg equilibrium is a pair $(g_1^s, G_2(g_1^s))$ for which g_1^s solves

$$\max_{g_1} \ u_1(g_1 + \max\{f_2(w_2 + g_1) - g_1, 0\}, w_1 - g_1).$$

We want to compare the solutions of these two sets of equations. This comparison is made simpler by noting that Bergstrom-Blume-Varian (1986) have proved that under the normality assumption we have made there is a *unique* Nash equilibrium. There will also be one Stackelberg equilibrium for each ordering of the agents.

17.7 Results for general utility functions

We have three sets of results. The first set of results concerns who contributes and who free rides. The second set of results concerns the effect of redistributions of wealth. The third set of results concerns how the amount of the public good provided in the Stackelberg equilibrium compares to the amount provided in the Nash equilibrium.

Free riding

Fact 2.   *If the standalone contribution is less than the complete crowding out contribution $(\bar{g}_1 < g_1^c)$ then both agents must contribute in the Stackelberg equilibrium.*

Proof. Evaluate the right derivative of agent 1's utility function at g_1^c. We have
$$\frac{\partial u_1(g_1^c, w_1 - g_1^c)}{\partial G} - \frac{\partial u_1(g_1^c, w_1 - g_1^c)}{\partial x_1} < 0.$$
The inequality follows since the derivative equals zero at $\bar{g}_1$, and $g_1^c > \bar{g}_1$. (Recall that $u_1(g_1, w_1 - g_1)$ is a concave function.) It follows that agent 1's utility will increase if he contributes less than g_1^c, even if he is the only one to contribute. The fact that the other agent will also contribute can only increase the first agent's utility. Hence the Stackelberg equilibrium must involve contributions by both agents. ∎

Fact 3.   *If there is a Nash equilibrium with $g_1^n = 0$, then this is also a Stackelberg equilibrium.*

Proof. By definition of Nash equilibrium, agent 2 is on his reaction curve, so we only need to show that agent 1 is on his reaction curve. If agent 1 contributes 0, then agent 2 will contribute $\bar{g}_2$. Let $g_1 > 0$ be any other possible contribution by agent 1. Then we have :
$$u_1(\bar{g}_2, w_1) > u_1(g_1 + \bar{g}_2, w_1 - g_1) > u_1(g_1 + G_2(g_1), w_1 - g_1).$$
The first inequality follows from the Nash assumption. The second inequality follows since $G_2(0) = \bar{g}_2$ and $G_2(g_1)$ is a nonincreasing function. ∎

Wealth redistribution

Fact 4.   *Suppose that we have a Stackelberg equilibrium (g_1^s, g_2^s). Let $(\Delta w_1, \Delta w_2)$ be a redistribution of wealth from the leader to the follower such that $g_i + \Delta w_i \geq 0$ for $i = 1, 2$ with $\Delta w_1 < 0$. Then the Stackelberg equilibrium after this redistribution is $(g_1^s + \Delta w_1, g_2^s + \Delta w_2)$ and the total amount of the public good remains unchanged.*

Proof. The first-order condition for the Stackelberg equilibrium is

$$\frac{\partial u_1(g_1 + g_2, w_1 - g_1)}{\partial G} f_2'(w_2 + g_1) - \frac{\partial u_1(g_1 + g_2, w_1 - g_1)}{\partial x_1} = 0.$$

Let (Δw_i) be a redistribution of wealth and let agent i change his contribution by $\Delta g_i = \Delta w_i$ for $i = 1, 2$. Note that since $\Delta w_1 + \Delta w_2 = 0$ we must have $\Delta g_1 + \Delta g_2 = 0$. Now simply observe that if each agent changes his contribution in this way the first-order condition is still satisfied. ∎

Warr (1983) and Bergstrom-Blume-Varian (1986) show that essentially the same result holds in an (interior) Nash equilibrium. Interestingly, a transfer from the follower to the leader may not be neutral since the leader's objective function is not concave and a transfer may induce a discontinuous response.[3]

Bergstrom-Blume-Varian (1986) also investigate the boundary cases in some detail. In the two-agent context we are investigating here the analysis of the boundary cases is quite straightforward so we simply state the result.

Fact 5.   *Suppose that person 1 is contributing and person 2 is not. Then a redistribution from 2 to 1 will increase the amount of the public good, while a redistribution from 1 to 2 can decrease or increase the amount of the public good.*

Comparison to the Nash equilibrium

Theorem 2.   *The amount of the public good contributed by agent 1 in the Stackelberg equilibrium is never larger than the amount provided by agent 1 in the Nash equilibrium. That is, $g_1^s \leq g_1^n$.*

---

[3] See Rudolf Kerschbamer and Clemens Puppe, "Sequential Contributions to Public Goods: A Note on the Structure of the Equilibrium Set," Working Paper, University of Vienna, July 1998.

Proof. There are two cases to consider, the case where $g_2^n = 0$, and the case where $g_2^n > 0$. In the first case, it follows from Fact 3 that the Nash equilibrium is also a Stackelberg equilibrium. Hence, $g_1^n = g_1^s$.

As for the second case, let $V_1(g_1) = u_1(g_1 + G_2(g_1), w_1 - g_1)$. The derivative of $V_1(g_1)$ evaluated at the Nash equilibrium is:

$$V_1'(g_1^n) = \frac{\partial u_1(G^n, w_1 - g_1^n)}{\partial G}[1 + G_2'(g_1^n)] - \frac{\partial u_1(G^n, w_1 - g_1^n)}{\partial x_1}$$

$$= \frac{\partial u_1(G^n, w_1 - g_1^n)}{\partial G} G_2'(g_1^n) < 0.$$

This follows since $\partial u_1/\partial G - \partial u_1/\partial x_1 = 0$ at the Nash equilibrium and $G_2'(g_1^n)$ is strictly negative when $g_2^n > 0$. This shows that agent 1's utility will increase by decreasing his contribution from which it follows that $g_1^s < g_1^n$. ∎

Corollary. *The total amount of the public good in the Stackelberg equilibrium is less than or equal to the total amount provided in the Nash equilibrium.*

Proof. According to Fact 1, the function $H(g_1) = g_1 + G_2(g_1)$ is an increasing function. Therefore,

$$H(g_1^n) = g_1^n + G_2(g_1^n) = g_1^n + g_2^n \geq g_1^s + G_2(g_1^s) = H(g_1^s).$$

The corollary follows. ∎

17.8 Public goods and general utilities

Here we describe some generalizations of the two-person subsidy-setting game described earlier. Each mechanism is a variation on the compensation mechanism described in Varian (1989b).

Subsidy setting with more than two agents

The subsidy-setting game described earlier only works for two agents with quasilinear utility. If there are more than two agents, each agent still prefers that the other agents' contributions be subsidized—but each agent wants someone else to do the subsidizing. However, by adjusting who subsidizes whom, it is possible to overcome this sort of free-riding in subsidy setting.

The trick is to have agent 1 set the rate at which agent 2 will subsidize agent 3's contributions. Agent 2, in turn sets the rate at which agent 3 will subsidize 1's contributions, and so on. More specifically, let s^i_j be the subsidy facing agent j as set by agent i. As before, let x_1 be agent 1's private consumption, and g_1 be his contribution to the public good. If there are 3 agents doing the contributing, agent 1's budget constraint will be:

$$x_1 + (1 - s^2_1 - s^3_1)g_1 = w_1 - s^3_2 g_2 - s^2_3 g_3.$$

Note that, unlike the two-person case, the prices agent i faces are independent of the prices he sets.

In order to establish the result, we need a regularity assumption on demand functions: they must be be locally invertible functions of the subsidy rates. This means that if agent 1 wants agent 2 to contribute a little more or a little less to the public good, there is some subsidy rate that he can set that will induce agent 2 to do this. Local invertibility will be satisfied if the derivative of each agent's demand function with respect to price is not zero at the equilibrium.[4]

Theorem 3. *Let each agent have continuous convex preferences. Assume that the demand functions are locally invertible. Then the subgame perfect equilibria of the subsidy setting game are Lindahl allocations.*

Proof. We prove the theorem for 3 agents, but the idea extends to an arbitrary number of agents. Let (x^*_i, g^*_i) be a subgame perfect equilibrium of this game, and let (x'_i, g'_i) be an allocation that Pareto dominates it. Since preferences are convex and continuous, we can assume that (x'_i, g'_i) is arbitrarily close to (x^*_i, g^*_i).

Agent i chooses his own contribution directly and chooses the other agents' contributions through the subsidy rates that he sets for them. If each agent prefers (x'_i, g'_i) to (x^*_i, g^*_i), then this allocation must not be affordable for each agent at the equilibrium subsidy rates. This yields three inequalities:

$$x'_1 + (1 - s^2_1 - s^3_1)g'_1 > w_1 - s^3_2 g'_2 - s^2_3 g'_3$$
$$x'_2 + (1 - s^1_2 - s^3_2)g'_2 > w_2 - s^1_3 g'_3 - s^3_1 g'_1$$
$$x'_3 + (1 - s^1_3 - s^2_3)g'_3 > w_3 - s^1_2 g'_2 - s^2_1 g'_1.$$

Adding these inequalities gives

$$\sum_{i=1}^{3} x'_i + \sum_{i=1}^{3} g'_i > \sum_{i=1}^{3} w_i,$$

which shows that the Pareto dominating allocation is not feasible.

---

[4] This is automatically satisfied if utility is quasilinear and strictly concave.

Next we show that the equilibrium is Lindahl. Agent 1 can choose g_1 directly and choose g_2 or g_3 indirectly, through the subsidy he sets for the other agents. Since the contributions are perfect substitutes in consumption, they must have the same equilibrium price. Hence we can define $p_1 = 1 - s_1^2 - s_1^3 = s_3^2 = s_2^3$. From this it follows that agent 1's budget constraint can be written as

$$x_1 + p_1(g_1 + g_2 + g_3) = x_1 + p_1 G = w_1,$$

which shows that the allocation is Lindahl. ∎

It is worth observing that this mechanism is balanced both in and out of equilibrium. The proof that the equilibrium is Lindahl is essentially the proof given in Varian (1989b) for general externalities, specialized to the case of public goods.

Another mechanism for implementing Lindahl allocations

Here is another two-stage mechanism that implements Lindahl allocations. The message space in this mechanism is much smaller than in the previous mechanism since each agent has to name only a single number.

The price setting stage. Each agent i announces a number q_i. The price for agent i's contribution to the public good is the average of the numbers named by the other agents:

$$p_i = \frac{1}{n-1} \sum_{j \neq i} q_j.$$

The contribution stage. Each agent i chooses (x_i, g_i) to maximize his utility subject to the budget constraint

$$x_i + p_i g_i = w_i - p_i \sum_{j \neq i} g_j - Q(p),$$

where the penalty term is given by $Q(p) = \left(\sum_{j=1}^n p_j - 1 \right)^2$.

In the second stage we have each agent choosing a contribution to the public good for which he pays a price $p_i g_i$. But agent i must also make a payment based on the amount of the good contributed by the *other* agents.

Since the total amount of the public good is $G = g_i + \sum_{j \neq i} g_j$, we could also write agent i's budget constraint as $x_i + p_i G = w_i - Q(p)$.

It is easy to show that the Lindahl allocation (p_i^e, G^e) is *an* equilibrium of this game. To do this we only need to show that if every agent makes announcements which lead to the Lindahl prices, agent i cannot increase his utility by announcing something that yields non-Lindahl prices for the other agents.

To prove this we first observe that since the Lindahl prices (p_i^e) result in an efficient amount of the public good, the penalty term, $Q(p)$, must be zero by the standard Samuelson efficiency condition.[5] Suppose that agent i, announces some numbers that change the price vector p^e to p' and that this change results in some possibly different amount of the public good, G'. Note that agent i can only affect the prices facing the other agents, not the price he faces.

We have

$$u_i(G^e, w_i - p_i^e G^e) \geq u_i(G', w_i - p_i^e G') \geq u_i(G', w_i - p_i^e G' - Q(p')).$$

The first inequality comes from the fact that we start with a Lindahl allocation; the second inequality comes from the fact that $Q(p') \geq 0$. This argument shows that agent i is at least as well off announcing prices that lead to the Lindahl prices (p_j^e) as any other prices; i.e., that Lindahl allocations are an equilibrium to the mechanism. In the appendix I show that there can be no other equilibria of the mechanism.

I've described this mechanism in terms of setting prices. However, it can also be described in terms of setting subsidies, which makes it look more like the mechanisms described earlier. In the subsidy-setting framework, each agent i names a number $1 - s_i$ which turns out in equilibrium to be the rate at which agent i's contributions are subsidized *and* the rate at which agent i subsidizes everyone else's contributions. We denote the contributions by everyone except agent i by $G_{-i} = \sum_{j \neq i} g_j$. The budget constraint facing agent i then can be written as

$$(1 - \sum_{j \neq i} s_j) g_i + x_i = w_i - (1 - \sum_{j \neq i} s_j) G_{-i} - (1 - \sum_{j=1}^{n} s_j)^2.$$

It can be shown that in equilibrium $s_i + \sum_{j \neq i} s_j = 1$, so that agent i ends up being subsidized at the rate $1 - s_i$ and subsidizing the other agents at the same rate.

Related literature

Danziger-Schnytzer (1991) have independently examined a subsidy-setting mechanism similar in spirit to this one. In the Danziger-Schnytzer mechanism, each agent names a rate at which he will subsidize the other agents'

---

[5] We assume that it is efficient to provide a positive amount of the public good.

contributions. In in my mechanism, the rate at which each agent subsidizes the other agents is set by the *other* agents. Furthermore, my mechanism requires a penalty function while a penalty is not necessary in the Danziger-Schnytzer mechanism. The Danziger-Schnytzer mechanism is therefore a bit simpler in the case of pure public goods. However, I show in Varian (1989b) that my mechanism also works for general externalities problems.

17.9 Incomplete information

Up until now we have examined games where each agent knows the preferences and wealth of the other agent. Here we consider a model where each contributor has incomplete information about the other contributor. In our game the second contributor reacts passively, making his optimal choice given the first agent's contribution. Hence it is irrelevant whether or not he knows anything about the first contributor. The only interesting uncertainty concerns the first contributor's knowledge of the second contributor's preferences.

Consider the quasilinear model examined earlier. In this case all that is relevant from the first contributor's point of view is the value of $\bar{g}_2$—how much the second person will contribute if the first person contributes zero. Suppose that the first contributor has a prior distribution on how much the other person will contribute and seeks to maximize expected utility.[6]

The expected utility of the first contributor is

$$
\begin{aligned}
V_1(g_1) &= \int_0^\infty [u(g_1 + \max\{\bar{g}_2 - g_1, 0\}) - g_1] f(\bar{g}_2) \, d\bar{g}_2 \\
&= \int_0^{g_1} [u(g_1) - g_1] f(\bar{g}_2) \, d\bar{g}_2 + \int_{g_1}^\infty [u(\bar{g}_2) - g_1] f(\bar{g}_2) \, d\bar{g}_2 \\
&= [u(g_1) - g_1] F(g_1) + \int_{g_1}^\infty [u(\bar{g}_2) - g_1] f(\bar{g}_2) \, d\bar{g}_2.
\end{aligned}
$$

Differentiating this expression with respect to g_1 and simplifying yields

$$
V_1'(g_1) = u_1'(g_1) F(g_1) - 1.
$$

Note that when $g_1 = 0$, the probability that $\bar{g}_2$ is less than g_1 is zero, so that $V_1'(0) = -1$. If g_1 is large enough so that agent 1 is certain that $\bar{g}_2$ is less than g_1, then $V_1'(g_1) = u_1'(g_1) - 1$. Hence, agent 1's utility as a function of his gift is similar to the shape depicted in Figure 2. Depending on the beliefs of agent 1 about agent 2's maximum contribution, agent 1

---

[6] We assume that the von Neumann-Morgenstern utility function takes the quasilinear form. This is restrictive, but seems necessary for a simple analysis.

will either choose to free ride, or to contribute an amount g_1^* that satisfies the condition

$$u_1'(g_1^*)F(g_1^*) - 1 = 0.$$

This marginal condition is quite intuitive. If agent 1 decides to contribute a bit more of the public good, he will get $u_1'(g_1^*)$, but only if agent 2 has $\bar{g}_2 < g_1^*$. Otherwise, agent 1 will get no incremental utility from his contribution—since his contribution would just crowd out some of the public good that agent 2 would have contributed anyway. Hence the *expected* marginal utility of agent 1's contribution is $u_1'(g_1^*)$ times the probability that $\bar{g}_2 < g_1^*$, which is just $u_1'(g_1^*)F(g_1^*)$. The optimal contribution is determined by the condition that this expected marginal utility must equal the (certain) marginal cost of the contribution.

How does this amount compare to $\bar{g}_1$, which is what agent 1 would contribute under certainty? Note that $V_1'(\bar{g}_1) = u_1'(\bar{g}_1)F(\bar{g}_1) - 1 = F(\bar{g}_1) - 1$. As long as there is some possibility that agent 2 will have $\bar{g}_2 > \bar{g}_1$, we will have $F(\bar{g}_1) < 1$ and $V_1'(\bar{g}_1)$ will be negative. If $V_1(g_1)$ is concave this implies that the equilibrium contribution in the presence of uncertainty is less than the contribution under certainty. Intuitively, the *possibility* that agent 2 may value the good more than agent 1 leads agent 1 to reduce his contribution to the public good, hoping to free ride on agent 2's contribution.

17.10 Summary

We have examined some sequential games involving contributions to a public good. If preferences are quasilinear, then:

1. The sequential equilibrium of the contribution game will provide the same or less of the public good than the simultaneous move game.

2. The player who likes the public good least will bid the most to move first.

3. Each player would like to subsidize the other player's contributions. If both players choose subsidy rates and then play the voluntary contribution game, a Lindahl equilibrium is the unique subgame perfect equilibrium of this two-stage game.

4. The equilibrium of the sequential move game is independent of small redistributions of wealth.

5. If the first agent is uncertain about the type of the second agent, he will tend to contribute less to the public good.

In the case of general utility functions, the amount of the public good supplied in the Stackelberg game will never be more than in the Nash game. Furthermore, there are several generalizations of the subsidy setting game that yield Lindahl allocations.

17.11 Appendix. Proof of uniqueness

Here we provide a proof of the claim made in the text that the only equilibria of our price-setting mechanism are Lindahl allocations. We assume that for some agent the marginal rate of substitution between the private and the public good is infinite when $G = 0$ so that someone will always want to make a positive contribution to the public good. We also assume local invertibility of the sort described earlier: there is a set of prices that will result any desired (small) change in behavior. See Varian (1989b) for more discussion of the role of this assumption.

Let (p_i^*) be the set of prices that result from the equilibrium announcements (q_i^*). We first show that in equilibrium we must have $\sum_{k=1}^{n} p_k^* = 1$. Suppose not. We have assumed that least one agent i will choose a positive amount of the public good. Suppose that this agent changes his announcement q_i. This will change agent i's utility by

$$\left[\frac{\partial u_i}{\partial G} - \frac{\partial u_i}{\partial x_i} p_i^* \right] \frac{\partial G}{\partial q_i} - 2 \frac{\partial u_i}{\partial x_i} \left(\sum_{k=1}^{n} p_k^* - 1 \right).$$

Since agent i is contributing a positive amount the bracketed expression vanishes by the envelope theorem, leaving us with a term that is, by assumption, nonzero. Hence there is some change in i's announcement that will increase his utility, contradicting the assumption of equilibrium. It follows that $\sum_{k=1}^{n} p_k^* = 1$ in equilibrium.

Now suppose that the equilibrium allocation is not Pareto efficient. Then there is some other feasible allocation (x_i', G') that all agents prefer. By continuity and convexity, we can take this allocation to be arbitrarily close to the equilibrium allocation. Local invertibility implies that there is some announcement of prices that each agent can make that will implement this dominating allocation. If they choose not to do so, it must be because the dominating allocation violates their budget constraint,

$$x_i' + p_i G' > w_i.$$

Summing over the agents and using the fact that $\sum_{k=1}^{n} p_k^* = 1$, we have

$$\sum_i x_i' + G' > \sum_i w_i,$$

which contradicts the assumption that the dominating allocation is feasible.

References

Admati, A. & Perry, M. (1991). Joint projects without commitment. *Review of Economic Studies, 58*, 259–276.

Bergstrom, T. (1989). Love and spaghetti, the opportunity cost of virtue. *Journal of Economic Perspectives, 3*(2), 165–173.

Bergstrom, T., Blume, L., & Varian, H. (1986). On the private provision of public goods. *Journal of Public Economics, 29*, 25–49.

Buchanan, J. M. (1975). The Samaritan's dilemma. In Phelps, E. S. (Ed.), *Altruism, Morality, and Economic Theory.* The Sage Foundation.

Cornes, R. & Sandler, T. (1986). *The Theory of Externalities, Public Goods, and Club Goods.* Cambridge University Press, Cambridge, England.

Danziger, L. & Schnytzer, A. (1991). Implementing the Lindahl voluntary-exchange mechanism. *European Journal of Political Economy, 7*, 55–64.

Forsyth, A. (1986). *A Natural History of Sex.* Charles Scribner's Sons, New York.

Groves, T. (1979). Efficient collective choice when compensation is possible. *Review of Economic Studies, 46*, 227–241.

Groves, T. & Ledyard, J. (1977). Optimal allocations of public goods: A solution to the 'free rider problem'. *Econometrica, 45*, 783–809.

Groves, T. & Ledyard, J. (1987). Incentive compatibility since 1972. In Groves, T., Radner, R., & Reiter, S. (Eds.), *Information, Incentives and Economic Mechanisms.* University of Minnesota Press, Minneapolis.

Guttman, J. (1978). Understanding collective action: Matching behavior. *American Economic Review, 68*, 251–255.

Guttman, J. (1986). Matching behavior and collective action: Some experimental evidence. *Journal of Economic Behavior and Organization, 7*, 171–198.

Guttman, J. (1987). A non-Cournot model of voluntary collective action. *Economica, 54*, 1–19.

Hurwicz, L. (1979). Outcome functions yielding Walrasian and Lindahl allocations at Nash equilibrium points. *Review of Economic Studies, 46*, 217–225.

Jackson, M., & Moulin, H. (1992). Implementing a public project and distributing its cost. *Journal of Economic Theory, 57,* 125–140.

Ledyard, J. (1995). Public goods: A survey of experimental research. in *Handbook of Experimental Economics,* John Hagel and Alvin Roth (eds.), Princeton University Press.

Lindbeck, A. & Weibull, J. W. (1988). Altruism and time consistency: the economics of fait accompli. *Journal of Political Economy, 96*(6), 1165–1182.

Moore, J. (1991). Implementation in environments with complete information. Tech. rep., Suntory-Toyota International Centre for Economics, London School of Economics.

Roberts, R. (1987). Financing public goods. *Journal of Political Economy, 95,* 420–437.

Varian, H. (1982). Pensions and public policy. Tech. rep., University of Michigan.

Varian, H. (1989). A solution to the problem of externalities when agents are well-informed. Tech. rep., CREST Working Paper.

Walker, M. (1981). A simple incentive compatible scheme for attaining Lindahl allocations. *Econometrica, 48,* 56–73.

Warr, P. (1983). The private provision of a public good is independent of the distribution of income. *Economic Letters, 13,* 207–211.

Chapter 18

A SOLUTION TO THE PROBLEM OF EXTERNALITIES WHEN AGENTS ARE WELL-INFORMED

I describe a class of simple two-stage mechanisms that implement efficient allocations as subgame perfect equilibria for economic environments involving externalities. These mechanisms, known as compensation mechanisms, solve a wide variety of externalities problems including implementation of Lindahl allocations, regulation of monopoly, and efficient solutions to the Prisoners' Dilemma.

Consider an economic environment in which agents take actions that impose benefits or costs on other agents. The agents involved know the relevant technology and the tastes of all other agents. However the "regulator," who has the responsibility for determining the final allocation, does not have this information. How can the regulator design a mechanism that will implement an efficient allocation?

In this paper I describe a class of simple two-stage games whose subgame perfect equilibria implement efficient allocations in this sort of environment. In addition to implementing efficient outcomes, the mechanisms also achieve desirable distributional goals. In the case of public goods, the mechanisms implement Lindahl allocations; in the case of a negative externality the injured parties are compensated. Because payment of "compensation" is an important feature of the mechanisms I describe, I refer to the general class of mechanisms as *compensation mechanisms*. These mechanisms appear to work in a broad variety of economic environments and do

This work was supported by National Science Foundation grant SES-8800114, a Fulbright grant and the IRIS Research Program. I wish to thank Mark Bagnoli, Ted Bergstrom, Ken Binmore, Alan Kirman, Paul Milgrom, Diego Moreno, Arthur Robson, Steve Salant, Mark Walker, Michael Whinston and two anonymous referees for their comments and suggestions. I also wish to thank the European University Institute and the University of Siena for their hospitality during the period in which I conducted this research.

not involve substantial restrictions on tastes or technology. They are also quite simple to describe and analyze.

The fact that multi-stage games and subgame perfect equilibria may be useful in implementation problems was suggested by Crawford (1979) , Moulin (1979, 1981) and extensively analyzed by Moore and Repullo (1988). Moore and Repullo show that in economic environments, almost any choice rule can be implemented by subgame perfect equilibria. However, as Moore and Repullo point out, "...the mechanisms we construct ...are far from simple; agents move simultaneously at each stage and their strategy sets are unconvincingly rich. We present such mechanisms to show what is possible, not what is realistic." (p. 1198) Moore and Repullo also show that in certain "economic environments" it is possible to use somewhat simpler mechanisms. However, the compensation mechanism appears to be much simpler than the examples Moore and Repullo examined. For a thorough review of the recent literature on implementation in complete information environments see Moore (1991).

It should be emphasized that the solution concept of subgame perfection requires the agents to be informed about the technology and tastes of the other agents. This is, of course, more restrictive than one would like. However, there is a broad set of cases for which this assumption may be plausible. For example, consider a group of agents who must design a constitution that describes a mechanism to make group decisions for problems that will arise in the future. At the time the mechanism is chosen, the agents may not know the relevant tastes and technologies, but they will know these things when the mechanism is actually used. In this circumstance, the compensation mechanism may be a useful mechanism. See Moore and Repullo (1988) and Maskin (1985) for further discussion of these issues.

I first describe a very simple example of the compensation mechanism in a two-agent externalities problem and discuss in an intuitive way why the method works. The following sections show how the method can be extended to work in more general environments.

18.1 A simple example of the compensation mechanism

Consider the following externality problem involving two agents. For simplicity we think of each agent as a profit-maximizing firm. Firm 1 produces output x so as to maximize profit

$$\pi_1 = rx - c(x),$$

, where r is the competitive price of output and $c(x)$ is a differentiable, positive, increasing, and convex cost function.

Firm 1's choice of output imposes an externality on firm 2; in particular, firm 2's profits are

$$\pi_2 = -e(x),$$

where $e(x)$ is a differentiable, positive, increasing, and convex function of x. All of this information is known to both agents, but is not known by the regulator. In general, the level of output chosen by firm 1 will not be efficient, since firm 1 ignores the social cost its choice imposes on firm 2. There are three classic solutions to this problem of externalities.

One class of solutions, associated with Coase (1960), involves negotiation between the agents. Coase claims that if transactions costs are zero and property rights are well-defined, agents should be able to negotiate their way to an efficient outcome. But this is an incomplete solution to the problem of externalities since Coase does not describe a specific mechanism for negotiation. The compensation mechanism described below provides a structure for such negotiations, and therefore can be viewed as being complementary to the Coase approach.

A second class of solutions, associated with Arrow (1970), involves setting up a market for the externality. If a firm produces pollution that harms another firm then a competitive market for the right to pollute may allow for an efficient outcome. From the Coasian point of view, a competitive market is a particular institution that allows agents to "negotiate" their way to an efficient outcome. However, as Arrow points out, the market for allocating a particular externality may be very thin—in many cases of interest such markets involve only two participants.

However, a thin market does not necessarily mean a non-competitive market. There are both theoretical and empirical reasons to believe that certain kinds of market interaction can be competitive even though only a small number of agents are involved. For example, a Bertrand model of oligopoly yields a more-or-less competitive outcome with only two firms. The real-life implementation of Bertrand competition—competitive bidding— seems to work reasonably well even if there are only a small number of bidders. This suggests that markets for externalities with price-setting agents may be a useful model for negotiations among agents. This is a key insight behind the compensation mechanism.

A third class of solutions, associated with Pigou (1920), involves intervention by a regulator who imposes a Pigovian tax. The difficulty with this solution is that it requires the regulator to be able to compute the correct level of the Pigovian tax; in many cases the regulator may not have access to this information, so the Pigovian solution is also incomplete. The compensation mechanism solves this problem, since it gives the regulator a method to induce the participants to reveal the information necessary to construct the optimal Pigovian tax.

Returning to our example, we note that if the regulator had full information, internalizing the externality would be easy. One solution would be for the regulator to impose the costs of the externality on firm 1 by charging it a "tax" of $e(x)$ if it produces x units of output. Firm 1 would then solve the problem

$$\max_{x} \ rx - c(x) - e(x).$$

Let x^* be solution to this problem; then x^* satisfies the first-order condition

$$r - c'(x^*) - e'(x^*) = 0.$$

Because of our curvature assumptions on $e(x)$, the regulator could just as well set a "Pigovian tax," $p^* = e'(x^*)$ and let firm 1 solve the problem

$$\max_{x} \ rx - c(x) - p^*x.$$

However, we have assumed that the regulator doesn't know the externality cost function and therefore cannot determine the appropriate value of p^*. The regulator's problem is to design a mechanism that will induce the agents to reveal their information about the magnitude of the externality and achieve an efficient level of production. Here is a version of the compensation mechanism that solves the regulator's problem.

Announcement stage. Firm 1 and firm 2 simultaneously announce the magnitude of the appropriate Pigovian tax; denote the announcement of firm 1 by p_1 and the announcement of firm 2 by p_2.

Choice stage. The regulator makes sidepayments to the firms so that the two firms face profit maximization problems:

$$\Pi_1 = rx - c(x) - p_2 x - \alpha_1(p_1 - p_2)^2$$
$$\Pi_2 = p_1 x - e(x).$$

The parameter $\alpha_1 > 0$ is of arbitrary magnitude.

In this mechanism firm 1 is forced to pay a tax based on the marginal social cost of the externality as reported by firm 2, and firm 2 receives compensation based on the marginal social cost of the externality as reported by firm 1. Firm 1 must also pay a penalty if it reports a different marginal social cost than firm 2 reports. Any penalty that is minimized when the reports are the same will work, but we have chosen a quadratic penalty for simplicity. Note in particular that the penalty can be arbitrarily small.

294 A SOLUTION TO EXTERNALITIES

18.2 Analysis of the compensation mechanism

There are many Nash equilibria of this game; essentially any triple (p_1, p_2, x) such that $p_1 = p_2$ and x maximizes firm 1's objective function is a Nash equilibrium. However, if we use the stronger concept of subgame perfect equilibrium we get a much smaller set of equilibria. In fact, the *unique* subgame perfect equilibrium of this game has each agent reporting $p_1 = p_2 = p^*$ and firm 1 producing the efficient amount of output.

In order to verify this, we must work backwards through the game. We begin with the choice stage. Firm 1 maximizes its profits, given the Pigovian tax announced in stage 1, which implies that firm 1 will choose x to satisfy the first-order condition

$$r = c'(x) + p_2. \tag{18.1}$$

This determines the optimal choice, x, as a function of p_2, which we denote by $x(p_2)$. Note that $x'(p_2) < 0$—the higher the tax that firm 2 announces, the less firm 1 will want to produce.

We next examine the price-setting stage of the game. We first examine firm 1's choice problem. If firm 1 believes that firm 2 will announce p_2, then firm 1 will want to announce

$$p_1 = p_2 \tag{18.2}$$

This is clear since p_1 only influences firm 1's payoff through the penalty term, and the penalty is minimized when $p_1 = p_2$.

Consider now firm 2's pricing decision. Although firm 2's announcement has no *direct* effect on firm 2's profits, it does have an *indirect* effect through the influence of p_2 on firm 1's output choice in stage 2. Differentiating the profit function of firm 2 with respect to p_2, and setting it equal to zero we have

$$\Pi_2'(p_2) = [p_1 - e'(x)]x'(p_2) = 0. \tag{18.3}$$

Since $x'(p_2) < 0$ we must have $p_1 = e'(x)$.

Combining (18.1), (18.2) and (18.3) we have

$$r = c'(x) + e'(x),$$

which is the condition for social optimality. Hence, the unique subgame perfect equilibrium to this game involves firm 1 producing the socially optimal amount of output.[1]

---

[1] We have not considered the possibility of mixed strategies. However, since the stage 1 game is supermodular and has a unique pure strategy equilibrium, the results of Milgrom and Roberts (1991) can be applied to show that there are no mixed strategy equilibria.

18.3 Why the compensation mechanism works

The intuition behind the mechanism is not particularly difficult. Firm 2 effectively chooses x by setting the price firm 1 faces. If we are to have an equilibrium, we must have $p_1 = e'(x)$; otherwise firm 2 would want to change its announcement of p_2 in order to induce firm 1 to change x. Furthermore, firm 1 will always want to set $p_1 = p_2$ so as to minimize its penalty. The only configuration compatible with these conditions is the efficient outcome.

For example, suppose that firm 1 thinks that firm 2 will report a large price for the externality. Then, since firm 1 is penalized if it announces something different from firm 2, firm 1 will also want to announce a large price. If firm 1 announces a large price, firm 2 will be "overcompensated" for the externality—so it will want firm 1 to produce a large amount of output. But the only way firm 2 can give firm 1 an incentive to produce a large amount of output is by reporting a *small* price for the externality. This contradicts our original assumption that firm 1 thinks that firm 2 will report a large price for the externality. The only equilibrium for the mechanism is where firm 2 is just compensated (on the margin) for the cost that firm 1 imposes on it; at this point firm 2 doesn't want firm 1 to increase or decrease its level of production.

18.4 Extensions of the basic example

Balance

The compensation mechanism, in the form presented above, is balanced in equilibrium but not out of equilibrium. However, if there are at least three agents it is easy to choose transfers to balance the mechanism. As Moore and Repullo point out, we can simply distribute the surplus or deficit generated by each agent's choice among the other agents. Since this lump sum distribution is independent of agent i's choice, there are no resulting incentive effects.[2]

Let's see how this works in the simple example considered above. We now suppose that agent 1 imposes an externality on agents 2 and 3. Use the notation p_{ij}^k to represent the price announced by agent k that measures (in equilibrium) the marginal cost that agent j's choice imposes on agent i.

---

[2] This idea seems to have been first used by Groves-Ledyard (1987). Since then it has been used by a number of other authors.

The basic compensation mechanism for this problem has payments of the form

$$\Pi_1 = rx - c(x) - [p_{21}^2 + p_{31}^3]x - \|p_{21}^1 - p_{21}^2\| - \|p_{31}^1 - p_{31}^3\|$$
$$\Pi_2 = p_{21}^1 x - e_2(x)$$
$$\Pi_3 = p_{31}^1 x - e_3(x).$$

If we distribute payments so as to balance the budget out of equilibrium, the payoffs become

$$\Pi_1 = rx - c(x) - [p_{21}^2 + p_{31}^3]x - \|p_{21}^1 - p_{21}^2\| - \|p_{31}^1 - p_{31}^3\|$$
$$\Pi_2 = p_{21}^1 x - e_2(x) + [p_{31}^3 - p_{31}^1]x + \|p_{31}^1 - p_{31}^3\| \qquad (18.4)$$
$$\Pi_3 = p_{31}^1 x - e_3(x) + [p_{21}^2 - p_{21}^1]x + \|p_{21}^1 - p_{21}^2\|.$$

Straightforward addition shows that this game is balanced. Using the same sort of arguments as before, it is possible to verify that the unique equilibrium of this mechanism is the efficient outcome. In fact, it is not necessary to have penalty terms when there are more than two agents. To see this, set the penalty terms in (18.4) equal to zero and differentiate the relevant objective functions with respect to the choice variables x, p_{21}^2, and p_{21}^3:

$$r - c'(x) - [p_{21}^2 + p_{31}^3] = 0$$
$$[p_{21}^1 - e_2'(x) + p_{31}^3 - p_{31}^1]x'(p_{21}^2 + p_{31}^3) = 0$$
$$[p_{31}^1 - e_3'(x) + p_{21}^2 - p_{21}^1]x'(p_{21}^2 + p_{31}^3) = 0.$$

Since the derivative of x must be non-zero due to strict convexity of the cost function, the terms in brackets must be zero. Adding the bracketed expressions in the last two equations together and substituting into the first equation shows that the equilibrium is efficient.

Yet a third way to balance the mechanism is to allow agent 2 to name the cost that 1 imposes on 3 and vice versa. This is a bit less natural in terms of the information requirements but it yields a very simple mechanism:

$$\Pi_1 = rx - c(x) - (p_{21}^3 + p_{31}^2)x$$
$$\Pi_2 = p_{21}^3 x - e_2(x)$$
$$\Pi_3 = p_{31}^2 x - e_3(x).$$

Differentiating with respect to each of the choice variables as above shows that the equilibrium of this mechanism is efficient, and it is obviously balanced. Each of these ways of balancing the compensation mechanism works in general as we shall see below.

Adjusting to equilibrium

There is a natural adjustment process for the compensation mechanism that will lead naive agents to the subgame perfect equilibrium. Suppose that two agents play the game repeatedly. In period $t + 1$ agent 1 sets p_1 to be whatever price agent 2 announced last period, and agent 2 moves p_2 in a direction that increases its profits if agent 1 sets the same price as it did last period. In the choice stage, agent 1 chooses output to maximize profits, given the current prices. This gives us a simple discrete dynamical system:

$$
\begin{aligned}
p_1(t+1) &= p_2(t) \\
p_2(t+1) &= p_2(t) - \gamma[p_1(t) - e'(x(p_2(t)))].
\end{aligned}
\tag{18.5}
$$

Here $\gamma > 0$ is a speed of adjustment parameter. The differential equation analog of this system is

$$
\begin{aligned}
\dot{p}_1 &= p_2 - p_1 \\
\dot{p}_2 &= -\gamma[p_1 - e'(x(p_2))].
\end{aligned}
\tag{18.6}
$$

It is easy to show that that (18.6) is locally stable; the difference equation version described in (18.5), will be locally stable if γ is small enough to avoid "overshooting." Note that if the agents use this adjustment procedure neither one needs to know anything about the other agent's technology. All that information is subsumed in the price messages that the agents send back and forth.[3]

Nonlinear taxes and compensation functions

The basic compensation mechanism described above uses linear pricing. Linear prices are fine in a convex environment, but if the environment is not convex, linear prices will not in general be able to support efficient allocations. However, this difficulty is no problem for a suitable generalization of the compensation mechanism.

Announcement stage. Firm 1 and firm 2 each announce the externality cost function for firm 2. Call these announcements $e_1(\cdot)$ and $e_2(\cdot)$.

---

[3] This is, of course, a very special adjustment process. However, Milgrom and Roberts (1991) show that for dominance solvable games every adjustment process consistent with adaptive and/or sophisticated learning converges to the dominance solvable equilibrium. Hence it may reasonably be expected that a wide class of adjustment mechanisms will work when the second-stage game is dominance solvable (as it is in this case.)

Choice stage. Firm 1 chooses x and each firm receives payoffs given by:

$$\Pi_1(x) = rx - c(x) - e_2(x) - \|e_1 - e_2\|$$
$$\Pi_2(x) = e_1(x) - e(x)$$

Here $\|e_1 - e_2\|$ signifies any norm in the appropriate function space. All that is required is that it is minimized when both agents report the same function.

To see that this works, simply note that in equilibrium, firm 1 will always want to report the same function as firm 2, so $e_1(x) \equiv e_2(x)$. Maximization of profit by firm 1 in the choice stage implies

$$rx^* - c(x^*) - e_2(x^*) \geq rx - c(x) - e_2(x) \quad \text{for all } x. \tag{18.7}$$

However, in the announcement stage, firm 2 can induce any level of x that it wants by appropriate choice of the function e_2. Hence, the equilibrium choice of x must also maximize firm 2's profits:

$$e_1(x^*) - e(x^*) \geq e_1(x) - e(x) \quad \text{for all } x. \tag{18.8}$$

Adding (18.7) and (18.8) together, and using the fact that $e_1(x) \equiv e_2(x)$ in equilibrium, we have

$$rx^* - c(x^*) - e(x^*) \geq rx - c(x) - e(x) \quad \text{for all } x, \tag{18.9}$$

which shows that x^* is the socially optimal amount.

This argument shows that all equilibria of the mechanism are efficient. However, in general there will be many equilibria of this game. To see this, observe that if e_1 and e_2 are equilibrium announcements, so are $e_1 + F$ and $e_2 + F$ for arbitrary values of F. In order to get uniqueness of equilibrium, it is necessary to restrict the class of allowable messages.[4]

One way to do this is to parameterize the cost function.[5] Suppose that the set of possible externality costs is $e(x, t)$, where t is a real-valued index of type. Suppose that the true type of firm 2 is t_0. In the announcement stage of the game, each firm simply announces the type of firm 2, and firm 1 pays a penalty if its announcement is different from that of firm 2. If t_1 is firm 1's announcement and t_2 is firm 2's announcement, the payoffs will be

$$\Pi_1(x) = rx - c(x) - e(x, t_2) - (t_1 - t_2)^2$$
$$\Pi_2(x) = e(x, t_1) - e(x, t_0)$$

---

[4] One could also refine the solution concept. In this example it may be reasonable for agent 1 to assume that agent 2 will announce the largest possible value of F consistent with agent 1's participation.

[5] In the convex case one can think of the efficiency prices as being a particularly convenient parameterization for the type space.

Differentiating with respect to x, t_1, and t_2, we have

$$r - c'(x) - \frac{\partial e(x, t_2)}{\partial x} = 0$$

$$t_1 - t_2 = 0$$

$$\left[\frac{\partial e(x, t_1)}{\partial x} - \frac{\partial e(x, t_0)}{\partial x} \right] x'(t_2) = 0.$$

Assuming that $x'(t_2) \neq 0$, it is easy to see that these equations imply

$$r = c'(x) + \frac{\partial e(x, t_0)}{\partial x},$$

which is the condition for social efficiency.

Of course, this argument requires sufficient regularity so that the various derivatives exist. If the environment is not suitably convex an argument can be constructed along the lines given above in inequalities (18.7)–(18.9). Note that in a nonconvex environment we need to assume that firm 2 can induce firm 1 to choose any desired level of x by choosing an appropriate value of t_2; this is simply a "global" version of the assumption that $x'(t_2) \neq 0$.

18.5 A general externalities problem

The externalities problem we have examined up until now is rather special. Only one agent makes a choice, and both agents have quasilinear objective functions so there are no income effects. In this section we consider a more general externality problem. For simplicity, we continue to examine a two-agent problem but the argument is easily generalized to n agents.

In the general model there are two choices, x_1 and x_2, and one transferable good, y. Agent i makes choice x_i, and has a quasiconcave utility function $u_i(x_1, x_2, y_i)$. Initially, agent i has w_i units of the transferable good, which can be thought of as money.

Efficient choices

In the absence of any transfers between the agents, agent i will choose x_i to maximize his own utility. The first-order condition characterizing these choices can be written as

$$\frac{\partial u_1 / \partial x_1}{\partial u_1 / \partial y_1} = 0$$

$$\frac{\partial u_2 / \partial x_2}{\partial u_2 / \partial y_2} = 0.$$

By contrast, an efficient allocation of choices must satisfy the first-order conditions

$$\frac{\partial u_1/\partial x_1}{\partial u_1/\partial y_1} + \frac{\partial u_2/\partial x_1}{\partial u_2/\partial y_2} = 0$$

$$\frac{\partial u_2/\partial x_2}{\partial u_2/\partial y_2} + \frac{\partial u_1/\partial x_2}{\partial u_1/\partial y_1} = 0.$$

(18.10)

These conditions simply require that the sum of the marginal-willingnesses-to-pay for activity i should be zero.

Define

$$p_{ij} = \frac{\partial u_i/\partial x_j}{\partial u_i/\partial y_i} \quad \text{for } i \neq j$$

Then we can write the efficiency conditions (18.10) as

$$\frac{\partial u_1/\partial x_1}{\partial u_1/\partial y_1} + p_{21} = 0$$

$$\frac{\partial u_2/\partial x_2}{\partial u_2/\partial y_2} + p_{12} = 0$$

This form suggests that the efficient allocation can be achieved if each agent faced the correct "price" for his choice. The problem is how to determine the correct price. Here is a description of the general compensation mechanism that solves this problem.

Announcement stage.   Agent 1 announces p_{12}^1 and p_{21}^1, and agent 2 announces p_{12}^2 and p_{21}^2.

Choice stage.   Each agent chooses x_i and y_i so as to maximize utility subject to a budget constraint:

$$\max_{x_1, y_1} u_1(x_1, x_2, y_1)$$

$$\text{such that } p_{21}^2 x_1 + y_1 = w_1 + p_{12}^2 x_2 - \|p_{21}^1 - p_{21}^2\|,$$

and

$$\max_{x_2, y_2} u_2(x_1, x_2, y_2)$$

$$\text{such that } p_{12}^1 x_2 + y_2 = w_2 + p_{21}^1 x_1 - \|p_{12}^2 - p_{12}^1\|.$$

We show below that the subgame perfect equilibria of this game are precisely the efficient allocations that satisfy the budget constraints. However, before providing that proof, let us make a few observations.

First, each agent i is facing a price, p_{ji}^j, for his own choice x_i. He is also receiving compensation $p_{ij}^j x_j$ for the choice that the other agent makes.

Both prices p^j_{ji} and p^j_{ij} are set by the *other* agent. Each agent i also pays a penalty based on how different his announced price, p^i_{ji}, is from the price that the other agent j announced for i's choice, p^j_{ji}.

As one might suspect, in equilibrium we must have $p^i_{ji} = p^j_{ji}$. This means that no penalties will be paid and that the payment made by agent i for his action will just be equal to the compensation paid to agent j. Hence, in equilibrium, the aggregate budget constraint will balance.

Let us now show that the equilibrium of this game must be efficient. We provide two proofs. The first proof simply involves writing down the first-order conditions for the utility maximization problems. There are three choice variables for each of the two agents, x_i, p^i_{ij}, and p^i_{ji}, so we have six first order conditions. Choosing the quadratic norm for computational simplicity, the first-order conditions are:

$$\frac{\partial u_1}{\partial x_1} - \frac{\partial u_1}{\partial y_1} p^2_{21} = 0 \qquad (18.11)$$

$$\left(\frac{\partial u_1}{\partial x_1} - \frac{\partial u_1}{\partial y_1} p^2_{21}\right)\frac{\partial x_1}{\partial p^1_{12}} + \left(\frac{\partial u_1}{\partial x_2} + \frac{\partial u_1}{\partial y_1} p^2_{12}\right)\frac{\partial x_2}{\partial p^1_{12}} = 0 \qquad (18.12)$$

$$\left(\frac{\partial u_1}{\partial x_1} - \frac{\partial u_1}{\partial y_1} p^2_{21}\right)\frac{\partial x_1}{\partial p^1_{21}} + \left(\frac{\partial u_1}{\partial x_2} + \frac{\partial u_1}{\partial y_1} p^2_{12}\right)\frac{\partial x_2}{\partial p^1_{21}}$$
$$-2\frac{\partial u_1}{\partial y}(p^1_{21} - p^2_{21}) = 0 \qquad (18.13)$$

$$\frac{\partial u_2}{\partial x_2} - \frac{\partial u_2}{\partial y_2} p^1_{12} = 0 \qquad (18.14)$$

$$\left(\frac{\partial u_2}{\partial x_2} - \frac{\partial u_2}{\partial y_2} p^1_{12}\right)\frac{\partial x_2}{\partial p^2_{21}} + \left(\frac{\partial u_2}{\partial x_1} + \frac{\partial u_2}{\partial y_2} p^1_{21}\right)\frac{\partial x_1}{\partial p^2_{21}} = 0 \qquad (18.15)$$

$$\left(\frac{\partial u_2}{\partial x_2} - \frac{\partial u_2}{\partial y_2} p^1_{12}\right)\frac{\partial x_2}{\partial p^2_{12}} + \left(\frac{\partial u_2}{\partial x_1} + \frac{\partial u_2}{\partial y_2} p^1_{21}\right)\frac{\partial x_1}{\partial p^2_{12}}$$
$$-2\frac{\partial u_2}{\partial y_2}(p^2_{12} - p^1_{12}) = 0 \qquad (18.16)$$

Here we have assumed that the equilibrium choices in the second stage are differentiable functions of the price announcements made in the first stage. As we shall see in the next section, this is not necessary for the argument, but it does help to see why the method works. Note that when agent 1 chooses p^1_{12}, for example, he recognizes that both his own choice, x_1, and the other agent's choice, x_2, may respond to changes in p^1_{12}.

We must assume that $\partial x_2/\partial p^1_{12}$ and $\partial x_1/\partial p^2_{21}$ are not zero. Now simply observe that this assumption and (18.11)–(18.13) together imply that $p^1_{21} = p^2_{21}$. Similarly, (18.14)—(18.16) imply that $p^1_{12} = p^2_{12}$. Finally, combine (18.11) and (18.15) to get:

$$\frac{\partial u_1/\partial x_1}{\partial u_1/\partial y_1} + \frac{\partial u_2/\partial x_1}{\partial u_2/\partial y_2} = 0,$$

and combine (18.12) and (18.14) to get:

$$\frac{\partial u_2/\partial x_2}{\partial u_2/\partial x_2} + \frac{\partial u_1/\partial x_2}{\partial u_1/\partial y_1} = 0.$$

These are precisely the first-order conditions given in (18.10). Therefore, the subgame perfect equilibrium is efficient.

Note that the equilibrium is a *particular* efficient allocation, namely one that satisfies the "natural" budget constraint involving the efficiency prices. In general, such allocations will be a small subset of all efficient allocations. By analogy with the public goods literature, we call these allocations *generalized Lindahl allocations*. We show below that when the externalities problem is a public goods problem, the prices in the compensation mechanism are Lindahl prices.

A more general proof

The above proof shows clearly why an equilibrium of the compensation mechanism must be an efficient allocation. However, being a calculus proof, it doesn't deal very well with corner solutions, additional constraints, non-differentiabilities, etc. Here is another argument that handles these difficulties easily.

We need one assumption for our proof, an invertibility assumption that says that each agent can set a price for the other agent that will induce the other agent to make any desired choice. That is, if agent 1 would like agent 2 to make some choice there is some price that agent 1 can set that will induce agent 2 to make this choice. This is analogous to the assumption that $\partial x_2/\partial p_{12}^1 \neq 0$ in our previous proof. As in the differentiable case, the demand functions only need to be locally invertible if the environment is suitably convex.

Local Invertibility Assumption. Let $x = (x_1, x_2)$ be the outcome of some set of price announcements. Let $\hat{x}_i$ be a choice close to x_i that agent j prefers to x_i. Then there is some $\hat{p}_{ji}^j$ that agent j can announce that will make $\hat{x}_i$ an optimal choice for agent i.

Local invertibility says that agent i can manipulate agent j's choices through agent i's price announcements. This is a very weak assumption. If the agents' demands are differentiable functions of price with nonzero derivatives then the Inverse Function Theorem implies local invertibility.

Theorem.   *Let preferences be convex and continuous. Then every subgame perfect equilibrium of the compensation mechanism is Pareto efficient.*

Proof. Let (x, y, p) be a subgame perfect equilibrium of the compensation mechanism. First we show that in equilibrium $p_{21}^1 = p_{21}^2$. To see this, consider the agents' budget constraints:

$$p_{21}^2 x_1 + y_1 = w_1 + p_{12}^2 x_2 - \|p_{21}^1 - p_{21}^2\|$$
$$p_{12}^1 x_2 + y_2 = w_2 + p_{21}^1 x_1 - \|p_{12}^2 - p_{12}^1\|.$$

Note that agent 1 can influence agent 2's choice of x_2 through both the "income term," $p_{21}^1 x_1$, and the "price term," p_{12}^1. However, by the Local Invertibility Assumption, any choice of x_2 that can be achieved through the income term can also be achieved by an appropriate choice of the price term, p_{12}^1.

Suppose that there were an equilibrium in which $p_{21}^1 \neq p_{21}^2$. Let agent 1 set $p_{21}^1 = p_{21}^2$ and adjust p_{12}^1 so as to induce the original equilibrium value of x_2. This must reduce agent 1's penalty, and thereby increase agent 1's utility. This contradicts the assumption that we had an equilibrium. It follows that an equilibrium must exhibit zero penalty terms for all agents.

Suppose now that (x', y') is a feasible allocation that Pareto dominates the equilibrium allocation. We will show that the existence of such an allocation leads to a contradiction. By convexity and continuity of preferences, we can assume that (x', y') is arbitrarily close to the equilibrium allocation. According to the Local Invertibility Assumption agent 1 can induce agent 2 to choose x_2' simply by choosing an appropriate level of p_{12}^1; furthermore, agent 1 can directly choose (x_1', y_1'). If agent 1 decides *not* to choose this preferred allocation, it must be because it lies outside his budget set. The same argument applies to agent 2, and this gives us the inequalities

$$p_{21}^2 x_1' + y_1' > w_1 + p_{12}^2 x_2'$$
$$p_{12}^1 x_2' + y_2' > w_2 + p_{21}^1 x_1'.$$

Summing these inequalities and using the fact that $p_{ji}^i = p_{ji}^j$, we have

$$y_1' + y_2' > w_1 + w_2,$$

which shows that the Pareto dominating allocation must be infeasible. ∎

Note that the logic of this proof is quite general. In particular, the taxation and compensation functions do not need to be linear functions. All that is necessary is that each agent can manipulate the other agent's choice without incurring any cost himself. If the economic environment is convex, we only need local invertibility; if the economic environment is non-convex, we may need global invertibility.

It can also be shown that if the environment is convex, then any Pareto efficient allocation is an equilibrium of this game for a suitable choice of initial endowments. The proof is a simple variation on the second welfare theorem and is omitted for sake of brevity.

18.6 Balancing the mechanism

We have seen that in the simple example discussed earlier that the compensation mechanism can be balanced by distributing the budget surplus generated by each agent among the other agents. The same procedure works in general; here we examine the simple case of quasilinear utility.

The appropriate payoff to agent i is

$$u_i(x) + \sum_{j=1}^{n} B_{ij} - T_i,$$

where

$$B_{ij} = p_{ij}^j x_j - p_{ji}^j x_i - \|p_{ji}^i - p_{ji}^j\|$$

$$T_i = \frac{1}{n-2} \sum_{k \neq i} \sum_{j \neq i} B_{kj} = \frac{1}{n-2} \left[\sum_{k=1}^{n} \sum_{j=1}^{n} B_{kj} - \sum_{j=1}^{n} B_{ij} - \sum_{j=1}^{n} B_{ji} \right].$$

It is obvious that $B_{ii} = 0$ and it is not hard to show that

$$\sum_{i=1}^{n} \left[\sum_{j=1}^{n} B_{ij} - T_i \right] = 0. \tag{18.17}$$

Note that B_{ij} depends on the vector of prices and the vector of choices. It is important to observe that the only price term that agent i determines is the price in the penalty term, p_{ji}^i; all other prices are independent of i's choices. To emphasize the fact that the payment depends on x, we write $B_{ij}(x)$ in the following paragraphs.

By local invertibility, each agent can induce any desired allocation in the choice stage by choosing the appropriate prices in the announcement stage. Hence a subgame perfect equilibrium allocation must satisfy

$$u_i(x^*) + \sum_{j=1}^{n} B_{ij}(x^*) - T_i(x^*) \geq u_i(x) + \sum_{j=1}^{n} B_{ij}(x) - T_i(x),$$

for all x. Summing over the agents and using equation (18.17), we see that

$$\sum_{i=1}^{n} u_i(x^*) \geq \sum_{i=1}^{n} u_i(x),$$

for all x which shows that the subgame perfect equilibrium is Pareto efficient.

Note that this argument does not use the linear structure of the $B_{ij}(x)$ terms; indeed, the only feature used is that agent j can report a $B_{ij}(x)$ term that will induce agent i to make the choice x_i that agent j wants him to make. In a convex environment linear prices will generally have this property, but in other environments other sorts of pricing functions may be necessary

Note further that this argument for efficiency does not use the penalty terms; if all the penalty terms are set equal to zero, the proof of efficiency still goes through. However, the penalty terms will in general be necessary if we want the equilibrium allocation to be a Lindahl allocation. Why? In order to be a generalized Lindahl allocation each agent must satisfy his budget constraint when each choice is priced at its supporting efficiency price. For this to be the case, the $T_i(x)$ term must be zero in equilibrium. If the penalty terms are present, each agent will have an incentive to set $p_{ji}^i = p_{ji}^j$ which will ensure that this will occur.

18.7 A different information structure

The compensation mechanism described above is appropriate for a "bilateral" information structure: if agent i imposes costs on agent j, both i and j know the magnitude of these costs. Another structure that one might imagine is that there is some third party, k, who knows the magnitude of these costs. In this case, we can use a slightly different type of compensation mechanism to achieve efficient outcomes.

Consider the following example with three agents. Agent i chooses x_i, holds "money" y_i, and has a quasilinear utility function $u_i(x_1, x_2, x_3) + y_i$. The prices that support an efficient allocation will have the form $p_{ij} = \partial u_i(x)/\partial x_j$. Let p_{ij}^k denote the report of person k about the appropriate magnitude of the price p_{ij}, and let $x = (x_1, x_2, x_3)$ be the vector of choices.

In this variant of the compensation mechanism the payoffs to the agents will be:

$$u_1(x) - (p_{31}^2 + p_{21}^3)x_1 + p_{12}^3 x_2 + p_{13}^2 x_3$$
$$u_2(x) - (p_{32}^1 + p_{12}^3)x_2 + p_{21}^3 x_1 + p_{23}^1 x_3 \qquad (18.18)$$
$$u_3(x) - (p_{23}^1 + p_{13}^2)x_3 + p_{31}^2 x_1 + p_{32}^1 x_2.$$

Note the payoffs are balanced, even out of equilibrium. No sidepayments or penalties are necessary in this case.

One way to prove that the subgame perfect equilibrium is efficient is to differentiate the payoffs with respect to each of the choice variables. However, we can also apply the logic of the previous section. Simply replace the definitions used there with

$$B_{ij}^k(x) = p_{ij}^k x_j - p_{ji}^k x_i$$
$$T_i(x) = 0,$$

where k takes on all possible values $1, \ldots, n$, but $k \neq i, j$. Note that when $n = 3$ we have the payoffs given in (18.18). These definitions imply that

$$\sum_{i=1}^{n} \sum_{j=1}^{n} B_{ij}^{k}(x) = 0,$$

and this is all that is required for the proof given in the previous section to work. The resulting allocation is automatically Lindahl.

18.8 Examples of the compensation mechanism

We have described the general form of the compensation mechanism; here we illustrate how it works in some specific cases.

Pure public goods

The special case of a pure public good is of some interest, since it is a well known and much studied example of a particular type of externality. Let x_1 and x_2 be two agents' monetary contributions to a public good. Let y_i be agent i's private consumption. In the absence of any transfer mechanism, agent 1's maximization problem in a public goods contribution game takes the form[6]

$$\max_{x_1, y_1} u_1(x_1 + x_2, y_1)$$

$$\text{such that } x_1 + y_1 = w_1$$

$$x_1 \geq 0.$$

Since there is now a positive externality between the agents, it is natural to think of the agents as subsidizing each other rather than taxing each other. Applying the subsidy payments appropriate for the compensation mechanism, the budget constraint facing agent 1 becomes:

$$(1 - p_{21}^2) x_1 + y_1 = w_1 - p_{12}^2 x_2 - \| p_{21}^1 - p_{21}^2 \|.$$

Here agent 1's contributions are subsidized at a rate p_{21}^2 which is chosen by agent 2; this subsidy is recovered by a tax on agent 2. Agent 1 also sets the rate at which 2's contributions should be subsidized, and in equilibrium he ends up paying $p_{12}^2 x_2 = p_{12}^1 x_2$ to cover this subsidy. In the compensation mechanism the taxes and subsidies that each agent faces are chosen by

---

[6] The nonnegativity constraint is natural in a model of voluntary contributions: one may choose to contribute a positive amount to a public good, but one is typically not able to make a *negative* contribution. The equilibrium of this contribution game has been studied extensively by Bergstrom, Blume and Varian (1986).

the other agent(s). See Danziger (1991) and Varian (1994) for similar mechanisms where the agents set some of the subsidy rates for themselves. Guttman (1978) describes a related mechanism where agents choose the rate at which they will match other agents' contributions to a public good. Guttman's mechanism is of some interest since matching contributions are a commonly used method to encourage contributions to a public good.

Since public goods are just a special kind of externality, the proof of efficiency given earlier still applies. Note that the non-calculus proof is the appropriate version here, due to the presence of the nonnegativity condition. However, given the special form of the public goods externality, we can say a bit more about the equilibrium prices. Suppose that we have an interior solution to the public goods game so that x_1 and x_2 are both positive. Since x_1 and x_2 are perfect substitutes in consumption, they must have the same price in equilibrium.

By inspection of the budget constraint it follows that $(1 - p_{21}^2) = p_{12}^2$. Therefore the budget constraint facing agent 1 can, in equilibrium, be written as

$$p_{12}^2[x_1 + x_2] + y_1 = w_1.$$

It follows that an equilibrium value of p_{12}^2 is simply the Lindahl price of the public good for agent 1, and the equilibrium allocation is simply a Lindahl allocation. Hence, the compensation mechanism gives a way to decentralize Lindahl allocations by giving each agent the incentive to reveal the appropriate Lindahl prices.

Pure private goods

Agent 1 is a consumer who consumes an x-good and a y-good and has a quasilinear utility function $u(x) + y_1$. Agent 2 is a monopolist that can produce the x good at cost $c(x)$; it's objective function is $y_2 - c(x)$. How can we induce the monopolist to produce the socially optimal output?

If we are only interested in efficiency, this is not terribly difficult: simply have one of the agents dictate a production level and a transfer. In this full information environment we will get an efficient amount of x regardless of which agent chooses it; only the transfer will be different. However, if we want to get a *particular* efficient allocation—say the competitive outcome—it is not so obvious how to proceed. However, the compensation mechanism solves the problem quite readily.

Announcement stage. The consumer announces how much he values the good, p_1, and the producer announces how much the consumer values the good, p_2.

Choice stage. The producer chooses x and the payoffs are

$$\Pi_1 = u(x) - p_2 x$$
$$\Pi_2 = p_1 x - c(x) - \|p_2 - p_1\|$$

Note that this problem is very similar to the simple externalities problem used to motivate the compensation mechanism, illustrating the Coasian point that externalities are just a special case of private goods.[7] Applying the standard argument shows that in equilibrium

$$p_1 = p_2 = u'(x) = c'(x),$$

which are the conditions that characterize the competitive allocation.

Regulation of duopoly

There are now three agents: the consumer (indexed by 0) and two firms. Firm 1 produces x_1 at cost $c_1(x_1)$, firm 2 produces x_2 at cost $c_2(x_2)$ and the consumer has utility function $u(x_1, x_2) + y_0$. The standard compensation mechanism involves payoffs of the form

$$\Pi_0 = u(x_1, x_2) - p_{01}^1 x_1 - p_{02}^2 x_2$$
$$\Pi_1 = p_{01}^0 x_1 - c_1(x_1) - \|p_{01}^1 - p_{01}^0\|$$
$$\Pi_2 = p_{02}^0 x_2 - c_2(x_2) - \|p_{02}^2 - p_{02}^0\|$$

Here the consumer is setting the prices that the firms face, and the firms are setting the prices that the consumer faces.

However, in the case of duopoly it is natural to think that the firms may know more about each other's technology than the consumer knows. Hence it makes sense for each firm to report the price that the *other* firm should face. This yields payoffs of the form

$$\Pi_0 = u(x_1, x_2) - p_{01}^2 x_1 - p_{02}^1 x_2$$
$$\Pi_1 = p_{01}^2 x_1 - c_1(x_1)$$
$$\Pi_2 = p_{02}^1 x_2 - c_2(x_2).$$

Note that the consumer chooses both x_1 and x_2 and that each firm sets the price for the *other* firms' product.

The arguments given earlier show that the competitive allocation is the unique equilibrium of this game. But it is useful to think about how it

---

[7] Or is it the other way around?

works here. Consider the classic Bertrand case where the two goods are perfect substitutes. Suppose that each firm has announced the competitive price. Why wouldn't firm 1 want to raise the price of firm 2's product, creating more demand for its own output? If firm 1 raised the price facing firm 2, then the consumer would demand more output from firm 1, which it would be *forced* to supply. But since the price that firm 1 faces equals its marginal cost this would reduce firm 1's profit.

Prisoners' dilemma

Consider the following asymmetric prisoners' dilemma:

		Column	
		Cooperate	Defect
Row	Cooperate	5, 5	2, 6
	Defect	7, 1	3, 3

How can we induce the Pareto efficient outcome? Let $x_i = 1$ if agent i cooperates, and $x_i = 0$ if agent i defects and let $u_i(x_1, x_2)$ be the payoff to agent i taken from the above game matrix.

Announcement stage. Agent 1 names p_{12}^1, how much agent 1 should be paid if he cooperates, and p_{21}^1, how much agent 2 should be paid if he cooperates. Similarly agent 2 names p_{21}^2 and p_{12}^2.

Choice stage. Each agent chooses whether to cooperate or defect. The agents receive payoffs

$$\Pi_1 = u_1(x_1, x_2) + p_{21}^2 x_1 - p_{12}^2 x_2 - \|p_{21}^1 - p_{21}^2\|$$
$$\Pi_2 = u_2(x_1, x_2) + p_{12}^1 x_2 - p_{21}^1 x_1 - \|p_{12}^2 - p_{12}^1\|$$

Note the sign change: since there is now a positive externality between the two agents, it is natural to subsidize good behavior rather than penalize bad behavior.[8] Using the by now standard argument, it can be shown that the it is a subgame perfect equilibrium for both players to cooperate. The supporting prices satisfy the conditions

$$4 \geq p_{21}^1 = p_{21}^2 \geq 2$$
$$3 \geq p_{12}^1 = p_{12}^2 \geq 1.$$

(If the inequalities are strict, the cooperative equilibrium will be unique.) As usual the compensation mechanism produces an efficient outcome in this game—or in any game, for that matter.

---

[8] We could also formulate this problem so as to have each agent announce how the other agent should be fined if he defects.

18.9 Related literature

There is a vast literature on mechanism design that is concerned with how to implement various social choice functions. Much of this literature is concerned with whether a particular social choice function can be implemented by a decentralized game. Our concern is not so much with the *existence* of a mechanism, but rather finding a suitably simple mechanism. Most of the attempts to find "simple" solutions to externalities problems have been concerned with the case of public goods, so we provide a very brief review of that literature insofar as it relates to the work described here. Moore provides a thorough review of the recent literature.

The well-known demand revealing mechanism of Clarke (1971) and Groves (1976) implements the efficient amount of a public good via a dominant strategy equilibrium. However, this mechanism only works with quasilinear utility, and is not balanced, even in equilibrium. Furthermore, it does not in general yield a Pareto efficient outcome.

Groves and Ledyard (1977) describe a quadratic mechanism that yields efficient Nash equilibria for the public goods problem, but the equilibrium allocations are not Lindahl allocations. Hurwicz (1979) and Walker (1981) also describe mechanisms that implement Lindahl allocations. In the Hurwicz mechanism, each agent proposes an amount of the public good and a Lindahl price; agents pay a quadratic penalty if they announce different levels of the public good. Walker's (1981) mechanism avoids such penalty terms. Groves (1979) and Groves-Ledyard (1987) provide a nice survey of these results.

Turning to the more recent literature on simple mechanisms, Bagnoli-Lipman (1989) and Jackson-Moulin (1992) examine the special case of a discrete public good with quasilinear utility. The Bagnoli-Lipman mechanism is very simple: each agent offers a voluntary contribution. If the sum of the contributions covers the cost of the public good, it is produced, otherwise the contributions are returned. This mechanism implements the core of the public goods game in undominated perfect equilibria.

The Jackson-Moulin mechanism implements an efficient allocation using undominated Nash equilibria. They also describe a variation using subgame perfect equilibrium. Their mechanism is reasonably simple and works with a broad family of cost-sharing rules. However, it appears that both the Bagnoli-Lipman and Jackson-Moulin mechanisms work only in the special case of indivisible public goods and quasilinear utility.

Varian (1989a) describes some mechanisms for the public goods problem that are closely related to the compensation mechanism. In the case of two agents with quasilinear utility there is a very simple mechanism that achieves a Lindahl allocation: in the first stage each agent offers to subsidize the contributions of the other agent. In the second stage, each agent makes a voluntary contribution and collects the promised subsidies from the other agent.[9] Varian describes some other variations on the compensation mechanism for public goods problems involving many agents and general utility functions.

18.10 Summary

The compensation mechanism provides a simple mechanism for internalizing externalities in economic environments. Transfer payments can be chosen so that the compensation mechanism is balanced, and penalty payments, when they are used, can be chosen to be arbitrarily small. The main problem with the mechanism is that it requires complete information by the agents. In many cases a simple dynamic adjustment model will converge to the subgame perfect equilibrium.

References

Arrow, K. (1970). The organization of economic activity: Issues pertinent to the choice of market versus non-market allocation. In Haveman, R. H., & Margolis, J. (Eds.), *Public Expenditures and Policy Analysis*, pp. 59–73. Markham.

Bagnoli, M., & Lipman, B. (1989). Provision of public goods: fully implementing the core through private contributions. *Review of Economic Studies, 56*, 583–602.

Bergstrom, T., Blume, L., & Varian, H. (1986). On the private provision of public goods. *Journal of Public Economics, 29*, 25–49.

Clarke, E. (1971). Multipart pricing of public goods. *Public Choice, 11*, 17–33.

Coase, R. H. (1960). The problem of social cost. *Journal of Law and Economics, 3*, 1–44.

Crawford, V. (1979). A procedure for generating pareto efficient egalitarian-equivalent allocations. *Econometrica, 47*, 49–60.

Danziger, L., & Schnytzer, A. (1991). Implementing the Lindahl voluntary-exchange mechanism. *European Journal of Political Economy, 7*, 55–64.

---

[9] This mechanism is related to the mechanism of Guttman, which involves offering to match contributions. See also Danziger and Schnytzer for a related model.

Groves, T. (1979). Efficient collective choice when compensation is possible. *Review of Economic Studies*, *46*, 227–241.

Groves, T., & Ledyard, J. (1977). Optimal allocations of public goods: A solution to the 'free rider problem'. *Econometrica*, *45*, 783–809.

Groves, T., & Ledyard, J. (1987). Incentive compatibility since 1972. In Groves, T., Radner, R., & Reiter, S. (Eds.), *Information, Incentives and Economic Mechanisms*. University of Minnesota Press, Minneapolis.

Groves, T. (1976). Information, incentives, and the internalization of production externalities. In Lin, S. (Ed.), *Theory and Measurement of Economic Externalities*. Academic Press, New York.

Guttman, J. (1978). Understanding collective action: Matching behavior. *American Economic Review*, *68*, 251–255.

Hurwicz, L. (1979). Outcome functions yielding Walrasian and Lindahl allocations at Nash equilibrium points. *Review of Economic Studies*, *46*, 217–225.

Jackson, M., & Moulin, H. (1992). Implementing a public project and distributing its cost. *Journal of Economic Theory*, *57*, 125–140.

Maskin, E. (1985). The theory of implementation in Nash equilibrium. In Hurwicz, L., Schmeidler, D., & Sonnenschein, H. (Eds.), *Social Goals and Social Organization*, pp. 173–204. Cambridge Univeristy Press, Cambridge.

Milgrom, P., & Roberts, J. (1991). Adaptive and sophisticated learning in repeated normal form games. *Games and Economic Behavior*, 82–100.

Moore, J. (1992). Implementation, contracts, and renegotiation in environments with complete information. In Laffont, J. J. (Ed.), *Advances in Economic Theory: 6th World Congress*, pp. 182–281. Cambridge University Press, Cambridge, England.

Moore, J., & Repullo, R. (1988). Subgame perfect implementation. *Econometrica*, *56*, 1191–1220.

Moulin, H. (1979). Dominance solvable voting schemes. *Econometrica*, *47*, 1337–1351.

Moulin, H. (1981). Implementing just and efficient decision making. *Journal of Public Economics*, *16*, 193–213.

Pigou, A. C. (1920). *The Economics of Welfare*. Macmillan, London.

Varian, H. (1994). Sequential contributions to public goods. *Journal of Public Economics*, *53*(2), 165–186.

Walker, M. (1981). A simple incentive compatible scheme for attaining Lindahl allocations. *Econometrica*, *48*, 56–73.

Chapter 19

ECONOMIC INCENTIVES IN SOFTWARE DESIGN

I examine the incentives for software providers to design appropriate user interfaces. There are two sorts of costs involved when one uses software: the fixed cost of learning to use a piece of software and the variable cost of operating the software. I show that a monopoly provider of software generally invests the right amount of resources in making the software easy to learn, but too little in making it easy to operate. In some extreme cases a monopolist may even make the software too easy to learn.

The market for computer software is large and rapidly growing. Despite this, there has been little theoretical investigation of the unique economic features of the software market. In this paper I investigate an important aspect of software economics: the extent to which the providers of software have the right incentives to design an appropriate interface for their software.

19.1 User costs

An important feature of software is that there are large costs to the consumer of using it. First, one must learn how to use a particular software package. Even if one only wants to use the package occasionally, one has to read the documentation, practice a bit, and invest time and energy in learning the basics of how to use the package. This cost of learning the software is a *fixed cost* to the user: it is more-or-less independent of the amount of use that the software gets.

This should be contrasted with the *variable cost* of operating a software package. These are costs that are incurred every time one uses the software. The most obvious of these costs are time costs, such as a delay in loading or saving a file. If it takes 10 seconds to start the package every time you use it, this is 10 seconds of lost time each time the package is used. If one

This work was supported by the National Science Foundation. I also wish to thank the Dipartimento d'economia politica at the Universitá di Siena for their hospitality during the period of this research. I would like to thank Jim Adams, Paul Courant and Judy Olson for their comments on an earlier draft of this paper.

has to wade through an elaborate menu structure to perform a simple task, then this is a cost that must be borne every time the task is undertaken.

People who use a particular software package every day incur a large amount of these variable costs, while people who use this software rarely incur little variable costs. However, everyone incurs roughly the same fixed cost of learning the program.

Reviews of software often talk about "ease of use." The above distinction suggests that there are two dimensions to ease of use: ease of learning and ease of operation. Software that is easy to learn has a lot of menus and elaborate help screens. It provides user prompts and error messages. The documentation is easy to read. Software that is easy to operate generally has fewer menus, replacing them with command key combinations. This means that a given command can be executed quite quickly—once the user has made the investment in learning the appropriate keystrokes. In this sense, the command driven interface is easy to operate, although the menu interface is easy to learn.[1]

Another aspect of ease-of-operation is *performance:* how quickly and how well the software does the job it is supposed to do. When we turn to modeling consumer choice of software we will be interested in the *net performance* of the software: the difference between the benefits from the task the software does and the costs of making the software perform that task.

These two aspects of ease-of-use—being easy-to-operate versus being easy-to-learn—are not mutually exclusive. A well-designed software package can satisfy both goals. However the software designer still has to decide how much effort to put into improving each aspect of the user interface. If the software is supposed to be delivered in one week, is that week better spent improving the speed of some calculation or fine-tuning the menu structure? The answer presumably depends on how improvements in these two dimensions affect profits ... which is where the economic analysis comes in.

In terms of our previous discussion, the cost of learning a piece of software is a fixed cost, while the cost of using a piece of software is a variable cost. The software provider would like to minimize both sorts of user costs, in order to make the software more attractive to consumers, but it is costly to do so. The question of interest to an economist is whether the market provides the right incentives to the software provider. Will the provider of software invest the socially correct amount of resources in minimizing each type of user cost?

Although we have discussed user costs in terms of software design, it is

---

[1] I first heard of this distinction in a discussion with Paul Scott. For some background concerning design of user-friendly software, see Nakamura (1990). See Mantei-Teorey (1988) for a discussion of benefit-cost analysis of software design from the viewpoint of software purchases by large corporations.

clear that it also applies to other types of goods. Consider for example, sporting equipment. Equipment designed for casual users may be very different from equipment designed for intensive users. An easy-to-learn tennis racket may be loosely strung, while an easy-to-use racket may be tightly strung. Or consider other sorts of hobbyist equipment such as cameras. Again, a camera for a casual user has a very different design than a camera for a professional user.

19.2 Market structure

However, there is an important distinction between the market for sporting equipment and the market for software. The market for tennis rackets and cameras seem to be reasonably competitive. There are a number of different types of products provided, and a given consumer can choose the type of product that is best for him. A casual user wants a product that is easy to learn; an intensive user wants one that is easy to operate, and the market provides both types of products.

The market for software is a bit different. It appears that for some products at least, the market is very highly concentrated. For example, in the database market, Ashton-Tate has over 50 percent of the market. In the wordprocessor market, WordPerfect appears to have over 60 percent of the market, and Microsoft controls another 25 percent. Until recently Lotus had a 75 percent share of the spreadsheet market.[2]

At a more aggregated level the market for personal computer software seems to be becoming more concentrated. According to the 1990 SoftLetter 100 list, Microsoft had 25% of industry revenue and the next 3 companies (Lotus, Novel, and WordPerfect) had another 25%. The top 12 companies had 77% of industry revenue, as compared to 66% in 1985.[3] This concentration has not gone unnoticed in Washington; the FTC is currently examining Microsoft looking for evidence of unfair trade practices.

In addition, there are compelling theoretical reasons to believe that the software market is unlikely to be a perfectly competitive market, due to the presence of increasing returns to scale. In the production of software, nearly all of the costs are fixed costs—the costs involved in designing, writing, debugging, documenting and marketing the software. Furthermore, most of these fixed costs are sunk costs—they are not recoverable if the firm exits the industry. The variable costs—the costs of duplicating, packaging, and distributing the software—are very small by comparison. The

---

[2] Data is for the MS-DOS market only. Database figures come from *Computer Reseller News,* July 15, 1991. Wordprocessing figures come from *Standard & Poor's Industry Surveys,* April 1991. Spreadsheet figures come from *Datamation,* December 15, 1990.

[3] Data from Bulkeley (1991); see also Fisher (1992).

fact that total costs are much larger than variable costs indicates that the likely equilibrium market structure will involve producers of mass-market software having a considerable amount of market power.

Another factor that suggests markets for software will be highly concentrated is the presence of network externalities among users. It is advantageous to me to have the same software as my colleagues since it makes it easier to share files, expertise, etc., and this tends to give the largest firm in the industry an advantage in selling more software.

Here we examine the admittedly extreme case of a monopolist. The case of monopolistic competition is certainly highly relevant, and I hope to examine it in future work, but it is beyond the scope of this paper. In any event, the phenomenon we examine here will apply in monopolistically competitive markets as well. Indeed, it will arise in any market where the producer has some degree of market power. The essential phenomenon we will discuss arises in any market where the producer faces a downward sloping demand curve for its product.

However, it is important for the following results that the manufacturer does not engage in product differentiation. That is, our model assumes that the producer sells only a single version of its product. This appears to be plausible in the case of software provision. There are some exceptions to this rule, such as WordPerfect and LetterPerfect, but these are rare. Generally, there is a single version of the product which is sold to a whole spectrum of users. This is quite different from the behavior of a typical manufacturer of tennis rackets, skis, or cameras.

19.3 The basic idea

The basic idea that I want to capture can be stated quite simply. We may think of ease-of-learning and ease-of-operation as two different dimensions of software "quality." It is well-known from the work of Spence (1975) that a monopolist does not in general have the right incentives to provide the appropriate amount of quality. Roughly speaking, the monopolist is interested in how a change in quality affects the willingness-to-pay of the marginal consumer, while the willingness-to-pay of the average consumer is the appropriate concern for social welfare.

Consider a monopolist contemplating investing an additional dollar in software design. Should the dollar go to making the software easier to operate or easier to learn? If the monopolist makes the software easier to learn then he will acquire additional customers—those consumers who previously weren't willing to invest in learning how to use the product, but now find the investment worthwhile. If the monopolist makes the software easier to operate, he will also acquire *some* new customers ... but most of the benefits of the improvements in ease of operation accrue to the people who would have bought the software anyway. Since the monopolist cannot capture the full marginal benefits from making the product easier to operate, it will, in general, underinvest in this aspect of software design. However, since the monopolist can expand its market by making the software easy to learn, it will have the correct social incentives in this dimension.

19.4 Design of a word processor

Take, for example, the design of a word processor. Some users may have need for a word processor only once a week. Whether or not they buy a word processor depends on how difficult they think that it will be to learn to use it effectively. How quickly it reformats paragraphs or spell-checks is not of great significance to them. However, these features could be very important to a person who uses the word processor everyday. For an intensive user, the learning costs are small relative to the costs of operation; for a casual user, the learning costs are the dominant consideration.

Ideally, there would be "friendly" wordprocessors for casual users and "powerful" wordprocessors for intensive users. But if there is only one wordprocessor for both casual and intensive users there is an inevitable tradeoff in the design of such software. Should there be a special command to transpose two words? This could be useful to an intensive user, but probably not very useful to an occasional user. Providing and documenting such a command is costly to the software developer. In at least the first release of the software, the developer would probably concentrate more on the quality of the documentation and user interface rather than investing much time in adding rarely-used features. Similarly, the casual user would probably not be too concerned with how rapidly the document could be reformatted, or how quickly the spell-checker worked. But these factors could be very important to an intensive user.

People who use software on an occasional basis don't want a lot of choices—they are willing to give up some features in order to make the software easy to learn. People who use the software intensively are willing to invest in learning a variety of features since they will probably find occasion to use them.

Another important example of this distinction is in user support. "Hand-holding" support is critical to casual users, but not nearly so important to intensive users. In fact, intensive users would probably prefer to see a company devote more of its resources to improving software performance rather than providing increased handholding for new users. But it's the new users who bring in the new dollars—and that's why software companies invest in activities that can reduce the costs facing new users.

When we look at the evolution of personal computer software, we see improvements in both the ease-of-learning and the ease-of-use of software. The current behavior of software providers seems to be much more focussed on the ease-of-learning aspect of software design. In order to sell software to consumers who don't have it already, they have to make the software easier to learn. The attraction of user-friendly shells, such as MS-Windows, to software developers lies in the fact that once users have mastered the shell environment, the fixed costs of learning a new piece of software are much smaller for them. Hence one can expect that the demand for software products will increase.

Contrast the reaction of software vendors to MS-Windows with the reaction, say, to an increase in CPU speed. This might make getting things done a lot easier for intensive users of some software packages, but it probably wouldn't sell much new software. Of course, developers might redesign their software to add help features that were not feasible before—but that simply shows what is important to the software producers.

19.5 Monopoly provision of quality

The producer of a product chooses both the price and the characteristics of the product he produces. Most work in economics is concerned with the pricing decision. However, considerations of product design are also of great importance. Spence (1975) and Sheshinski (1976) consider the incentives facing a monopolist in choosing the "quality" of its product. Here quality should be thought of as a variable that shifts the demand curve for the product; in our application, "quality" is the ease-of-learning and the ease-of-operation described above.[4]

Spence (1975) computes the derivative of consumers' surplus minus costs evaluated at the monopoly position and derives two conditions sufficient to sign this derivative. The first involves comparing the impact of a quality change on the marginal versus the average consumer: if the average consumer values the change in quality more than the marginal consumer then the monopolist underprovides quality. The second involves examining the sign of $\partial^2 p(x,q)/\partial x\partial q$. These conditions provide an answer to the question, but it is hard to interpret precisely what they mean. As Schmalensee (1979) puts it: "It is very hard to form any general intuition about the sign (let alone the magnitude) of the crucial cross-derivative P_{QX}."

In order to determine the sign it is helpful to develop a microeconomic model of consumer choice, a task I pursue below. However, before doing that it may be useful to derive the Spence-Sheshinski result. The derivation below is different from the method used by Spence and Sheshinski and has the advantage that it focuses attention on the crucial aspect of the problem relevant to the case at hand.

---

[4] The most common example of quality in the literature is "durability." See the seminal work of Swan (1970) and the survey by Schmalensee (1979). See also the textbook treatment by Tirole (1988).

Let x denote the quantity and q the quality of some product. Let $u(x,q)$ be the utility of the product and $c(x,q)$ be the cost of providing it. Let $p(x,q) = \partial u(x,q)/\partial x$ be the inverse demand curve for the product. The social objective function is defined to be

$$W(x,q) = u(x,q) - c(x,q)$$

which is simply benefits minus costs. The monopolist's objective function is given by profit:

$$\Gamma(x,q) = p(x,q)x - c(x,q).$$

Let (x^m, q^m) denote the monopolist's profit-maximizing choice of output and quality. We are interested in the derivative of welfare evaluated at the monopolist's choice.

Write the welfare function as

$$W(x,q) = [u(x,q) - p(x,q)x] + [p(x,q)x - c(x,q)] = CS + PS.$$

This is simply the sum of consumer surplus plus producer surplus. If we differentiate with respect to q and evaluate the derivative at the monopolist's optimum, we see that the derivative of producer surplus must be zero—since the monopolist is already maximizing profits. Hence the derivative of welfare with respect to quality is simply the derivative of consumers' surplus with respect to quality. This is a significant simplification since it means that we don't have to model the cost side of things at all.[5]

How does consumer surplus change as quality changes? This derivative is given by

$$\frac{\partial W(x_m, q_m)}{\partial q} = \frac{\partial u(x_m, q_m)}{\partial q} - \frac{\partial p(x_m, q_m)}{\partial q} x_m.$$

We can write this expression as

$$\frac{\partial W(x_m, q_m)}{\partial q} = x_m \frac{\partial}{\partial q} \left[\frac{u(x_m, q_m)}{x_m} - p(x_m, q_m) \right].$$

Hence the sign of the derivative of the welfare change is just the sign of the term in brackets. The first term in the brackets is the total willingness-to-pay divided by the number of consumers who purchase the good; this is the average willingness-to-pay. The second term in the expression is the price—the marginal willingness-to-pay. The welfare effect of the quality

---

[5] This observation also has global implications. Start at the profit-maximizing position and consider a "large" change in quality. Profits go down since we've moved away from the profit-maximizing choice; if consumers' surplus also goes down, welfare unambiguously decreases.

change depends on how a quality change affects the *difference* between these two terms. This proves the first of Spence's observations.

Note that no calculations are necessary; all that is required is the observation that the derivative of profit is zero at the monopoly solution and the observation that consumers' surplus is proportional to the difference between an average and a marginal quantity. We now go on to ask what it is about demand that determines the sign of this quantity. In other words, how does consumers' surplus change as the demand curve moves? As shown in Figure 1, we can decompose a movement of the demand curve into a parallel "shift" and a "tilt." The shift doesn't change consumers' surplus at all; only the tilt matters. It is easy to see that if the demand curve gets flatter consumers' surplus decreases and if it gets steeper, consumers' surplus increases.[6]

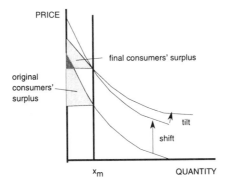

Figure 1. Decomposing the change in demand into a shift and a tilt.

Thus what matters is how a change in quality affects the *slope* of the demand curve; this is given by

$$\frac{\partial}{\partial q}\frac{\partial p}{\partial x} = \frac{\partial^2 p(x,q)}{\partial q \partial x}$$

This is, of course, simply the Spence-Sheshinki condition. However, the interpretation in terms of shifts and tilts turns out to be quite useful below.

We can also relate this back to the earlier discussion of marginal versus average valuations. Changes in quality that shift the demand curve have no effect on welfare since they don't affect the difference between the average

---

[6] The "tilt" terminology is slightly misleading since the normal usage of tilt implies a *constant* change in slope. Of course this is not necessary for the result; all that is required is that the change in q either increases or decreases the slope of the demand curve at every point—not that it changes the slope of the demand curve by the same amount at every point.

and marginal valuation. To affect the average and marginal consumer differently, the change in quality must affect the *slope* of the demand curve.

It follows that to answer the question of how a change in quality affects welfare, we need to construct a micro-model of consumer behavior and see how the quality variable enters the demand curve. Quality variables that shift the demand curve have no effect on welfare; variables that tilt the demand curve increase or decrease welfare depending on which way they tilt the demand curve.

19.6 The model

I now present a formal model of ease of learning versus ease of operation. I model the user costs in the following way. I suppose that there are a number of different users, each of whom uses the software more or less intensively. Let n be the number of times that a consumer uses a piece of software in some given time period, and let $g(n)$ be the number of consumers who use the software this often. For simplicity we take the frequency-of-use of the software to be independent of the ease-of-operation, although this can be relaxed.

Each time the software is run, the user bears a cost v. This is a variable cost of operation: it could refer to the time it takes to run the program, the complexity of the keystrokes necessary to run it, etc. High-intensity users—those who use the software a lot—pay a high variable cost.

Let F be the fixed cost of running the program. This is the cost that the user must pay regardless of his intensity of use. If she runs the program once or a hundred times, she must pay the same cost F. This should be thought of as the cost of learning to use the program. A program that is easy to learn has a low value of F; a program that is easy to operate has a low value of v.

Let $c(x, v, F)$ be the cost to the manufacturer of selling x copies of a program that has user costs of (v, F). For simplicity, we will suppose that the cost function has the separable form $c(x, v, F) = c_x(x) + c_v(v) + c_F(F)$. The term $c_x(x)$ measures the cost of producing x units of the software. The term $c_v(v)$ is the cost of designing software with variable costs v. The term $c_F(F)$ is the cost of designing software with fixed user costs F. This separable structure is not necessary for most of the results, but it makes the analysis simpler.

For simplicity we assume that the marginal costs of production are constant, and set $c_x(x) = c_x x + K$. Here c_x is the marginal cost of producing an extra copy of the software, once it has been created, and K is the fixed cost of producing the software. We should think of the fixed costs as being large relative to the variable costs of production. Note that the cost functions c_v and c_F should be *decreasing* functions of their argument since it should cost more to make a package with smaller user costs. It is natural to assume that both of these functions are convex, since the marginal cost of improving a package should increase the better the package is to start with.

Let b be the gross benefit to the user each time he or she uses the program. If a user runs the software n times, the net benefit accruing to the user is then $(b - v)n - F$. This is the gross benefit per use minus the user costs. If the package sells for a price of p, then a person who uses the software n times has a consumer surplus of $(b - v)n - F - p$.

The benefit, b, measures the *performance* of the software. In our formulation, all that matters to the consumer is the difference between the performance, b, and the ease-of-operation, v. We might think of this as the *net performance* of the software: the net benefit of the software per use. In general b is a choice variable—the producer can invest more or less effort in order to increase b. But since all that matters to the consumer is $b - v$, an increase b is equivalent to a decrease in v. Hence there is no need to carry out a separate analysis of the choice of b.

We suppose that a person who has positive consumer surplus will purchase the product, and a person who has negative consumer surplus will not. The marginal user will be the person who has a net surplus of zero. If n^* is the intensity of use by this consumer, then it must satisfy the equation

$$(b - v)n^* - F - p = 0,$$

which implies

$$n^* = \frac{F + p}{b - v}. \tag{19.1}$$

This gives us a relationship between the characteristics of the software, (v, F, p), and the number of *uses*. We want to convert this into a relationship between the price and the number of *users* in order to determine how many consumers will buy the product.

Let $G(n)$ be defined by

$$G(n) = \int_n^\infty g(t)\, dt.$$

This measures the number of people who use the software at least n times per period. If the number of uses by the marginal user is n^*, as defined in equation (19.1), and there are x users in total, x must satisfy the equation

$$G(n^*) = x. \tag{19.2}$$

Let $H(x)$ be the inverse function of $G(n)$. The function $H(x)$ measures the number of uses by the marginal person if x units are sold. Applying H to both sides of (19.2) and using (19.1), we can write

$$n^* = H(x) = \frac{F + p}{b - v}.$$

Solving for p as a function of x we have the inverse demand function

$$p(x) = (b - v)H(x) - F.$$

Since $G(n)$ is a monotonic decreasing function, so is its inverse, $H(x)$. Hence the inverse demand function is a decreasing function of price. Note that the variable cost affects the *slope* of the demand curve, while the fixed user cost merely *shifts* the demand curve.

This is quite reasonable. If the a software package becomes easier to operate, then all users are willing to pay more for it. But the high intensity users' willingness-to-pay goes up by more than the other users, since they use it more often. On the other hand, if the software becomes easier to learn, then everyone will be willing to pay more for it, regardless of their intensity of use.

We are now in a position to apply the preceding analysis concerning the welfare effect of changing v and F. However, it is useful to spell out the welfare analysis in slightly more detail.

In order to do this we first derive an expression for consumers' surplus. If x users buy the software the gross surplus (the area under the demand curve) is:

$$u(x) = \int_0^x p(t)\, dt = \int_0^x [(b - v)H(t) - F]\, dt.$$

If each package is sold at a price of $p(x)$, the net consumers' surplus is

$$u(x) - p(x)x = \int_0^x [(b - v)H(t) - F]\, dt - [(b - v)H(x) - F]x$$

$$= (b - v)\left[\int_0^x H(t)\, dt - H(x)\right]. \qquad (19.3)$$

Note that F drops out of this expression; it follows immediately that the derivative of consumers' surplus with respect to F is zero. Furthermore, since $H(x)$ is a decreasing function, it is easy to see that the expression in brackets is positive. A reduction in v helps the average consumer more than the marginal consumer since the average consumer uses the software more intensively than the marginal consumer.

The monopolist has the correct incentives with respect to ease-of-learning, but the wrong incentives with respect to ease-of-operation. Why? Essentially, the reason is the standard monopoly distortion pointed out by Spence (1975): the monopolist cares about the marginal consumer, not the average consumer. In our framework, the marginal consumer values ease-of-learning in exactly the same way as the average consumer; hence, there is no distortion in this aspect of the product design. But the marginal consumer in our model uses the product less intensively than the average consumer; hence the monopolist has too little incentive to invest in reducing this sort of user costs. From the monopolist's point of view, the high-intensity user will buy the product anyway, and the monopolist has no incentive to make the product easier to operate for them. But the monopolist has just the right incentive to make the product easy to learn, since this increases the size of its market, and makes *all* users willing to pay more for the product.

The problem discussed above arises due to the fact that in our model the monopolist doesn't have a way to extract any payment from the infra-marginal users, even though they would be willing to pay for improvements in ease-of-operation. In real life, the monopolist does have such an option: it can offer software upgrades. Intensive users will be willing to pay for those upgrades if they offer improved capabilities.[7]

However, typically a new release of the software is sold to both new and existing customers. When trading off investment in ease-of-use and ease-of-learning the software producer will still face the incentives described above: it will be willing to invest less in features valued by consumers who are sure to buy the product anyway. In any event, the fact that software can be upgraded is unique among products and is worth examining in its own right.[8]

The distortion in this model depends on the fact that the consumer cares about the number of *uses* while the monopolist cares about the number of *users*. If the monopolist could charge a price per use, there would be no distortion. To see this, imagine that the software is run on a mainframe computer so that the software provider can monitor the number of uses. The monopolist sets a schedule $\pi(n)$ that indicates the charge per use. The price schedule is given by

$$\pi(n) = \begin{cases} \infty & \text{if } n \leq F/(b-v) \\ (b-v)n + F & \text{if } n > F/(b-v). \end{cases}$$

It is easy to check that this price schedule extracts all the consumers' surplus from the users of the software. Hence the monopolist will choose the socially optimal levels of F and v.

19.7 Software that is too easy to learn

In the above analysis we've seen an example where the product of the monopolist has too little quality (too hard to operate) and just the right amount of quality (appropriate ease of learning). It would be nice to complement this with an example where a monopolist provides too *much* quality.

In order to do this, let us change the model slightly. Suppose now that there is no difference in intensity of use among consumers. For simplicity

---

[7] For some background on upgrades, see Bulkeley (1990).

[8] I intend to investigate software upgrades in future work.

suppose that all consumers use the program only once, and each gets the *same* net benefit $b - v$.[9] However, users differ in how difficult it is to learn to use a new program. To be specific, the net surplus from use of the computer program is

$$b - v - \gamma F - p.$$

Here F is a measure of the how easy the software is to learn –the fixed costs—and γ measures the capability of a given individual to learn the software. People with high values of γ find it more costly to learn a new piece of software than individuals with low values of γ We suppose that γ is distributed in the population according to some cumulative distribution function $J(\gamma) = \int_0^\gamma j(t)\, dt$.

The marginal purchaser of the program satisfies the condition that benefits are just equal to the price of the software,

$$b - v - \gamma F - p = 0,$$

so

$$\gamma^* = \frac{b - v - p}{F}.$$

Everyone with a smaller γ buys the software, so the total sales are

$$x = J(\gamma) = J((b - v - p)/F).$$

Letting K be the inverse of J, we have

$$K(x) = \frac{b - v - p}{F},$$

which implies that the inverse demand function is

$$p = b - v - FK(x).$$

Note that $K'(x) > 0$ since it is the inverse of a cumulative distribution function.

For this form of demand, changes in v shift the demand function and changes in F tilt the demand function. According to our previous analysis, the monopolist produces the right ease-of-operation, but the wrong ease-of-learning. In fact $\partial^2 p / \partial x \partial F < 0$. From our previous analysis, this implies that welfare increases if F increases—that is, welfare goes up if the software is made harder to learn! In this model the monopolist *overinvests* in making the software easy to learn.

Why is this? In this model the marginal consumer is one who finds the software harder to learn than the average consumer. Hence making the software a little easier to learn benefits the marginal consumer more than the average consumer. Hence the monopolist tends to invest too many resources in attracting marginal consumers rather than, say, improving the functioning of the program for the inframarginal consumers.

---

[9] An example that fits this model might be tax preparation software. You use this software only once a year, so that there is little difference in intensity of use across the population. Whether or not you choose to use the software depends primarily on how easy it is to learn.

19.8 Policy implications

What are the implications of the easy-of-operation/ease-of-learning distortion from a policy perspective? Obviously it is premature to draw definitive conclusions from such a simple model, but it is worthwhile raising the question to see where a more in-depth analysis may lead.

Since we are examining a monopolist, it is always in the social interest to increase output. One possibility would be to pursue antitrust actions to eliminate the monopoly power. However, it is far from clear that this would be appropriate since it would affect incentives to innovate and perhaps lead to excessive product differentiation.

Accordingly, we adopt the viewpoint that the monopoly output distortion should be tolerated. However, the above arguments suggest that even if the monopoly output remains constant there still will be social benefits to encouraging changes in the monopolist's provision of "quality."

In different models of quality, different tools may be appropriate. For example, in some models, setting minimal (or maximal!) quality standards may be appropriate. However, this instrument seems implausible in our model of software.

One interesting policy choice is to subsidize the provision of software "quality." In practice this would be done by publicly sponsored research grants. We suppose that social policies such as this will reduce the cost of providing software that is easy-to-learn and software that is easy-to-use. What will be the impact of such subsidies on social welfare?

We first examine the original model where consumers differ in the intensity of use. Suppose that we subsidize the cost of developing easy-to-learn and easy-to-operate software at rates s_v and s_F respectively. Welfare can be written as

$$W(x, v, F) = [u(x, v, F) - p(x, v, F)x] + [p(x, v, F)x - (1 - s_v)c_v(v)$$
$$- (1 - s_F)c_F(F)] \quad - [s_v c_v(v) + s_F c_F(F)].$$

The three bracketed terms in this expression are consumer surplus, producer surplus, and government expenditure respectively. Differentiating this expression with respect to s_v and s_F and evaluating the derivative at the monopoly equilibrium with $s_v = s_F = 0$ we have

$$\frac{dW}{ds_v} = -\frac{\partial p}{\partial x}\frac{\partial x}{\partial s_v} + \left[\frac{\partial u}{\partial v} - \frac{\partial p}{\partial v}x\right]\frac{\partial v}{\partial s_v} + \left[\frac{\partial u}{\partial F} - \frac{\partial p}{\partial F}x\right]\frac{\partial F}{\partial s_v}$$

$$\frac{dW}{ds_F} = -\frac{\partial p}{\partial x}\frac{\partial x}{\partial s_F} + \left[\frac{\partial u}{\partial F} - \frac{\partial p}{\partial F}x\right]\frac{\partial F}{\partial s_F} + \left[\frac{\partial u}{\partial v} - \frac{\partial p}{\partial v}x\right]\frac{\partial v}{\partial s_F}.$$

In calculating these derivatives several terms drop out due to utility maximization and profit maximization. The remaining terms are composed of two effects: the direct effect on consumers' surplus of changing v and F and the indirect effect of the induced output change and the cross effect of the subsidy.

We have already calculated the direct effect; it is zero for changes in F and positive for reductions in v. I show in the appendix that both the output effect and the cross effect have a positive effect on utility. Hence there is a case to be made for imposing (small) subsidies on both cost functions. However, in terms of the impact on output, a reduction in F is exactly equivalent to imposing an output subsidy on the monopolist. Hence the social benefits of making the software easier to learn are just the same as the benefits from an output subsidy. This is to be compared to the effects of subsidizing v. In this case the subsidy benefits consumers both through the increase in output *and* through the improvement in "quality."

Another way to observe this is to consider the case where $F = 0$. In this case the profit-maximization problem for the monopolist becomes

$$(b - v)H(x) - (1 - s_v)c_v(v).$$

The first-order condition for output is

$$(b - v)H'(x) = 0,$$

which is independent of s_v. Hence output doesn't change when ease-of-operation is subsidized. Nevertheless, welfare increases due to the impact of the quality change on the inframarginal consumers.

We turn now to the second model, where consumers differ in the cost of learning. We show in the appendix that $dx/ds_F > 0$ in this case as well. Hence the impact on social welfare is composed of two effects: the benefit from having more output and the cost from the monopolist investing "too much" in making the software easy-to-learn. The combination is ambiguous, but at least it forces attention on the proper tradeoff: one would have to expect a big output effect from a subsidy in order for it to be worthwhile from a social point of view.

I interpret this as saying that it is reasonable to use public funds to subsidize research on how to make software easy to operate. However, there is no particular argument, in the context of this model at least, to subsidize research on how to make software easier to learn—the market gives the monopolist the right incentives with respect to this choice already, at least conditional on the output chosen by the monopolist. Of course, there may be other reasons to subsidize research on this aspect of software design. For example, there may be economies of scale in research, or there may be problems with appropriability of intellectual property that could cause problems for developing easy-to-operate software in the private sector. Or it may be that there are lower costs to developing easy-to-learn software in an educational environment. It would clearly be premature to make policy pronouncements without careful consideration of these possibilities.

19.9 Appendix. Comparative statics of the profit maximization problem

Here we study the impact of subsidizing research on ease-of-learning and ease-of-operation. We assume that this research lowers the cost of providing easier-to-operate and easier-to-learn software. We model this cost reduction as being equivalent to subsidies of s_v and s_F on the cost functions. Letting $R(x) = H(x)x$, we can write the monopolist's profit maximization problem as

$$\max_{x,v,F} (b - v)R(x) - Fx - (1 - s_v)c_v(v) - (1 - s_F)c_F(F).$$

Note that we have set the cost of production equal to zero. Alternatively we could incorporate a constant marginal cost of production into F.

The first-order conditions for this problem are

$$(b - v)R'(x) - F = 0$$
$$-R(x) - (1 - s_v)c_v'(v) = 0$$
$$-x - (1 - s_F)c_F'(F) = 0.$$

Totally differentiating this system and evaluating the derivatives at $s_v = s_F = 0$ we have

$$\begin{pmatrix} (b - v)R'' & -R' & -1 \\ -R' & -c_v'' & 0 \\ -1 & 0 & -c_F'' \end{pmatrix} \begin{pmatrix} dx \\ dv \\ dF \end{pmatrix} = \begin{pmatrix} 0 \\ -c_v' ds_v \\ -c_F' ds_F \end{pmatrix}.$$

In the case of a regular maximum the second-order conditions imply that the determinant of the Hessian matrix on the left-hand side of this expression will be negative and all principal minors of order 2 will be positive. This latter condition implies

$$(b - v)R''(x)c_v''(v) + R'(x)^2 < 0$$
$$(b - v)R''(x)c_F''(F) + 1 < 0 \tag{19.4}$$

These conditions are useful in signing the comparative statics effects.

Let $H < 0$ denote the value of the determinant of the Hessian and solve for the various differentials.

$$dF = \frac{-ds_v R'(x)c_v'(v) + ds_F c_F'(F)\left[(b - v)R''(x)c_v''(v) + R'(x)^2\right]}{H}$$

$$dv = \frac{-ds_F R'(x)c_F'(F) + ds_v c_v'(v)\left[(b - v)R''(x)c_F''(F) + 1)\right]}{H}$$

$$dx = \frac{ds_v R'(x)c_v''(v)c_F''(F) + ds_F c_F'(F)c_v''(v)}{H}$$

It is straightforward to verify

- dv/ds_v and dF/ds_F are negative. Hence subsidizing ease-of-learning or ease-of-operation will tend to lead to improvements in those variables.

- dx/ds_v and dx/ds_F are positive. Hence the subsidies tend to increase output.

- dv/ds_F and dF/ds_v are negative. Hence subsidizing ease-of-learning will lead to an improvement in ease of operation and vice versa.

The other model discussed in the text was based on differences among the consumers in ease of learning. The profit maximization problem in that case is:

$$\max_{x,F} (b-v)x - FK(x)x - (1-s_F)c_F(F).$$

The first-order conditions are

$$(b-v) - FR'(x) = 0$$
$$-R(x) - (1-s_F)c_F'(F) = 0,$$

where $R(x) = K(x)x$. Totally differentiating this system and evaluating the result at $s_F = 0$ we have

$$\begin{pmatrix} -FR'' & -R' \\ -R' & -c_F'' \end{pmatrix} \begin{pmatrix} dx \\ dF \end{pmatrix} = \begin{pmatrix} 0 \\ -c_F'ds_F \end{pmatrix}.$$

From this we find

$$\frac{dx}{ds_F} = \frac{\begin{vmatrix} 0 & -R' \\ -c_F' & -c_F'' \end{vmatrix}}{\begin{vmatrix} -FR'' & -R' \\ -R' & -c_F'' \end{vmatrix}} > 0.$$

References

Bulkeley, W. (1990). Software users are beginning to rebel against the steady stream of upgrades. *Wall Street Journal*, B4.

Bulkeley, W. (1991). Software industry loses start-up zest as big firms increase their domination. *Wall Street Journal, August 27*, B1.

Fisher, L. (1992). Business turns tough in software. *New York Times, December 14.*

Mantei, M., & Teorey, T. (1988). Cost/benefit analysis for incorporating human factors in the software lifecycle. *Communications of the ACM, 4,* 428–439.

Nakamura, R. (1990). The x factor. *Infoworld, November 19,* 51–55.

Schmalensee, R. (1979). Market structure, durability, and quality: a selective survey. *Economic Inquiry, 42,* 177–196.

Sheshinski, E. (1976). Price, quality and quantity regulation in monopoly situations. *Economica, 43,* 127–137.

Spence, M. (1975). Monopoly, quality and regulation. *Bell Journal of Economics, 6*(2), 417–429.

Swan, P. (1970). Durability of consumer goods. *American Economic Review, 60,* 884–894.

Tirole, J. (1988). *The Theory of Industrial Organization.* MIT Press, Cambridge, MA.

Chapter 20

PRICING CONGESTIBLE NETWORK RESOURCES

We describe the basic economic theory of pricing a congestible resource such as an ftp server, a router, a Web site, etc. In particular, we examine the implications of "congestion pricing" as a way to encourage efficient use of network resources. We explore the implications of flat pricing and congestion pricing for capacity expansion in centrally planned, competitive, and monopolistic environments.

The Internet is now involved in a major transformation from a government sponsored project to a private enterprise. Privatization and commercialization of the Internet means that providers of network connectivity and services will have to confront issues of pricing and cost recovery. When connectivity was provided to users via government subsidies, little attention was paid to these issues. Suddenly, they have become quite significant. At the same time, new problems in resource allocation are emerging as other telecommunication network technologies begin to converge.

We think that economic modeling can play a significant role in thinking about the consequences of various issues facing decisionmakers. Given the current paucity of economic data about the Internet, economic analysis is unlikely to give precise numerical answers to many questions of interest. Still explicit economic models can serve as a useful guide to "how to think" about some of these issues.

For example, consider the problem of providing bandwidth which will be shared by many users. As network technology and availability advances, there will likely be places and periods when bandwidth is scarce and periods when it is abundant. When the supply of bandwidth far exceeds the demand, there is little role for economics. But when the demand for bandwidth exceeds the supply, the fundamental issues of resource allocation become important.

There are many network resources whose performance suffers when there is "overuse": the switching capacity of the routers, the bandwidth of the transport medium, the disk and CPU capacity of popular servers, etc. When users access such resources they presumably take into account their

Co-authored with Jeff MacKie-Mason. We are grateful to Marvin Sirbu and Scott Shenker for their comments. This work was supported by the National Science Foundation grant SES-93-20481.

own costs and benefits from usage, but ignore the congestion, delay, or exclusion costs that they impose on other users. Economists refer to this phenomenon as a "congestion externality"; in ecology, it is known as the "problem of the commons" (Hardin (1968)).

There are many ways to deal with congestion externalities. One way is to establish social norms that penalize inappropriate behavior. Such norms can work well in small groups where there is repeated interaction, but they often do not scale well to a system with millions of users.

Another way to deal with congestion is to establish rationing or quota systems. (Bohn (1993)). One appeal of rationing is that is relatively easy to implement. Indeed, it is common today to see file servers, Web servers, and other network services that reject additional users when the load is too high.

Despite the simplicity of rationing and quotas, economists tend to favor pricing mechanisms as a way of alleviating congestion. One important feature of congestion prices is that they not only discourage usage when congestion is present, but they also generate revenue for capacity expansion. Indeed, it has long been recognized that under certain conditions the optimal congestion prices for a fixed amount of capacity will automatically generate the appropriate amount of revenue to finance capacity expansion.

In previous work we have proposed some simple pricing schemes to deal with congestion (MacKie-Mason (1993a, 1993b)). Here we examine the issue of how the pricing scheme chosen affects industry structure and performance. Our framework is that of "club theory," a term used by Buchanan (1965) to deal with the provision of shared goods. A textbook treatment of club theory can be found in Cornes (1986). The papers in the literature that are closest to the treatment here are Scotchmer (1985a, 1985b); we will describe the relationship of our work to this literature in more detail below.

20.1 Notation

Let x_i denote person i's use of the network resource and $X = \sum_{j=1}^{n} x_j$ the total use of the resource. The user cares about her own use, x_i, and the delay that she encounters. Delay should be interpreted as a general congestion cost: it can include the cost of exclusion, congestion, and so on. Delay depends on the *utilization* of the resource, which we define to be total use divided by capacity: $Y = X/K$. We summarize the preferences of the user by a utility function $u_i(x_i, Y) + m_i$, where m_i is money that the user has to spend on other things. We assume that $u_i(x_i, Y)$ is a differentiable, concave function of x_i and a decreasing concave function of Y.[1]

---

[1] Later on we consider a special form of this function, $u_i(x_i, Y) = v_i(x_i) - D(Y)$, where $D(Y)$ is interpreted as a delay cost. However, we will not introduce this specification until it is necessary.

The critical feature of this specification is the relationship between usage and capacity: if total usage (X) is doubled and capacity (K) is also doubled, then utilization $Y = X/K$ and hence delay remain constant.[2] We let $c(K)$ measure the cost of providing capacity. For simplicity we take this to be the only cost of providing the service.[3]

This specification is general enough to capture the essence of many network resources. Consider the specific example of an ftp server. In this context x_i could be the number of bytes transferred to user i, K would be the capacity of the server in terms of how many total bytes it can transfer in a given time period, and X would be total bytes transferred to all users. It is natural to suppose that user i cares about the total amount of material she retrieves and the delay involved in retrieving it. A router is another example. In this case x_i would be the bytes sent to (and/or received from) the router by user i, X would be the total use of the router, and K would be the maximum throughput of the router.

20.2 Efficient use and capacity

We first examine the efficient pattern of usage given some given capacity K. By definition, the efficient pattern maximizes the sum of benefits minus costs. Denoting aggregate net benefits by $W(K)$ we have:[4]

$$W(K) = \max_{x_j} \sum_{j=1}^{n} u_j(x_j, Y) - c(K). \tag{20.1}$$

The optimal solution must satisfy the first-order condition

$$\frac{\partial u_i(x_i, Y)}{\partial x_i} = -\frac{1}{K} \sum_{j=1}^{n} \frac{\partial u_j(x_j, Y)}{\partial Y} \tag{20.2}$$

This says that user i should use the system until the marginal benefit from her usage equals the marginal cost that she imposes on the other users.

---

[2] Delay is fully determined by average utilization only under certain traffic conditions. More generally delay may depend on peak utilization or the variance of utilization. Generalizing the model to account for such effects is clearly of interest, but is beyond the scope of this paper.

[3] In principle, costs could also depend on the amount of usage (X) and on the number of users (n), but we omit these in order to keep the model simple. Capacity costs are normally the dominant costs for most services of interest to us.

[4] We maximize total benefits minus total costs, without making any particular distributional judgments. We could, of course, allow for lump-sum transfer payments to the agents that reflected such concerns. However, such transfer payments would not modify the form of the solution to the benefit-cost problem considered here.

We can decentralize this solution by defining a "shadow price"

$$p_e = -\frac{1}{K}\sum_{j=1}^{n}\frac{\partial u_j(x_j, Y)}{\partial Y}, \tag{20.3}$$

which measures the total marginal congestion cost that an increase in x_i imposes on the users; note that this is independent of i. Suppose that consumer i is charged a price p_e for usage. Then she would want to solve the following problem

$$\max_{x_i}\ u_i(x_i, Y) - p_e x_i.$$

The solution to this problem is characterized by

$$\frac{\partial u_i(x_i, Y)}{\partial x_i} + \frac{1}{K}\frac{\partial u_i(x_i, Y)}{\partial Y} = p_e. \tag{20.4}$$

Referring to the definition of p_e in equation (20.3), we see that for large n the second term on the left-hand side will be negligible relative to the right-hand side of the equation. For large n this expression is essentially the same as the first-order condition for the social optimum given in (20.2), and thus the decentralized solution corresponds with the social optimum.

To see this more explicitly, consider the special case where $u_i(x_i, Y) = v_i(x_i) - D(Y)$. Then the social optimum in equation (20.2) is described by

$$u_i'(x_i) = \frac{n}{K}D'(Y),$$

and the individual optimization in equation (20.4) is

$$u_i'(x_i) = \frac{n+1}{K}D'(Y).$$

For large n these are virtually the same.

Economists say that the price p_e "internalizes" the externality by making the user face the costs that she imposes on the other users. The point of introducing the shadow price is to emphasize the fact that each user should face (essentially) the *same* price for usage—the sum of the marginal congestion costs that each user imposes on the other users.

Capacity expansion

In the maximization problem (20.1) we used $W(K)$ to denote the maximum welfare given an arbitrary capacity K. What happens to welfare as we expand capacity? Differentiating (20.1) with respect to K, we have[5]

$$W'(K) = -\sum_{j=1}^{n} \frac{\partial u_j(x_j, Y)}{\partial Y} \frac{X}{K^2} - c'(K).$$

Using the shadow price defined above, we can write this as

$$W'(K) = p_e \frac{X}{K} - c'(K). \tag{20.5}$$

From this it follows that $W'(K) > 0$ if and only if $p_e X - c'(K)K > 0$. This means that expanding capacity will increase welfare if and only if the revenue from the congestion fees $(p_e X)$ exceeds the value of capacity $(c'(K)K)$, where capacity is valued using the marginal cost of capacity.

Hence the shadow price p_e plays a dual role: it provides a measure of the social cost of increased usage for an given capacity, but it *also determines the value of a change in capacity*. The fact that congestion fees send the right economic signals to expand capacity under certain conditions was noted by Mohring (1962) and Strotz (1965); it takes various forms in the literature and is considered a classic principle of congestion pricing.

20.3 Pricing in a competitive market

The above discussion describes optimal pricing in a utopian world of welfare maximization. In the brave new world of deregulated, privately-provided information network services we would expect to see provision of network resources by profit-seeking firms. What kind of prices would emerge in such a market environment?

The answer depends on the details of market structure: clearly a monopoly or oligopoly structure will result in different (presumably higher) prices than a competitive market. We begin with the admittedly special case of a competitive market with many independent producers; later we examine monopoly provision.

We suppose that each producer uses a "two-part tariff" for pricing: a "subscription/attachment" fee of q per user per month, say, plus a usage fee of px_i. A representative producer's profits can then be written as

$$\pi = pX + nq - c(K)$$

Here pX is the revenue collected by usage-sensitive fees, nq is the revenue collected from connection fees, and $c(K)$ is the cost of providing capacity K. This appears to be a natural form for pricing network access and usage. Of course, pure connection pricing, in which $p = 0$, and pure usage pricing, in which $q = 0$, are special cases of this pricing form.

---

[5] Note that terms involving $\partial x_j / \partial K$ drop out due to the first-order conditions given in (20.2). This is an instance of what economists call the envelope theorem. (See Varian (1992)).

Consumer optimization

The utility maximization problem for consumer i is to choose which network resource to use and how much to use it. We suppose that there are (potentially) many suppliers with possibly different utilization levels. Suppliers with lower levels of utilization can charge more due to the better service they provide. We write the price offerings of a representative supplier with utilization Y as $(p(Y), q(Y))$, where $p(Y)$ is the usage fee and $q(Y)$ is the subscription fee.[6]

The utility maximization problem for a representative consumer now becomes

$$\max_{x_i, Y} \; u_i(x_i, Y) - p(Y)x_i - q(Y).$$

That is, the consumer chooses which provider to use (represented by Y) and how much to use (represented by x_i). For convenience, we assume that the menu of offered prices can be treated as a continuous and differentiable function of Y. The consumer's optimization problem has first-order conditions

$$\frac{\partial u_i(x_i, Y)}{\partial x_i} - p(Y) = 0$$

$$\frac{\partial u_i(x_i, Y)}{\partial Y} - p'(Y)x_i - q'(Y) = 0. \tag{20.6}$$

The first equation shows that each user will use the resource until the value of additional usage equals its price. The second equation shows that the consumer's choice of delay satisfies the condition that the marginal utility cost of increased delay must be compensated by a reduced expenditure, $p'(Y)x_i + q'(Y)$. Adding this last equation up across consumers gives us an expression that we will use below,

$$p'(Y)X + nq'(Y) = \sum_{j=1}^{n} \frac{\partial u_j(x_j, Y)}{\partial Y}. \tag{20.7}$$

Producer optimization

A representative producer chooses its capacity K and how much bandwidth to supply to users. We assume that there are many competing producers, each of whom takes the price-quality schedules $(p(Y), q(Y))$ as being outside of its control; i.e., determined by the competitive market.

---

[6] For simplicity, we assume that each firm offers only one class of service; this can easily be generalized.

The profit maximization problem facing a representative producer is to choose X and K to maximize profits given the price-quality schedules available in the market

$$\max_{X,K} p(Y)X + nq(Y) - c(K),$$

The first-order conditions are

$$p(Y) + p'(Y)\frac{X}{K} + n\frac{q'(Y)}{K} = 0$$

$$-p'(Y)\left(\frac{X}{K}\right)^2 - nq'(Y)\frac{X}{K^2} = c'(K).$$

Collecting terms we can write:

$$p(Y) + [p'(Y)X + nq'(Y)]\frac{1}{K} = 0 \qquad (20.8)$$

$$-[p'(Y)X + nq'(Y)]\frac{X}{K^2} = c'(K). \qquad (20.9)$$

Using equations (20.6) and (20.7), we can further simplify these equations to

$$p(Y) = \frac{\partial u_i(x_i, Y)}{\partial x_i} = -\frac{1}{K}\sum_{j=1}^{n}\frac{\partial u_j(x_j, Y)}{\partial Y} \qquad (20.10)$$

$$-Y\sum_{j=1}^{n}\frac{\partial u_j(x_j, Y)}{\partial Y} = c'(K)K \qquad (20.11)$$

Comparing (20.10) to (20.2) we see that the competitive price will result in the optimal degree of congestion. By combining (20.10) and (20.11) we can write

$$p(Y)X = c'(K)K, \qquad (20.12)$$

which leads to the same rule for optimal capacity that we obtained in equation (20.5).

In this model a competitive supplier is forced to charge the socially optimal price for the quality of service that he offers. Why is the competitive market price equal to the sum of congestion costs? The term $-(1/K)\sum_j \partial u_j/\partial Y$ is how much the other users of the resource would be willing to pay the provider to *refrain* from selling additional usage. If this is less than the price a user is willing to pay for additional usage, the competitive supplier would want to allow more usage. The producer would stop providing additional usage when the price that a user is willing to pay for additional use is balanced with the amount that the other users are willing to pay for a reduction in total usage.

Free entry

If there are no restrictions on entry, firms will enter the industry until profits are driven to zero:

$$p(Y)X + nq(Y) - c(K) = 0.$$

Substituting the expression for $p(Y)$ derived above, we can write the zero-profit condition as

$$nq(Y) = c(K) - c'(K)K.$$

Dividing through by $c(K)$ we have

$$\frac{nq(Y)}{c(K)} = 1 - \frac{c'(K)}{c(K)/K} = 1 - \frac{1}{e},$$

where e is the *elasticity of scale* (average cost over marginal cost). If the marginal cost of capacity is small relative to the average cost, subscription fees will cover most of the cost of providing the service. If the marginal cost of capacity is large, then usage fees will contribute more to recovering total costs.

Scotchmer (1985a) examines a model of two-part pricing of a congestible resource that has some features in common with the one described above. In her model, congestion depends on the number of users, not the total usage, and the capacity of the club is fixed. (This is natural for the kinds of clubs that motivated her study: golf courses, ski clubs, swimming lanes, etc.; it is less natural in our context.) She considers an oligopolistic model with a finite number of firms and examines the limiting behavior as the number of firms increases. She finds that the connection fee goes to zero as the number of firms is increased. Although this result is derived under the assumption that the technology of each firm has fixed capacity, it appears that something similar to this will occur for the more general technology we consider here.

We should emphasize that we have examined the functioning of an idealized competitive industry—a market structure with many firms each having a small market share. There is a very real question of whether the provision of network services will actually have this industrial structure. A full examination of this issue is beyond the scope of this paper, but it is worth observing that a critical consideration is the nature of the cost function for providing network services. If larger firms can produce at lower unit cost, then a large firm will be able to undercut the price of a small firm and there will a tendency to end up with a single firm dominating the market.[7] We

---

[7] This is known as the case of a natural monopoly; see Sharkey (1982) for a detailed treatment.

should emphasize that this is only a tendency: antitrust policy, regulation, and other tools can be used to influence the ultimate outcome.

We conjecture that a primary factor in determining the industry structure of digital communication networks will be the ease of interconnection. If it is costly or difficult for networks to interconnect, large providers will have an automatic advantage in competing for customers. If this view is correct, there may well be a case for government policy to help coordinate interconnection agreements so as to ensure a healthy competitive environment.

Customer sorting and multiple qualities of service

Nothing in this model implies that there will be a single "optimal" quality of service offered. If all users were identical then the joint solution of equations (20.6) would yield a single quality Y^*, and associated prices $(p(Y^*), q(Y^*))$. However, user preferences for most services are often heterogeneous: some users may be very intolerant of delay while others may prefer to wait but pay low prices.

When customers have heterogeneous preferences for quality, social welfare is generally *not* maximized by having a single, "high quality" service or product available. Typically, there will be users who would prefer to accept lower quality in exchange for a price reduction—they value the quality difference less than they value the other goods and services they can buy with the savings. Competition with free entry will then force each quality level to be priced efficiently. Some suppliers will have low prices and high congestion, while others offer high prices and low congestion.

How does a competitive market arrive at the socially optimal variety of price-quality choices? Suppose that there are two types of user: delay-tolerant and delay-intolerant, but only one "average" quality of service is initially offered by all the firms. When would it pay for a firm to offer a different quality of service than its competitors?

By offering a quality of service optimized for one of the groups, a deviating firm could attract all the customers from that group. If the revenue from this deviation exceeds the cost of providing the new quality, this would increase the deviant firm's profits. If there are no fixed costs to creating different qualities we would expect to see as many different qualities as there are types of consumer preferences.

But what if there are large fixed costs to adding new service qualities? In this case it may well not be profitable for a deviant firm to provide a different quality since the entrant may have trouble extracting sufficient profits to cover its costs. Hence the equilibrium number of firms and variety of qualities of service offered will depend on the fixed costs of creating new qualities of service.[8]

When individual users have heterogeneous preferences

Thus far we have considered what happens if different users have different preferences for the resource. What if a single user has different willingness to pay for a resource when using it for different purposes? For example, a user may place a high value on the e-mail access from her network service provider, but a lower value on the ability to engage in real-time video conferencing. If there were small costs of connecting to more than one service provider, then we might see a "restaurant" equilibrium: various providers offering different service qualities at different prices, with a single consumer using more than one provider for different purposes.

However, there may be significant costs of accessing additional providers. For example, it might require having multiple lines running into the home or office, as we now have with telephone, cable and electric lines. If the costs of having multiple providers for multiple services get high enough, then we might expect to see single providers who offer multiple qualities of service. There has been considerable recent interest in the development of integrated services networks; see Braden-Clark-Shenker (1994) for a proposed multiple quality-of-service architecture for the Internet. Pricing is likely to be an effective mechanism for allocating different service qualities to appropriate uses, although the type of pricing that emerges will depend crucially on the evolution of the technological infrastructure (MacKie-Mason-Varian (1994a)).

Adding capacity

We saw earlier that the efficient congestion prices send the right signals for capacity expansion. Let us see how this works in a competitive market.

Suppose that a competitive firm must decide whether to add additional capacity ΔK. We consider two scenarios. In the first scenario, the firm contemplates keeping X fixed and simply charging more for improved quality of service due to the reduced delay. The extra amount it can charge user j is:

$$[q'(Y) + p'(Y)x_j]\frac{dY}{dK}\Delta K.$$

---

[8] Another factor that influences the number of firms is the presence of "network externalities." These occur when one consumer's utility of connecting to a network depends positively on the number of other users who are connected to the network. See Katz and Shapiro (1985) and Economides (1994) for an analytical treatment of this effect.

Using equation (20.6) this becomes

$$-\frac{1}{K}\frac{\partial u_j}{\partial Y}\frac{X}{K}\Delta K.$$

Summing this over all consumers and using equation (20.10) we have

$$p\frac{X}{K}\Delta K.$$

This will increase profits if the increase in revenue is greater than the cost of capacity expansion:

$$p\frac{X}{K}\Delta K - c'(K)\Delta K = \left[p\frac{X}{K} - c'(K)\right]\Delta K > 0.$$

Comparing this to equation (20.5) we see that profits will increase if and only if net social benefits increase.

In the second scenario, the firm expands its capacity and keeps its price fixed. In a competitive market it will then attract new customers due to the reduction in delay. In equilibrium this firm must have the same delay as other firms charging the same price. Suppose that in the initial equilibrium $X/K = Y$. Then the additional usage must satisfy $\Delta X = Y\Delta K$. It follows that the increase in in profit for this firm is given by

$$pY\Delta K - c'(K)\Delta K = \left[p\frac{X}{K} - c'(K)\right]\Delta K.$$

Again we see that capacity expansion is optimal if and only if it increases profits.

20.4 Equilibrium without usage fees

In this model usage fees play two critical roles—they determine both the efficient level of usage and the efficient level of capacity. However, usage-based pricing itself is expensive—it requires an infrastructure to track usage, prepare bills, and collect revenues. These transactions costs may be substantial, and a general examination of usage-based pricing must compare the benefits from improved resource allocation with the costs of accounting and billing. We do not attempt that exercise here. However, it is of considerable interest to examine how a model might function that has no usage fees, but only attachment/subscription fees.

It is convenient to specialize the model described above to a specific form for utility:[9]

$$u_i(x_i, Y) = v_i(x_i) - D(Y).$$

---

[9] We make this choice primarily to simplify the exposition; most of the results can be obtained without it, but with somewhat more effort.

Here $D(Y)$ is directly identified as the "delay costs" from congestion. We assume that $D(Y)$ is an increasing, differentiable, convex function. This says that the delay costs increase with utilization, and that they increase at an increasing rate. Note that this additive form implies that additional delay does not affect the marginal benefits from usage—an admittedly extreme assumption.

For this form of utility, the equilibrium values of (K^e, Y^e) in the world with usage based pricing can be written as

$$v_i'(x_i^e) = \frac{n}{K^e} D'(Y^e)$$
$$nD'(Y^e)Y^e = c'(K^e)K^e. \tag{20.13}$$

The conditions are found simply by writing the conditions (20.10–20.11) for the special form of the utility function that we have adopted.

Let us now consider what would happen if only attachment pricing were available. Since access is priced, but there is no price for usage we assume that agent i satiates at some point x_i^a. This determines $X^a = \sum_{j=1}^n x_j^a$.

User i's utility maximization problem for Y is

$$\max_Y \; v_i(x_i^a) - D(Y) - q(Y),$$

which leads to the first-order condition

$$-D'(Y) = q'(Y).$$

Adding up across the consumers gives us

$$nq'(Y) = -nD'(Y). \tag{20.14}$$

The supplier's profit-maximization problem is

$$\max_K \; nq(Y) - c(K),$$

which has first-order conditions

$$-nq'(Y)\frac{X}{K^2} = c'(K).$$

Combining this with equation (20.14) we see that the equilibrium solution with no attachment pricing only must satisfy the equilibrium condition

$$nY^a D'(Y^a) = c'(K^a)K^a. \tag{20.15}$$

Comparing this to equation (20.13) we see that the form of the equation that determines equilibrium capacity is the same with and without usage-based pricing: in either case the amount of capacity will be determined by the willingness to pay for reduction in delay.

However there is one subtlety: even though the *form* of the equation is the same in both cases, it may be that the equilibrium magnitudes of the relevant variables are different. In particular, it can easily happen that the number of users is different with and without usage-based pricing. We must therefore compare the equilibria under the two different scenarios: when the number of users is the same and when the number of users is different.

The number of users is the same

For fixed X, the equilibrium capacity is determined by

$$nD'(X/K)\frac{X}{K} = c'(K)K. \tag{20.16}$$

The convexity of $D(Y)$ implies that the left-hand side of this equation is a decreasing function of K. The right-hand side will be an increasing function of K, as long as $c''(K)$ is not too negative. Putting these facts together, we have Figure 1A.[10] Certainly equilibrium usage with a zero usage price, X^a, is larger than the equilibrium usage with a positive usage price, X^e. Decreasing X shifts the $nD'(X/K)X/K$ curve down, so equilibrium capacity with usage-based pricing will be less than the equilibrium capacity without usage-based pricing.

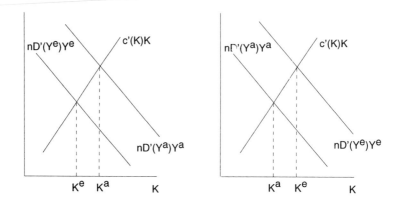

Figure 1. Determination of equilibrium capacity.

Will equilibrium congestion be higher or lower? With zero usage prices each user uses the resource more. But we have just shown that capacity will be higher, too, so it is not obvious what happens to utilization. Consider equation (20.16) again. Since $D(Y)$ is convex, $nD'(Y)Y$ is increasing in Y. If we write $K = X/Y$, it is easy to see that $c'(X/Y)X/Y$ is decreasing in Y as long as $c(K)$ is convex. Thus we can determine equilibrium congestion as in Figure 2. The increase from X^e to X^a causes $c'(X/Y)X/Y$ to move up, so with no usage pricing there is higher equilibrium congestion.

---

[10] The curves could be nonlinear; the straight lines are to simplify the presentation.

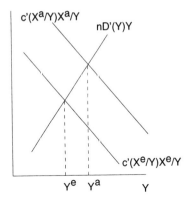

Figure 2. Determination of equilibrium congestion.

The number of users is different

Now we consider the case where the number of users changes. The equilibrium utility of a user without usage-based pricing is

$$v_i(x_i^a) - D(X^a/K^a) - q(Y).$$

This utility could be greater or less than the corresponding utility with usage-based pricing since there is more usage without prices, but there is also more congestion.

Suppose that there is some alternative service that provides the user with utility level u_i^*. Then voluntary participation requires that

$$v_i(x_i^a) - D(X^a/K^a) - q(Y^a) \geq u_i^*,$$

or,

$$v_i(x_i^a) - u_i^* \leq D(X^a/K^a) + q(Y^a).$$

That is, a user will stop using the network under access-only pricing if her net benefit from high usage is less than her congestion cost (including the access fee).[11]

Reducing the number of users will reduce $nD'(Y)Y$. This shifts *down* the corresponding curve in Figure 1B, and could result in an equilibrium amount of capacity that is *less* than one would have under usage-based

---

[11] We should note that there may also be users who do not consume a usage-priced resource, but *do* consume if there are only access prices. These would be users who want to generate a high volume of low-value traffic.

pricing.[12] One might call this a Yogi Berra equilibrium—after his famous remark that "it's so crowded that no one goes there anymore." In this case, however, the remark is apt: in this equilibrium there are a small number of intensive users with high tolerance for congestion, and therefore low willingness to pay for capacity expansion. The high-value users prefer to exit to alternative services.

20.5 Market power

What does utilization and capacity look like if there is market power? Suppose, for example, that a resource provider has a monopoly on the resource it provides: e.g., it is the only source for a certain kind of information. In this case it will typically have an incentive to restrict output in order to raise price. How does this affect its choice of optimal capacity?

If the provider prices only on the basis of usage, the answer is pretty straightforward. Generally output will be lower and price higher under a monopoly than under competition. Lower output means that the curve labelled $nD'(X/K)X/K$ will shift down in Figure 1, which implies less capacity.

However, this analysis is based on the assumption of usage pricing only. We have suggested that a combination of attachment and usage pricing would be a fairly common configuration for information and network service providers. The implications of such a two-part tariff are significant.

Identical tastes

For example, suppose that all users have the same tastes. In this case, the maximum connect fee that the monopolist can charge is the fee that makes the user indifferent between using the service and not using it. For simplicity, we normalize the utility of no use to zero, so the participation condition becomes

$$u(x, Y) - px - q = 0.$$

The profit maximization problem of the monopolist is

$$\max_{K,x} n[q + p(x, Y)x] - c(K).$$

Substituting from the participation condition we have

$$\max_{K,x} nu(x, Y) - c(K),$$

---

[12] Reducing n also reduces X^a (which is equal to the sum of satiation usage by all participating consumers), but the convexity of $D(Y)$ ensures that this indirect effect also works to shift $nD'(Y)Y$ downward.

which is just the problem of maximizing social welfare. It follows that the optimal policy of the monopolist is to set the use-price equal to the optimal congestion fee, charge the user $q = u(x^e, Y^e) - p^e x^e$ for usage, and make the socially optimal investment in capacity. This observation is the classic two-part tariff result of Oi (1971) See Schmalensee (1981) for a detailed exposition, and Varian (1989) for a survey of this and related results.

Different tastes

However, the assumption that all users—which really means all *potential* users—have identical tastes is rather unrealistic. Let us investigate the more realistic case of heterogeneous users. This case is well-treated in the literature on two-part tariffs cited above, but we need to see how it works for the congestion pricing problem we are examining here.

Let t be a parameter indexing tastes and write the utility function as $u(x, Y, t) = v(x, t) - D(Y)$. Let $f(t)$ be the density of type t and let $F(t)$ be the CDF. Choose the parameterization so that $u(x, Y, t)$ is decreasing in t.

The marginal consumer—the consumer who is just indifferent between using the service or not, denoted by T—is characterized by the condition

$$v(x, T) - D(Y) - q - px(p, T) = 0. \tag{20.17}$$

For any given p, the monopolist's choice of q is, effectively, a choice of the marginal consumer. Let $X(p, T)$ be the total demand of the consumers who use the service:

$$X(p, T) = \int_0^T x(p, t) f(t) \, dt.$$

The profit maximization problem of the monopolist is

$$\max_{T, p, K} qF(T) + pX(p, T) - c(K), \tag{20.18}$$

where q is defined in (20.17). Substituting, we have

$$\max_{T, p, K} [v(x, T) - D(Y)]F(T) + p[X(p, T) - x(p, T)F(T)] - c(K).$$

It is worth observing that if the demand of marginal consumer equals the demand of the average consumer, the bracketed term in the middle cancels out and we are back in the previous case.

The first-order conditions for p and K are

$$\left[\frac{\partial v}{\partial x} \frac{\partial x}{\partial p} - D'(Y) \frac{\partial X / \partial p}{K} \right] F(T) + p \left[\frac{\partial X}{\partial p} - \frac{\partial x}{\partial p} F(T) \right] +$$

$$[X(p, T) - x(p, T)F(T)] = 0$$

$$D'(Y)YF(T) = c'(K)K. \tag{20.19}$$

Define the elasticity of demand of the serviced customers as

$$\epsilon = -\frac{p}{X(p,T)}\frac{\partial X(p,T)}{\partial p}.$$

After some manipulations we can write the first-order condition as

$$\frac{p - c'(K)/Y}{p}\epsilon = 1 - \frac{x(p,T)}{X(p,T)/F(T)}.$$

The last term on the right-hand side is the ratio of the demand of the marginal consumer to the demand of the average consumer. If all consumers have the same tastes, then this fraction is 1, and we find that pricing at marginal congestion cost is optimal, as we have already observed. The interesting cases are when the marginal and the average consumer have different tastes.

Recall that by construction the marginal consumer has a lower total value for a given level of usage than the average consumer. Normally, one would think that a consumer with lower total value would want to consume less than a consumer with higher total value. In this case, the monopolist who uses a two-part tariff would set price higher than marginal congestion cost. However, if the marginal consumer wants to consume *more* than the average consumer, it is quite possible that the monopolist would want to set the price *lower* than marginal congestion cost. This is the "auto salesman equilibrium"—the monopolist prices the service so low that he loses money on every sale but makes up for it in volume! Unlike an automobile dealer, our monopolist really may be willing to do this since it collects a uniform subscription fee from each user which can make up for the lost usage fees.

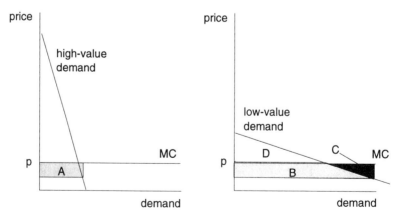

Figure 3. Pricing less than marginal cost may be optimal.

To see how this can happen consider Figure 3, which is based on Oi (1971). There are two users. One has a very high value for the service, but only wants to use a little of it. (Think of ASCII email.) The other user has a low willingness-to-pay for the service but wants to consume a very large amount of it. (Think of a teenager downloading MTV videos.) The teenager is the marginal user, and the connection fee—which is paid by both users—reflects his (relatively low) valuation.

For simplicity, we take the marginal cost of congestion to be constant. Suppose initially that the monopolist prices at the marginal congestion cost; we will show that under some circumstances monopoly profits will increase if the monopolist reduces its price.

If the monopolist sets price equal to marginal cost, the low-value user will achieve net consumer surplus of area D, while the high-value user achieves consumer surplus that is larger than D. The monopolist can therefore charge *each* of them a connection fee of D yielding profits of $2D$.

Now suppose that monopolist reduces its price to some amount *below* marginal cost. The monopolist can now increase the connection fee to $2(D + B)$. However, costs increase as well due to the increased use by both parties. The high-value user imposes additional costs of A and the low-value user imposes additional costs of $(B + C)$. The net increase in profits is $2B - A - (B + C) = B - A - C$. This area may easily be positive, as it is in the case illustrated.

The teenager's utility is larger since he can now download more videos, so he is willing to pay more for the connection; the monopolist extracts this additional surplus through the increased connection charge B. Although the teenager's utility increase (B) is less than the reduction in usage revenues $(B+C)$, the email user *also* has to pay the subscription increase (B). In addition the email user will impose costs on the monopolist of an amount A due to his additional usage. Hence if the subscription increase from the high-value user is greater than the usage revenue losses $(B - A - C > 0)$, profits will increase when price is set below the marginal congestion cost.

This is the same effect observed by Oi (1971) in his classic article. In the literature it is commonly regarded as a perverse effect that is unlikely to occur in reality. But in our context this effect appears to be quite plausible: it can easily happen that relatively low-valued services can require a huge amounts of bandwidth. In order to capture revenues from such uses, the monopolist may find it profitable to *underprice* the congestion they create, thereby imposing potentially significant congestion costs on high-value, low-bandwidth users.

20.6 Summary

We have argued that many network resources are congestible: that is, they can be used by more than one person but increasing usage degrades their quality. One person's use creates an externality: it lowers the value of usage for everyone else. Economists long have proposed pricing to internalize this externality: such a price should reflect both the direct and external costs of usage, so that consumers will use the resource efficiently.

In this paper we have developed this theory for a model of the type of congestible resources typically found in an information network. We found that if the resource is provided in a competitive market with connect fees and usage prices, the equilibrium price and capacity will maximize net social benefits. If there is a monopoly provider, however, the profit-maximizing usage price could be either higher or lower than the socially optimal price (with offsetting adjustments in the connection fee), depending on the value that different users put on the resource.

The extent to which the market is competitive ultimately depends on the cost structure of providing the network resource. Whether a given provider will offer a single or multiple qualities of service will depend both on the cost structure and the extent to which an individual user has preferences for multiple qualities of service.

Currently, the most common form of Internet pricing is pricing by access, with no usage-sensitive prices. With a fixed set of users, we expect to see greater capacity when usage is not priced, but also greater congestion. However, with greater congestion, congestion-sensitive users might not use the resource; the resulting "Yogi Berra" equilibrium might actually have lower usage (but higher congestion) than when usage is priced.

References

Bohn, R., Braun, H.-W., Claffy, K., & Wolff, S. (1993). Mitigating the coming Internet crunch: Multiple service levels via precedence. Tech. rep., UCSD, San Diego Supercomputer Center, and NSF.

Braden, R., Clark, D., & Shenker, S. (1994). Integrated services in the Internet architecture: an overview. Tech. rep., IETF. RFC 1633.

Buchanan, J. (1965). An economic theory of clubs. *Economica*, *32*, 1–14.

Cornes, R., & Sandler, T. (1986). *The Theory of Externalities, Public Goods, and Club Goods*. Cambridge University Press, Cambridge.

Economides, N. (1994). Critical mass and network size. Tech. rep., New York University Stern School of Business, New York.

Hardin, G. (1968). The tragedy of the commons. *Science*, *xx*, 1243–47.

Katz, M., & Shapiro, C. (1985). Network externalities, competition and compatibility. *American Economic Review*, *75*, 424–440.

MacKie-Mason, J. K., & Varian, H. (1993). Some economics of the Internet. Tech. rep., University of Michigan.

MacKie-Mason, J. K., & Varian, H. (1994a). Pricing the Internet. In Kahin, B., & Keller, J. (Eds.), *Public Access to the Internet*. Prentice-Hall, Englewood Cliffs, New Jersey.

MacKie-Mason, J. K., & Varian, H. R. (1994b). Economic FAQs about the Internet. *Journal of Economic Perspectives, 8*(3).

Mohring, H., & Hartwiz, M. (1962). *Highway Benefits: An Analytical Approach*. Northwestern University Press, Evanston.

Oi, W. (1971). A Disneyland dilemma: two-part tariffs for a Mickey Mouse monopoly. *Quarterly Journal of Economics, 85*, 77–96.

Schmalensee, R. (1981). Monopolistic two-part pricing arrangements. *Bell Journal of Economics, 12*, 445–466.

Scotchmer, S. (1985a). Profit-maximizing clubs. *Journal of Public Economics, 27*, 25–45.

Scotchmer, S. (1985b). Two-tier pricing of shared facilities in a free-entry equilibrium. *Rand Journal of Economics, 16*(4), 456–472.

Sharkey, W. W. (1982). *The Theory of Natural Monopoly*. Cambridge University Press, New York.

Strotz, R. H. (1965). Urban transportation parables. In Margolis, J. (Ed.), *The Public Economy of Urban Communities*, pp. 127–169. Resources for the Future, Washington, D.C.

Varian, H. R. (1989). Price discrimination. In Schmalensee, R., & Willig, R. D. (Eds.), *Handbook of Industrial Organization*, Vol. I of *Handbooks in Economics*, chap. 10, pp. 597–654. Elsevier Science Publishing, New York.

Varian, H. R. (1992). *Microeconomic Analysis*. W. W. Norton & Co., New York.

Chapter 21

WHAT USE IS ECONOMIC THEORY?

I examine how neoclassical economic theory can be helpful as a guide to economic policy. I also describe what I view as the role of economic theory in the practice of economics.

Why is economic theory a worthwhile thing to do? There can be many answers to this question. One obvious answer is that it is a challenging intellectual enterprise and interesting on its own merits. A well-constructed economic model has an aesthetic appeal well-captured by the following lines from Wordsworth:

"Mighty is the charm
Of these abstractions to a mind beset
With images, and haunted by herself
And specially delightful unto me
Was that clear synthesis built up aloft
So gracefully."

No one complains about poetry, music, number theory, or astronomy as being "useless," but one often hears complaints about economic theory as being overly esoteric. I think that one could argue a reasonable case for economic theory on purely aesthetic grounds. Indeed, when pressed, most economic theorists admit that they do economics because it is fun.

But I think purely aesthetic considerations would not provide a complete account of economic theory. For theory has a *role* in economics. It is not just an intellectual pursuit for its own sake, but it plays an essential part in economic research. The essential theme of this essay is that economics is a *policy science* and, as such, the contribution of economic theory to economics should be measured on how well economic theory contributes to the understanding and conduct of economic policy.

21.1 Economics as a policy science

Part of the attraction and the promise of economics is that it claims to describe policies that will improve peoples' lives. This is unlike most other physical and social sciences. Sociology and political science have a policy component, but for the most part they are concerned with understanding the functioning of their respective subject matters. Physical science, of course, has the potential to improve peoples' standards of living, but this is really a by-product of science as an intellectual activity.

In my view, many methodologists have missed this essential feature of economic science. It is a mistake to compare economics to physics; a better comparison would be to engineering. Similarly, it is a mistake to compare economics to biology; a better comparison is to medicine. I think that Keynes was only half joking when he said that economists should be more like dentists. Dentists claims that they can make make peoples' lives better; so do economists. The methodological premise of dentistry and economics is similar: we value what is useful. None of the "policy subjects"— engineering, medicine, or dentistry—is much concerned about methodology, and economists, by and large, aren't either.

When you think about it, it is quite surprising that there isn't more work on the methodology of engineering or medicine. These subjects have exerted an enormous influence on twentieth century life, yet are almost totally ignored by philosophers of science. This neglect should be contrasted with with other social sciences where much time and energy is spent on methodological debate. Philosophy of science, as practiced in philosophy departments, seems to be basically concerned with physics, with a smattering of philosophers concerned with psychology, biology, and a few social sciences.

I think that many economists and philosopher who have written on economic methodology have not given sufficient emphasis to the policy orientation of most economic research. One reason for this is the lack of an adequate model to follow. There is no philosophy of engineering, philosophy of medicine or philosophy of dentistry—there is no model of methodology for a policy science on which we can build an analysis. The task of constructing such a theory falls to economists. This is, in my view, one of the most interesting problems for those concerned with methodological issues and the philosophy of the social sciences.

21.2 Role of theory in a policy science

Given my view that economics is a policy science, if I want to defend a practice in economics, then I must defend it from a policy perspective. So I need to argue about how economic theory is *useful* in policy. The remainder of the paper will consists of a list of several such ways. The list is no doubt incomplete, and I would welcome additions. But perhaps it can help focus some discussion on *why* economists do what they do, and how theory helps them do it.

Theory as a substitute for data

In many cases we are forced to use theory because the data that we need are not available. Suppose, for example, we want to determine how a market price will respond to a tax. We could estimate this effect by running a regression of market price against tax rates, controlling for as many other variables as possible. This would give us an equation that we could use to predict how prices respond to changes in taxes.

We rarely have data like this; taxes just don't change enough. But if people only care about the total price of a good, inclusive of tax—a theory—then we can use estimated price elasticities to forecast the response of price to the imposition of a tax.

This uses a theory about behavior—people will respond to the imposition of a tax in the same way that they respond to a price increase—in order to allow data on price responses to be useful. We can use the theory to forecast the outcome of an experiment that has never been done.

Here is another, slightly more esoteric example. Consider the assumption of transitivity of preferences mentioned briefly above. This theory asserts that if A chosen when $\{A, B\}$ is available and B is chosen when $\{B, C\}$ is available, then we can predict A will be chosen when $\{A, C\}$ is available. This is certainly a theory about behavior; it may or may not be true.

If we had data on choices between all pairs of A, B, and C, then the theory wouldn't be necessary. When we want to predict the choice out of the set $\{A, C\}$ we would simply look at how the person chose previously—that is, we would just use brute induction. And we know why induction works—it has always worked in the past!

But we rarely observe all possible choices; typically we observe only a few of the possible choices. Theory allows us to *interpolate* from what we observe to what we don't observe. In the case of the $\{A, B, C\}$ example brute induction requires observing all choices the consumer could make from the various proper subsets available, which requires 3 choice experiments. But if the assumption of transitivity holds, then 2 choice experiments are all we need. The theory of consumer choice allows us to economize on the data.

Naive empiricism can only predict what has happened in the past. It is the theory—the underlying model—that allows us to extrapolate.

Theory tells what parameters are important

The Laffer curve depicts the relationship between tax rates and tax revenue. At some tax rates tax revenue decreases when the tax rate increases. It has been said that the popularity of the Laffer curve is due to the fact that you can explain it to a Congressman in six minutes and he can talk about it for six months.

The Laffer analysis demonstrates both good and bad economic theory. The bad theory is the inference that because the Laffer effect *can* occur it *does* occur. The good theory is that we can use simple supply and demand analysis to determine what magnitudes the elasticity parameters have to be for the Laffer effect to occur. We can then compare the magnitudes of estimated elasticities to estimated labor supply elasticities. In the simplest model a marginal tax rate of 50% requires a labor supply elasticity of 1 to get the Laffer effect. The theory tells us what the relevant parameters are; without the theory, one would have no idea of the relevant parameters are. Indeed, if one examines the rather sordid history of the use of the Laffer curve in public policy debates in the U.S. this becomes painfully clear.

For another example, consider the theory of investment in risky assets. I take it as given that risk is a "bad." Therefore when wealth goes up, people may want to purchase less of it. On the other hand, you can afford to bear more risk when you have more wealth. So an argument based on intuition alone shows that investment in a risky asset can go up or down when wealth increases. A systematic theoretical analysis shows what the comparative statics sign depends on: how risk aversion changes with wealth. So the risk aversion parameter is the one you want to estimate in order to predict how investment in risky assets changes with wealth. Conversely how investment changes with wealth tells you something about how risk aversion changes with wealth.

Theory helps keep track of benefits and costs

I indicated above that the sorts of optimizing models used by economists serve the purpose of providing guidance for policy choices. Indeed one of the important roles of economic theory is to keep track of benefits and costs. The idea of opportunity cost is a fundamental one in economics, and would be very difficult to use without a theoretical model of economic linkages.

This brings up the important point that the correct way to measure an economic benefit or cost can only be determined in light of a theoretical model of choice: a specification of what objectives and the constraints facing an economic agent.

Consider for example, the practice of computing present value or risk adjusted rates of return. These computations are only meaningful in light of a model of choice behavior. If the model of behavior does not apply, the policy prescription cannot apply either.

Benefit-cost analysis is only one small field of economics. But the *idea* behind benefit-cost analysis permeates all of economics. If economic agents are making choices to maximize something, then we can get an idea of what is being optimized by looking at agents' choices. This objective function can then be used as an input to making policy decisions. In some cases, one may need a quantitative estimate of the objective function. In other cases, one may want to show that one kind of market structure, or tax structure, may do a better job of satisfying consumers' objectives than another. But the basic framework of moving from individual objectives, to individual choice, to social objectives and social choice is common to many, many economic studies.

Theory helps relate seemingly disparate problems

If one describes a model in a purely mathematical way, it often happens that the underlying equations will describe a rich set of economic phenomena. The classic example of this phenomenon is the Arrow-Debreu general equilibrium model. The concept of "good" can be interpreted as a physical commodity available at different times, locations, or states of nature. One theoretical model can thereby provide a model of intertemporal trade, location, and uncertainty.

Another example from general equilibrium theory is the First Welfare Theorem. This result shows the intimate relationship between the apparently distinct problems of equilibrium and efficiency.

A third example is that a formal analysis of the problem of second-degree price discrimination shows that it is equivalent to the design of an auction or the determination of optimal provision of qualities. Quality discrimination, auction design, and nonlinear price discrimination are essentially the same sort of problem.

Each of these insights came from examining an abstract theory. Once the the "irrelevant" details are stripped away, its becomes apparent that the same essential choice problem is involved.

Theory can generate useful insights

Let me illustrate this role of economic theory with an example. In the U.S. most interest receipts are taxable income, but many kinds of interest payments are tax deductible. This policy has been criticized as "subsidizing borrowing." Does it?

The answer depends on the tax brackets of the marginal borrowers and lenders. If the tax brackets are the same, for example, the policy has no effect at all on the equilibrium after-tax interest rate. The supply curve tilts up due to the tax on interest income, but the demand curve tilts up by the same amount due to the subsidy on interest payments. This is a simple insight, but it would be very difficult to understand without a model of the functioning of the market for loans.

A theory that is wrong can still yield insight

Pure competition is certainly a "wrong" theory for many markets; pure monopoly is a wrong theory for other markets. But each of these theories can be very useful for yielding significant insights for how a particular market functions. No theory in economics is ever exactly true. The important question is not whether or not a theory is true but whether it offers a useful insight in explaining an economic phenomenon.

In my undergraduate textbook I examine a very simple model of conversion of apartments to condominiums. One result of the model is that converting an apartment to a condominium has no effect on the price of the remaining apartments—since demand and supply each contract by one apartment.

This result can hardly be thought of as literally "true." There are a host of reasons why converting an apartment to a condominium might influence the rent of remaining apartments. Nevertheless, it focuses our attention on a crucial feature of such conversions: they affect both the supply *and the demand* for apartments. The simple supply-demand framework shows us how to start thinking about the impact of condominium conversion on apartment prices.

Theory provides a method for solving problems

I take the method of neoclassical microeconomics to be 1) examine an individual's optimization problem; 2) look at the optimal equilibrium configuration of individual choices; 3) see how the equilibrium changes as policy variables change.

This methods doesn't always work—the models of behavior or equilibrium may be wrong. Or it may be that the specific phenomenon under examination is not fruitfully viewed as an outcome of optimizing, and/or equilibrium behavior. But any method is better than none. In the words of Roger Bacon: "More truth arises through error than confusion."

Methodological individualism is a limited way of looking at the world, no question about it. It probably doesn't do very well in describing phenomenon such as riots or class loyalty. Certainly this sort of individualistic methodology works better for describing some sorts of behavior than others. But it is likely to add insight to *all* problems.

Theory is an antidote to introspection

Most people get their economic beliefs from introspection and their personal experience—the same place that they get their beliefs about most things.

Economic theory—and indeed science in general, can serve as an antidote to this kind of introspection.

Consider, for example, the widely held belief that all demand curves are perfectly inelastic. If the price of gasoline increases by 25%, a layman will argue that no one will change their demand for gasoline. He bases this argument on the fact that *he* would not change his demand for gasoline.

Indeed, it is perfectly possible that *most* people wouldn't change their demand for gasoline... but some would. There are always some people at the margin; these people would change their demand. At any one time, most people are inframarginal in most of their economic decisions. The marginal decisions are the ones that you agonize over. If the price were a little higher or a little lower, the results of your agonizing might be different, and this is what causes the aggregate demand curve to slope downward.

Another nice example of this phenomenon is free trade. It's hard to convince a layman of the advantages of free trade since it is easy to see where the dollars go, but difficult to see where they come from. People have personal experience with imports of foreign goods; but they rarely encounter their own country's exports unless they travel abroad extensively. Only by abstracting from introspection can we see the total picture.

A third example is the bias in perceptions of inflation: price moves are perceived to be exogenous from the viewpoint of the individual, but wage movements are personalized. Even if prices and wages move up by the same amount, people may *feel* worse off since they think that they would have gotten the wage increases anyway.

Verifying that something is obvious may show that it isn't

One of the criticisms that economists have to deal with is that they spend a lot of time belaboring the obvious. Isn't it obvious that demand curves slope down and supply curves slope up? But many theories that seem to be obvious turn out not to be. It may be obvious that demand curves slope down—but as the theoretical analysis shows, it is possible to have demand curves that don't.

Economic theory shows that a profit-maximizing firm will decrease its supply when the output price decreases. But farmers often claim that removing milk price supports will increase the supply of milk since farmers will have to increase output to maintain the same income. The second effect *sounds* like it might be possible—after all, farmers wouldn't advance the claim unless it had some plausibility. However, theory shows us that this particular claim cannot be true if the farmers attempt to maximize profits.

Strategic interactions are a good source of counterintuitive results. A simple analysis of a two-person zero-sum game shows that improving your backhand in tennis may lead to your using it less often.

It would seem that a public offer to match any competitor's price is a sign of a highly competitive market. But when you think about the problem facing a cartel it is not so obvious. The prime problem facing a cartel is how to detect cheating on the agreed-upon prices and quotas. Offering to match a competitor's price is a cheap way to gain information about what your competitors are doing. What appears to be a highly competitive tactic can easily be viewed as a device to support collusion.

Theory allows for quantification and calculation

According to Lord Kelvin, "When you cannot measure it, when you cannot express it in numbers, your knowledge is of a meagre and unsatisfactory kind."[1]

Theoretical economics gives us a framework to calculate and quantify economic relations. Consider the Laffer curve mentioned above. Laffer gave the existence proof, but it took some theoretical calculations to see what magnitudes were important.

In fact, one of the major differences between economics and the other social sciences is that in economics you can *compute*. There is very little computation in sociology, political science, history or anthropology. But economics is filled with computation.

Economic theory is useful since you can use it to compute answers to problems. They aren't always the *right* answers—that depends on whether the model you have is right. (Or, at least, whether it is good enough for the purposes at hand.) But a desideratum of a good model is that you can compute with it: the model can be *solved* to determine some variables as a function of other variables.

In my view, it is impossible to learn economic theory without solving lots of problems. Richard Hamming, a highly prolific electrical engineer, once gave me some excellent advice about how to write a textbook. He told me to assemble the exams and problem sets that you want the students to be able to solve by the time they had finished the course, and then write the book that would show them how to solve them. In general, I have tried to follow this advice, with, I think, some success.

Economics is amenable to experimental verification

Because neoclassical economic models enables one to compute answers to problems, it is possible to compare the answers you get with the outcomes

---

[1] However, the same poet whose praise for abstraction and synthesis I quoted in the introduction also once said: "... High Heaven rejects the lore of nicely calculated less or more."

of controlled experiments. In my view, experimental economics has been one of the great success stories of the last 20 years. We now have rigorous ways to test models of human behavior in the laboratory. Some standard models, such as supply and demand, have turned out to be much more robust than we would have thought 20 years ago. Other models, such as expected utility, have turned out to be less robust.

But this is to be expected—if there were no surprises from experiments, they wouldn't be worth doing. The growth of experimental economics has led many theorists to construct theories that are simple, concrete and testable, rather than theories that are complex, abstract, and general. And experience in observing human subjects in the laboratory has no doubt contributed to the current emphasis on investigating models of learning. Laboratory observations have also been instrumental in alerting us to theoretical dead ends, such as some of the more convoluted refinements of game-theoretic equilibrium concepts.

I expect that the interaction between theory and experimentation will continue to grow in the future. As economists become more comfortable with experimentation in the laboratory, they will also become better at identifying "natural experiments" in real-world data. Such developments can only lead to better models of economic behavior.

21.3 Summary

I have argued that in order to why economic theorists behave in the way they do one has to understand the role of economic theory's contribution to policy analysis. The fact that economics is fundamentally a policy science allows one to explain many aspects of economic theory that are quite mysterious otherwise.

Chapter 22

HOW TO BUILD AN ECONOMIC MODEL IN YOUR SPARE TIME

This is a little article that I wrote to describe how I work. It contains the advice that I wish I had received when I was just starting out, and it is meant to be entertaining as well as instructive.

Most of my work in economics involves constructing theoretical models. Over the years, I have developed some ways of doing this that may be worth describing to those who aspire to practice this art. In reality the process is much more haphazard than my description would suggest—the model of research that I describe is an idealization of reality, much like the economic models that I create. But there is probably enough connection with reality to make the description useful—which I hope is also true for my economic models.

22.1 Getting ideas

The first step is to get an idea. This is not all that hard to do. The tricky part is to get a *good* idea. The way you do this is to come up with lots and lots of ideas and throw out all the ones that aren't good.

But where to get ideas, that's the question. Most graduate students are convinced that the way you get ideas is to read journal articles. But in my experience journals really aren't a very good source of original ideas. You can get lots of things from journal articles—technique, insight, even truth. But most of the time you will only get someone else's ideas. True, they may leave a few loose ends lying around that you can pick up on, but the reason they are loose is probably that the author thought about them a while and couldn't figure out what to do with them or decided they were too tedious to bother with—which means that it is likely that you will find yourself in the same situation.

362 HOW TO BUILD AN ECONOMIC MODEL IN YOUR SPARE TIME

My suggestion is rather different: I think that you should look for your ideas outside the academic journals—in newspapers, in magazines, in conversations, and in TV and radio programs. When you read the newspaper, look for the articles about economics ... and then look at the ones that aren't about economics, because lots of the time they end up being about economics too. Magazines are usually better than newspapers because they go into issues in more depth. On the other hand, a shallower analysis may be more stimulating: there's nothing like a fallacious argument to stimulate research.[1]

Conversations, especially with people in business, are often very fruitful. Commerce is conducted in many ways, and most of them have never been subjected to a serious economic analysis. Of course you have to be careful not to *believe* everything you hear—people in business usually know a set of rules that work well for running their own business, but they often have no idea of where these rules come from or why they work, and this is really what economists tend to find interesting.

In many cases your ideas can come from your own life and experiences. One of my favorite pieces of my own work is the paper I wrote on "A Model of Sales". I had decided to get a new TV so I followed the ads in the newspaper to get an idea of how much it would cost. I noticed that the prices fluctuated quite a bit from week to week. It occurred to me that the challenge to economics was not why the prices were sometimes low (i.e., during sales) but why they were ever high. Who would be so foolish as to buy when the price was high since everyone knew that the item would be on sale in a few weeks? But there must be such people, otherwise the stores would never find it profitable to charge a high price. Armed with this insight, I was able to generate a model of sales. In my model there were two kinds of consumers: informed consumers who read the ads and uninformed consumers who didn't read the ads. The stores had sales in order to price discriminate between the informed and uninformed consumers.

Once I developed the model I had a research assistant go through a couple of years' worth of the *Ann Arbor News* searching for the prices of color TVs. Much to my delight the general pattern of pricing was similar to that predicted by the model. And, yes, I did manage to get a pretty good deal on the TV I eventually bought.

22.2 Is your idea worth pursuing?

So let's assume (a favorite word of economists) that you have an idea. How do you know if it is any good? The first test is to try to phrase your idea in a way that a non-economist can understand. If you can't do this

---

[1] But which sources to read? I read the *New York Times*, the *Wall Street Journal* and the *Economist*; these are probably good places to start.

it's probably not a very good idea. If you can phrase it in a way that a noneconomist can understand, it still may be a lousy idea, but at least there's hope.

Before you start trying to decide whether your idea is correct, you should stop to ask whether it is interesting. If it isn't interesting, no one will care whether it is correct or not. So try it out on a few people—see if they think that it is worth pursuing. What would follow from this idea if it is correct? Would it have lots of implications or would it just be a dead end? Always remember that working on this particular idea has an opportunity cost—you could be spending your time working on a different idea. Make sure that the expected benefits cover that opportunity cost. One of the primary purposes of economic theory is to generate insight. The greatest complement is "Ah! So that explains it!" That's what you should be looking for—forget about the "nice solid work" and try to become a Wizard of Ahs.

22.3 Don't look at the literature too soon

The first thing that most graduate students do is they rush to the literature to see if someone else had this idea already. However, my advice is to wait a bit before you look at the literature. Eventually you should do a thorough literature review, of course, but I think that you will do much better if you work on your idea for a few weeks before doing a systematic literature search. There are several reasons for delay.

First, you need the practice of developing a model. Even if you end up reproducing exactly something that is in the literature already you will have learned a lot by doing it—and you can feel awfully good about yourself for developing a publishable idea! (Even if you didn't get to publish it yourself . . .)

Second, you might come up with a different approach than is found in the literature. If you look at what someone else did your thoughts will be shaped too much by their views—you are much more likely to be original if you plunge right in and try to develop your own insights.

Third, your ideas need time to incubate, so you want to start modeling as early as possible. When you read what others have done their ideas can interact with yours and, hopefully, produce something new and interesting.

22.4 Building your model

So let's skip the literature part for now and try to get to the modeling. Lucky for you, all economics models look pretty much the same. There are some economic agents. They make choices in order to advance their objectives. The choices have to satisfy various constraints so there's something that adjusts to make all these choices consistent. This basic structure suggests a plan of attack: Who are the people making the choices? What are the constraints they face? How do they interact? What adjusts if the choices aren't mutually consistent?

Asking questions like this can help you to identify the pieces of a model. Once you've got a pretty good idea of what the pieces look like, you can move on to the next stage. Most students think that the next stage is to prove a theorem or run a regression. No! The next stage is to work an example. Take the simplest example—one period, 2 goods, 2 people, linear utility—whatever it takes to get to something simple enough to see what is going on.

Once you've got an example, work another one, then another one. See what is common to your examples. Is there something interesting happening here? When your examples have given you an inkling of what is going on, *then* you can try to write down a model. The critical advice here is KISS: keep it simple, stupid. Write down the simplest possible model you can think of, and see if it still exhibits some interesting behavior. If it does, then make it even simpler.

Several years ago I gave a seminar about some of my research. I started out with a very simple example. One of the faculty in the audience interrupted me to say that he had worked on something like this several years ago, but his model was "much more complex". I replied "My model was complex when I started, too, but I just kept working on it till it got simple!"

And that's what you should do: keep at it till it gets simple. The whole point of a model is to give a simplified representation of reality. Einstein once said "Everything should be as simple as possible ... but no simpler." A model is supposed to reveal the essence of what is going on: your model should be reduced to just those pieces that are required to make it work.

This takes a surprisingly long time—there are usually lots of false starts, frustrating diversions, and general fumbling around. But keep at it! If it were easy to do, it would have already been done.

22.5 Generalizing your model

Suppose that you've finally made your model as simple as possible. At this point your model is probably *too* simple to be of much interest: it's likely just an example or a special case. But if you have made your model as simple as possible, it will now be much easier to see how to generalize it since you know what the key pieces are that make the model work.

Here is where your education can be helpful. At last you can use all those techniques you learned in graduate school. Most of the time you were a student you probably studied various canonical models: things like consumer choice, and producer choice, general equilibrium, game theory and so on. The professor probably told you that these were very general models that could encompass lots of special cases.

Well, it was all true. Over the last fifty years economists have come up with some very general principles and models. Most likely your model is a special case of one of these general models. If so you can immediately apply many of the results concerning the general model to your special case, and all that technique you learned can help you analyze your model.

22.6 Making mistakes

This process—simplify to get the result, complexify to see how general it is—is a good way to understand your model. Most of the time that I spend modeling is involved in this back-and-forth process. Along the way, I make a lot of mistakes. As Piet Hein puts it:

The road to wisdom? Well it's plain
and simple to express:
Err
and err
and err again
but less
and less
and less.

This back-and-forth iteration in building a model is like sculpting: you are chipping away a little bit here, and a little bit there, hoping to find what's really inside that stubborn block of marble. I choose the analogy with sculpting purposely: like sculpture most of the work in building a model doesn't consist of adding things, it consists of subtracting them.

This is the most fun part of modeling, and it can be very exciting when the form of the idea really begins to take shape. I normally walk around in a bit of a daze at this stage; and I try not to get too far away from a yellow pad. Eventually, if you're lucky, the inner workings of your model will reveal itself: you'll see the simple core of what's going on and you'll also understand how general the phenomenon really is.

22.7 Searching the literature

At this point you can start doing your literature search. Tell your professors about what you've discovered—nine times out of ten they'll tell you to look in the "1983 *AER*" or "*Econometrica* 77" or some textbook (maybe even one of mine). And lots of the time they'll be right. You'll look there and find "your" model—but it will be much better done, much more fully developed, and much clearer.

Hey, no one said research would be easy. But this is a point where you really have a chance to learn something—read the article(s) carefully and ask yourself "Why didn't I do that?" If someone started with the same idea as you and carried it further, you want to see what you missed.

On the other hand, if you really followed the advice I gave you above to keep it simple, you may have come up with something that is much clearer than the current treatments. Or, maybe you've found something that is more general. If so, you may have a worthwhile insight. Go back to your advisor and tell him or her what you have found. Maybe you've got a new angle on an old idea that is worth further exploration. If so, congratulations—you would never have found this if you did the literature search right away.

Maybe what you've figured out is not already in the literature. The next possibility is that you are wrong. Maybe your analysis isn't right, maybe the idea is just off the wall. This is where your advisor can play a big role. If you've really made your analysis as simple as possible, it is a) less likely to contain an error, and b) any errors that remain will be easier to find.

This brings me to another common problem. When you've worked on a topic for several months—or even several weeks—you tend to lose a lot of perspective ... literally. You're just too close to the work to really get a picture of what is going on. This lack of perspective takes one of two forms: first, you may think something is obvious when it really isn't. It may be obvious to *you,* but you've been thinking about this issue for several months—it probably isn't so obvious to someone who doesn't have the benefit of that experience.

The other possibility is that you may think something is complicated when it is really obvious—you've wandered into a forest via a meandering path. Maybe there's a nice clear trail just a few feet away that you've totally missed.

So at this point you've got to start getting some independent judgment of your work. Talk to your advisor, talk to your fellow students, talk to your wife, husband, girlfriend, boyfriend, neighbor, or pet... whoever you can get to listen. And here's what you'll find: they've got no idea of what you are talking about (especially your pet). So *you* have to go back to trying to figure out what you really are talking about: what *is* the fundamental idea of your model?

22.8 Giving a seminar

After you've bored your friends, relatives and pets to death, you should give a seminar. This is a really important phase: the more you can talk about your work, the better the final paper will be. This is because a talk forces you to *get to the point.* If you want your audience to listen to you, you've got to make your idea clear, concise, and organized—and the experience that you gain by doing this is extremely useful for writing your paper.

I listen to a lot of stupid ideas—but that's what I'm paid to do. Lots of people listen to stupid ideas from me, too: my colleagues get paid to do it, and the students get examined on it. But most people don't have to listen to you. They don't have to read your paper. They won't even have to glance at the abstract unless they have a reason to.

This comes as a big shock to most graduate students. They think that just because they've put a lot of work and a lot of thought into their paper that the rest of the world is obliged to pay attention to them. Alas, it isn't so. Herb Simon once said that the fundamental scarcity in the modern world was scarcity of attention—and brother, is that the truth. There are demands for everybody's attention, and if you want someone to pay attention to you, you have to give them a reason to do so. A seminar is a way to get them to pay attention, so be sure to exploit this opportunity to get people to listen to you.

The useful thing about a seminar is that you get immediate feedback from the audience. An audience won't put up with a lot of the things that authors try to write in papers: turgid prose, complex notation, and tedious details. And, believe it or not, readers won't put up with these things either! The trick is to use the seminar to get all those things out of your paper—that way, it may actually get read.

Controlling the audience

I've seen it claimed that one of the greatest fears that most people have is speaking before a group. I imagine that most assistant professors have this problem, but after many years of giving lectures before several hundred students it goes away.

In fact, lecturing can become downright addictive (as my family often reminds me.) As the mathematician R. H. Bing once said: "When I was young, I would rather give a lecture on mathematics than listen to one. Now that I am older and more mature I would rather give *two* lectures on mathematics than listen to one." Giving lectures is a bit like eating oysters. Your first one requires some courage, but after you develop a taste for them, it can be hard to stop.

There are three parts to a seminar: the introduction, the content, and the conclusion. My advice about introductions is simple: don't have one. I have seen many seminars ruined by long, pretentious, contentless introductions. Just say a few sentences about the big picture and then get down to business: show them what you've got and why it's important. The primary reason to get down to business right away is that your audience will only remember about twenty minutes of your talk—and that is usually the *first* twenty minutes. So make sure that you get some useful information into that first twenty minutes.

As for conclusions, the most common problem is letting the seminar trail off into silence. This can ruin a good talk. I always like to spend the last couple of minutes summarizing what I accomplished and why the audience should care. After all, this is what they will walk away with, so you might as well tell them what they should remember rather than make them figure this out for themselves

Nowadays everyone seems to use overheads for their lectures. The downside of this is that the seminar isn't very spontaneous—but the upside is that the seminar is usually better organized. My advice is to limit yourself to one or two slides for a introduction and one for a conclusion. That way you will be forced to get to *your* contribution sooner rather than later. And make your overheads *big*; use large type and don't try to say too much on each one.

There are two things to avoid in your presentation: don't let your audience go to sleep, and don't let them get too lively. You want the audience to hear what you have to say. They won't hear your message if they are sleeping, and they won't hear your message if they are talking more than you are. So don't loose control of your seminar!

The key to maintaining control is to establish credibility early on. The way to do is to go into great detail in the presentation of your first result—a theorem, a regression, a diagram, whatever. Spell out each aspect of your result in excruciating detail so no one can possibly misunderstand. When you do this you will certainly get questions like "Will this generalize to n agents?" or "Have you corrected for heteroskedasticity?"

If you know the answer to the question, go ahead and answer it. If you don't know the answer—or the questions is totally off the wall—say "That's a good question; let me come back to that at the end of the seminar." (Of course you never will.) Don't get sidetracked: the point of going through the initial result in great detail is to establish credibility.

Once you've presented your result and you see that the audience has understood the point—their heads are nodding but not nodding off—you can go on to the generalizations and elaborations. If you've done a good job at establishing your credibility initially now the audience will believe anything you say! Of course you shouldn't abuse this trust, but it is useful to exploit it in the rest of your presentation. This is the fundamental reason for starting simple: if you start out with a delicate argument, it will be hard for the audience to understand and you will never establish trust.

When you are done with your talk you should take a few minutes to jot down some notes: what was difficult for people to understand? What questions did they ask? What suggestions did they make? What references did they give you? You may think that you will remember these points, but quite often you won't. The audience is a very useful resource for clarifying your thoughts—make sure you use it well.

22.9 Planning your paper

Almost everyone writes on computers these days. I know that computers are great time savers: I get almost as much work done now as I got done before I started using computers.[2]

I thought that I would spend a bit of time talking about how I use computers, not because it is all that important, but because no one else ever discusses such mundane matters. Since I am well known as a computer nerd, people always ask me what I use, and I figure I can save time by pointing them to this article. Undoubtedly this will all look incredibly archaic in a few years, but that's the cost of being on the bleeding edge of technology.

I currently use a Unix machine, but most of what I say applies equally well to other environments. I have a directory on my computer called `Papers` and when I start to work on a new topic I create a subdirectory under papers. (For example, this paper is in a directory `Papers/how-I-work`.) When I create the directory I create a `notes.txt` file: this contains my initial ideas, a rough outline, whatever. For example, the `notes.txt` file for this paper initially had entries in it like:

```
*read the newspaper
*simplify
*write and talk
**if you don't grab them in the first page, they won't read it
```

I create a notes file like this when I first start to work on a topic—I jot down the initial ideas I have, which are usually pretty sketchy. In the following days and weeks I occasionally take a look at this outline. When I look at it I move things around, add material and so on. I rarely take anything out completely—I just move material to the end of the file. After all, I might want those notes again.

After organizing these ideas for several weeks or months I am ready to write the first draft of the paper. I usually try to do this in a day or two, to keep it all fresh. I normally put the notes in one window and the paper

---

[2] If a train stops at a train station, what do you think happens at a work station?

in the other and write the paper while I refer back and update the notes to keep them in sync with the paper.

Once the paper is written I put it aside for a couple of weeks. Papers need to age like fine cheese—it's true that mold might develop, but the flavor is often enhanced. More importantly, it gives your subconscious mind a chance to work on the idea—maybe it will come up with something your conscious mind has missed.

When I come back to the paper I try to read it with a fresh mind, like someone who has never seen it before.[3] On rare occasions I like what I read, but usually I have lots of criticisms. Whenever I have to pause and think "what does that mean?" I rewrite—I add more explanation, change the notation, or whatever is necessary to make the paper clearer. When I'm done with this process I have a first draft.

I next check this draft into a revision control system. This is a piece of software that keeps track of the revisions of a paper. It documents all of the changes you make and allows you to restore any previous version of a paper. I use the Unix utility `rcs` but I know there are many other systems available. Revision control systems are especially valuable if you are working with a coauthor since they keep track of which person made which changes when.

I then repeat the process: let the paper sit for a few more weeks or months, then come back to it, read it with a fresh mind and revise it accordingly.

It is particularly useful to do a revision right after you give a seminar. Remember those notes I told you to write after your seminar ended? Sit down with the paper and go over the questions the audience had and the suggestions they made. Can you answer their questions in your paper? Can you incorporate their suggestions? Be sure to modify the notes/outline/slides for your talk when you incorporate the audience's suggestions.

Bibliographic software

One very useful computer tool is a bibliographic system. This is a piece of software designed to managed a list of references. There is a master database of references that is stored on your computer. You assign a key to each article like `Arrow70` or `ArrowRisk`. When you want to refer to a paper you use the key, by saying something like `\cite{Arrow70}`. The bibliographic program then looks up the appropriate citation in your database and puts it in the list of references at the end of your article.

I use the system called BibTeX, since it works well with TeX. However, there are many other systems available that work for other wordprocessing

---

[3] This is much easier once you reach middle age.

packages. It's a good idea to get in the habit of using a system like this. Over the years you will build up a comprehensive bibliography for the areas you work in.

But where do you get your references in the first place? Well, one way is to ask people: your adviser, your colleagues, your friends, and so on. This is still one of the most reliable ways. But nowadays there are a number of computerized databases available online or on CDs that allow for easy search. You can open the CD for the *Journal of Economic Literature*, type in a few key words like "price discrimination" and get the last 10 years' worth of abstracts of published articles that contain the words "price discrimination." As you look at these articles you will see a few "classic" articles cited. When you identify these classic articles go to the *Social Science Citation Index* and search for all the recent papers that have cited these classics. This process should give you an up-to-date bibliography pretty quickly. Often you can download the citations you get directly into your bibliography database program.

22.10 The structure of the paper

There's an old joke about academic papers. They are all supposed to have three parts. The first part, everyone can understand. The second, only a handful of readers can understand. The last part no one can understand— that's how the readers know it's a serious piece of work!

The big mistake that authors make these days is to leave out the first part of the paper—that part that everyone can understand. But the introduction is the most important part of the paper. You've got to grab the reader on the first page. No matter how brilliant the rest of the paper is, it won't be noticed if no one reads it. And no one will read it if you don't get their interest in the first few paragraphs. If you really know what your paper is about, you shouldn't find it hard to explain this to your readers in a couple of paragraphs.

My basic advice is to make your paper look like your talk. Get to the point. Use examples. Keep it simple. Tell people why what you did is important after you've done it. Put the tedious stuff in the appendix. End with a summary of what you have accomplished. If you have really written a good paper, people won't have to listen to your seminar to find out what you have done: they can just read it in your paper.

22.11 When to stop

You can tell when your work is getting ready for publication by the reactions in the seminars: people stop asking questions. (Or at least, the people who have read your paper stop asking questions.) If you've followed my advice, you've already asked their questions—and answered them—in your paper.

Once you've made your point, stop. Lots of papers drag on too long. I said earlier that people only remember about 20 minutes of your seminar (if you're lucky), and they only remember about 10 pages of your paper. You should be able to say most of what you want to say in that length.

Once your paper is written, you can submit it to a journal. I don't have too much to say about this; Dan Hamermesh has written a nice article that describes the procedure better than I can.[4] All I can say is to echo his advice that you go over the article with a fine tooth comb before sending it in. Nothing turns off an editor or a referee more than to find typos, missing references and sloppy editing in the articles they deal with.

22.12 Writing textbooks

Most of what I've had to say so far has to do with writing articles. But I suppose I really should say a bit about the other kind of writing I've done: textbooks.[5]

My first text, *Microeconomic Analysis* really wasn't planned; it just happened. When I first started my professional career at MIT in 1973 I was asked to teach the first year graduate micro course. The text, such as it was, consisted of about 20 pages of notes written by Bob Hall, maybe 40 pages of notes from Dan McFadden and Sid Winter, and a few journal articles. The notes were awfully sketchy, and the journal articles were much too advanced for first year students. So I had to write my own notes for the students.

The first year I wrote about 50 pages; the next year another 50, and the year after that another 50. The students who used them were great. They read them carefully and told me what was wrong: where the obscurities were, where the errors were, what was too advanced, and what was too simple. I owe much of the success of that book to the fact it was class tested before a highly critical audience.

During this period I happened to meet Richard Hamming, an electrical engineer who had written several texts. He gave me a key piece of advice: "Get together the problems that you want your students to be able to solve after they've read your book—and then write the book that will teach them how to solve them."

---

[4] Daniel S. Hamermesh, "The Young Economist's Guide to Professional Etiquette", *Journal of Economic Perspectives*, 6: 1, 169–180.

[5] The reader may recall Disraeli's warning: "An author who speaks about his own books is almost as bad as a mother who talks about her own children."

This was great advice. I followed it to some degree with the graduate text, but later, when I wrote the undergraduate text, I followed it religiously—but more about that below.[6]

One day a publisher came into my office and asked (as they often do) "Are you writing a book?" I said that would be a silly thing for an assistant professor to do but as a matter of fact, I did have some class notes that I had been working on for a few years.

Next thing I knew, I had several publishers interested in my notes. I spent a semester at Berkeley in 1977 and used that opportunity to hammer them into shape. Much to my surprise the notes eventually become a book and ended up being very widely used. I did a second edition in 1983 and I *should* have done a revision in 1987 or so—but instead I decided to write an undergraduate text.

I wanted to write an undergraduate book because I was fed up with the books I had been using. I had tried several different ones, but couldn't find any I really liked. I remember one semester I sat down and tried to write a midterm exam—but the book I had been using was so vapid that I couldn't think of any problems that the students could solve using the tools that had been presented in the book! At that point I figured I could produce something better.

About the same time one of my undergraduates had picked up a workbook by Marcia Stigum called, I believe, *Problems in Microeconomics*. The student found this very helpful in understanding the concepts of economics, and I remembered what Hamming had told me about how to write a textbook. So I asked my colleague Ted Bergstrom if he would like to work with me to create a serious workbook.[7] Ted created problems as the text was being written, and I had to make sure that the text contained everything necessary to solve the problems he created. I created problems too, but those were automatically coordinated with the textbook—the external stimulus imposed by Ted's problems was much more important in shaping the content of the book. If the students weren't able to solve the problems, I had to add explanations to the text until they could—and if we couldn't create a problem to illustrate some point, the point probably wasn't important enough to put in the text.

It's a pity that most workbooks are created as afterthoughts. Creating the workbook really should be an integral part of the writing process, as Hamming suggested. You want the students to be able to *use* the material

---

[6] The general principle that I followed (and still follow) with the graduate text is that it should give the student the information they need to know to read a microeconomics paper in the *American Economic Review*. Every now and then I go through a few issues of the *AER* and note topics that should go in the next edition of the book.

[7] As it turned out, it wasn't quite as serious as I had expected—in fact, I think that it is quite funny, but that is due to Ted's unique sense of humor rather than my intentions.

you teach them, so the first order of business is to figure out what it is that you want them to be able to do. The latest buzzword in education is "learning by doing" but as far as I'm concerned that's always been the only way to go.

The undergraduate text turned out to be pretty successful as well. And the workbook has ended up selling two or three times as much as any of its competitors—which goes to show that there still is a market for a quality product in the textbook market.

22.13 Summary

I said that every talk should have a summary—so I suppose I have to follow my own advice. Here are the points to take away:

- Look for ideas in the world, not in the journals.

- First make your model as simple as possible, then generalize it.

- Look at the literature later, not sooner.

- Model your paper after your seminar.

- Stop when you've made your point.

And now my points have been made, so I'm duty bound to stop. Go forth and model!

INDEX

Economists of the Twentieth Century

Monetarism and Macroeconomic
Policy
Thomas Mayer

Studies in Fiscal Federalism
Wallace E. Oates

The World Economy in Perspective
Essays in International Trade and European
Integration
Herbert Giersch

Towards a New Economics
Critical Essays on Ecology, Distribution and
Other Themes
Kenneth E. Boulding

Studies in Positive and Normative
Economics
Martin J. Bailey

The Collected Essays of Richard E. Quandt
(2 volumes)
Richard E. Quandt

International Trade Theory and Policy
Selected Essays of W. Max Corden
W. Max Corden

Organization and Technology in Capitalist
Development
William Lazonick

Studies in Human Capital
Collected Essays of Jacob Mincer, Volume 1
Jacob Mincer

Studies in Labor Supply
Collected Essays of Jacob Mincer, Volume 2
Jacob Mincer

Macroeconomics and Economic Policy
The Selected Essays of Assar Lindbeck
Volume I
Assar Lindbeck

The Welfare State
The Selected Essays of Assar Lindbeck
Volume II
Assar Lindbeck

Classical Economics, Public Expenditure
and Growth
Walter Eltis

Money, Interest Rates and Inflation
Frederic S. Mishkin

The Public Choice Approach to Politics
Dennis C. Mueller

The Liberal Economic Order
Volume I Essays on International Economics
Volume II Money, Cycles and Related Themes
Gottfried Haberler
Edited by Anthony Y.C. Koo

Economic Growth and Business Cycles
Prices and the Process of Cyclical Development
Paolo Sylos Labini

International Adjustment, Money and Trade
Theory and Measurement for Economic Policy
Volume I
Herbert G. Grubel

International Capital and Service Flows
Theory and Measurement for Economic Policy
Volume II
Herbert G. Grubel

Unintended Effects of Government Policies
Theory and Measurement for Economic Policy
Volume III
Herbert G. Grubel

The Economics of Competitive Enterprise
Selected Essays of P.W.S. Andrews
*Edited by Frederic S. Lee
and Peter E. Earl*

The Repressed Economy
Causes, Consequences, Reform
Deepak Lal

Economic Theory and Market Socialism
Selected Essays of Oskar Lange
Edited by Tadeusz Kowalik

Trade, Development and Political Economy
Selected Essays of Ronald Findlay
Ronald Findlay

General Equilibrium Theory
The Collected Essays of Takashi Negishi
Volume I
Takashi Negishi

The History of Economics
The Collected Essays of Takashi Negishi
Volume II
Takashi Negishi

Studies in Econometric Theory
The Collected Essays of Takeshi Amemiya
Takeshi Amemiya

Economics and Social Justice
Essays on Power, Labor and Institutional
Change
David M. Gordon
Edited by Thomas E. Weisskopf
and Samuel Bowles

Practicing Econometrics
Essays in Method and Application
Zvi Griliches

Economics Against the Grain
Volume One
Microeconomics, Industrial Organization and
Related Themes
Julian L. Simon

Economics Against the Grain
Volume Two
Population Economics, Natural Resources and
Related Themes
Julian L. Simon

Advances in Econometric Theory
The Selected Works of Halbert White
Halbert White

The Economics of Imperfect Knowledge
Collected Papers of G.B. Richardson
G.B. Richardson

Economic Performance and the Theory of
the Firm
The Selected Papers of David J. Teece
Volume One
David J. Teece

Strategy, Technology and Public Policy
The Selected Papers of David J. Teece
Volume Two
David J. Teece

The Keynesian Revolution, Then and Now
The Selected Essays of Robert Eisner
Volume One
Robert Eisner

Investment, National Income and Economic
Policy
The Selected Essays of Robert Eisner
Volume Two
Robert Eisner

International Trade Opening and the
Formation of the Global Economy
Selected Essays of P. J. Lloyd
P. J. Lloyd

Production, Stability and Dynamic
Symmetry
The Selected Essays of Ryuzo Sato
Volume Two
Ryuzo Sato

Variants in Economic Theory
Selected Works of Hal R. Varian
Hal R. Varian

Political Economy, Oligopoly and
Experimental Games
The Selected Essays of Martin Shubik
Volume One
Martin Shubik

Money and Financial Institutions
A GAME THEORETIC APPROACH
The Selected Essays of Martin Shubik
Volume Two
Martin Shubik